WITHDRAWN

D0207844

Africa in Literature for Children and Young Adults

Recent Titles in
Bibliographies and Indexes in World Literature

Africa in Literature for Children and Young Adults

An Annotated Bibliography of English-Language Books

MEENA KHORANA

Bibliographies and Indexes in World Literature, Number 46

GREENWOOD PRESS
Westport, Connecticut • London

Library of Congress Cataloging-in-Publication Data

Khorana, Meena.
   Africa in literature for children and young adults : an annotated
bibliography of English-language books / Meena Khorana.
      p.   cm.—(Bibliographies and indexes in world literature,
ISSN 0742–6801   ;   no. 46)
   Includes indexes.
   ISBN 0–313–25488–5 (alk. paper)
   1. Children's literature—Bibliography.   2. Young adult
literature—Bibliography.   3. Africa in literature—Bibliography.
I. Title. II. Series.
Z3508.C5K48   1994
[DT3]
016.96—dc20   94–34223

British Library Cataloguing in Publication Data is available.

Library of Congress Catalog Card Number: 94–34223
ISBN: 0–313–25488–5
ISSN: 0742–6801

First published in 1994

Greenwood Press, 88 Post Road West, Westport, CT 06881
An imprint of Greenwood Publishing Group, Inc.

Printed in the United States of America

The paper used in this book complies with the
Permanent Paper Standard issued by the National
Information Standards Organization (Z39.48–1984).

10 9 8 7 6 5 4 3 2 1

To my parents

Contents

Preface

This annotated bibliography of English-language books set in Africa is intended for scholars, teachers, librarians, parents, students, and general readers. While much critical attention has been showered on adult literature, African literature for children and young adults still remains a neglected area. The existing critical studies mainly focus on thematic analyses, denunciation of imitative writing, and difficulties of publishing for children in postcolonial Africa. The major thrust of this study is to initiate a serious investigation of this body of literature from a number of critical approaches: influence of political, economic, and social conditions; current literary theories and African historiography; and the impact of indigenous oral structures on African children's writers.

The books listed in this bibliography, dating from 1873 to 1994, represent both African and Western authors. Only those books that are either originally written in English or translated into English are included. These books represent three broad phases in the representation of Africa in books for children and young adults: colonial literature, postcolonial Western literature, and postcolonial African literature. With the numerous English-language books published on Africa, this bibliography does not claim to be exhaustive. However, the books were carefully selected from existing bibliographies, *Books in Print*, *African Books in Print*, *African Book Publishing Record*, and publishers' catalogs to give a fair representation to the various regions and countries of Africa, literary genres, prominent authors and books, and literary trends and themes. A concerted attempt was made to include all available books published in the 1980s and 1990s. Of the books listed, approximately two hundred represent children's publishing in Africa, mainly Nigeria, Kenya, Ghana, Zimbabwe, and South Africa.

The books included in this bibliography, published both in Africa and in Western countries, were easily available through Interlibrary Services, the Library of Congress, and Afrocentric bookstores. However, for the most recent books published in Africa, say within the last three years, the bookstore of the Smithsonian Museum of African Art in Washington, D.C. and publishers and distributors in Africa and Great Britain proved helpful.

The nearly seven hundred entries are arranged in six chapters according to region: General Books, North Africa, West Africa, East Africa, Central Africa, and Southern Africa. An additional 120 books are either mentioned or briefly discussed in the various annotations. Each chapter is further subdivided by genre: traditional literature, fiction (including historical, realistic, and fantasy), poetry, drama, biography and autobiography, and informational books. While the entries are numbered consecutively throughout the bibliography, individual titles are listed alphabetically by author under each genre. In the traditional literature segments, retellers and compilers of folktales have not been identified as such. If, however, the author has also collected the folktales, the annotation makes note of that fact. Separate indexes on authors, illustrators, titles, and subjects are provided to assist both the general reader and the researcher. The subject index lists the major themes, national figures, deities, historical sites, ancient civilizations, and events mentioned in the annotations. It does not attempt to categorize books by literary themes and motifs. The introductory essay provides an in-depth historical and critical analysis of the three phases of African literature for children and young adults.

Each book listed in the bibliography was carefully read and evaluated. The annotations provide a plot/content summary, thematic analysis, and literary evaluation. In biographies of prominent national figures, only the first entry contains a detailed summary of the content. Subsequent entries only mention the scope of the book and any distinctive features of the author's style or treatment. The books were also examined for sensitivity to multicultural and international issues. For instance: Does the book reflect an ethnocentric attitude? Are cultural details presented respectfully and in their proper contexts? Is there stereotyping in characterization, plot, and themes? Is there any distortion, omission, or misinterpretation of facts? In evaluating informational books, Beverley Naidoo's *Censoring Reality: An Examination of Books on South Africa* was most useful in identifying two types of bias in nonfiction: bias by commission and bias by omission.

A major dilemma in writing the annotations was whether to substitute pejorative words like Pygmies, Bushmen, and Hottentots with San, Mbuti, and Khoi Khoi. As a researcher, I felt disadvantaged because these terms are often used loosely, and it is beyond the scope of this bibliography to identify the precise ethnic group and geographical region intended by the author. For instance, in using the term Pygmies, the author could be referring to any one of a number of ethnic groups such as the Mbuti, Tswa, or Twa. Being cognizant of the reconstructionist mode of modern historiography and the changes occurring in vocabulary to accurately define African cultures and peoples, I hesitated to use African terms loosely. Thus, the individual summaries of books present the terminology and perspective of the authors. In the case of spellings of African names and terms, the generally accepted spellings were used. The subject index makes note of the various spellings of significant words.

In developing a theoretical paradigm for books by African authors, close attention was paid to the pedagogical debate on the appropriate criteria for evaluating African literature. Should the literature be examined by Western or African standards? On the one hand, Eustace Palmer argues that since the novel is not an indigenous African genre, and since African novelists were influenced by the Western novel, they should be judged by Western literary standards. Palmer states in *The Growth of the African Novel*: "Our considerations must be literary and cultural rather than ideological, nationalistic or political" (2). In judging books by purely sociological and historical standards, he continues, "works of a dubious literary value would be treated with respect because of their sociological relevance" (7). Likewise, Adrian Roscoe, in *Mother is Gold*, contends that if an African writes in English, he should be judged by the standards of English letters (x). On the other hand, Afrocentric writers feel that to be judged by Eurocentric methodology is a form of cultural neoimperialism. In a polemical attack against Euromodernist criticism by both African and Western critics, Chinweizu, Onwuchekwa Jemie, and Ihechukwu Madubuike emphasize in their book, *Toward the Decolonization of African Literature*, that "African literature *is* an autonomous entity separate and apart from all other literatures. It has its own traditions, models and norms" (4). They specifically refer to the charges of thin plot, brevity, situational themes, too many autobiographical or culture conflict novels, inadequate description, lack of character development, unrealistic and awkward dialogue, problems with the handling of time and space, and didacticism brought against the African novel (7-8). They argue that recent developments in the form and structure of the modern novel have shown that "the novel is an open form, and that there is no ideal form to which all novels must conform" (88).

Hence, in examining books by African authors, the relevant social, political, cultural, and literary contexts of the works were discussed in the annotations. Each book was analyzed for excellence in writing: Are the characters and plot presented in an interesting manner? How effectively have themes of love and hate, growing up, and problems of identity been treated? Is the book well written? How has African society been portrayed? Is the book well edited and produced? Are the illustrations accurate and aesthetically pleasing? If African idioms, speech patterns, and elements of storytelling such as songs, ideophones, and culture-specific metaphors and imagery are employed, the book was not evaluated by Western standards but by its ability to convey African experiences and values in an engaging manner.

This bibliography would not have been possible without the help extended to me by scholars, friends, and family in Africa and the United States. I express my sincere thanks to Abiola Odejide, Steve Chimombo, Asenath Bole Odaga, Debbie Adiv, Deepa Khanna, and Osayimwense Osa for their valuable suggestions and help in procuring books from Africa. For their assistance in locating library books, I am grateful to Betsy Van Auker and the Interlibrary staff, Howard County Public Library; John Z. Hugh, Interlibrary Department, Parlett Moore Library at Coppin State College; and Margaret N. Coughlan, Children's Department, Library of Congress. Sincere thanks are also due to Eugenia Collier, Chair, Department of English and Language Arts, and Burney Hollis, Dean of Arts and Sciences, Morgan State University, for their strong support of my research by granting me release time and convenient class schedules. I also thank my former colleagues at Coppin State College, especially Ibrahim Kargbo who served as consultant for this bibliography. For their help in preparing the manuscript for publication, I am indebted to Audrey and Martin Peter for their meticulous work in typsetting and preparing the camera-ready copies; to Wanda Adams for help with typing; and to Rohini Khorana for so diligently preparing the indexes. Finally, for their encouragement and patience, I thank the editors at Greenwood Press, Marilyn Brownstein and George F. Butler, and my husband, Shamsher, and daughters Shobna and Rohini.

Meena Khorana
August 1994

Introduction

The children's literature set in Africa that is surveyed in this bibliography reflects how Africans and others have defined, interpreted, and promoted Africa, its cultures and peoples, its religions and beliefs, and its worldview to themselves and to the world. African children's literature represents a multiplicity of viewpoints from nineteenth century books by Europeans to contemporary literature by both African and Western writers. This body of literature, like literature anywhere in the world, is influenced by political, economic, and social conditions, philosophic ideologies, and the hopes and beliefs of the cultures that gave rise to it. Central to this study is an examination of authenticity as determined by audience, purpose, and environment. This introductory essay is a critical analysis of the three major phases of African children's literature: colonial literature, postcolonial Western literature, and postcolonial African literature.

Edward Said's definition of the European attitude toward the Orient as a form of colonial superiority that makes "statements about it, authorizing views of it, describing it, by teaching it, settling it, ruling over it . . ." outlines eloquently and aptly the European attitude toward Africa (3). The exploitation of the African colonies by Western nations for industrial raw material, markets for manufactured products, cheap labor, and territorial expansion led to a literary exploitation as well. Nancy Schmidt points out that "while fiction is a creation of individuals' imaginations, all individuals live in culturally defined worlds which influence the directions in which their imaginations develop" (*Children's* 194). The political, economic, social, and intellectual climate of mid-nineteenth to early twentieth century Europe and America had a dominant influence on colonial writers. The distorted picture of Africa that emerged provided a psychological rationalization for imperialism and exploitation on "scientific authority." Theories on evolution, Social Darwinism, environment versus heredity, origin of religious thought, political organization of society, and the progressive social movements against slavery were given fictional life by authors.

Even before the scramble for empire began in 1880, exciting tales of "strange" lands and peoples with exotic rituals and customs had been filtering into Europe and America through the accounts of traders, missionaries, and explorers. These tales gave rise to a popular new genre in literature: colonial literature set in Africa.[1] George Henty's fictionalized South African war stories; Rene Guillot's fantasies of the spiritual harmony between "natural" man and the wild animals and terrain of Africa; Hugh Lofting's charming and beguiling animal fantasies set in Western Africa; Rider Haggard's romantic search for lost kingdoms; Edgar Rice Burroughs' and Roy Rockwood's jungle adventures; R. M. Ballantyne's antislavery-- though imperialistic--stories set in East Africa; and, more recently, American author Reba Mirsky's account of the social life of Zulus, to name a few, belong to this literary tradition.[2] Their blatant Eurocentrism is obvious: "primitive" Africans are judged according to the norms of Western civilization and culture, and their traditional societies are pitted against the military might of the colonial nations.

COLONIAL LITERATURE

Written solely for domestic consumption, colonial literature, as Jeffrey Richards states in *Imperialism and Juvenile Literature*, "legitimises, glamorises and romanticises particular mindsets" (1). It perpetuates myths and misconceptions about the geography, social organization, peoples, cultures, and civilizations of Africa by introducing stereotypical themes, characters, and plots in book after book.[3]

Colonial literature presents a contradictory picture of the geography of Africa. On the one hand, Africa is stereotyped as a "dark" and forbidding continent of deserts, inhospitable coasts, and impenetrable jungles. Every conceivable danger of the wild is fully exploited in these stories: intolerable heat, blinding desert storms, predatory animals, hostile natives, and tribes of cannibals. European domination of Africa is, thus, justified on the grounds that an untamed land and peoples are being "civilized." Lest Europeans become fearful of living in this environment, they are quickly assured of their ability to survive and overcome its discomforts. As Brian Street writes in *The Savage in Literature*: "For the popular writer, the debate between heredity and environment is more important for reaffirming the superiority of the white man" (116). Thus, in adventures like *Tarzan of the Apes* and *Bomba, the Jungle Boy and the Cannibals*, the white heroes survive the harsh environment due to their congenital superiority.[4] When Lord Greystoke and his wife are stranded on the shores of Western Africa in the Tarzan story, they are consoled with: "are we not armed with ages of superior knowledge, and have we not the means of protection, defence and sustenance which science has given us, but of which they are totally ignorant?" (17). In addition, the white heroes' oneness with the African environment enables them to endure and conquer every life-threatening danger that they are confronted with. Yet, this fantasy of the "noble savage," as Street points out, is always embodied in white characters who "combine the splendid physical qualities of the jungle native with the intellectual and moral superiority of an Anglo-Saxon heritage" (8).

On the other hand, readers are enticed with Africa's mineral riches, exotic wildlife, great sport, and romantic adventures, so that they can be tempted to visit and settle it. George Henty's *The Young Colonists* reads like a travelogue on the attractions of Africa:

> I wonder sometimes that gentlemen in England . . . do not more often come out for a few months' shooting here . . . the trip would be a novel one, and every comfort could be carried in the wagons, while the sport, when the right country was reached, would be more abundant and varied than in any other part of the world. Lions may be met, deer of numerous kinds, giraffes, hippopotami, crocodiles, and many other animals, not to mention an occasional gallop after ostriches. (245)

Mrs. Huxley writes in her autobiographical book, *The Flame Trees of Thika*, that her father was tempted to East Africa by the prospect of making a fortune in coffee plantations. Kenya was presented to him as having a "Wonderfully healthy climate, splendid neighbours, magnificent sport, thousands of years of untapped fertility locked up in the soil" (7).

Colonial literature also inculcates a sense of pride in the glory of an overseas empire. Darwin's theory of evolution and natural selection offered a justification for exploitation and colonization. The Anglo-Saxon race considered itself capable of governing the "primitive" peoples of America, Africa, and Asia; otherwise, the subject races would enslave themselves and a state of anarchy would result. Through imperialistic books, children are conditioned to regard "the non-white population of the world . . . as composed not only of inferior, but of conquered peoples, who are destined to remain subject to the economic and social domination of those who have vanquished them" (Dingwall 114). Far from describing conditions in Africa accurately, or portraying the political, economic, and social institutions as being of any intrinsic value, colonial writers depict African nations as violent and war-mongering. Ethnic groups and social organizations are called "tribes," a derogatory word connoting lawless, disorganized bands of people. In actuality, Africa had nationalities of varying sizes with great differences in culture and values. As Jocelyn Murray points out, there were multiethnic states, as in Ethiopia in the nineteenth century and in Mali in the fourteenth century, under a single political authority. In some cases, single ethnic groups comprised a political unit such as the Zulus; while there were some groups like the Chagga of Kilimanjaro that were divided into several tiny political units (24).

The history of African civilizations is not presented as a time of glorious conquests and achievements, but as a time of despotism and bloodshed. For instance, Shaka, the founder of the Zulu empire, is condemned in all children's stories for his "senseless" bloodshed, burning and looting, and tyrannical treatment of innocent people. These books fail to recognize the irony that European nations also used force to maintain and expand their colonial possessions in Africa, Asia, and the Americas. Judged historically, Shaka was perhaps the first African ruler who attempted to unify South African nations into a strong empire against the advancing powers of Europe. Even the credit for the superbly organized army of Shaka is given to the Zulu contact with Europeans in books like *Sons of the African Veld*. The political authority--the chief or Arab sheik--is invariably undermined in colonial literature as cruel, violent, and self-serving.

Justification for the colonization of African nations is further based on the theory of survival of the fittest in the struggle between nations and races. "This conflict," according to social scientists, "far from being an evil thing, was nature's indispensable method for producing superior men, superior nations, and superior races" (Gossett 145). In Victor Pohl's *Farewell, the Little People*, a fictionalized study of the near-extinction of the "Bushmen," the idyllic existence of the San people is threatened by the coming of the tall blackmen, the Zulus, from the north; the yellowmen, or "Hottentots" (Khoi Khoi), from the south; and the mysterious, clothed whitemen from across the seas. Although the author presents San culture as advanced and refined, it is not fitted to survive in the Darwinian sense against the "superior" races. This novel perpetuates the myth--and the European view of African history--that African nations were in a constant state of flux and did not have a permanent residence, hence, no real claim to the land which the Europeans believed they had won by virtue of conquest, hard work, and perseverance.

Colonial stories perpetuate the stereotype that Africans are unable to govern their kingdoms competently or effectively; it is the white characters who administer the native territories in a tactful and sympathetic manner, hence bringing peace and order to a basically cruel and warlike people. In *King Solomon's Mines*, all the political problems of Kukuanaland are resolved, and a golden age predicted, when Ignosi promises to rule by British standards:

> when I sit upon the throne of my fathers, bloodshed shall cease upon the land. No longer shall ye cry for justice to find slaughter, no longer shall the witch-finder hunt ye out so that ye be slain without a cause. No man shall die save he who offendeth against the law. (156)

In *Doctor Doolittle's Post Office*, Hugh Lofting depicts the lack of administrative order in the kingdom of Fantippo. When Doctor Doolittle arrives on the scene, however, he organizes the domestic and foreign mail to be run by birds, and he settles the affairs of Chief Nyam-Nyam of the neighboring country by defeating his enemies and establishing a lucrative pearl trade with the help of cormorants. The white heroes in these fantasy-like adventures single-handedly gain leadership of the native population. In Roy Rockwood's *Bomba the Jungle Boy and the Cannibals*, the protagonist is able to protect an entire "tribe" of "Pygmies," whom Rockwood describes as, "brave in the fight, yet unstable as children in their decision" (192). As a leader, Bomba selflessly provides for those under his care, and animals and humans alike idolize him. The author makes it plain that "the responsibility thrust upon him [Bomba] called into play all his remarkable qualities of body and brain," because "He knew that he was different from the dark-skinned natives who surrounded him. He felt the tug of his white blood" (14-15). Rockwood would have readers believe that

Bomba, who is only a teenager, is more mature than adult Africans because of his "superior" racial heritage.

Similarly, novels on the British Navy's efforts to end the slave trade in East Africa invariably blame slavery on the Arab traders, the greed of African chiefs for money and Western goods, and the lawlessness of "tribal" society. In *Black Ivory*, the white characters are heroic saviors who free Africans from bondage because of their humanitarian and Christian civilization; ironically, there is seldom any mention of the European trade in slaves on the west coast.

Both African and European characters are stereotyped in colonial novels in order to rationalize territorial conquest. Darwin's biological theory of evolution gave validity to the doctrines of social scientists like Gobineau, Franklin Frazer, and Herbert Spencer that human beings had evolved from the ape in a unilinear fashion and that each race had its place in the hierarchial evolutionary ladder. The idea that Anglo-Saxons were on the topmost rung and the "savage" Africans were at an earlier stage of civilization through which the Europeans had already passed, took firm root in intellectual circles from the end of the nineteenth century to the early part of the twentieth century (Street 9). Culture and human experience were ignored and race was defined in purely biological terms. Racial superiority was graded by visible physical characteristics such as skin color, shape of the nose and forehead, brain size, and limb length. As Ruth Benedict states in *Race and Racism*: "They considered the evolutionary process a ladder, each rung of which has marked some advance upon the ape. Thus the apes have broad, flat noses, as have also the Bushmen, Negroes, and Australians; Europeans have narrow, prominent noses. More prominent configuration of the nose and lessened limb length were therefore end results of evolution and were characteristics of the white race" (64). *Thirty One Brothers and Sisters*, a fictional work by Reba Mirsky, implies that the "Pygmies" are the missing link in the evolutionary chain:

> Their arms seem too long for their bodies; their legs were short; their feet were very large, but their toes were the most remarkable of all. They were so long that they looked more like fingers than toes. How wonderful they must be for climbing trees. (158-59)

Ballantyne in *Six Months at the Cape? or Settler and the Savage* reduces "Bushmen" to the level of animals when he discusses how they differ from apes: "The highest type of monkey suggests--thanks, or, rather blame to Darwin--the lowest type of man in Africa . . . he is very far removed from the baboon. He has no tail, for certain, at least if he has, he conceals it effectually. He wears garments, which no monkey does, and he speaks, which no monkey ever did." Other novels describe "Bushmen" as crawling inside a dead elephant, eating raw meat, and growling like animals.

Through descriptions, white is associated with goodness and beauty, while black is evil and ugly. The romantic Prince Bumpo in *The Story of Doctor Doolittle* yearns to be white and to have blue eyes so that he can marry Sleeping Beauty. Doctor Doolittle makes Prince Bumpo soak his face in a mixture of chlorine, animal pigment, and zinc ointment and, to everyone's surprise, his face does turn as white as snow and his eyes turn from mud-colored to a "manly gray." When the doctor expresses misgivings about how long this "magic" will last, Dab-Dab the duck says, "Serve him right if he does turn black again! I hope it's a dark black" (105). This episode has the serious racial implication that "the black man, quite naturally wishes to be white but he can never become white with all that whiteness signifies, no matter how hard he tries, and how great his longing" (Dixon 106).

Apart from physical attributes, theories on the psychological evolution of the mind led Europeans to believe that Africans were inferior mentally as well. In *The African Colony*, a lengthy book discussing the possibility of political and social equality for Africans, John Buchan writes, "Mentally he is as crude and naive as a child, with a child's curiosity and ingenuity, and a child's practical inconsequence. Morally he has none of the traditions of self-discipline and order, which are implicit, though often in a degraded form, in white people. In a word, he cannot be depended upon as an individual save under fairly vigilant restraint" (290). Isak Dinesen, who spent many years on her coffee plantation in Kenya, echoes the Spencerian belief in the intellectual limitations of Africans:

> The dark nations of Africa, strikingly precocious as young children, seemed to come to a standstill in their mental growth at different ages. The Kikuyu, Karvirondo and Wakamba, the people who worked for me on the farm, in early childhood were far ahead of white children of the same age, but they stopped quite suddenly at a stage corresponding to that of a European child of nine. (11-12)

Brian Street points out that in colonial literature when Europeans are placed in the same circumstances as Africans, their superior heredity enables them to rise above the cultural and intellectual level of Africans (177). Edgar Rice Burroughs, in the story of Tarzan's evolution from ape-child to a "civilized" gentleman, illustrates that cultural characteristics are inherited genetically and that heredity is stronger than environment. When exposed to the trappings of Western culture, Tarzan is instinctively attracted to books and letters; makes tools and sliding knots; wants to wear clothes and take baths; and evolves sophisticated ideas on religion. He teaches himself to read and write English through picture books, primers, and dictionaries when he has never even heard the English language, or any human language being spoken. He journeys through the various "stages" of human evolution in a matter of four or five years.

On the strength of such "scientific" evidence, writers make generalizations about African characters. Africans are stereotyped as gullible, lazy, childish, simple-minded, indolent, cruel, and corrupt. In contrast, the white characters are invariably virtuous, brave, selfless, and disciplined. In children's fiction, even adult Africans are portrayed as childish or as grotesque caricatures of human beings; they are irresponsible and fearful, and they take childish glee in trinkets and toys. For example, King Dingaan plays with a telescope in *The Broken Spear* and King Koko in *Doctor Doolittle's Post Office* sits at the palace door sucking his lollipop. In *Kintu*, the chief delights over a coil of telephone wire that he has purchased from the white trader for four leopard skins and a pair of elephant tusks.

The idea that individual races inherit certain character traits depending on climate also gained popularity. Hence, the San and Mbuti ethnic groups are idealized because of their symbiotic relationship with the environment; the Zulus are termed bloodthirsty and cruel perhaps because they offered resistance to Europeans; the Bwa Bwa "dwarfs" and "cannibals" are considered hostile and dangerous; and the Arabs are seen as cunning, deceptive, and cruel. All interactions between Africans and whites are reduced to the level of superior and inferior, master and servant, or protector and child. In fictional works, Africans are usually minor characters holding menial jobs as servants, faithful followers, or warriors and chiefs who oppose the benevolent whites. Even in *Ambari!*, where Forbes-Watson narrates the exploits of two brave and intelligent East African boys, the ultimate resolution comes from their white friends and the colonial administration.

In colonial literature, African society and culture are trivialized and judged according to Western standards. In the area of religion, Africans are considered superstitious and highly susceptible to nonrational beliefs in their constant fear of the *idolozi,* or ancestral spirits, and the *inyanga,* called the "witch doctor." Religious practices are denounced as magical worship of demons and spirits. The *inyanga* is a favorite subject of ridicule and verbal abuse, instead of being considered a healer or a wise spiritual leader. The stereotypical "witch doctor" is a hideous and deformed embodiment of evil, who cunningly plays on the gullibility and superstitious beliefs of the people. In one novel, he is frequently referred to as "baboon," "old hyena," and "old buzzard." Books abound in descriptions of *inyangas* in grotesque costumes, engaged in meaningless ceremonies and inhuman rites. In *Seven Grandmothers,* the *inyanga's* hair is adorned with:

> five dried gall bladders, striped feathers in the . . . straggly reddened hair and a tuft of black fur that stuck out from the back of her head like a bushy tail. (10)

There is no systematic investigation of the intrinsic value of these rituals to Africans through a study of their culture and symbols. The message clearly reads that Western civilization and Christianity will bring salvation and prosperity to the savage land. Exotic features of African cultures such as polygamy, bride price, initiation rites, circumcision rites, body painting, clothing, and eating habits are represented in great detail, but without a true understanding of their religious and social value. In *Seven Grandmothers,* Mirsky states that Zulus have many beautiful and useful customs, "But there are others that are no longer sensible" (177).

Colonial literature has an obvious Christian agenda to convert "heathen" souls by recruiting prospective missionaries for the churches in Africa and by urging the homebound to contribute generously to missionary societies. A series of biographies and autobiographies of Western and African missionaries like David Livingstone, Thomas Comber, Mary Slessor, Canon Apolo, and Bishop Ajayi Crowther recount pioneering journeys into the interior of Africa. These individuals are portrayed as courageous, hardworking, and steadfast in their devotion. Missionary novels denounce traditional religions as primitive and cruel in order to promote

Christianity. In *Children of the Chief*, Mabel Shaw narrates the story of a mission school and how the students are transformed from rowdy, thoughtless girls to well-behaved and truthful women once the "white mama" introduces them to "Chief Jesus." In *Mpengo of the Congo*, a Christian family goes to live in a non-Christian village to set an example of fellowship and self-sacrifice, and to expose how the "witch doctor" exerts control by exploiting the villagers' belief in evil spirits and superstition.

The language and tone of these books also distort readers' view of Africans and their culture by using pejorative words like Pygmies, Hottentots, Bushmen, underdeveloped, jungle, bush, tribe, savage, primitive, bloodthirsty, ebony hide, and culturally deprived. Africans are the continual butt of racist insults. Throughout the Doolittle books, animals and birds are depicted as being smarter than Africans, and they engage in verbal abuse of Africans. In *Vengeance of the Zulu King*, Jenny Seed writes, "the men of Zulu rolled their eyes in alarm," and "The royal women were pushing and tearing at each other and shrieking as if they were in a state of madness" (72, 105). Such descriptions reduce Africans to the level of wild and senseless beings. African characters are named Flumbo, Sambo, Bumpo, Toto, and Loko-Moto to indicate that they are parodies of human beings.

While negative comments can be made about colonial literature, in all fairness, the painstaking work of numerous missionaries and anthropologists who recorded, collected, and translated folktales from various regions of Africa must be mentioned. In fact, a number of contemporary collections and pictures books are based on the field work of pioneering folklorists such as Leo Frobenius, George Herzog, R. S. Rattray, Heli Chatelain, A. C. Hollis, W. H. I. Bleek, and F. W. T. Possett. Jan Knappert has studied the diaries of travelers and accounts of early missionaries to piece together fragments of oral tradition and obtain a coherent picture. This task is especially difficult, he says, because the most deeply held religious beliefs cannot be revealed or discussed with strangers, and because "The early explorers did not realize this nor did the early missionaries, who described Africans as idolaters and barbarians" (12). While these collections of traditional stories are interesting, frequently, the introductory essays reflect the collectors' lack of understanding of the culture and beliefs. Rennie Bere's *Crocodile's Eggs for Supper*, based on thirty years' service in Uganda, reflects the author's Western perspective toward Acholi culture.

Colonial literature for children and young adults is clearly a rationalization for the economic, political, and religious exploitation of African nations. However, after World War I, there was a definite shift in paradigm, and consciousness against the colonial attitude was raised by enlightened philanthropists, writers, missionaries, and politicians. The doctrines of unilinear evolution, heredity and genetics, and brain size were proven to be unscientific. Modern race studies state: "No great civilization has been the work of a pure race, and neither history nor psychology, biology, nor anthropology can render decisions about the future destiny of any present human breed" (Benedict 141). In 1941, the British statesman, Clement Atlee, announced in the Labour Party Manifesto:

> We in the Labour Party have always been conscious of the wrongs done by the white races to the races with darker skins. We have always demanded that the freedom which we claim for ourselves should be extended to all men.

With this shift in the intellectual climate, colonial literature declined as African nations, beginning with Ghana in 1957, started to gain independence from Britain and other European powers.

POSTCOLONIAL WESTERN LITERATURE

The end of colonial rule did not signal an end to Western influence in Africa. Both independent African nations and the former powers wanted to continue the relationship. While African nations desired Western aid and technical assistance, Western countries wanted to maintain their trade monopolies, procure raw materials and markets for their products, and exert political influence on the new governments. Hence, Africa continues to be of interest to the Western world for political, economic, technological, humanitarian, and missionary reasons. Postcolonial Western literature reflects this renewed interest in Africa and shift in perspective. For adult readers, the tradition established by the humanistic novels of E. M. Foster, Joseph Conrad, and Graham Greene led to the caustic fiction and nonfiction of V. S. Naipaul and Shiva Naipaul who condemn the cultural and psychological damage done to the subject peoples. Regrettably, in the field of children's literature, some of the colonial stereotypes persist in postcolonial Western literature.

Most fictional works published after the 1960s continue to reflect the former prejudices, as well as creating some new stereotypes. The setting, presentation of African culture, plot, characterization, themes, and language and tone have to be analyzed carefully for any signs of covert bias because of the beguiling and charming exteriors of these novels. The jungle-type environment is still a favorite setting for books on Africa. Even books published in the last decade prefer a premodern, rural, or primitive setting, while modern city life, with its inherent adjustment to postcolonial realities, is totally ignored. It is the mysterious, Edenic, or traditional Africa that Western writers try to evoke. The exotic atmosphere of ancient Egypt and its monuments and the harshness of the Sahara Desert are also exploited in adventure and mystery novels like *Fear in Algeria, Bess and the Sphinx, Riders of the Wind, Cliffs of Cairo, The Dragon and the Thief, Tales of a Dead King,* and *King Tut's Game Board.* While the mysteries surrounding ancient tombs and artifacts are interesting to read about, the daily lives of North Africans are not explored.

Likewise, African culture is not represented in an authentic manner. Most authors focus on exotic ethnic groups such as the Zulus, Bantus, San, Masai, Watusi, or Mbuti. The cultural background is a superficial treatment of manhood ceremonies, rituals of witch doctors, polygamy and bride price, and clothing and bodily adornment. For instance, the ceremonies and social role of the Poro Tribal Council in *Salah of Sierra Leone* are not explained in depth; hence, its decisions appear to be arbitrary and cruel. *Lurk of Leopards* displays no negative stereotypes about Africa; yet, there are some vital omissions. It makes no reference to African culture and lifestyle and does not have a single native character who is vital to the story. The author seems to consider only African wildlife as worthy of consideration.

Postcolonial Western literature is also concerned with progress and development in Africa and European assistance to the newly emerging nations in the form of technology, education, and democracy. Hence, the plots of a number of books focus on the superiority of Western civilization. Willard Price's animal adventures are liberally sprinkled with derogatory episodes on governmental incompetence, political chaos and civil unrest, and rigid adherence to outmoded customs and beliefs. Set in 1966, *Salah of Sierra Leone* focuses on tribal jealousies and political turmoil; it is the Freetown Creoles who represent goodness and civilized Western ways. Similarly, Loren Graham in *I, Momolu* extols the advantages of bringing American culture, Western medicine and technology, Christianity, and the English language to Liberia. *Fear in Algeria* condemns the persecution of Christian missionaries by the fundamentalist Islamic government of Algeria without adequately exploring the postcolonial duality between the need for trained personnel from the West and maintaining their national pride and cultural heritage. Another missionary novel, *African Adventure*, focuses on the efforts of Christian organizations in combatting poverty, food shortages, and health care crisis in Chad. The white characters are do-gooders who selflessly serve in Chad, while President Timbabel's government is portrayed as dictatorial and unconcerned with human rights. The need for education is another favorite theme in novels of progress such as *The Village that Allah Forgot* and *Bisha of Burundi* because it spreads new ideas on more scientific methods of farming for the community and personal freedom for the characters.

In the area of characterization, the perspective and experiences of white characters in Africa and the conflict between Western and African values are depicted. In *Elephant Adventure*, Price describes "Pygmies" as: "This small, bare, dark-skinned creature of the forest with large head and old face seemed more like a chimpanzee than a man" (38). Price invariably focuses on the adventure and thrill of capturing live animals, while African characters are denounced as insensitive and unreliable. Still other novels perpetuate the stereotype of the elemental man who is in perfect harmony with the wild animals and untamed environment of Africa. They glorify primitivism and the mystical union with nature. For example, in *Bushbabies* William Stevenson dehumanizes Tembo, the older and wiser African character, by placing him in a subservient role to the rather impulsive eleven-year-old British protagonist. Tembo is portrayed as an idealized "natural" man, instead of as a citizen of a newly independent country who has to contend with changing political and social realities.

Happily, not all Western books published in the past thirty years suffer from an ethnocentric bias. There are some children's stories that view life from the perspective of Africans and depict their aspirations, conflicts, and triumphs. *Omoteji's Baby Brother* presents traditional family life as an integral part of growing up; *Lion Yellow*, set in Mbuyu Game Park, employs several metaphors that symbolize the changes facing independent Kenya; and *Mogo's Flute* is a delightful account of the inner development of a puny little boy who learns to balance his personal needs with the collective needs of family and community. The heroine of *Bisha of Burundi* represents the conflict between traditional religion and Christianity, one-party political system and Tutsi feudalism, formal education and oral tradition, and national unity and ethnic loyalties. In the last decade, there have been some outstanding books like *Story for a Black Night*, *Song of the Giraffe*, *The Captive*, and *Ajeemah and His Son*. *Captives in a Foreign Land* provides sensitivity toward the Arab world and dispels the stereotype of Arabs as unreasonable, violent, and narrowminded in their strict adherence to Islam.

The late 1980s saw another paradigm shift in the publishing world when eight of the Doctor Doolittle books were reissued by Dell in the Yearling Centenary Editions. In the Afterword to the book, Christopher Lofting states that the decision was a challenging one:

> Is it appropriate to reissue the *Doctor Doolittle* books exactly as written and stand on principle at the expense of our obligation to respect the feelings of others? Should future generations of children be denied the opportunity to read the *Doctor Doolittle* stories because of a few minor references in one or two of the books that were never intended by the author to comment on any ethnic group, particularly when the references are not an integral or important part of the story? (152-153)

In deference to the changing political climate and sensitivity toward ethnic groups, the publishers and Christopher Lofting, son of Hugh Lofting, took the opportunity to rewrite or delete the objectionable episodes, words, and illustrations from the original versions. For instance, *The Story of Doctor Doolittle* has been rid of all verbal abuse of Africans, offending descriptions, and pejorative adjectives that identify characters as black or white. The entire Sleeping Beauty and Prince Bumpo episode has been rewritten. This decision by Dell raises the issue of censorship: Should colonial literature be distorted, changed, and rewritten to make it acceptable to contemporary readers? Are modern critics being fair to writers like Lofting who wrote in a totally different political, social, economic, historical, and literary context? Should these works be relegated to their appropriate stage in the evolution of children's literature, as MacCann and Woodard suggest, and be placed in historical research collections rather than in the children's sections of libraries (6)? Now that the Hugh Lofting books are rid of their racist content, they seem to have revived the motif of a kindly doctor visiting Africa. William Steig's recent book, *Doctor DeSoto Goes To Africa,* is reminiscent of Doctor Doolittle's concern for animals.

While the number of novels set in Africa has decreased in the past decade, picture books on Africa that reflect painstaking artwork, research of cultural details, and a blend of Western artistic techniques and African motifs and styles have increased. Prominent among them are alphabet and counting books and collections of folktales and single tales from a variety of cultures like the Nuer, Zulu, Tos, Nandi, and Asante. *The Ox of the Wonderful Horns and Other African Folktales, How Many Spots Does a Leopard Have?, The Orphan Boy, What's So Funny, Ketu?, The Egyptian Cinderella, The Winged Cat, A Story, A Story, The Sabbath Lion, Tower to Heaven,* and *Traveling to Tondo* celebrate the traditions and beliefs of Africa. The joys and sorrows of childhood in modern Africa are represented through books like *The Day of Ahmed's Secret,* a series of books on the inner life of a girl named Osa, and *The Old, Old Man and the Very Little Boy,* an intergenerational story of wisdom and old age. The African American protagonists of *Africa Brothers and Sisters, Masai and I, Africa Dream, Cornrows, The Black Snowman,* and *Joshua's Masai Mask* search for their cultural identity by connecting with their African heritage, clothing, music, dance, and rituals. *When Africa was Home* is the story of a white American child who longs for his home, friends, and familiar surroundings in Malawi. *Oba of Benin* and *Aida* provide information on African history and achievements. *The Dancing Masks of Africa* explains the symbolic role of masks in West African traditions when masked male dancers mystically assumed the powers of their animal and spiritual deities. These picture books are especially distinctive because their exquisite illustrations represent a variety of techniques and styles. For instance, David Wisniewski in *Sundiata* follows a complicated process of cut-outs which are assembled with photo mountings and foam tape and then photographed to lend depth and perspective; Gerald McDermott in *Anansi the Spider* draws sequential movements to represent the frames of a movie film; Deborah Nourse Lattimore in *The Winged Cat* creates the impression of reading a papyrus manuscript; and Leo and Diane Dillon in *Aida* capture the glory and grandeur of ancient Egypt.

For factual information on individual countries and topics of special interest, there are numerous good quality nonfiction books for children. Biographical works, however, are restricted to well-known people who figure in the news. By focusing on Winnie and Nelson Mandela, Desmond Tutu, Abdel Gamal Nasser, Anwar Sadat, Haile Selassie, Muammar Qaddafi, Jomo Kenyatta, and Kwame Nkrumah, a very limited view of the shapers of African history, politics, and society is presented to children. More numerous are the pseudo biographies in series such as Children of Other Lands, Families the World Over, Families Around the world, A Family In, We Live In, and A Village In. Using a young child as a point of entry, these series provide a superficial sociological investigation into the family life, social roles, economic conditions, and beliefs and values of the area under scrutiny.

Informational books, in contrast, are more varied. Although there is an emphasis on wildlife, there are books on nearly every aspect of Africa. Series such as African Animal Discovery, Wildlife, Habits, and Habitats, Animal Friends Book, Books for Young Explorers, Easy Menu Ethnic Books, and Discovering Our Heritage range from books for preschoolers to secondary school children. The most interesting books, however, provide an in-depth account of specific cultural groups like the San, Masai, Zulu, Asante, Berber, Bedouin, and Mbuti; of special topics like the origin of humans, mummies, crafts and foods, and sociomathematics in Africa; of the achievements of ancient kingdoms such as Egypt, Meroe, Aksum, and

Zimbabwe; and of geographical topics like the Suez Canal, ecology of national parks, and endangered animal species.

Enchantment of the World, Portraits of the Nations, Places and Peoples of the World, Today's World, Let's Visit, A First Book, Conflict in the 20th Century, Where We Live, and A New True Book series focus attention on individual countries and regions of Africa. The Visual Geography series, originally published by Sterling, has been revised by Lerner for current information and statistics, African perspective of the subject matter, and elimination of biased diction and tone. Typically, informational books have page restrictions and rigid formats which dictate that the material be organized under such topics as land and geography, peoples and cultures, history and government, economy and industry, arts and crafts, and village and city life. While the information is easily accessible and clear, the text does not provide firsthand experience of life in that country. Furthermore, rigid conformity to page length and structure invites a judgmental approach by the author as to what is important and what is not. Also, information that is unique to a particular country may be omitted if it does not fit in the prescribed framework. The Enchantment of the World and Scholastic World Cultures seem to be the only series that are flexible enough to give a multifaceted portrait of each country. The information in each chapter is extended by brief prose essays on related topics.

Informational books published after the mid-1980s are concerned with dispelling the old myths and stereotypes about Africa. They trace history from the earliest known times, emphasize precolonial achievements, outline the reasons for European explorations and colonization, and portray modern political, economic, social, and cultural realities. While there are individual books like Alexander Creed's *Uganda* that contain oversimplifications of African history and a colonial bias, by and large these books tend to present a fair and objective picture of Africa. They acknowledge the paucity of research and the validity of oral histories and accounts of travelers in charting the early history of Africa; and the disruptive social, economic, and political influence of the slave trade and European colonization. They just as frankly discuss the problems confronting the newly independent nations: political instability, official corruption, and repressive governments; lack of capital; need for industrial development and technical training; inadequate health care; inadequate infrastructure for transportation and communication; and lack of trained teachers. They also point out that African nations do not necessarily have to seek a Western-style, multiparty democracy in order to progress, and that a one-party government, dictatorship, or military regime may be more suitable. Various forms of neocolonialism in the continent are also discussed.

Illustrations in nonfictional works, likewise, display a new awareness of and sensitivity to African pride by not giving an imbalanced or distorted impression. An attempt is made to depict all aspects of life in Africa: urban and rural, traditional and modern, subsistence farming and large agricultural projects, and cottage industries and modern factories. Attractive photographs and drawings, maps, list of facts, index and glossary are also included. Some of the material in the Visual Geography Series, however, is recycled. The nineteenth century colonial map of Africa, statistics on urban population, life expectancy, and literacy levels are inserted in each book.

Moreover, many black-and-white pictures from the old editions are interspersed with the more recent color photographs.

Pan-African Children's Literature

With the recent emphasis on books that reflect the multicultural makeup of society, children's publishing has seen the emergence of books on Africa that are written, illustrated, and published by African Americans. Small Afrocentric publishing houses such as Marral Enterprises, Karia Press, Red Sea Press, Black Classics Press, Africa World Press, African Islamic Mission, and Bellerophon Books celebrate their African roots and identity. Further incentive is provided to black writers and illustrators for children through the Coretta Scott King Award, established in 1969. Meant to empower the black community, these books are marketed through nonconventional methods at fairs, conventions, church groups, minority bookshops, and private homes (Igus 14-18).

The Positive Image Education series published by Afro-Vision, in particular, is committed to addressing the issue of negative self-image among African Americans by publishing informational books that offer "positive, accurate, and readable lessons from Black history." Daud Malik Watts, the founder of Afro-Vision, states: "We have found that the records of history abound with positive images of Black people, and that the history of Africans is one from which *all* people can gain knowledge, wisdom, and pride" (cover page). Books like *My First Trip to Africa, Afro-Bets First Book About Africa, Story of Africa's Flags to Color, 100,000 Horsemen*, and *Roots of Time* set the record straight by outlining the reasons for European expansion in Africa, the impact of colonialism, and the misinformation or Eurocentric interpretation of African history. They also describe the achievements of precolonial Africa in the areas of science, industry, mathematics, statesmanship, medicine, engineering, architecture, horsemanship, art, and writing and literature. These books also portray the rich and diverse life in traditional Africa by examining communal organizations, supportive family life, psychological effect of rituals, age-sets, respect for environment, noncompetitive economy, kinship ties, and marriage customs. Daud Malik Watts' *Gifts of the Nile* examines the geography, history, religion, culture, scientific achievements, and architecture of Egypt with the specific purpose of establishing that ancient Egypt was populated by or had direct contact with the African heartland. References to primary Egyptian, Greek, Roman, and Biblical sources support the above claim. The convention of visiting Africa for spiritual sustenance is a powerful theme in children's literature. Eight-year-old Atlantis Tye Browder's *My First Visit to Africa* depicts the young author's pride in discovering her African heritage when she visits Egypt. Atlantis Tye is particular about giving the original names of places, people, and objects. Readers are challenged to consider the importance of names and the subversive politics of changing African names.

Collections of folktales and single tales celebrate the ancient wisdom, rituals, religious ideologies, and inherent beliefs that gave meaning and dignity to the lives of Africans. Jamal Koram, the storyteller, directs his retellings of African fables specifically at innercity children to emphasize the need to be principled, courageous, and true to oneself. He also stresses the concept of oneness of family and of living and working together as Africans in the global community. These folktales also dispel the myth that African religions are superstitious and primitive; rather, they are a celebration of life, creation, and the human community. The African American holiday of Kwanzaa is inspired by these beliefs and the harvest rituals of ancient Africa.

Like the books published by white authors, African American publications also tend to focus on rural Africa. Instead of presenting the realities of life in modern Africa, they prefer to go back to their roots, to the Africa that was when their ancestors were chained and brought to America. Their objective, however, is not to portray an exotic or backward Africa, but to affirm their African origins and to celebrate traditional African culture. These books aspire to counteract the self-hatred and negative stereotypes perpetuated as a consequence of slavery, exploitation, and continued racism. The social agenda of these authors is that once the above attitudes of group pride are ingrained, a strengthened African American community can then attend to the pressing problems of innercity violence, disillusionment of black youth, poverty, and illiteracy.

South African Children's Literature

Children's literature published in South Africa, which has deliberately been placed in this section because it represents the literature of and for the white elite, reflects a relaxation of censorship rules and a change in attitude. From the openly racist and derogatory books that perpetuated the implacable Afrikaner attitude of exclusive rights in South Africa, white South African writers have recently begun to voice the suffering and hopes of black South Africans.[5] The tradition of revolt established by adult authors like Nadine Gordimer, Etienne Leroux, and Andre Brink is permeating into children's books as well. There is a definite shift in the intellectual climate that emphasizes that the interests of South Africa's varied racial groups do not have to be incompatible. In an effort to ''contribute towards the creation of a just, democratic and non-racial country,'' courageous publishers like Ravan, Skotaville, and Maskew Miller Longman explore the sensitive themes of racial prejudice against blacks, demands for a fair and equitable educational system in the townships, interracial friendship, and participation of white pacifists in the liberation struggle (Randall 5).

Recent books by these publishers attempt to describe the problems and experiences of black protagonists in a sensitive manner. However, the open-ended plots, restrained tones, failure to depict the anger and resentment of blacks, lack of direct condemnation of governmental policies, and powerlessness of the characters imply the inability of authors/publishers to take a definite stand. In *Wake Up Singing*, *Kayaboeties*, and *PIG*, the youthful idealism of white liberals is presented as something that they will outgrow when confronted with adult realities; they must learn to ''tow the line'' despite private sympathies. The interracial friendship in these stories is one-sided, with the white characters taking leading roles and the blacks merely passive recipients. *Love, David* gives the impression that apartheid is a just and fair system for blacks, and the alienation of the protagonist is blamed on his confusion and family situation. Still other authors like Jenny Seed (*Ntombi's Song*), Niki Daly (*Not So Fast Songololo*), Isadora Rachel (*At the Crossroads* and *Over the Green Hills*), and Ruth Craft (*The Day of the Rainbow*) either do not address the political issues, or minimize the difficulties of living in an apartheid society; instead, they present the universal or pleasanter aspects of life and growing up in homelands and racially segregated cities. Marguerite Poland's restraint in *Once at KwaFubesi* is obvious as she delicately maneuvers readers' sympathy by using metaphors and analogies from the world of nature to describe the migrations of tribes in South Africa, power struggle among races, and survival of the fittest. These books are set within the social and political framework of apartheid, and the solution or outcome is always within the hegemonic culture. Rory Ryan cautions that this inability to condemn apartheid is a literary stance that actually perpetuates white superiority: "The institutionalization of an imperialist discursive form under the guise of a neutral (objective, truth-serving, self-evident, ideologically disinterested) rationality is the source of current cultural-social power in the South African academy" (4). He further states that in such novels the oppositional voices are trivialized, controlled, dismissed, and marginalized by presenting reactionary behavior as socially ill-mannered, hysterical, Marxist, and rebellious (7).

However, there are some exceptional books like *Ghamka, Man-of-Men*, which provides a respectful treatment of traditional social organization, religious beliefs, and social customs prior to Portuguese landings in South Africa; *Summer's End*, set in a future ice age, which depicts South Africans as a happy blend of African and European characteristics, whose society resembles precolonial Africa; and *Tutti and the Black Iron*, which is a fantasy linking modern South Africa with the iron-making skills and technical achievements of ancient Africans. However, all three books are set far enough in the past or future so as not to offend political sensibilities, or to make an impact on contemporary values. They do not subvert or deconstruct the power of the state. It is only when "the mechanisms of humanist-colonial power-preservation are exposed," says Ryan, that literature can hope to become a real instrument of change (13). Gladys Thomas' *Spotty Dog and Other Stories* is, perhaps, the only book published in South Africa that reveals the daily humiliations and inner despair of township children.

While the literary scene in South Africa may appear to be more relaxed in the 1980s, there is very little writing by black South Africans, and it is generally nonpolitical and nonsubversive. Prominent among children's books are some folktales by Gcina Mhlope, picture books by Maria Mabeota, and a few collections of protest poems by Zindzi Mandela and Mlungisi Mkhize. The most outstanding book is *Two Dogs and Freedom*, a collection of writings by the children of Soweto, because it chronicles the experiences of black children under oppression and voices their dreams and aspirations. The protest and revolutionary literature by black South Africans like Zindzi Mandela (*Black as i am*), Peter Magubane's photo essays, Mark Mathubane (*Kaffir Boy*), and Oswald Mtshali (*Sounds of a Cowhide Drum*) were all published abroad. According to Martin Trump, black writers offer a different view of history: Black struggle against colonial capitalism, continuity between precapitalist and capitalist black societies, and the experiences and memories of a collectivist society, or communal past form a significant part of the black South African's consciousness and vision (163-165). However, protest literature by both blacks and whites is inaccessible to black readers. Dorothy Driver suggests that the censor's decision to permit the publication of political and realistic books that censure apartheid if addressed to a literary audience, only means that "much writing by black writers is banned, while most writing by whites is accessible" (171).

For truly political works for children, one has to read books by expatriate South Africans who live and publish outside South Africa. In *Free As I Know,* Beverley Naidoo writes that at the age of eighteen she "became conscious of the artificially-constructed blinkers of racist prejudice which were distorting my vision as a white South African . . . Much of what I saw was deeply painful and was a direct result of the system which gave me and my white community its privileges" (6). When she left for England to study, she became actively involved in the struggle to end apartheid through her research, teaching, and writing. In particular, she reveals the plight of women under apartheid in *Journey to Jo'burg* and *Chain of Fire*: feeding and clothing the family; nursing sick and dying children; caring for the elderly; and, quite often, leaving families in homelands to seek domestic employment in white cities. Sheila Gordon, Hugh Lewin, Toeckey Jones, and Donald Woods also speak out against the ills of apartheid. In *The Middle of Somewhere* and *Waiting for the Rain*, Gordon depicts the feelings of black characters as they are forcibly removed from their homes and relocated in homelands; as their anger and dreams find expression in protest marches and rallies; and as they attempt to bring pride and dignity to their lives through small symbolic acts. *Skindeep* by Jones explores the inner feelings of a colored who passes as white. Lewin, in contrast, nostalgically captures his love for South Africa through a series of romantic books about Jafta, who lives in a homeland. Lewin presents Jafta's spiritual affinity with nature and his cultural heritage, as well as describing indirectly and gently the effects of apartheid on the little boy's life. Woods' biography of Steven Biko is a scathing relevation of the apartheid infrastructure and institutionalized racism. South African authors in exile are committed to exposing the impact of apartheid on the lives of all South Africans--black, colored, Asian, and white.

POSTCOLONIAL AFRICAN LITERATURE

The history of literature written and published specifically for African children began in the 1960s with independence from colonial rule. Precolonial literature for children was oral in nature, passed down by adults in the form of folktales, myths, songs, riddles, and proverbs. During the colonial period, children's reading was confined to textbooks and Western literature which promoted Western culture and values. As was the case with the newly emerging nations of Asia, political independence led to the development of an intellectual climate that firmly insisted that children's literature should "work outward from the home base" of the African students so that they will not become "culturally stateless persons" (Roscoe, *Mother* 133).

In the 1960s and 1970s, a series of seminars and conferences were held throughout Africa to address the problems of colonial bias in school curricula and textbooks; to develop relevant classroom material; to publish trade books with a suitable African content; to write in African languages; and to determine the role of national governments in promoting and assisting a children's book industry.[6] At the Ife Conference on Publishing in Africa in the Seventies (1973) and the Legon Conference on children's literature (1976), a strategy for forging an indigenous African consciousness through children's reading was outlined. At the Ife Conference, McLean and Oluwasanmi pointed out that the vacuum of Afrocentric reading material for children was "filled with books which are written for European or North American children. African children are unable to relate to these books. What is needed are children's books that are relevant to their own environment in textual content and illustration" (qtd. in Osa, *Nigerian* 15). Thus, the development of a typically African children's literature was the direct result of the need to "repatriate" the school system and revise the textbooks.

Not surprisingly, in the early years of independence, the publishing industry in Africa was dominated by overseas firms like Macmillan, Longman, Heinemann, and Evans, which propagated a new form of colonialism that determined what Africans could read or write--hence, think (Nottingham 103). Since these multinational companies were in Africa to make money, they focused mainly on textbooks where they were assured a ready market for their products, or they published only those indigenous writers and books that would sell internationally. A study of publishing trends in postcolonial nations indicates that, "The multinationals do not always work to the benefit of the Third World. They are concerned basically with the profitability of the corporation and not of the host country, and their publishing decisions are made with their own interests in mind" (Altbach and Gopinathan 17).

Sensitive to neocolonialism in the publishing business and eager to take economic, cultural, and ideological control, Africans indigenized these companies in the 1970s in order to establish a strong publishing industry "where both policy and editorial control" were in African hands (Nottingham 105). They believed that cultural independence would become a reality only when Africans discarded their "colonial hangover" and started writing for Africans and not for foreign publishers. The Ife Conference, in particular, led to cooperation among publishers, writers, and booksellers throughout Africa to outline the problems of publishing and to devise a plan to overcome them. They sought to increase the pool of competent, well-trained editors and printers, especially in the latest technical advances; to devise strategies to overcome rising prices and shortage of printing paper; to encourage young and unknown authors; to solicit active involvement by publishers in campaigns to eradicate illiteracy; to form professional booksellers' associations to improve distribution, marketing, and promotion; to widen the role of libraries and teachers' organizations in developing the book reading and book buying habit; and to stress the necessity for cooperation among publishers at the national, regional, and continent-wide levels (Rathgeber 57-59).

In response to the above needs, several established writers such as Meshack Asare, Asenath Bole Odaga (Lake Publishers & Enterprises), Kola Onadipe (Natona Press), Buchi Emecheta, Chinua Achebe, Mabel Segun, and Flora Nwapa (Tana Press) sought to fill the void in children's publishing by either starting their own independent publishing companies, or by dedicating themselves to writing books that embody African themes and forms. Today, in addition to these small independent publishers and the indigenized foreign publishers, there are several firms like Adwinsa, Afram, African Universities Press, Baobab, DUCA, East African Publishing House, Edupress, Ethiope Publishing Corporation, Fourth Dimension, Ghana Publishing Corporation, Ibadan University Press, Jacaranda Designs, Obobo Books, Onibonoje, Phoenix, Sedco, Spectrum, Uganda Publishing House, Unimax, Waterville, and Y-Books that are committed to publishing children's books. Adrian Roscoe believes that these writers and publishers are taking

> responsibility for the rehabilitation of a *whole* society and not merely for the adult segment of it. In the kind of cultural battle they are waging, no effective strategy could exclude the rising generation of schoolchildren who are always felt to carry the promise of a better tomorrow. (*Mother* 132)

The hurdles that continue to thwart the development of a viable book industry for children, however, are problems associated with publishing. Due to a lack of widespread readership; low per capita income; poor purchasing power of parents, especially for nontextbooks; low literacy throughout the continent; dependence on industrialized nations for reasonably priced, good quality imported books; poor infrastructure for distribution; emphasis on textbook publication; lack of sophisticated publishing technology; and almost no children's libraries and no training for children's librarians, children's publishing is a risky financial venture ("IBBY News" 35). Also, technology for producing superior books with colorful illustrations does not exist on a wide scale with the result that the books are poorly produced and unattractive. Because children's books are expensive due to limited print runs for a small community of English-language readers, because foreign books are readily available in libraries and bookstores, and because buying trade books is considered a waste of money and time by the general public, it is especially difficult to promote and encourage children's literature. Sugh Loho, in a revealing article, analyzes the role of the traditional social structure in discouraging the reading habit among children (143-144).

In order to offset some of the problems associated with children's publishing, individual countries have engaged in unique experiments to make children's books available to a wider population. Because of the reality of low literacy, priority is given to reading for literacy so that a reading culture can be established. In Ghana, the Ghana Library Board, established in 1950, set up children's reading rooms in public libraries in cities and provided children with books through the mobile library service (Pellowski 267). In Nigeria, the Nigeria Library Association, founded in 1978, is responsible for organizing readership promotion campaigns. In Zimbabwe, the Home Libraries Project, which received the 1990 IBBY-Asahi Reading Promotion Award, has established mini-libraries in private homes where an adult member of the family serves both as storyteller and librarian. In addition to making printed material available to children, this project preserves African oral traditions, encourages children's creativity to formulate stories, motivates parents and the community to inculcate an appreciation for books, and encourages new literates to use their reading skills ("IBBY News" 35-37). In Mali, Operation Lecture Publique, founded in 1977, won the 1992 IBBY-Asahi Reading Promotion Award for establishing a network of forty-six public libraries, especially in remote rural communities. This project makes books available to children and their families, organizes extensive book related activities, publishes children's books and magazines, and records and collects folklore in the local languages ("Focus IBBY"). In Malawi, the National Library Service and the Malawi National Commission for UNESCO organized a training seminar in 1992 for writers of children's books and launched a project, "Writing for Children," which ensures quality publications for children (Chimombo, "A Brief Report"). In Egypt, the eighth IBBY-UNESCO workshop and international symposium on reading was held in Cairo in 1992 to discuss various aspects of publishing for children and to launch the Portable Libraries Project to make books available to rural children (Maissen).

Significant improvements have also been made in the field of children's publishing. The Second Pan African Children's Book Fair that was held in 1993 indicates that positive developments are taking place in the area of children's literature. Recent publications by Skotaville (South Africa), Baobab Books (Zimbabwe), Fourth Dimension (Nigeria), and Jacaranda Designs (Kenya) show improvement in the quality of the paper, printing techniques, binding, editing, and overall book design. Picture books, in particular, display a remarkable improvement in the technical artistry of the illustrations; creativity of the paintings by award winning artists like Joel Oswaggo (Kenya) and Colleen Cousins (Zimbabwe); complexity of colors used; and overall reproduction of the illustrations in the printing process. The promotional brochure of Jacaranda Designs claims that only top quality illustrations based on authentic African designs and art forms and original paintings and drawings are acceptable. Jacaranda Designs and Longman Zimbabwe are especially sensitive to the dearth of adequate reading material for preschool and early elementary age groups. Jacaranda Designs has initiated a carefully structured and expanding program for beginning learners through a series of books on the alphabet, numbers, colors, story books, poems, and fun books. The books are intended to stimulate language development, creative and critical thinking skills, and a dignified view of themselves and their cultural diversity.

Closely related to the problems of publishing and low readership is the language controversy, which has been heatedly debated by intellectuals since the end of the colonial era. To the Kenyan author Ngugi wa Thiong'o, the question of whether or not to write in English (or French or Portuguese) symbolizes the struggle between two mutually opposed forces in Africa today: an imperial tradition that continues to define itself in terms of the languages of the colonizers, and the resistance to the neocolonial control of the economy, politics, and culture offered by patriotic students, writers, and thinkers who seek to usher in an era of self-determination (2-4). Ngugi regrets that even the most radical pro-African writers have sought the renaissance of Africa through the languages of Europe (5). He maintains that writing in non-African languages denies the urban poor and rural populations access to knowledge and information, and it creates an elite class that is distanced from the mainstream of Africa (83-85). Above all, detractors of writing in English emphasize that the colonial mentality has succeeded in weakening African self-respect to the extent that everything British or foreign is respected. They want to "end all foreign domination of African culture, to systematically destroy all encrustrations of colonial and slave mentality, to clear the bushes and stake out new foundations for a liberated African modernity" (Chinweizu 1).

Supporters of writing in English, in contrast, point out that English has become a language of communication with the international community, among African nations, and within the same country because of linguistic diversity. Adrian Roscoe, in analyzing the problem of English and the vernaculars, states in *Uhuru's Fire*: "It is well known that the wealth of language Africa has inherited from the past hangs on the continent like a mill-stone, obstructing basic communication, exasperating central governments, confusing education systems, and making the overall task of development hopelessly tough and expensive" (1). Anglophone writers emphasize that the former British colonies in Africa have adopted English as the official language of communication and as the medium of instruction in schools because of political expediency, because no one indigenous language is universally understood or has wide readership, and because English is a cohesive and unifying force in the continent. As a result, English is the language that leads to success in the professional, business, and social worlds.

Chinua Achebe, in defending the use of English, stated that "colonialism in Africa . . . gave [Africans] a language with which to talk to one another. If it failed to give them a song, it at least gave them a tongue, for sighing. . ." (qtd. in Cott 164). Writing in favor of the "domestication" of English in Nigeria, Osayimwense Osa writes: "Using English language does not mean an illicit dependence or passive imitation relieved by no adaptive originality of usage. The Nigerian does not have to use English language as a British or as an American. But he has to adapt it for its communicative use—'a new English, still in full communion with its ancestral home but altered to suit its new African or Nigerian surroundings'" ("Wither" 148). The writings of Amos Tutuola are a case in point. Tutuola has developed a vigorous prose style in English based on Igbo and Yoruba idioms and syntax to give this borrowed colonial language an African flavor. However, the popularity of his works in the Western world has offended and embarrassed many educated Nigerians who condemn his writing as bad grammar and his popularity as an act of condescension by racists (Lindfors, ''Tutuola'' 140).

In the context of children's books, the language debate is fraught with controversy. The Kenyan author Asenath Odaga points out that children's literature, which is an extension of the English-based school system, contradicts and undermines the African languages that are used in most homes. Although Odaga writes both in Luo and English, she believes that ''the use of English from the lowest classes or grades continues to hamper the evolution of an authentic literature for children and young people that has values and images relevant to the emergent Kenyan society.'' She further states that there are ''certain values of a people which they can only pass on to their youth in the original language in which the culture itself functions and is promoted'' (*Literature for Children* xiii).

Some questions raised by the language issue are: Who is the audience for African books in English? Are African writers who publish abroad trying to write to the demands of the Western reader, or are they being true to their African identities? Can English-language books represent African culture in an authentic manner? Do these books empower young Africans? Does publishing in English increase the sales of imported books to the detriment of African writers? Because readership is small in African languages, because English has become the *lingua franca* of the educated classes, and because the English-language book buying public is more able financially to purchase nontextbook material for their children, publishing for children in English is more vibrant and progressive than in the national languages.

Publishing in the indigenous languages has, nevertheless, made some progress. Since independence in 1950, Ghana has ushered in a period of aggressive publishing to produce inexpensive, quality books for neoliterates, especially children, and the general public in nine Ghanaian languages (Djoleto 76). North African countries, in general, have a negligible amount of English-language books available for children, mostly reprints of British and European classics intended as supplemental English readers. Children's reading needs, however, are fulfilled through a sophisticated Arabic-language publishing industry based in Egypt, or through imported books from other Islamic countries like Lebanon and Pakistan. In Ethiopia, children's books are published mainly in Amharic. In Zimbabwe, Baobab Books is committed to publishing texts simultaneously in four languages --English, Ndebele, Shona, and Tonga--making them available to a wider audience and reducing production costs by using the same color plates for the illustrations. In Kenya, Jacaranda Designs has started publishing books simultaneously in English and Kiswahili. In Malawi, children's books in both English and Chichewa are being encouraged under the ''Writing for Children'' project.

Major Themes

African children's literature in English represents a split identity because it is the product of dichotomous forces: African versus Western, traditional versus modern, rural versus urban. On the one hand, children's authors are engaged in restoring cultural pride by reconnecting with their roots, and, on the other hand, they recognize the pressing need to pursue the benefits of Western civilization through formal education, science, and technology. This duality in children's literature, often embodied in works by the same author, is the result of the search for a typical African consciousness.

Traditionalists place great emphasis on oral legacy as an effective medium through which a common set of values and an African worldview can be transmitted to children. Wanjiku Kabira writes, "It is therefore of great importance to study the oral literature if we are to appreciate the people's feelings, hopes, fears, aspirations, philosophy and aesthetics. In other words the totality of the people's way of life" (3). In *African Religions and Philosophy*, John Mbiti analyzes the connection between traditional cultures and religions and their influence on Africans' understanding of themselves and the world around them: "Only religion is fully sensitive to the dignity of man as an individual. . . who has both physical and spiritual dimensions. . . In practical terms, religion has a role to play in cultivating reconciliation, harmony, peace and security with and within oneself, the community, the nation and the universe" (274).

Perhaps, the strongest expression of pride in African culture is reflected in the efforts of scholars and folklorists from all over Africa to collect, record, translate, and publish their oral heritage. Their efforts are timely because African folklore is fast disappearing due to the impact of Western civilization and culture; the rejection of traditions by the younger generation; modern means of communication and entertainment; rising literacy and book buying culture; and rapid urbanization and industrialization. In Malawi, Adrian Roscoe and Ellis Singano have worked on behalf of the University of Malawi to collect folktales; in Kenya, Asenath Odaga, Wanjiku Kabira, and Karega Mutahi are committed to recording and translating Luo and Gikuyu tales in English; in Nigeria, Chinua Achebe and Cyprian Ekwensi celebrate Yoruba myths; in Southern Africa, Chisiya, Marguerite Poland, Charles Mungoshi, and Chiman Vyas have recorded tales from all the major language groups; in Egypt, Hasan El-Shamy has collected and translated Arab prose tales from the Nubian, Bedouin, and Berber groups; in Sierra Leone, the People's Educational Association is a leader in this venture; and in The Gambia, Charlotte Collin has recorded and translated Gambian children's games from various ethnic groups. Collectors like Dan Kabele and Asenath Odaga have also developed a systematic methodology to record the oral material; to examine the difficulties of collection, transcription, and translation; and to study existing genres, transmission techniques, circumstances of presentation, and analysis and interpretation of the recorded material. In Malawi, Steve Chimombo has examined the theory of *ulimbaso,* the verbal aesthetics and linguistic models of the Bantu-speaking peoples of Southern Africa.

In children's literature, this vast fund of recorded material has found expression in folktales, novels which embody the style and form of oral narratives, translations of traditional poetry and songs, historical plays and novels, and biographies. By far, the most popular genre is the retellings of folktales, legends, and myths. In fact, in Nigeria, 233 percent of children's books are folktales, stated Abiola Odejide in a paper delivered to the

Institute of African Studies (7). Recent years have seen the publication of several outstanding collections for children by Chinua Achebe, Cyprian Ekwensi, Amos Tutuola, Charles Mungoshi, Abayomi Fuja, Dannabang Kuwabong, Ken Saro-Wiwa, Diana Pitcher, and Tim Matthews. In recreating an actual storytelling experience, they incorporate the circumstances of the storytelling; songs which are an essential element of a performance; explanatory remarks on the historical and social background; and verbal exchanges with the listeners. There are tales and songs for all occasions--birth, naming ceremony, initiation, marriage, death--which lend dignity and meaning to life. Oral literature offers an understanding of past history, develops strategies for facing the daily problems of survival, presents behavioral codes for community living and personal happiness, instills respect for ancestral spirits, as well as raising some complex ethical and philosophic issues. Adrian Roscoe states in *Tales of Old Malawi*, "What rises vividly from the stories, then, is a basic truth (often forgotten in the complexities of industrial societies) that codes of morals and systems of values arise from, and speak to, real human situations and are not the mere dreams of sages and divines" (viii).

In the area of fiction, Tutuola's novels resemble oral narratives in their recounting of the exploits of a central character who faces supernatural beings, human foes, and physical obstacles while fulfilling a quest. Around these first person accounts, Tutuola organizes a vast array of folklore, Yoruba and Igbo proverbs, rich details of animal and plant life, descriptions of fabulous ancient kingdoms, cultural beliefs, and religious rituals. In *The Brave African Huntress*, *Feather Woman of the Jungle*, *The Palm-Wine Drunkard*, *Simbi and the Satyr of the Dark Jungle* and other heroic adventures, he rejects the conventions of Western literature and culture to present an African aesthetic and worldview. Cyprian Ekwensi's *An African Night's Entertainment* and *The Passport of Mallam Ilia*, although they can be charged with being exotic, also follow the structure of an oral history. Readers are held captive by the continual action, sensational episodes, and wealth and power of the protagonists as they pursue a life of revenge over a beautiful woman.

Still other writers search for the pastoral idyll and a traditional lifestyle as answers to the ills of society. In *The Moonlight Bride* and *The Wrestling Match*, Buchi Emecheta presents the rural setting as a place of family values, community solidarity, respect for the authority of elders, and the intertwining of rituals and customs in an individual's life. In *The Storm*, a village youth's visit to his grandparents provides Odaga with an ideal framework for introducing Kenyan children to the myths, folktales, and historical legends associated with the Yimbo region. In *Simbi Nyaima*, Odaga dramatizes the myth of the deluge when the village of Simbi was believed to have totally submerged under water.

Historical novels and biographies infuse pride in past achievements and the modern struggle for independence. Emecheta's *The Rape of Shavi*, a modern fable set in the imaginary kingdom of Shavi, examines how Western civilization stripped Shavians of their natural resources, dignity, and harmonious existence among themselves and with neighboring communities. Meja Mwangi's *Jimi the Dog* and *Little White Man*, both set during the Mau Mau Movement, describe British exploitation of Kenya and shatter the colonial myth that the guerrilla fighters were inhuman and bloody murderers. In Ngugi wa Thiong'o's political allegories, also set during the Kenyan nationalistic movement, history, fantasy, and heroic myth intertwine with the protagonist's experiences to expose the evils of colonialism and celebrate the sacrifice of patriots. In Zimbabwe, the Chimurenga War and the glory and heroism of its martyrs are the subjects of historical novels, dramas, and informational books.

Biographies of past heroes provide children with suitable role models and demonstrate the relationship between national service and individual responsibility. Young readers are introduced to historical personages like Oluyole the Basorun, Emotan of Benin, Nii Ayi Bontey, Menelick I, Osei Bonsu, Queen Nzinga, Horombo, Mzee Nyachote, Khema of Botswana, and Betty and Kenneth Kaunda. These biographies, while they do not meet the standards of literary excellence, set the record straight by emphasizing the wisdom, bravery, and leadership qualities of the subjects; the economic self-sufficiency and humanistic goals of traditional communities; and the achievements of African kingdoms and their efforts to end slavery and introduce reforms.

Modernity in children's literature, in contrast, is primarily embodied in an imitation of Western literary forms, themes, and sensibilities. This tendency is easily discernible in nursery rhymes and picture books, some drama, mystery and adventure stories, school stories, stories of growing up, and stories of social progress. Perhaps, the most blatantly imitative books are picture books like *Sam and His Blue Train*, a copy of "The Little Engine That Could," and *Dabodabo Akosua*, a variation of the "Ugly Duckling" story. Most nursery rhymes reflect the Euromodernist tendency to use Western rhyming patterns and imported diction and imagery, while the vast fund of traditional themes, symbols, and poetic idioms and forms remain untapped. Collections like *Children's Stories and Riddles*, *Sing Me a Song*, *Lots of Wonders*, and *Beneath the Rainbow* contain nature and animal poems, but they also give voice to the postcolonial aspirations for progress through education, medical doctors, and social responsibility of youth.

Adventure and mystery stories, based on the Enid Blyton and R. L. Stevenson models, use formula plots, stereotypical characters, and hackneyed themes that have been "domesticated" to fit the African setting. *Juju Rock*, *The Adventures of Souza*, *Akpan and the Smugglers*, *The People from the Sea*, *Inspector Rajabu Investigates*, *Ehanna and Friends*, *Adventure in Mombasa*, and *Adventure in Nakuru* are some of the better examples. What Bernth Lindfors writes in connection with Ekwensi's adventure stories can be applied universally: "He has mastered the conventions and commonplaces of foreign juvenile adventure fiction and knows how to domesticate them. His is a literature of imitation and adaption, not a literature of imagination and original invention" ("Cyprian Ekwensi" 7).

Boarding school stories, a popular subgenre of the school stories, portray the life of students in dormitories under strict regulations; in conflict with teachers and prefects when rules are broken; in friendships and rivalries; and in overcoming obstacles to acquire an education. With the exception of a few cultural details, these stories could easily have been set in Britain. *Growing up in Lina School*, in particular, reads like an issue of the *School Girl* or *Girl's Crystal* magazines that were so popular in

Western-style girls' schools throughout the British empire. Similarly, in stories of character building and growing up such as *Without a Silver Spoon*, *The Drums of Joy*, *Chike and the River*, *The Adventures of Souza*, *Footsteps in the Dark*, *The Prize*, and *Youth Day Parade*, the protagonists are either victims of deception, or they are caught in circumstances that lead to their personal maturity and self-knowledge. While these are universal themes that all good literature should explore, the emphasis on plot and theme, sparse prose, and superficial character delineation results in stories that lack vigor, imagination, and skill.

As was typical of the early postcolonial Western novels set in Africa, African children's writers also stress the need for social progress and the role of youth in effecting change. These stories reflect both the aspirations of newly independent African nations to acquire the comforts of Western civilization and the tenacious hold that colonial attitudes have on modern Africans. These social consciousness novels depict postcolonial African societies trying to achieve modernity through education (*Village Boy!*, *Eze Goes to School*, *Kofi Mensah*, *The Potter's Wheel*, *A Lucky Chance*); Western medicine (*The Boy Doctor*); and reform of social evils like infanticide, abandonment of twins and hunchback babies, and human sacrifice (*Zandi and the Wonderful Pillow*, *Koku Baboni*, and *The Angry Flame*). The feminist themes of bride price, second class status of women, and neglect of girls' education are the subjects of Asenath Odaga's *Jande's Ambition*, Buchi Emecheta's *The Moonlight Bride*, and Teresa Meniru's *Unoma*. Odaga was among the first children's novelists to portray an exemplary female character who is strong, makes mistakes, and learns from them. In an interview with Adeola James, Odaga explains: "What I do not like is the way men writers handle female characters in their books, in a way that makes them stupid or lazy or sensual. . . I hope when more African women write they will try to give the African woman the dignity she deserves" (129).

Recent years have also seen the emergence of the Macmillan's Pacesetters and the Fontana/Collins Paperbacks series which claim to reflect the contemporary issues and problems of African adolescents: personal and family problems, marriage, search for identity, unemployment and money, success, government corruption, and deterioration of morals. These novels, under the guise of realism, employ sensationalism, rather than a serious investigation of issues to attract their Westernized, urban readers. Convinced that these contemporary young adult novels do not embrace the concerns of African youth, Jurgen Martini in an essay entitled, "Sex, Class and Power: The Emergence of a Capitalist Youth Culture in Nigeria," argues that these books emphasize the values of a rising capitalist bourgeoisie: class consciousness, aggressive materialism, sex, Westernized atmosphere of "ex-pat" culture, suggestive titles, and formulaic romances.

While the traditionalists and Eurocentric writers take divergent approaches to children's literature, ironically, their common overarching goals are that books should educate and influence the character, thinking, and morals of children. Both Western and African critics condemn this didacticism; yet, that is precisely the function African authors intend children's literature to serve. Writing in favor of transmitting traditional values through folktales, Onyango-Ogutu states: "The small closely-knit societies of traditional Africa could ill afford to risk the chaos and turmoil which might result from blunt public correction. Hence the need for devious, painless admonition, for moral castigation that is handed out discreetly, hinted at rather than handed down in open court" (30). Writers who support modern themes and genres maintain that the "Novelist in Africa today should deliberately attempt to regenerate his society by directing his message to impressionable young people, especially school-children" (Lindfors, "Achebe" 128). In response to critics who denounce the moralizing in children's books, Achebe states in an interview: "But to say that a good story is weakened because it conveys a moral point of view is absurd, because in my view all the great stories do convey such a point. A tale may be fascinating, amusing--creating laughter and delight and so forth--but at its base is a sustaining morality, and I think this is very important" (Cott 175).

While the moral edification of children remains a primary concern, some contemporary writers are attempting to heal the split identity manifested in children's literature by honestly depicting the clash between traditions and modernity. At the 1983 Seminar on Creative Writing and Publishing for Children in Africa Today, Meshack Asare emphasized that children's books should "stress the importance of the child as an individual . . . with a mind of his own, with feelings and ideas to express and the driving desire to succeed" (17). He believes that books can inspire a child to "explore with his mind and create with his hands" only if he can "reconcile the events of the story with his own experience." Asare regrets that because of the "magical" elements and prescriptive tone of traditional stories, "the efficacy of our folklore in reinforcing the individual character then is questionable" (18). Likewise, at the 4th Zimbabwe International Book Fair, held in Harare in 1987, both Chinua Achebe and Mabel Segun called for a reexamination of some ancient values and social lessons that are transmitted and reinforced through traditional stories. They denounced folktales that propagate such outmoded ideas as the superior status of male children, unquestioned obedience to elders even when a child's health is at risk, and the passive role of children in society (Osa, "African" 39). In a paper delivered at the fair, "Fantasy and Reality in Children's Books," Segun stated that such traditional tales "tended to retard the progress of developing countries" (qtd. in Osa, "African" 39).

Focusing specifically on Kenya, Odaga points out that today colonial literature and African oral traditions exist side by side and have encouraged the formation of a postcolonial literature that reflects African values, situations, and experiences (*Literature for Children* xvii). Perhaps, the convention of the "been-to," as outlined by William Lawson in *The Western Scar: The Theme of the Been-to in West African Fiction*, best explains the divergent trends in contemporary children's literature and the search for a compromise and self-realization. In examining the African character who has been to the West to study, Lawson states: "The crisis of reentry or, more precisely, the entire experience of the conflict between the individual's African and Western selves serves as a metaphor for Africa's still dynamic assimilation of Western countries" (2). In children's literature, the identity crisis is not necessarily caused by the characters' residence in Europe or America, but by their Westernized educations at home and their assimilation of Western norms and culture. Some of the features of the "been-to" convention that can be found in recent works, especially those directed at an adolescent audience, are political adjustment after colonial rule, urbanization and encroaching modernity, psychological disruption, conflicting values of the older generation and the Westernized younger generation, problems of entry into the adult community, and the representation of the West as evil and an agent of disorder (Lawson 2-4).

In these thought-provoking novels, the city invariably represents modernity and Westernization, whereas the village stands for traditional values. Cyprian Ekwensi, known chiefly for his novels of city life, presents the dynamic confrontation of his protagonists with their loss of traditional values. In *The Motherless Baby*, the suffering and death of the heroine stem from the growing independence of youth, disrespect toward parents and elders, and influence of Western culture and education. Ekwensi probes the emotions of the unwed teenager and her guilt at abandoning her baby. Bernard Chahilu's protagonist in *The Herdsman's Daughter* also suffers loss of pride and humiliation because her mission school education leaves her sadly lacking in knowledge of human nature. Likewise, the difficulty of integrating traditional manhood rituals with formal education under the changed political, economic, and social circumstances of postcolonial Africa is a powerful theme in Musa Nagenda's *Dogs of Fear* and Henry Kulet's *To Become a Man* and *Is It Possible*.

In *Flowers and Shadows* by Ben Okri, the city of Lagos symbolizes power politics, corruption, moral decadence, and hedonism of the Westernized elite. The sensitive hero's rejection of this world represents the ability of youth to regenerate society. Meja Mwangi, like Okri, focuses his adolescent novels on "examining the human consequences of economic exploitation in the post-colonial era by detailing the lives of laborers, vagabonds, and slum dwellers, who face their daily battle for survival with ingenuity and resilient humor" (Lindfors, "Kenyan" 86). His in-depth character delineation, detailed descriptions of the urban setting, and impact of environment on characters expose human exploitation and suffering. In *Kill Me Quick*, for example, the city is not a place of temptation as in Ekwensi, but an impersonal place where the hopes and dreams of rural youth are shattered as they plunge into poverty, a life of crime, and loss of values. Themes of governmental corruption and materialism are also the subjects of plays like *This is Our Chance*, *The Incorruptible Judge*, and *The One Honest Man*. In the play, *Duogo*, Christianity and modern medicine are pitted against traditional religions and the healing practices of spiritualists.

What distinguishes these recent books is their graphic realism, their spirit of stressing commonalities, and their attempt to provide abiding values to young readers in the face of contemporary realities. As books for adult African readers have done since the beginning of the negritude movement, children's literature finally seems to be moving in the direction of portraying the reality of children's lives in a postcolonial Africa. As Ngugi wa Thiong'o emphasizes, the difficult task facing Africans is "the importance of fusing old and new, traditional and western, so that Africans could progress politically without losing their cultural identity" (Lindfors, "Kenyan" 85).

Postcolonial African children's literature thus is a literature in various stages of development. It reflects the many problems, concerns, aspirations, and fears of a continent trying to reevaluate and redefine itself. Children's literature spans the entire range from serving as a means of achieving literacy and child welfare, to being associated with the government's educational and supplemental reading programs, to sophisticated writing that satisfies the recreational needs of African children. As Nancy Schmidt, the foremost scholar of sub-Saharan African children's literature, states:

> The colonial dominance of African children's literature has been broken, innovations in the creation of African children's literature are taking place and in due course their cumulative effect will enable African children's literature to make a contribution to world literature. ("Africanization" 16)

CONCLUSION

The above survey of English-language books set in Africa clearly indicates that both African and Western authors have responded to the shifting political, economic, and social paradigms of their respective societies and the changing needs of the reading public. Ironically, some of the same comments can be made of books published in Africa and in Western countries.

African children's literature presents a limited range in terms of genres and subject matter. As Nancy Schmidt has pointed out, "Basically two types of literature are available, folklore, primarily folk tales, and fiction, primarily novels" ("Resources" 126). Citing Gail Haley's *A Story, A Story* as an example, Schmidt believes that African folklore for Euro-American children is merely a vehicle for artist-authors to make drawings, while the folktales are generally destylized plots summaries ("Resources" 130). Abiola Odejide of Nigeria also regrets that "the demands of the curriculum have shaped the forms of these renditions. The retention of the subject-matter and theme of the folklores has not been matched by the preservation of the vibrant languages and performer's art." Very few writers, she continues, are able to achieve "the controlled cadence, the local flavour of the language and the creation of an aura of performance involving listener and story teller" (7-8). In the area of fiction, a majority of the writers adhere to stereotypical characters, themes, and plots. In recent years, however, African authors have begun to forge an African identity in response to the problems of living in a postcolonial society; they explore the world of the contemporary child, conscious of the dual pressures of modernity and traditions. In the 1980s and 1990s, Western writers have also become sensitive to African perceptions, although still focusing on traditional village life. The plight of diaspora Africans, in particular, is the subject of recent novels that portray the inner feelings of enslaved Africans.

Besides fiction and traditional literature, there is very little drama, poetry, and other types of oral literature for children. Both African and Western writers need to embody oral poetic forms, technical intricacies, styles of arrangement and delivery, themes, rhythm, and figurative language in poetry for children. Geormbeeyi Adali-Mortty outlines the rich source of creative material that needs to be discovered in West African poetry: "madrigals, songs sung by children at play in the moonlit village squares, drum songs and drum language, hunters' songs, lullabies and cradle songs, songs for outdooring a maiden, songs to illustrate stories, songs of *asafos* (youths' warrior organisations) and songs of battle, songs of challenge and of abuse, words of libation, religious prayers and songs" (11). Such a poetic tradition has already emerged for adults. Likewise, the great tradition of communal drama, religious dance dramas, and masquerades can also inspire a uniquely African drama for children. Mphahlele states that it is "inconceivable that people can write plays if they do not see plays on the stage" (45). While there is a viable theater movement emerging in Malawi, thanks to the competitions organized by the Secondary Schools Drama Festival, experimentation in dramatic art needs to be encouraged by providing children with the opportunity to attend dramatic performances, theater workshops and courses, drama festivals, and participation in competitions (Mphahlele 45-46).

Children's literature can capture some of the diversity of the continent through translations from various African languages, techniques of oral performance, religious and moral writing in Ge'ez, and the Arabic literary models and artistry of expression. Through a collaboration between African and Western writers, establishment of a strong copublication program, and literary innovations, African children's literature can enter a new phase which is truly representative of the richness and complexity of African literatures and artistic styles. Both African and Western writers need to develop the "do-cultures" mentality that Rajat Neogy envisaged for a postcolonial Africa: "Do-cultures are permissive, experimental, vigorous and challenging. They attract attention and other experimenters. They absorb a great deal of techniques from outside their orbits and use them for their own ends. They are new yet operate with a base of traditional certitude" (109).

NOTES

1. Colonial literature, according to Jeffrey Meyers, is categorized into two types: the adventure-filled journeys of English heroes into far-off tropical jungles, and the more thought-provoking novels of E. M. Forster, Joseph Conrad, and Graham Greene who discuss issues of race relations and the decline of Western civilization. It is the former that is considered true colonial literature.

2. Novels by South African authors such as Jenny Seed are included here because they display the typical narrative structure of the imperial novel and because they defend and promote the subjugation of Africans by whites. With the entrenchment of apartheid in South Africa and with the severing of political and moral ties with Europe, South Africa represents an "intransigent internal colony" (Stotesbury 129).

3. Brian Street in *The Savage in Literature* gives an in-depth analysis of the parallel between colonial literature for adults and the various theories on the biological, social, religious, and political evolution of humankind.

4. Only those children's books that are not included in the bibliography are listed in the "Works Cited."

5. Refer to this author's article, "Apartheid in South African Children's Fiction." *Quarterly* 13. 1 (Summer 1988): 52-56.

6. The most prominent conferences were the Tananarive Conference (Nigeria, 1962); two conferences sponsored by the Congress for Cultural Freedom in Dakar and Freetown (1963); Seminar on African Culture and New East African Writings (Nairobi, 1965); Lagos Conference (1969); Ife Conference on Publishing in Africa in the Seventies (1973); Seminar on Writing and Production of Literature for Children (Lagos, 1976); the 10th Annual Conference of Nigerian English Studies Association in 1979 was devoted entirely to children's literature; and the founding of the Children's Literature Association of Nigeria in 1977 and the Children's Literature Foundation in Ghana in 1978 (Osa, "Growth" 25).

WORKS CITED

Adali-Mortty, Geormbeeyi. "Ewe Poetry." *Introduction to African Literature: An Anthology of Critical Writing from "Black Orpheus,"* edited by Ulli Beier. Evanston, IL: Northwestern University Press, 1967. 3-11.

Altbach, Philip G., and S. Gopinathan. "Textbooks in the Third World: Challenge and Response." *Publishing in the Third World: Knowledge and Development*, edited by Philip G. Altbach, Amadio A. Arboleda, and S. Gopinathan. Portsmouth, NH: Heinemann, 1985. 13-24.

Asare, Meshack. "The African Writer in the Child's World." *Proceedings, Papers and Summaries of Discussions* at the Seminar on Creative Writing and Publishing for Children in Africa Today, January 12-14, 1983. Freetown: Sierra Leone Library Board, n.d. 13-19.

Benedict, Ruth. *Race and Racism*. London: Routledge, 1942.

Bleek, W. H. I. *Reynard the Fox in South Africa*. London: Trubner, 1864.

Buchan, John. *The African Colony: Studies in the Reconstruction*. London: William & Blackwood, 1903.

Chatelain, Heli. *Folk-Tales of Angola*. Boston and New York: G. E. Stechert, 1894.

Chimombo, Steve. "A Brief Report on Children's Literature on Malawi." Personal communication, October 1993.

_____. *Malawian Oral Literature: The Aesthetics of Indigenous Arts*. Zomba, Malawi: Centre for Social Research and University of Malawi, 1988.

Chinweizu, Onwuchekwa Jemie, and Ihechukwu Madubuike. *Toward the Decolonization of African Literature*. Volume 1. African Fiction and Poetry and Their Critics. Washington, D.C.: Howard University Press, 1983.

Cott, Jonathan. *Pipers at the Gates of Dawn: The Wisdom of Children's Literature*. New York: Random House, 1981, 1983.

Council on Interracial Books for Children. "Ten Quick Ways to Analyze Books for Racism and Sexism." *Bulletin* 5. 3 (1974): 178-181.

Dinesen, Isak. *Shadows on the Grass*. New York: Random House, 1961.

Dingwall, Eric John. *Racial Pride and Prejudice*. London: Watts & Co., 1946.

Dixon, Bob. *Catching Them Young: Sex, Race and Class in Children's Fiction*. London: Pluto Press, 1977.

Djoleto, Amu. "Publishing in Ghana: Aspects of Knowledge and Development." *Publishing in the Third World: Knowledge and Development*, edited by Philip G. Altbach, Amadio A. Arboleda, and S. Gopinathan. Portsmouth, NH: Heinemann, 1985. 76-86.

Driver, Dorothy. "South African Literature: In English." *African Literature in the 20th Century: A Guide*. Based on the *Encyclopedia of World Literature in the 20th Century*, Leonard S. Klein, General Editor. Harpenden, Herts, England: Oldcastle Books, 1988. 170-175.

"Focus IBBY." *Bookbird* 29. 4 (Nov. 1991): n.p.

Forbes-Watson, Reginald. *Ambari!* London: Oxford University Press, 1952.

Frobenius, Leo, and Douglas C. Fox. *African Genesis*. Harrisburg: Stackpole, 1937.

Gossett, Thomas F. *Race: The History of an Idea in America*. Dallas: Southern Methodist University Press, 1963.

Guidelines for Selecting Bias-Free Textbooks and Storybooks. New York: Council on Interracial Books for Children, 1980.

Herzog, George, and Charles G. Blooah. *Jobo Proverbs from Liberia*. London: Oxford University Press, 1936.

Hollis, A. C. *The Masai: Their Language and Folklore*. Oxford: Clarendon Press, 1905.

Huxley, Elspeth. *The Flame Trees of Thika*. New York: Morrow, 1959.

"IBBY News." *Writer and Illustrator* 9. 4 (July-Sept. 1990): 33-46.

Igus, Toyomi. "Publishing Books for Black Kids." *ABBWA Journal* 4.2 (Summer 1990): 14-18.

Jacobs, Sharron K. *Song of the Giraffe*. Boston: Little, Brown, 1991.

James, Adeola, ed. *In Their Own Voices: African Women Writers Talk*. London: James Currey/ Portsmouth, NH: Heinemann, 1990.

Kabele, Dan B. *Certificate Guide to Oral Literature Research*. Kisumu, Kenya: Lake Publishers & Enterprises, 1986.

Kabira, Wanjiku Mukabi, and Karega wa Mutahi. *Gikuyu Oral Literature*. Nairobi, Kenya: Heinemann, 1988.

Knappert, Jan. *Kings, Gods & Spirits from African Mythology*. World Mythologies Series. New York: Schocken Books/Vancouver and Toronto: Douglas and McIntyre, 1986.

Lawson, William. *The Western Scar: The Theme of the Been-to in West African Fiction*. Athens, Ohio: Ohio University Press, 1982.

Lindfors, Bernth. "Achebe, Chinua," "Kenyan Literature," and "Tutuola, Amos." *African Literatures in the 20th Century: A Guide*. Based on the *Encyclopedia of World Literature in the 20th Century*, Leonard S. Klein, General Editor. Harpenden, Herts, England: Oldcastle Books, 1988. 85-90, 126-129, 139-141.

_____. "Cyprian Ekwensi: An African Popular Novelist." *African Literature Today* 3 (1969): 7--?

Lofting, Christopher. "Afterword." *The Story of Doctor Doolittle* by Hugh Lofting. The Centenary Edition/A Yearling Book. New York: Dell, 1988. 151-156.

Loho, Sugh. "A Readership Promotion Campaign for Nigerian Youth." *Journal of Youth Services in Libraries* (Winter 1991): 141-148.

MacCann, Donnarae, and Gloria Woodard. *The Black American in Books for Children: Readings in Racism.* Metuchen, NJ: Scarecrow Press, 1972.

Maissen, Leena. "IBBY-UNESCO Workshop in Egypt." Focus IBBY, *Bookbird* 3 (1992): n.p.

Martini, Jurgen. "Sex, Class and Power: The Emergence of a Capitalist Youth Culture in Nigeria." *Journal of African Children's Literature* I (1989): 43-59.

Mbiti, John S. *African Religions and Philosophy.* London, Ibadan, Nairobi: Heinemann, 1969.

Meyers, Jeffrey. *Fiction and the Colonial Experience.* Totowa, NJ: Rowman & Littlefield, 1968.

Mphahlele, Ezekiel. "Drama in East Africa." *East Africa's Cultural Heritage.* Contemporary African Monographs Series No. 4. Nairobi, Kenya: East African Institute of Social and Cultural Affairs, 1966. 45-47.

Murray, Jocelyn, ed. *Africa.* Cultural Atlas of the World Series. Alexandria, VA: Stonehenge, 1991.

Naidoo, Beverley. *Censoring Reality: An Examination of Books on South Africa.* London: ILEA Centre for Anti-Racist Education and the British Defense and Aid Fund for Southern Africa, 1984.

_____. "Introduction." *Free As I Know*, edited by Beverley Naidoo. London: Bell & Hyman, 1987. 6-8.

Neogy, Rajat. "The Role of a Literary Magazine in the Development of Culture." *East Africa's Cultural Heritage.* Contemporary African Monographs Series No. 4. Nairobi, Kenya: East African Institute of Social and Cultural Affairs, 1966. 109-114.

Ngugi wa Thiong'o. *Decolonising the Mind: The Politics of Language in African Literature.* London: James Currey/Nairobi: Heinemann Kenya/ Portsmouth, NH: Heinemann Educational, 1986.

Nottingham, John. "The Book Trade in East Africa." *East Africa's Cultural Heritage.* Contemporary African Monographs Series No. 4.

Nairobi, Kenya: East African Institute of Social and Cultural Affairs, 1966. 103-108.

Odaga, Asenath Bole. *Literature for Children and Young People in Kenya.* Nairobi: Kenya Literature Bureau, 1985.

_____. *Yesterday's Today: The Study of Oral Literature.* Kisumu, Kenya: Lake Publishers & Enterprises, 1984.

Odejide, Abiola. "Nigerian Children's Literature: From Oral to Written Forms." Paper presented at the Institute of African Studies Seminar, January 23, 1985. 1-25.

Onyango-Ogutu, Benedict, and Adrian A. Roscoe. *Keep My Words.* Nairobi, Kenya: Heinemann, 1974.

Osa, Osayimwense. "African Children's Literature from the Legon Seminar to the 1987 Zimbabwe International Book Fair." *International Review of Children's Literature and Librarianship* 4.1 (1989): 34-41.

_____. "English in Nigeria: 1914-1985." *Foundation: Essays in Children's Literature and Youth Literature* by Osayimwense Osa. Benin City, Nigeria: Paramount Publishers, 1987. 129-133.

_____. "The Growth of African Children's Literature." *Journal of African Children's Literature 1 (1989): 20-29.*

_____. *Nigerian Youth Literature.* Benin City, Nigeria: Paramount Publishers, 1987.

_____. "Wither English in Nigeria." *Foundation: Essays in Children's Literature and Youth Literature*, by Osayimwense Osa. Benin City, Nigeria: Paramount Publishers, 1987. 134-151.

Palmer, Eustace. *The Growth of the African Novel.* London, Ibadan and Nairobi: Heinemann, 1979.

Pellowski, Anne. *The World of Children's Literature.* New York: R. R. Bowker, 1968.

Possett, F. W. T. *Fables of the Veld.* Oxford: Clarendon Press, 1929.

Randall, Isobel. "Publishing Children's Books in South Africa." *Bookbird* 27. 3 (Sept. 1989): 5-6.

Rathgeber, Eva M. "The Book Industry in Africa, 1973-1983: A Decade of Development?" *Publishing in the Third World: Knowledge and Development*, edited by Philip G. Altbach, Amadio A. Arboleda, and S. Gopinathan. Portsmouth, NH: Heinemann, 1985. 57-75.

Rattray, R. S. *Hausa Folk-Lore, Customs, Proverbs, Etc*. Oxford: Clarendon Press, 1913.

Richards, Jeffrey, ed. *Imperialism and Juvenile Literature*. Studies in Imperialism Series. Manchester and New York: Manchester University Press, 1989.

Roscoe, Adrian A. *Mother is Gold: A Study in West African Literature*. Cambridge, UK: Cambridge University Press, 1971.

_____. *Tales of Old Malawi*. Limbe and Lilongwe, Malawi: Popular Publications & Likuni Press, 1980.

_____. *Uhuru's Fire: African Literature East to South*. Cambridge, UK: Cambridge University Press, 1977.

Ryan, Rory. "Literary-Intellectual Behaviour in South Africa." *Rendering Things Visible: Essays on South African Literary Culture*, edited by Martin Trump. Athens, OH: Ohio University Press, 1990. 1-21.

Said, Edward. *Orientalism*. New York: Pantheon, 1978.

Schmidt, Nancy J. "The Africanization of Children's Literature in English-speaking Subsaharan Africa." *Journal of African Children's Literature* I (1989): 7-19.

_____. *Children's Fiction About Africa in English*. New York: Conch Magazine, 1981.

_____. "Resources on African Literature: Children's Literature." *The Teaching of African Literature*, edited by Thomas Hale and Richard Priebe. Washington, D.C.: Three Continents Press and The African Literature Association, 1989. 125-147.

Steig, William. *Doctor DeSoto Goes to Africa*. New York: HarperCollins, 1992.

Stotesbury, John A. "The Intransigent Internal Colony: Narrative Strategies in Modern South African Popular Fiction." *Literature and Imperialism*, edited by Robert Giddings. New York: St. Martin's Press, 1991. 128-149.

Street, Brian V. *The Savage in Literature*. Boston: Routledge and Kegan Paul, 1975.

Trump, Martin. "Part of the Struggle: Black Writing and the South African Liberation Movement." *Rendering Things Visible: Essays on South African Literary Culture*, edited by Martin Trump. Athens, OH: Ohio University Press, 1990. 161-185.

BIBLIOGRAPHIES CONSULTED

Adcock, June, and John Adcock, comps. *The World in Stories: Books for Young People Selected for Geographical Interest*. N.p.: School Library Association, 1972.

American Association for the United Nations. *Read Your Way to World Understanding*. New York: Scarecrow Press, 1963.

Barthold, Bonnie J. *Black Time: Fiction of Africa, The Carribbean, and the United States*. New Haven: Yale University Press, 1981.

Cooley, Maurice W. *Africa: An Annotated List of Printed Materials Suitable for Children*. N.p.: Information Center on Children's Cultures, American Library Association and African American Institute, 1963.

Coughlan, Margaret N. *Folklore from Africa to the United States: An Annotated Bibliography*. Washington, D.C.: Library of Congress, 1976.

Ettlinger, John, and Diane Spirt. *Choosing Books for Young People: Guide to Criticism and Bibliographies, 1945-1975*. Chicago: American Library Association, 1982.

Hill, Janet, ed. *Books for Children: The Homelands of Immigrants in Britain*. London: The Institute of Race Relations, 1971.

Kenworthy, Leonard S. *Studying Africa: In Elementary and Secondary Schools*. New York: Teachers College Press, Columbia UP, 1970.

Miller-Lachmann, Lyn. *Our Family, Our Friends, Our World: An Annotated Guide to Significant Multicultural Books for Children and Teenagers*. New Providence, NJ: R. R. Bowker, 1992.

Nkwocha, Philip. "Publishing for Children." In *Publishing in Nigeria*. Benin: Ethiope, 1972.

Paricsy, Pal. *Studies in Modern Black African Literature*. Budapest: Center for Afro-Asian Research, 1971.

Printed for Children: World Children's Book Exhibition. Munchen, New York, London, Paris: K. G. Saur, 1978.

Ragatz, Lowell Joseph. *The Literature of European Imperialism 1815-1939*. Ann Arbor, MI: Edwards Brothers, 1947.

Rollock, Barbara. *The Black Experience in Children's Books*. New York: The New York Public Library, 1984.

1   Introduction

Sewitz, Maureen Beatrice. *Children's Books in English in an African Setting, 1914-1964: A Bibliography.* Johannesburg: University of the Witwatersrand, 1965.

Schmidt, Nancy J. *Children's Books on Africa and Their Authors: An Annotated Bibliography.* New York: Africana, 1975.

_____. *Children's Fiction About Africa in English.* New York: Conch Magazine, 1981.

Sutherland, Zena, ed. *The Best in Children's Books: The University of Chicago Guide to Children's Literature, 1966-1972.* Chicago: University of Chicago Press, 1973.

Africa in Literature
for Children and
Young Adults

General Books

TRADITIONAL LITERATURE

001. Aardema, Verna. *Oh, Kojo! How Could You!* Illustrated by Marc Brown. New York: Dial, 1984. N.p. Grades K-3.
  The spendthrift Kojo is repeatedly duped by Ananse into buying his pet dog, cat, and dove in exchange for golddust. However, the trickster is tricked when the dove turns out to be the Queen Mother of her country. In return for freeing her, Kojo receives a magic ring which transforms him into a rich chief. Ananse once again tries to outsmart Kojo by sending his niece to steal the ring, but Kojo sends the cat and dog to get it back. This tale also explains that cats are favored over dogs in Asanteland because the dog did not assist the cat in retrieving the ring. Brown's illustrations sensitively portray the human element of the story through the expressions of the characters.

002. _____. *Tales for the Third Ear from Equatorial Africa.* Illustrated by Ib Ohlsson. New York: Dutton, 1969. 96p. Grades 3-5.
  Nine tales represent the varied folklore of the Hausa, Masai, and Asante peoples who live near the equator. There are trickster tales of animals and humans that uphold the moral order, a Swahili fairy tale of the ogre Zimwi, and a realistic story, "Kindai and the Ape," which teaches kindness to animals. Aardema's narrative style heightens the dramatic tension through dialogue and a fast-paced plot; draws characters with appealing human qualities; and makes the scene come alive through descriptive details.

003. Abrahams, Roger D. *African Folktales: Traditional Stories of the Black World.* Pantheon Fairy Tale and Folklore Library. New York: Pantheon, 1983. 352p. Grades 8-12.
  The ninety-four folktales selected and retold by Abrahams represent the diverse cultures and peoples of sub-Saharan Africa. Despite this variety, the tales reflect an underlying unity in thought, aesthetics,

and worldview. The stories are organized into five parts, with Part I devoted to Tales of Wonder and the remaining sections grouped around the uses of the stories rather than on form and content. These stories were traditionally used to introduce discussion of specific moral problems in order to keep the family and community together; entertain and depict the chaotic and unprincipled actions of tricksters; and praise great deeds in epics like "Gassire's Lute" and "The Mwindo Epic." Both the general introduction and introductions to the individual segments provide the geographical, economic, and cultural contexts of the tales, as well as explaining how these stories fit into the lives of storytellers and listeners. The general introduction, in particular, has an excellent segment on the difficulties of rendering a storytelling session in the written form.

Through the wonder tales, Abrahams emphasizes that Africa had connections with other areas of the ancient world. Influences of Mediterranean and Middle Eastern cultures brought in with Islam are evident in tale types like "Tortoise and the Hare," "Hansel and Gretel," "Ali Baba and the Forty Thieves," and "Jack and the Beanstalk." Although Africanized in form and content, these tales have all the familiar fairy tale motifs of transformations, tests, magical helpers, and charmed objects.

004. Arnott, Kathleen. *African Myths and Legends*. Illustrated by Joan Kiddell-Monroe. New York: Walck, 1962. 211p. Grades 6-12.
The thirty-four folktales in this volume represent the folklore of a variety of ethnic groups like the Bushong, Akan, Bantu, Hausa, Ibibo, Zulu, Tiv, Xhosa, Fulani, Chaga, Yoruba, and Swahili. The tales do not appear to be culture specific but represent the shared oral tradition of sub-Saharan Africa. There are stories that explain the origin of thunder and lightning, why the Bush-Fowl calls at dawn and Flies buzz, why the Sun and Moon live in the sky, and why Dog lives with Man; there are trickster tales that narrate the exploits of Spider, Hare, Tortoise, and Squirrel; and there are wonder tales about giants and witches, brave princes, enchanted animals and objects, and magical kingdoms. In addition to entertainment, each story offers guidance for acceptable human conduct within a family and the larger community. Hence, jealousy among siblings and co-wives always ends in disaster for the evil character; greed and selfishness are punished; and intelligence and wit, and courage and strength enable people to survive as long as they do not harm others. The stories also contain universal motifs like magical gourds ("Snake Magic"), giants who can smell humans ("The Tale of the Superman"), two brothers and two sisters who are opposites in nature ("The Two Brothers" and "The Snake Chief"), humans who can understand the speech of animals ("The Man Who Learned the Language of the Animals"), and a virtuous girl who breaks the spell binding a handsome prince ("The Snake Chief"). These motifs clearly indicate that African folklore is a response to the human need for survival, curiosity about natural phenomena, and desire for wonder and magic.

005. Bess, Clayton. *The Truth About the Moon.* Illustrated by Rosekrans Hoffman. Boston: Houghton Mifflin, 1983. 48p. Grades 2-5.
Folklore and modern science come together beautifully in this story of a young child's fascination with the moon. Sumu goes to his older sister, father, and mother to learn about the moon, and he is told traditional stories explaining that the moon changes its shape and size to represent the eternal cycle of life and death. Not satisfied, Sumu approaches the village chief to find out the truth about how many moons there are, why the moon waxes and wanes, and why the sun is hot and the moon is cold. The chief narrates a folktale about how the sun and moon had a race and the moon lost its heat and brightness, but Sumu remains dissatisfied with such explanations. Finally, the chief suggests that Sumu is ready for the rational stories only a teacher can tell from books. The chief hopes that as Sumu gains scientific knowledge, his ancient traditions will continue to provide him with roots and cultural enrichment.

006. Brown, Marcia, trans. *Shadow.* Illustrated by Marcia Brown. Translation of "La Feticheuse" by Blaise Cendrars. New York: Scribner's, 1982. N.p. Grades 1-5.
Winner of the Caldecott Medal, Brown's collages skillfully interpret and give material form to Cendrars' somewhat abstract view of Shadow. Set in traditional Africa, Shadow changes direction, size, and shape according to the position of the sun or the village fire. Cendrars takes readers to a more philosophic and psychological dimension as he tries to characterize Shadow: It is voiceless and blind; it is the mystery and darkness of the night; it is both prowler and dancer; and it is a trickster that can cast a spell for good or bad. The predominant blacks, blues, and reds of the illustrations heighten the mysterious tone of the text.

007. Bryan, Ashley. *Lion and the Ostrich Chicks and Other African Folk Tales.* Illustrated by reteller. New York: Atheneum, 1986. 87p. Grades 2-4.
Four stories representative of the Masai, San, Angolan, and Hausa cultures are narrated in Bryan's lively style that combines vigorous dialogue with songs and refrains. Three stories recount the exploits of the trickster mongoose, hare, and Spider Ananse, while the fourth one is a legend about the unusual friendship between a boy and the son of Wind. Each tale celebrates the triumph of universal moral values and common sense. Bryan's action-filled illustrations add a pleasing visual dimension to the book.

008. _____. *The Ox of the Wonderful Horns and Other African Folktales.* Illustrated by reteller. New York: Atheneum, 1971. 41p. Grades K-4.
Bryan's vigorous narrative and bold illustrations make these tales ideal for private reading as well as for storytelling. Based on earlier collections from Angola, Southern Africa, and the Akan-Asante region, the five tales in this collection are representative of the major motifs and tale types of sub-Saharan folklore. There are trickster tales of Ananse the Spider and Hare, both of whom are duped by even

cleverer tricksters; there is the lesser-known tale of a clever frog who outsmarts an elephant; there is a pourquoi tale which explains that the frog croaks because he is undecided and confused when his two wives invite him to eat at the same time; and there is a wonder tale of an ox with magical horns who helps a chief's worthy son. Bryan retains the oral character of African storytelling through his unique introductions and conclusions to each story, imitation of sounds, and insertion of verses that the audience can repeat.

009. Courlander, Harold. *The Crest and the Hide.* Illustrated by Monica Vachula. New York: Coward, McCann and Geoghegan, 1982. 137p. Grades 4-8.

A majority of stories in this collection are simplified versions of epics and heroic legends from a variety of cultural groups in Africa. Beginning with the account of how the profession of djeli, or bard, began among the Soninke of Mali, Courlander narrates the exploits of warrior heroes like Kirama, Karkejan, and Kene Bourama of the Soninke; Ngunza of Angola; Liongo of Tanzania; epic heroes of Wagadou; and Chief Khama of Botswana. Courlander's retellings are based on narrations by Ousmane Sako of Bamako, Mali; *African Genesis* (1937) by Leo Frobenius and Douglas Fox; *African Arts* (November 1978); *Swahili Tales As Told by Natives of Zanzibar* (1870) by Edward Steere; and *Folk Tales of Angola* (1894) by Heli Chatelain. The remaining stories in this collection are about visits to the underworld, how the giants of Eastern Africa left the earth, limits to friendship and loyalty, and the wise conduct of chiefs and ordinary people.

010. _____. *The King's Drum and Other African Stories.* Illustrated by Enrico Arno. New York: Harcourt, Brace and World, 1962. 125p. Grades 4-8.

Based primarily on retellings by individuals and collections of African folktales published in the late nineteenth or early twentieth centuries, the twenty-nine tales in this volume reflect the beliefs, customs, and wisdom of the diverse peoples of sub-Saharan Africa. There are tales of Ananse the trickster, tall tales, stories that illustrate proverbs, riddles that lead to philosophic discussions, and pourquoi tales that explain animal traits. There are also stories of heroes and humorous tales that poke fun at human pretensions. Collectively, the stories establish rules for living harmoniously in a village community: the king must rule wisely, the warrior must defend, and people must respect the rights of others. Disputes--both personal and communal --must be settled promptly with the help of a chief or elder, if necessary, because an unsettled grievance festers and grows. Similarly, there are specific marriage customs that ensure the stability of a union, good behavior of husband and wife, and a lasting bond between families. There are philosophic stories such as "How Poverty Was Revealed for the King of Adja," which rejects the notion that one has to be poverty-stricken to be virtuous. Courlander's notes on the individual stories provide background information on the culture, the basic story-structure, and variants in Africa, Asia, and the Middle East. While the morals taught by the stories are serious, Courlander's delightful narrative emphasizes the humor and irony.

011. Hambly, Wilfrid Dyson. *Talking Animals.* Illustrated by James A. Porter. Washington, D.C.: Associated Publishers, 1949. Reprinted in 1985. 100p. Grades 3-8.

As a scholar of African anthropology and curator of African Ethnology at the Chicago Natural History Museum, Hambly brings his vast scientific knowledge to this collection of African animal stories. The tales are arranged in eight chapters according to subject matter: storytellers, creation myths, stories about honey, adventures of Hare, tortoise stories, relationship between birds and boys, man-eaters, and tiny animals and insects. The narrative is enriched by Hambly's personal experiences in Africa and his observations of the customs and lifestyles of various African peoples. He eloquently establishes the possible rural settings and circumstances of the storytellers before beginning his narration: when the hunter returns home, he recounts his experiences; when women are tired from pounding corn, they rest and listen to stories; and when children ask questions or need to be entertained, they are told stories. The stories are skillfully narrated with close attention to details that make characters and scenes come to life.

012. Kaula, Edna Mason. *African Village Folktales.* Illustrated by reteller. Cleveland and New York: World, 1968. 155p. Grades 3-8.

This unique book contains traditional tales from twenty distinct regions of Africa such as the San of the Kalahari, Zulus of South Africa, Asante and Hausa of West Africa, Bemba of Zambia, and Pygmies of the Ituri Forest. Preceding each tale is an informative essay on the geography, village economy and lifestyle, religious rituals and social customs, and impact of industrialization on the region. While Kaula does mention life in the city, her focus is on village culture and the preservation of the art of storytelling. The twenty stories in this volume--which were collected by the author during her travels in Africa--include fables, pourquoi tales, trickster stories of the hare, tortoise, and monkey, and survival stories. The stories are not only as varied as the peoples they represent, but they also reflect the universal concerns of all farming peoples: living in harmony with the land, constant preoccupation with seasonal rains and drought, survival against the strong and powerful, and the need for a just and organized society to regulate behavior and ensure unity.

013. Knappert, Jan. *Kings, Gods & Spirits from African Mythology.* Illustrated by Francesca Pelizzoli. World Mythologies Series. New York: Schocken; Vancouver and Toronto: Douglas & McIntyre, 1986. 92p. Grades 6-10.

An expert on the languages and folklore of Africa, Knappert first provides a general introduction on the land, civilizations, religions, communal organizations, kinship ties, and animals of Africa. Next, representative stories of gods, spirits, ghosts, heroes, and animals from all the major language groups are organized according to type. There are creation myths from the Yoruba, Bakuba, Pangwe, Nubian, Yao, and Zulu groups; and legends of kings and kingdoms from Egypt, Napata (Sudan), Meroe, Zululand, Zimbabwe, Mali, Zaire, Wagadou, and Buganda. The world of spirits, or one's invisible being which survives death, is represented by stories of Orisha, the Yoruba Divine Spirit, roles of sorcerers, world of the ancestors, and rivers worshipped as gods. The collection also includes animal stories; tales of monsters and demons; and legends of the saints of Islam like Sidi Ahmed of Algeria and El-Magharibi of Morocco. Collectively, this book provides a coherent picture of the culture, religious beliefs, history, and soul of traditional Africa.

The full-page color illustrations and the black-and-white sketches by the award winning artist add a pleasant visual dimension to the book.

014. Koram, Jamal. *Aesop: Tales of Aethiop the African.*   Volume 1. Illustrated by Demba Mbengue. Beltsville, MD: Sea Island Information Group, 1989. 48p. Grades 2-5.

Twenty-nine fables interpret the wisdom of Aesop, a black man from Phyrygia, Asia Minor, who lived in ancient Athens. A brief account of Aesop's life and the achievements of African civilizations is provided to inspire racial pride in African Americans. Jamal Koram points out that Aesop was a respected orator, statesman, philosopher, counsellor, and student of the African "mystery school" who interspersed his public speeches and defended his clients in court with the wisdom of African fables. While these animal stories delighted and entertained the Greeks, they also carried political and moral messages which have become an integral part of Western thought and folklore.

Koram emphasizes the African features of the tales through descriptions of the African setting, African names, and phrases and terms from African languages. His intention is to educate readers through an Afrocentric account of the peoples, languages, and wildlife that Aesop could have used. As an educator, Koram focuses on restating or elaborating the "lesson" of each fable to make it relevant to the lives of his listeners and readers, especially African Americans. Hence, the popular fables of the boy who cried wolf and the donkey who tried to jump on the roof like a monkey emphasize the need to be principled, courageous, and true to oneself. Still other fables stress the concept of oneness of family and of living and working together as Africans in the global community.

The glossary and notes explain African terms, customs, and historical and geographical conditions. The illustrations by Mbengue --a leading artist at the DeCasa African Cultural and Heritage Center in Dakar, Senegal--further highlight the Afrocentric elements of the fables.

015. _____. *When Lions Could Fly*. Illustrated by Marcy Dunn Ramsey. African Lion Stories and Fables Series. Silver Spring, MD: Flying Lion Press, 1989. 49p. Grades 2-5.

The eleven folktales in this slim volume focus on the exploits of the lion as a royal, wise, and generous king of the forest. The stories include pourquoi tales that explain how the lion got his roar and why he lost the power of flight; trickster tales in which the sometimes devious lion is in turn hunted and outsmarted by weaker animals; and Aesop's fables that emphasize the qualities necessary for survival against clever adversaries. "The Lion and the Hyena," for instance, clearly illustrates that people can be exploited only as long as they allow it, but as soon as they seek freedom and assert themselves, they cease to be slaves.

Koram's narrative style follows the African traditions of storytelling. While he generously provides details of life in Africa and uses African terms and proverbs, the stories are directed at African American audiences, especially inner city children, to offer guidance by discussing friendship, relationships between husband and wife, and child-raising practices. Ramsey's graceful illustrations capture the action and emotions of the plot and provide details of the African setting.

016. Leaf, Munro. *Aesop's Fables*. Illustrated by Robert Lawson. New York: Heritage Reprints, 1941. 132p. Grades 2-6.

Published on the 2500th anniversary of Aesop's death, the hundred and one fables in this collection were written with the taste and culture of the Western child in mind. An introductory essay by Emile Van Vliet provides an account of Aesop's life (600 B.C.) from his years as a slave in the house of Iadmon, to his rise as Emperor Croesus' ambassador to Delphi, and to his lynching by the irate Delphians over the distribution of certain sums of money among them. Vliet also traces the history of the fables which were circulated by word of mouth from country to country until they were collected and written down for the first time in the third century A.D. by Babruis. A century later, Phaedrus Avianus translated forty-two of the fables into Latin, and in the ninth century Ignatus Diaconus wrote another version which included several Eastern fables. It is from this version that Maximus Planudes revised the fables that have been attributed to Aesop. Vliet betrays his racial bias when he calls Aesop ugly because of his African features.

Leaf maintains the swift action characteristic of fables, but he also deftly individualizes the characters and settings through a minimum of description. Despite the moral lessons, these fables are entertaining because of the vitality and energy of the dialogues. They also provide guidance for social behavior and interpersonal relationships. Unlike the gentler, more spiritual Buddhist *Jataka* fables of India, Aesop's fables are more akin to the *Panchatantra* stories, many of which have been incorporated in Aesop's fables, because they emphasize using intelligence to thwart one's enemies and to prevent exploitation of property and self.

Not all retellers, however, acknowledge that Aesop was a historical person, much less that he was an African. There are several versions of these fables for children, especially as picture books. A few prominent titles are Mitsumasa Anno's *Anno's Aesop* (Orchard, 1987), Fulvio Testa's *Aesop's Fables* (Barron's, 1989), and Roger L'Estrange's *Fables of Aesop* (Dover, 1967), originally published in 1692 with Alexander Calder's line drawings.

017. Leslau, Charlotte and Wolf, eds. *African Folk Tales.* Illustrated by Grisha Dotzenko. Mount Vernon, NY: Pauper, 1963. 62p. Grades 3-6.

Twenty-five stories from countries like Uganda, Kenya, Tanzania, Ethiopia, Madagascar, Senegal, and Nigeria represent the varied folklore of Africa. A majority are creation or pourquoi tales that explain the origin of the world and habits and physical features of animals. In addition, there are fairy tales, legends, and stories of common sense and wisdom. Although brief, the stories are told in an entertaining and appealing manner. Likewise, Dotzenko's woodcut illustrations are attractive.

018. Lester, Julius. *How Many Spots Does a Leopard Have? and Other Tales.* Illustrated by David Shannon. New York: Scholastic, 1989. 71p. Grades 2-4.

Lester's graceful adaptation of ten African and two Jewish folktales in the idiom and imagery familiar to American children reflects his truly multicultural heritage. The reteller focuses on the universal aspects of the stories that he as an American can respond to rather than on their African and Jewish cultural elements. The tales, thus, provide explanations for questions that have puzzled human beings about the heavenly bodies and animals that surround them; entertain by narrating the exploits of the trickster tortoise and adventures with monsters and dragons; and give moral guidance by exposing human greed, pride, and ignorance. Shannon's full-page color illustrations, however, portray the cultural details relevant to each tale.

019. Parrinder, Geoffrey. *African Mythology.* Library of the World's Myths and Legends Series. New York: Bedrick, 1967, 1982. 144p. Grades 8-12.

Based on recent collections by highly qualified researchers, the myths in this volume represent the religious beliefs, sacred history, and spiritual approach to life of sub-Saharan Africa. The central myth is the creation of the world according to the mythologies of various African peoples. Subsequent chapters narrate stories related to why God left the world, the first ancestors, the mystery of birth, the origin of death and the world beyond death, gods and spirits, oracles and divination, witches and monsters, and secret societies and ancestors. Parrinder also includes animal fables and legends of past heroes who provide models for human behavior. One hundred and fifty photographs of African paintings and sculptures illustrate the myths as well as testify to the richness and diversity of African art.

020. Pitcher, Diana. *The Calabash Child.* Illustrated by Meg Rutherford. Cape Town, South Africa: David Philip, 1980. 64p. Grades 4-8.

    Seventeen creation stories representing various ethnic groups from sub-Saharan Africa have been adapted and retold against the background of Zulu family life and customs. Beginning with the creation of First Man and First Woman, the book narrates how the first parents are gifted with flocks, herds, and a son so that they can establish their family. Their home becomes the microcosm of the world as they hunt, farm, and survive the threats of animals and nature. Beliefs, morals, folk wisdom, and mythology are passed down to young Vugiswe by First Woman in the form of highly entertaining stories told when they rest from work. Hence, Vugiswe--who later narrates these stories to his son--learns about the many exploits of the trickster Hare; why Sun and Moon stay up in the sky; story of the first drought and how Nkulumkulu, the creator, listened to First Woman's prayers and sent rain; taming of fire for domestic use; how dog became a helper to humans; and stories of animal traits.

    The book ends with the myth of the snake, the harbinger of death, when First Woman is old. Nkulumkulu sends the gift of everlasting life to humans through duiker, but the snake tricks God's messenger and keeps all the skins for renewal of body for himself and his children and his children's children. First Woman dies and her spirit escapes toward Manyeleti, the power of the Wind, and the sacred pool.

021. Suter, Joanne. *World's Myths and Legends: African.* Illustrated by James Balkovek. Belmont, CA: Fearon/Janus, 1992. 100p. Grades 3-5.

    Twenty-one tales reflect the values and vision of diverse ethnic groups who live south of the Sahara Desert. Organized into four broad categories--In the Beginning, The Sun and the Moon, Animal Tales, and The Mystery of Death--these myths are indicative of the human search for answers to metaphysical and philosophic questions. Whether the story belongs to the Yoruba, Lozi, Krachi, San, or Fang oral traditions, it affirms faith in a supreme god. The account of creation in "Olorun, Creator of Life" is quite similar to the Biblical version. Other interesting stories are "The First Man," which embodies the concept of the Holy Trinity and the distinction between body and soul, and "Naba Zid-Wende," which explains the existence of various races, division of the earth into countries, and strength leading to power. Suter's simple narrative style is well suited for private reading pleasure as well as for storytelling.

022. Yarbrough, Camille. *Cornrows.* Illustrated by Carole Byard. New York: Coward, McCann, and Geoghegan, 1979. N.p. Grades K-2.

    As Mama and Great-Grammaw braid cornrows for Sister and little brother MeToo, they talk of their African heritage. The children learn about the great creative spirit that expressed itself not only through intricate hairstyles, but also through woodcarvings, ritual masquerades, and approach to life which enabled Africans to endure the hardships of slavery. Great-Grammaw urges her great grandchildren to recognize and express this spirit through their own unique cornrow patterns in order to inform their lives with praise, courage, honor, and wisdom. Young readers are asked to reflect on the meaning of the spirit behind the symbol, which is not affected by time, place, class, fame, or even shame and hate.

FICTION

023. Appiah, Sonia. *Amoko and the Party.* Illustrated by Carol Olu Easmon. London: Andre Deutsch, 1991. N.p. Grades K-3.
Through the experiences of young Amoko at home and at play, this picture book portrays the life of a well-to-do contemporary African family. The highlight of the story is the family party for Amoko's cousin's birthday. The sparse plot lacks a meaningful central theme, a conflict to advance the story, and an opportunity for character development. Likewise, the illustrations, though accurate, are rigid; the lines lack grace and fluidity of movement.

024. Asare, Meshack. *Cat in Search of a Friend.* Illustrated by author. Brooklyn, NY and La Jolla, CA: Kane/Miller, 1986. Originally published in 1984 as *Die Katze Sucht Sich Einen Freund* by Verlag Jungbrunnen, Vienna. N.p. Preschool-Grade 2.
A beautiful cat with yellow fur, a bushy tail, and eyes the color of honey is in search of a friend and protector. At first, she joins a group of little monkeys, but when she sees that the chimpanzees are stronger, she joins them. Later, the cat befriends even stronger friends like the gorillas, leopard, lion, rhinoceros, elephant, and man with a gun. She finally attaches herself to the hunter's wife because the hunter fears her temper. The cat seems to have learned the lesson that even the most powerful creature is afraid of someone larger than himself, till the wife is frightened by a tiny mouse. When the cat is able to scare the mouse with just a "Pfff," she realizes that she does not need a protector, hence gaining self-knowledge and confidence in her own abilities. This thought-provoking story will generate discussion of gender roles, balance of nature, and awareness of strengths and weaknesses. The illustrations, which are done in various shades of brown, dark yellow, and gray, are dull and unattractive. The story has an African setting.

025. Berry, James. *Ajeemah and His Son.* New York: Perlman, 1991. Originally published in the collection *The Future-Telling Lady* by Hamish Hamilton. 83p. Grades 4-8.
Set in the early nineteenth century, the novel focuses on the experiences of Ajeemah and his son Atu who are kidnapped by slave traders while on their way to deliver the dowry for Atu's bride-to-be.

After days of walking in shackles and being penned in a fort, they make the long, humiliating journey to Jamaica, where they are sold to different plantation owners. The narrative alternates between the experiences of Ajeemah (now Justin) and Atu (now Simon) at adjoining farms: both resist their loss of freedom, plan to escape, and recall memories of loved ones in Africa to maintain composure and sanity. When their attempts at freedom are foiled, Atu commits suicide, while the unhappy Ajeemah finds consolation in the friendship of Bella, a fellow slave, whom he later marries. Both Atu and Ajeemah are triumphant: Atu dies with his dignity intact, while Ajeemah lives to see the slaves freed in Jamaica. When his daughter Sisi gets married, he gives her the two pieces of gold intended for Atu's bride, so that the couple can buy land and assimilate in the New World.

Despite this powerful theme and the romantic interest generated by Atu's longing for Sisi in Africa, the protagonists do not come alive as real individuals because of the author's style. With the exception of a few dialogues, the activities, experiences, thoughts, and feelings of Ajeemah and Atu are reported, instead of being unfolded or revealed in the narrative.

Two additional books that describe the plight of diaspora Africans in North America are *To Be a Slave* (Scholastic, 1968) by Julius Lester, which powerfully integrates the first person accounts of those who lived through slavery; and *The African* (Crown, 1967) by Harold Courlander, a fictional work narrating the traumatic life of Wes Hunu from the freedom of his home in Dahomey, to the indignity of captivity, to the degradation of slavery on a plantation in Georgia. Intended for young adults or older readers, the latter book brilliantly portrays how Wes Hunu's religious beliefs and myths sustain and inspire him through his tragic experiences.

026. Campbell, Peggy, Eric King, and Phillip Supersad. *Fadaka and Other Stories.* Illustrated by Errol Stennett. Leopard Readers Series. London: Collins, 1980. 32p. Grades 4-8.

Four short stories deal with the issue of the growing independence of children in contemporary Africa. Three stories uphold the rights of parents to control and discipline their children because of parental wisdom and experience. The feelings of adolescents, their need to socialize with peers, and their need to be treated as responsible individuals are not explored sensitively. The fourth story, "Match," is about sexual harassment. Olufemi takes his date to a football match, but he annoys her with his rude behavior and continual attempts to touch her. Aminatu takes charge of the situation by telling him to behave, and when he persists, by simply walking out of the stadium. The stories are sketchily written to emphasize their didactic themes; neither the characters nor the events are adequately developed. While the subject matter of at least three of the stories concerns adolescents, the vocabulary and sentence structure are at a primary reading level.

027. Easmon, Carol Olu. *Bisi and the Golden Disc*. Illustrated by author. New York: Crocodile Books, 1990. N.p. Grades K-3.

This fantasy is based on Easmon's memories of the many fairy tales, fables, legends, and romances she had heard as a child and read as an adult. The conflict centers on Princess Bisi's desire to marry the man she loves and the evil magician's schemes to manipulate her weak and greedy father to his own ends. With the help of a magical object and a guardian angel, Bisi's story ends happily. This fantasy also addresses the issue of daughters being forced into loveless marriages because of the material advantage to their parents.

The illustrations deftly integrate a variety of cultural details; however, they lack liveliness and movement.

028. Ekeh, Efanim. *How Tables Came to Umu Madu: The Fabulous History of an Unknown Continent*. Illustrated by Thomas Hamilton. Trenton, NJ: Africa World Press, 1989. 97p. Grades 6-10.

This deceptively simple modern myth/fable is in reality a brilliantly conceived and executed political allegory on the state of affairs in Africa after the coming of Europeans to the continent. The peaceful, harmonious life of the village of Umu Madu is lost forever when No Skin--a European--gifts a table for its communal feasts. The table, which symbolizes Western civilization, consumer goods, materialism, and elitism, introduces bitter strife, disunity, and competition into the village. As this elaborate metaphor traces the various phases of European colonization in Umu Madu/Africa from exploration and trade to missionary work, education, and political control, the citizens of Umu Madu lose their independence and self-respect. Their burning desire for the table, now a seven-tiered edifice, compels them to believe blindly in what No Skin tells them, because they are both in fear and awe of him. They are introduced to the notion of European racial superiority and their own subject status; to political hierarchy in society; and to corruption and control through military might. The metaphor is sustained through postcolonial times with Umu Maduans sacredly trying to uphold the values of the decaying and wobbly table. Political instability, military regimes, violence, corruption, elitism, and an outmoded educational system are all they have achieved since independence.

The message underlying this satire is self-evident: although African nations are free, they are still slaves of the colonial system. Far from condemning Europeans, Ekeh's ironic gaze is focused steadily on Africans, compelling them to evaluate their history and behavior and to empower themselves to establish institutions suited to their needs and traditions. The tongue-in-cheek humor, cutting satire, and interesting episodes prevent the book from degenerating into a mere didactic tract. Ekeh's superb manipulation of diction, at once mock-serious, exaggerated, and revealing, makes this an exceedingly entertaining and thought-provoking book. Among the most memorable scenes are those of the frivolous quarrel over lengthy titles, seeking the favor (''licking someone else's nyash'') of those in power, and the elaborate feast on the seven-tiered table. This humorous tone extends even to the title page where the author's name is prefaced by a string of titles: Chief-Doctor-General-Professor. The framed illustrations maintain the outward formality of the structure, while portraying the humorous content of the fable.

029. Emecheta, Buchi.   *The Rape of Shavi*.   London: Flamingo/Fontana Paperbacks, 1985. Originally published in 1983 by Ogwugwu Afor. 178p. Grades 9-12.

This is a more hopeful modern fable on the impact of Western civilization on Africa than the one described above. Set in the 1980s, the story focuses on how the simple and peaceful lives of the people of Shavi, an imaginary kingdom, change when an aeroplane carrying seven Europeans crashes in their midst. The ensuing rape and exploitation strip Shavians of their dignity, harmonious existence with each other and their environment, economic self-sufficiency, and mineral wealth. Dreams of power, war, and technological might temporarily blind the Crown Prince, Asogba, and his youthful followers till the kingdom is nearly destroyed. However, the wise Queen Mother advises Asogba not to hanker after Western values, but to make Shavi the highly civilized and cultured place it was before the arrival of the intruders.

Despite the fantasy element, Emecheta's skillful character delineation, intricate structure, and knowledge of Western culture make this a profound book. By shifting the perspective repeatedly between the two sets of characters--African and European--and presenting their different cultural backgrounds, values, speech, and behavior, Emecheta introduces both depth and meaning to the story.

030. Franklin, Kristine L.   *The Old, Old Man and the Very Little Boy*. Illustrated by Terea Shaffer. New York: Atheneum, 1992. N.p. Grades K-3.

This is a thought-provoking story of the inexorable passage of time and the blending of past, present, and future at the psychological and emotional levels. To the little boy who enjoys listening to Old Father's stories of adventure and love, it is inconceivable that the aged man has ever been young; yet, the old man insists that inside his ancient body lives a little boy. The wisdom of the old man is clear to the boy only when he becomes old himself and narrates stories to the young. Shaffer's oil paintings capture the vigor and confidence of youth and the loneliness and infirmity of old age.

031. Gray, Nigel.   *A Country Far Away*.   Illustrated by Philippe Dupasquier. New York: Orchard Books, 1989. Originally published in 1988 by Andersen Press, Great Britain. N.p. Grades K-3.

This unique picture book has a common text and two separate sets of illustrations that simultaneously portray the lifestyles of two boys from very different backgrounds, African rural and Western urban. The simple text outlines the boys' daily activities at home, at play, and at school, while the detailed illustrations reveal their cultural differences. The black African child lives in a mud hut, herds goats, fetches water, and goes to an open air school on a donkey; while the white Western boy lives in a large suburban house, helps with washing the family car and vacuuming the house, and goes to a well-equipped school by bus. The two boys do not meet in the story, but each reads a book about the other's country and longs to visit it. The illustrations, though warm and sensitive to both cultures, may unfairly focus attention on the lack of material amenities--cars, computers, supermarkets, parking garages--available to the rural child in Africa. Adult guidance is necessary to encourage young readers to look past the externals and recognize the similarities in the protagonists' basic experiences: both boys enjoy family security and physical comforts; have fun with friends; and have joyous, fulfilling lives.

032. Greenfield, Eloise. *Africa Dream.* Illustrated by Carole Byard. New York: Day, 1977. N.p. Grades K-3.
A young girl connects with her African roots in a dream that takes her to glorious ancient civilizations; to her ancestral village where she participates in communal singing and dancing; and to the arms of her "long-ago" grandmother. This dream nurtures the child's spirit as she feels one with her roots in Africa. Byard's black-and-white illustrations convey the dreamlike, surrealistic quality of the text.

033. Kent, Louise Andrews. *He Went With Vasco da Gama.* Illustrated by Paul Quinn. Boston: Houghton Mifflin, 1938. 258p. Grades 7-12.
Based on Vasco da Gama's diary of his first voyage to India in 1497 and Gaspar Correa's *Land of India,* Kent narrates the story of this historic voyage around the Cape of Good Hope to the western port of Calicut in India. Enroute, the Portuguese ships stop at St. Helena Bay, San Braz, Mozambique, Mombasa, and Malindi in Africa. Mombasa is described as a rich port which has brisk trade with India and other countries, and da Gama also acknowledges the peoples' knowledge of navigation and monsoon winds. The characters' attitudes toward the Africans and Moors they encounter reflect the general spirit of superiority prevalent at that time. The focal interest of the book, however, is not Africa, but the adventures of two fictional characters who accompany da Gama.

034. Muhammad, Alhaji Obaba Abdullahi. *Three Little Africans.* Illustrated by Russ McCollin. New York: African Islamic Mission, 1980. 35p. Grades K-3.
Set somewhere in Africa, this story is based on "The Three Little Pigs." There are three characters--Baba, Ahmad, and Keysa--who are nearing independence and adulthood. How they will lead their lives is symbolized by the building materials they select for their homes: Baba chooses the attractive wood, ebony; Ahmad builds rapidly with palm leaves; and Keysa keeps the future in mind by building a solid house of stone and clay. Instead of the wicked wolf, nature in the form of heavy rains destroys the first two homes. Ashamed and disheartened, the two young adults take the advice of an elder that the future offers hope if they are willing to change. And they do just that with the encouragement of Keysa.

Apart from the obvious didacticism, the story emphasizes traditional African values as being superior to Western civilization, especially in the form of parties and European hotels. In this regard, the story displays bias because temptations and human weaknesses are present in all cultures and societies.

035. Packard, Edward. *Africa: Where Do Elephants Live Underground?* Illustrated by Barbara Carter. Earth Inspectors Series. New York: McGraw-Hill, 1989. 104p. Grades 4-6.

The reader is invited to become an alien from Turoc, a more advanced planet than Earth, to find the mysterious place where elephants live underground. As the protagonist, the reader makes choices affecting the plot, setting, and mode of transportation. While the initial selection of a landing place where elephants are most likely to dwell demands some critical thinking, the remainder of the adventure shapes like an episodic plot requiring no reasoning ability. The protagonist may choose to visit the Pygmies in the Ituri Forest, go to Virunga National Park or Ngorongoro Crater, take a boat ride on the Zaire River, or fly to Arusha. After traveling all over sub-Saharan Africa, the explorer finds elephants licking salt in a cave in Kenya's Mount Elgon National Park.

If the adventure is without intellectual challenges and any real excitement, the reader does gain considerable information on the land, history, peoples, lifestyles, and customs of each city or country visited. Unfortunately, some of the details perpetuate the common stereotypes associated with the continent. Like the typical "spoilt" tourist who resents missing the comforts of home, the explorer makes unfavorable comments on the poor living conditions, lack of hot water, disrepair of roads, and the AIDS epidemic. Politically, independent African countries are seen as going through a "terrible time" since the end of colonialism because of tyrants like Mobutu in Zaire and Idi Amin in Uganda. Also, the details are replete with the Tarzan cliches: lush jungles and stifling heat; encounters with poisonous snakes, lions, and crocodiles; mosquitoes and filthy surroundings; and exotic foods like grilled caterpillars and smoked porcupine.

036. Sterne, Emma Gelders. *The Slave Ship.* Illustrated by David Lockhart. New York: Scholastic, 1953. Originally published as *The Long Black Schooner.* 188p. Grades 5-8.

This historical novel is based on the true story of one hundred slaves who were kidnapped from their homes in Africa and shipped to Cuba in 1839. The fifty-three healthy survivors were sold to two Spanish planters, even though treaties had been signed making the slave trade illegal. According to the novel, under the leadership of the majestic Cinque, the slaves take charge of the ship, Amistad, by killing the captain, although the crew and planters are spared. Unfortunately, their lack of familiarity with the compass and the night stars of the northern hemisphere forces them to accept the help of the Spaniards. During the day the Africans sail the boat toward Africa and the rising sun, while at night the tricky slave buyers turn it west. After zigzagging along the Atlantic coast for two months, the Amistad docks in Connecticut. Because of the captives' inability to communicate, the Spaniards convince the American authorities to imprison and try them. As the case is ruled in favor of the captives by the District Court, the Circuit Court, and, finally, the Supreme Court, the very foundations of the American Constitution--its belief in life, liberty, and the pursuit of happiness--are tested against vested interests. In April 1841, the captives are free to return to their homes in Africa aboard a British ship.

Sterne deftly integrates the historical background, the conflicting philosophies of the slaveowners and abolitionists, and the large profits to be made from the illegal trade in humans into the plot. The excitement and drama of the events is maintained through a fast-moving story. However, sufficient care has been taken to present the captives as real human beings with intelligent thoughts, feelings, and hopes. They maintain their pride, dignity, and love of freedom despite the humiliation of capture and sale on the block. Sterne's characters are quite unlike the passive, huddled masses portrayed in Paula Fox's stylistically superior novel, *The Slave Dancer* (Dell, 1973). The most recent historical novel on slavery in New England is *The Captive* (Scholastic, 1994) by Joyce Hansen. For more information on the Amistad Rebellion, refer to Helen Kromer's *The Amistad Revolt 1839* (Watts, 1973).

037. Zimelman, Nathan. *Treed by a Pride of Irate Lions.* Illustrated by Toni Goffe. Boston: Little, Brown, 1990. N.p. Preschool-Grade 3.
This is a humorous story about Father who, despite his best intentions, is not liked by the domestic animals on the family's farm. Envious of Mother, whom the animals adore, Father sets off for Africa to see if there is some special wild animal who will accept him. Faring no better with elephants, lions, crocodiles, boa constrictors, giraffes, and rhinoceroses, he returns home to his loving family, only to be bitten by the baby! The illustrations extend the tongue-in-cheek humor and whimsical aspects of this kindly man's desperate need to be liked by animals.

POETRY

038. "African Poetry." In *Trade Winds: Poetry in English from Different Cultures,* edited by R. B. Heath, 101-140. Harlow, Essex, England: Longman, 1989. Grades 7-12.
Twenty-two poems, either originally written in English or translated into English, represent the contemporary poetry of a variety of African nations like South Africa, Nigeria, Zambia, Angola, Malawi, and Zimbabwe. Varied in subject matter, the poems express pride in

African traditions; feelings of nationalism; need for political involvement; and a postcolonial identity crisis. Collectively, the poems scan African history and modern conditions to explore what is meant by the African "self." In addition to the above topics that are specific to the African experience, the poets also discuss universal subjects like love, nature, human suffering, exploitation, and peace and happiness. The works of well-known writers like Chinua Achebe, Leopold S. Senghor, Jack Mapanje, and Oswald M. Mtshali are included.

039. Allen, Samuel W., comp. *Poems from Africa.* Illustrated by Romare Bearden. New York: Crowell, 1973. 205p. Grades 8-12.
Selections from sub-Saharan poetry are organized into five broad categories representing oral tradition, West African poetry in English, West African poetry translated from the French, South African poetry, and East African poetry. Traditional poetry expresses the need to understand and respond to the mysteries of life. The modern poets, however, explore subjects like the repudiation of colonialism, rediscovery of Africa's glory, confrontation of ancient lore and twentieth century sensibilities, nostalgia for the ancestral way of life, and critical appraisal of modern African societies. Among the many prominent poets represented here are Aime Cesaire, Leopold Senghor, David Diop, Birago Diop, Gabriel Okara, J. P. Clark, Christopher Okigbo, Wole Soyinka, Kwesi Brew, Mabel Segun, Chinua Achebe, John Mbiti, and Okot p'Bitek.

040. Beier, Ulli. *African Poetry: An Anthology of Traditional African Poems.* Illustrated by Susanne Wenger. Cambridge, England: Cambridge University Press, 1966. 80p. Grades 4-6.
Compiled and edited by Beier from a variety of sources, some of them out-of-print, this collection of traditional African poetry is intended as an introductory work for school children. Beier regrets that the English translations are unable to capture the sound effects of African tonal languages and the subtleties and complexities of the rhythm. In an introductory essay, he establishes the cultural atmosphere that gave rise to the oral poetic tradition of African societies. Any family event such as birth, initiation, marriage, or death, or public celebration such as religious festivals or the installation of a chief was an occasion for praise singers, drummers, priests, and masqueraders to recite and invent poetry. Even ordinary people sang songs and made up verses as they hunted animals, pounded yams, or put babies to sleep.
The poems are organized thematically into nine sections: Religious Songs, Death, Sorrow, Praise Songs, War, Love, People, Animals, and Children's Songs. They are representative of a variety of ethnic groups and cultures, including the Yoruba and Ewe of West Africa, the Zulu and San of South Africa, Galla and Swahili of East Africa, and ancient Egypt. The diversity of the continent becomes apparent when reading about one topic from various cultural perspectives. For example, the supreme creator is referred to as eternal, sun, moon, and

bringer of light. The poems also testify to the common beliefs of all Africans in their respect for nature, worship of ancestral spirits, and manifold expressions of love and sorrow. The descriptions and imagery are unique to the African experience and environment. The spirits of the dead at the gates of the underworld are like "swarming mosquitoes in the evening"; the lover's heel and palm are "sweet to touch like liver"; and the beauty of a bull is "white like the shimmering crane bird on the river bank." The imagery also indicates that African poetry is part of a living tradition that is flexible enough to encompass new influences and ideas. Hence, there are references to guns, Turkish cannons, and Europeans. Wenger's graceful wood-block illustrations, inspired by the simplicity of African wood carvings, complement the poems.

041. Dhondy, Farrukh, ed. "Africa." In *Ranters, Ravers and Rhymers: Poems of Black and Asian Poets, 122-158.* London: Collins, 1990. Grades 9-12.

Representative poets from Nigeria, Zimbabwe, South Africa, Uganda, Tanzania, and Kenya express their postcolonial experiences. Only those black African poets who write in English--since colonialism had "stolen their original tongues," according to Dhondy--are included in order to explore the new idioms, imagery, and subject matter that they bring to English poetry. African poetry touches on varied subjects like exploitation of human beings; living in times of political and social torment; maintaining self-pride after slavery and colonialism; and inferior status of women. Perhaps, the most caustic poem is Wole Soyinka's "Telephone Conversation," in which a white landlady wants to find out how dark-skinned a prospective African tenant is. Collectively, these poems express a personal awareness of being politically independent. The tone is overwhelmingly serious; it is satiric, ironic, questioning, provocative, and revolutionary.

042. Nichols, Grace, comp. *Poetry Jump-Up.* Illustrated by Michael Lewis. New York: Puffin, 1990. Originally published in 1988 as *Black Poetry* by Blackie and Son. 143p. Grades 3-8.

The anthologist has extended the racial and cultural definition of "black" to include the broader "political color" of the term by including poetry from Africa, the Caribbean, America, Asia, and Great Britain. Nichols' objective is to expose children to the new sounds and tastes, new ideas, and new aesthetics that nonwhite cultures have contributed to the world's literary heritage. The selections from Africa embody diverse moods and subjects. There are poems that express ancient folk wisdom, confrontation with modernity, survival during droughts, and faith in the power of the Great Spirit. Especially touching is "My Country" by Zinziswa Mandela, daughter of Nelson and Winnie Mandela, written at the age of twelve on her father's life imprisonment on Robben Island. The poem does not dwell on her inner pain and loneliness, but it recognizes her mother's bravery in facing separation from her husband and her father's need to be comforted that he will be free someday.

043. *A Selection of African Poetry*. Introduced and annotated by Kojo E. Senanu and Theo Vincent. Harlow, Essex, England: Longman, 1976, 1988. 320p. Grades 8-12.

This revised and enlarged second edition is even more representative of the variety and quality of sub-Saharan poetry because it includes Liberian and Lusophone poets. The anthology begins with selections from traditional poems to establish the indebtedness of modern African poetry to oral themes and techniques. This is followed by selections from thirty-seven prominent writers whose poems symbolize the African process of subjecting European languages to the poetic traditions of Africa. In an introductory essay, Senanu and Vincent identify four phases of modern African poetry: The pioneering writers of the 1930s and 1940s such as Leopold Senghor, Birago Diop, and David Diop who protested for political and cultural independence; the postindependence poets like Abioseh Nicol, Gabriel Okara, Wole Soyinka, and Kwesi Brew who attempted to identify with Africa's physical, cultural, and sociopolitical environment; the literary experimenters like Kofi Awoonor, Christopher Okigbo, and Okot p'Bitek whose works embody oral forms; and the contemporary phase which symbolizes a further intensification of the appropriation of Africa's spiritual heritage. To enable students to experience the cultural and aesthetic aspects of African poetry, notes, questions, and commentaries accompany each poem. A glossary of poetic terms and short biographies of the poets are also included.

BIOGRAPHY

044. Dobler, Lavinia, and William A. Brown. *Great Rulers of the African Past*. Illustrated by Yvonne Johnson. Garden City, NY: Doubleday, 1965. 120p. Grades 4-6.

This book celebrates the nationalistic strategies and vision of five rulers from Western and Central Africa--Mansa Musa of Mali, Askia Muhammad and Sunni Ali Ber of Songhay, Affonso I of the Congo, and Idris Alaoma of Bornu. Each ruler looked beyond his own kingdom to the inventions, knowledge, skills, and culture of North Africa, the Middle East, or Europe to benefit his country; each strengthened trade and diplomatic relations with the outside world to establish a strong and powerful empire; and, above all, each sought to unify his people through religion (Affonso was a Catholic, whereas the other four were Muslims). Although Affonso I was the only one who failed in his mission, he is still remembered in songs and legends because he did not let his country disintegrate in the face of Portuguese exploitation and the disloyalty of his noblemen. Each biographical sketch successfully conveys the historical background, social and economic conditions, and the personality and accomplishments of the subject.

045. Kaula, Edna Mason. *Leaders of the New Africa.* Illustrated by author. Cleveland and New York: World, 1966. 192p. Grades 7-12.

Brief biographical sketches of leaders responsible for political movements in Africa are organized around broad regions such as the French Empire in West Africa, Equatorial Africa, British colonies on the west coast, provinces and protectorates of Portugal, Britain, and South Africa, and East Africa. In order to place individuals in their correct social contexts, each chapter discusses the land and peoples, history upto independence, cultural traits, and achievements prior to European colonization. The book is ambitious as it discusses *all* the important African leaders upto the 1960s such as Leopold Senghor, Kwame Nkrumah, Joseph Kasavubu, Patrice Lumumba, Moise Tshombe, Albert Luthuli, Robert Sobukwe, Holden Roberto, King Sobhuza II, Kenneth Kaunda, Jomo Kenyatta, Julius Nyerere, Edward Mutesa, Haile Selassie, Gamal Abdel Nasser, and Habib Bourguiba. Collectively, these biographies display an understanding of colonialism, a restored sense of pride in Africa, and the common transcendent purpose of providing equal opportunities for all.

While Kaula's account objectively represents the views of Africans, she discusses the history of South Africa from the perspective of the white minority government. She praises the apartheid policy of building townships, schools, and hospitals for blacks, but no comparative figures on educational standards within the country, or statistics on malnutrition and death are provided. Furthermore, Kaula neither explains what "separate development" stands for, nor sees the relationship between the creation of homelands and forced removals, poor living conditions, cheap labor for factories, and control by the white government. Her only regret is that black South Africans have no voice in their government.

046. Polatnick, Florence T., and Alberta L. Saletan. *Shapers of Africa.* New York: Messner, 1969. 184p. Grades 6-10.

By tracing the lives of five significant African heroes and heroines, chosen from a time span of almost seven hundred years, the authors recreate the unique and rich history of sub-Saharan Africa. The account begins with Mansa Musa, ruler of the Mali empire, and his decision in 1324 to set out on a *hadj,* or holy pilgrimage, to Mecca with sixty thousand pilgrims. The entire story focuses on the grand preparations, the travels of the royal entourage, and the lavish gifts of gold and other precious items distributed enroute. The account also provides insight into the confederation of independent states in the Mandingo political organization; the high standard of living of the common people; the influence of Islam and establishment of Islamic centers in Timbuktu and Gao in 1325; and the expansion and prestige of the Mali empire in Africa, the Western world, and the Middle East. Next, the authors trace the history of the valiant and tenacious freedom fighter from Angola, Queen Nzinga, as she challenged the Portuguese right to control her Ndonga territory. From 1622 onward, she led her people through warfare and exile, made treaties with both the Portuguese and Dutch on an equal footing, and refused to pay homage to foreign governments.

In the eighteenth and nineteenth centuries, one is inspired by the stories of Samuel Ajayi Crowther (1808-1891) and King Moshoeshoe (1790-1870). Crowther was taken as a slave from Nigeria when he was thirteen. He was rescued by a British patrol, taken to Sierra Leone, and educated by missionaries. Later, he was ordained as the first African bishop. Moshoeshoe, king of the Basuthos, was known for his pacifist philosophy, keen intelligence, skillful diplomacy, and commanding personality. The account ends in the twentieth century with Tom Mboya (1931-1969), the youthful Kenyan freedom fighter, labor leader, and politician.

Each biography reads like an interesting story with a vigorous plot, character development, and detailed descriptions of time, place, and culture. The only flaws in the treatment are references to the cruelty of King Shaka, without objectively portraying him as a nationalist, and an emphasis on the rewards of conversion to Christianity from traditional religions. However, the authors mean well and it is their intention to take an Afrocentric approach in introducing Western readers to the shapers of African history.

047. Walters, Jane G. *African Triumph*. London: Allen and Unwin, 1965. 94p. Grades 5-8.

This book of ten inspiring biographies of pioneers of African progress in Africa, the United States, and Haiti contains the accounts of Samuel Ajayi Crowther of Nigeria and James Emman Kwegyir Aggrey of Ghana. Like Samuel Crowther, James Aggrey (1875-1927) was a preacher and an educator who emphasized a practical approach to providing for the daily needs and national pride of Africans, instead of focusing just on formal education and spiritual salvation. Their outstanding achievements and their recognition by Western royalty, statesmen, churchmen, and scholars in a climate of slavery and racism are testimony to their extraordinary intelligence, ability, and success.

INFORMATIONAL BOOKS

048. Adrian, Mary. *Wildlife on the African Grasslands*. Illustrated by Bette J. Davis. New York: Messner, 1979. 64p. Grades 2-4.

With the daily activities of a pride of lions as a point of entry, Adrian provides a lively account of the varied animals that live on the African grasslands. Each wild animal depends upon another animal or plant for food. Lions, cheetahs, hyenas, and wild dogs, for instance, feed on grazers like antelopes, zebras, and buffaloes and plant eating animals like giraffes.

Adrian ends on a pessimistic note because humans have upset this food chain on the grasslands. Despite the many wildlife reserves and national parks, African governments have to choose between saving their priceless animal heritage or providing for the needs of a growing population.

049. *Africa and the Origin of Humans.*   History of the World Series. Milwaukee, WI: Raintree, 1989. Originally published in 1985 as *Origini dell'uomo e l'Africa* by Editoriale Jaca Book. 79p. Grades 8-10.

Aided by maps, charts, drawings, and supplementary insets, the extensively researched text traces the history of Africa from the origin of humans up to 300 A.D. Through scientific theories and fossil finds of Raymond Dart, Robert Broom, Louis and Mary Leakey and others, the physical, intellectual, social, and cultural evolution of humans is traced from Pre-Australopithecus (4,000,000 years ago) to Homo habilis, Homo erectus, Neanderthal man, and Homo sapiens. These hominids adapted to various African environments like the Sahara Desert (100,000 to 130,000 years ago), equatorial forest regions, open savannas, steppe and mountains, and coastal areas. Around 50,000 B.C. human populations in Africa were differentiating according to region; they became specialized in their environments and developed distinct cultures as can be seen from their habitats, tools, artifacts, rock paintings, and burial caves. Next, there follows an examination of the culture, arts, economy, government, religion, and lifestyle of four civilizations: Egyptian, Punic (Carthage), Kushite, and Aksum. In particular, mention of the scripts developed in Egypt, Meroe, Ethiopia, and Numidia dispels the myth that written language was unknown to the early peoples of sub-Saharan Africa. The account ends with the expedition of Alexander the Great (334 B.C.) and the Greek colonization of Libya and Egypt; the Roman conquest of Northern Africa (31 B.C.); and the spread of Christianity and the birth of the Coptic church.

The complexity and variety of the above information has created some "thought gaps" or confusion. For instance, it is not clearly stated that hominids spread to Europe and Asia *from* Africa, although it is implied. Such clarification is important in view of the conflicting theories on the origin of humans. There is at least one factual error in the statement that Christianity came to Aksum in 330 B.C. via Alexandria, because the text later states that Christianity spread in Alexandria in 190 A.D. In addition, it is not clear why a book on the development of humans and their civilizations in Africa should give such prominence to the Phoenician, Greek, and Roman colonization of Africa. European conquests tend to minimize the importance of African achievements. Furthermore, one brief section (seven paragraphs) dismisses the Bantu migrations and accomplishments (between 1000 B.C. and 1000 A.D.), spread of iron technology, development of towns in Djenne (about 300 B.C.) and in the Nok culture of Nigeria, and the creation of travel routes within the continent and across the Indian Ocean. The achievements of Eastern Africa--of Ethiopia and Kenya--are credited to Asian and Arabic contacts.

050. Bash, Barbara. *Tree of Life: The World of the African Baobab.*
Illustrated by author. San Francisco: Sierra Club Books; Boston: Little,
Brown, 1989. N.p. Grades K-3.

This unique informational book first narrates the !Kung myth of the
creation of the baobab before explaining the tree's importance to the
ecosystem of the dry savannas of Africa. With a life span of more
than one thousand years, the baobab is revered as an honorable
"mother," the giver of life. When it is full of blossoms and foliage, a
variety of creatures seek it for shelter and sustenance: birds build
nests in its branches; honey bees, caterpillars, worms, grasshoppers,
and other insects inhabit it; bushbabies and baboons make their
homes in it; and giraffes, elephants, and impalas eat the tender leaves
and flowers or munch the bark for moisture. Even when the leaves
are gone, the baobab continues to be the microcosm of life. Humans,
too, share in the bounty of this ancient gnarled and twisted tree. The
melon-shaped fruit is used for candy and drinks; the bark for baskets
and ropes; the leaves and roots for medicine; and the dry stump of the
dying tree for stored water and shelter. Bash, who is a specialist in
botanical illustrations, provides graphic pictures of the baobab's
ecology. Both text and illustrations display the clarity and organization of an informational book and the poetic grace of a creative work.

051. Baynham, Simon. *Africa from 1945.* Conflict in the 20th Century
Series. London: Franklin Watts, 1987. Originally published in 1987 by
Aladdin. 62p. Grades 6-8.

The problems of modern African countries are examined in the light
of European colonialism and the difficulties that have come to
epitomize the Third World. Colonial rule was responsible for the
creation of artificial national boundaries and the introduction of
political and economic institutions not suited to African conditions.
Postindependent conditions, in contrast, led to ineffective governments, armed conflicts and military coups, border disputes and
secession, and bitter civil wars. Baynham concludes that the future
seems bleak unless the immediate problems of a rapidly increasing
population, poverty, food shortages, widespread starvation, and
disease can be addressed by the individual governments and through
foreign aid.

Appendices on African personalities, apartheid, famine, foreign
intervention, and Rhodesian counterinsurgency focus the discussion
on specific topics and countries. Photographs, maps, charts, and a
chronology complement the informative text. An index and reading
list are also included.

052. Boyd, Allen R., and John Nickerson. *Tropical and Southern Africa.*
4th edition. Scholastic World Cultures Series. New York: Scholastic, 1986.
Originally published in 1973. 235p. Grades 6-9.

This book dispels the prevalent stereotypes about Africa by
discussing its varied geography, peoples and lifestyles, including
Europeans, Arabs, and Indians, and family loyalty, not ethnicity, as
the basis of larger social organizations like clans, villages, and

kingdoms. Modern Africans are confronted with the dilemma of loosening traditional loyalties, food production and jobs in a changing economy, problems of famine, and the importance of developing a national identity. Focusing on contemporary problems, the authors state that Africans are responding to the ''winds of change'' brought from outside: Islam and Christianity; formal education and mission schools; urbanization; and modern technology and industrialization. An insider's view is presented by interspersing the informative chapters with photographic essays, personal narratives of Africans, and prose essays on related topics. For example, counterpoint and extension of the main text are achieved through the story of a Zairean woman returning to her husband's home after the birth of her first child; details of an Ivory Coast couple's traditional marriage negotiations, marriage, and divorce; attempts of an Asante chief to change the traditional matrilineal inheritance laws through the modern law courts in order to preserve cocoa farming; and departure of a young Gikuyu from his village for the attractions of the city. The book concludes that whether the future will bring new dignity to the family system and provide a place for customs and traditions of the village, and whether Africans will be able to put new roots without destroying the old ones which remain, is yet to be seen.

Tropical and Southern Africa will make an excellent class text because each chapter, essay, and personal narrative is accompanied by maps, photographs with explanatory captions, review and discussion questions, suggestions for activities, and tables and charts.

053. Chiasson, John. *African Journey*. Photographs by author. New York: Bradbury, 1987. 55p. Grades 6-12.

Both text and color photographs record the influence of geography on the living conditions, religious beliefs, customs, and achievements of Africans. Chiasson's journey takes him to six distinct regions across the broadest part of Africa between the Sahara Desert to the north and the equator to the south. Beginning with the Sahel, a sandy strip of land along the southern edge of the Sahara Desert, Chiasson describes the nomadic lifestyle of two herding tribes, the Tuareg and the WooDaabe. Next, he visits a small farming village, GDobje, inhabited by a clan of the Yoruba tribe, on the densely populated and fertile coastal plains of Benin. The dependence of cities on nature is illustrated through the Senegalese capital of Dakar which relies on the farming, fishing, and mining industries that take place in the countryside. The influence of rivers is felt in Mopti, sometimes called the Venice of West Africa, whose inhabitants depend on the river for transportation, fishing, trade, and drinking water. Just how delicate the African ecosystem is can be seen in the chapter on Ethiopia, which focuses on the years 1983 to 1985 when the northern provinces were stricken by drought.

Because the continent has undergone tremendous changes in recent decades, Chiasson believes that Africans will have to adapt to new environments, new farming methods, and learn new technologies in order to tap their natural resources.

054. Corwin, Judith Hoffman. *African Crafts.* Illustrated by author. London: Franklin Watts, 1990. 48p. Grades 1-5.

Through useful, decorative, and expressive art objects, Corwin enriches readers' understanding of African history, peoples, and cultures. Using materials that are readily available in the house, she provides clear and simple directions on how to design masks, dolls, beads and good luck charms, Asante gold weights, and Nigerian cloth. In addition, instructions on how to make and play Mankala, a popular African game, and cook dishes from Algeria and Ethiopia are included. With each activity, Corwin gives background information on the social, religious, and spiritual meaning of the object. Attractive motifs of animals and geometric patterns capture the unique spirit of the continent.

055. Davidson, Basil, and the Editors of TIME-LIFE Books. *African Kingdoms.* Great Ages of Man Series. New York: TIME-LIFE Books, 1966. 191p. Grades 8-12.

The specific purpose of this book is to dispel the European stereotype of Africa as a dark and uncivilized continent. By piecing together written records made long ago in Africa, the Middle East, Europe, and China, Africa emerges as a continent with a long and distinguished record of achievements in adaptation to the environment, complicated political systems, profound religious beliefs, and close-knit social structures. The account begins with a discussion of the varied geography and evolution of humankind in Africa. Next, *African Kingdoms* enumerates the accomplishments of the civilizations of Egypt, Kush, Aksum, and Meroe in the Nile region; the sophisticated organization of village communities of the Pygmies, Dinka, and Tongo; the ruins of ancient civilizations at Zimbabwe and Kilwa; the trading empires of Ghana, Mali, Songhay, and Kanem-Bornu; and the forest kingdoms of the Congo, Benin, and Asante. A separate chapter discusses the religious thought and moral rules that guided social conduct, spiritual aspects of life, and communal harmony.

Each chapter is enriched by supplementary essays on topics such as Timbuktu, the bustling port of Kilwa, horsemen of Bornu, Saharan cave paintings (some as old as 4500 B.C.), initiation rituals of Nuba wrestlers, ancient trade routes, salt making in the Sahara, Christian churches in Ethiopia, and African wood sculpture. The book is profusely illustrated with photographs, drawings, maps, and charts.

056. Ellis, Veronica Freeman. *Afro-Bets First Book About Africa.* Illustrated by George Ford. Orange, NJ: Just Us Books, 1989. 31p. Grades 1-3.

Organized as a storytelling hour at school, this book provides basic information on the diverse history, geography, natural resources, wildlife, peoples, slavery, arts and crafts, religions, and cultures of the African continent. While there are no headings or subheadings, the storyteller's lecture and the children's questions provide the necessary transitions between topics. The Afro-Bets Kids learn of their African heritage through the ancient civilizations of Egypt, Kush, Ethiopia,

Ghana, Mali, Songhay, Zimbabwe, and the Zulu nation; trade and contacts with Arabia, China, India, and Europe; and the determination of modern Africans to free themselves from colonial rule. The children ask pertinent questions, express their awe and pride in Africa, and satisfy their curiosity. The above information is presented in an objective manner, placing events in their proper historical, economic, and social contexts. The text is abundantly illustrated with photographs and drawings.

057. Faul, Michael A. *The Story of Africa and Her Flags to Color.* Illustrated by Nancy Conkle. Santa Barbara, CA: Bellerophon, 1990. N.p. Grades 3-5.

The current national flags of the fifty-two countries represented in the Organization of African Unity are arranged alphabetically. An introductory section provides background information on the various parts of a flag, major historical and political terms, and the significance of the predominant colors. For example, several countries use the red, yellow, and green of the Ethiopian flag to show their respect for and solidarity with the oldest independent African country. Black is frequently used to represent pride in their race and unity with other African states. Diagrams of each national flag are provided, and children are required to follow directions in filling the colors.

The discussion of the symbols on each flag also includes a brief account of the country's history and culture, resistance and independence, and present leaders and government. A reading of this book will impress children with Africa's long tradition and history; diversity in races, cultures, and languages; enduring power to withstand the momentous events of the past; and youthful attitude in starting afresh and looking ahead to the future with hope and courage.

058. Garlake, Peter. *The Kingdoms of Africa.* The Making of the Past Series. New York: Bedrick, 1990. Originally published in 1978 by Elsevier Publishing, Lausanne. 152p. Grades 8-12.

Based on modern archeological sites and the accounts of early explorers, travelers, and archeologists, *The Kingdoms of Africa* provides a holistic survey of the peoples, resources, and settlements of entire regions of Africa. Individual chapters discuss the character of Africa, concepts of Africa, villagers and farmers, mines and courts of the South, cities on the eastern coast, and kingdoms of West Africa. The author recognizes the "autonomy, creativity and innovative dynamism of indigenous local societies" and their response to the many challenges and opportunities that they encountered. Visual essays on Meroe and Aksum, traditional architecture, ruins of Zimbabwe, and sculpture of Ife and Benin focus attention on specific achievements. The text is supplemented by photographs, maps, a glossary, an index, and a reading list.

059. Georges. D.V. *Africa*. A New True Book. Chicago: Children's Press, 1986. 48p. Grades 2-4.

> Organized by region, this beginning book introduces young readers to the land, peoples, history and achievements, and lifestyles of Africans. Both color photographs and text present a balanced and objective account of the continent. Georges, however, does present the Eurocentric view that Victoria Falls was "discovered" by David Livingstone in 1855.

060. Green, Carl R., and Willaim R. Sanford. *The African Lion*. Edited by Howard Schroeder. Wildlife, Habits and Habitat Series. Mankato, MN: Crestwood House, 1987. 47p. Grades 3-5.

> Beginning with the biological classification and history of lions on earth, the authors proceed to give details of the African lion's habitat, physical characteristics, behavior, and life cycle. The necessity of protecting the dwindling population--today, wild lions can be found only in Africa and the Gir Forest in Eastern India--from frightened farmers and trophy hunters has resulted in the lion being in a controlled environment in zoos and game preserves.
>
> The book ends with an account of the work of Joy and George Adamson of Kenya. Joy Adamson is author of *Born Free, Living Free,* and *Forever Free*, which narrate the story of the lioness Elsa's life with the Adamsons and the rescue of her cubs after her death.

061. Jefferson, Margo, and Elliott P. Skinner. *Roots of Time: A Portrait of African Life and Culture*. Illustrated by Jerry Pinckney. Trenton, NJ: Africa World Press, 1990. Originally published in 1974 by Doubleday. 127p. Grades 7-9.

> Relegating ethnic differences to the background, *Roots of Time* provides a comprehensive portrait of the quality of life in traditional Africa. Individual chapters discuss the rituals associated with birth and childhood, male and female initiation, and age-sets; economic systems based on respect for the environment; communal unity arising from kinship ties, arranged marriages, bride price, and the extended family; political stability and law and order maintained through the interdependence of descending layers of authority from the king down to the chiefs, village elders, and individual families; religious beliefs in a supreme god, ancestor worship, priests, and spiritualists; and the practical and spiritual aspects of artistic expression. "Africa Today" focuses on the clash between these traditional values and the imposition of new political, economic, religious, and social institutions. The account ends on a hopeful note because modern Africans are seeking to blend the best of the traditional with the best of the modern. Both the elegant prose and the black-and-white illustrations capture the dignity, diversity, and richness of traditional Africa.

062. Johnson, Sylvia A. *The Lions of Africa*. The Animal Friends Book Series. Minneapolis, MN: Carolrhoda, 1977. Originally published as *Les Lions* by Anne Marie Pajot. N.p. Preschool-Grade 2.

Information on the habitat, family structure, training of the young, and hunting techniques of African lions is presented in the form of a movie being shown by a wildlife expert. The photographs, informal dialogue, and questions and answers address the queries of young readers and engage their interest.

063. Kaula, Edna Mason. *The Bantus*. London: Franklin Watts, 1968. 90p. Grades 7-12.

Based on traditional legends and the studies of ethnologists and anthropologists, Kaula provides a comprehensive portrait of the Bantu speaking persons of Africa. Their origin is traced to Cameroon, from where over 2,000 years ago successive waves migrated into the Congo forest belt, the Great Lakes area of Central East Africa, and East Africa, undergoing ethnic and cultural changes because of contact with Hamites and Nilotes. When this region became overcrowded, the three strongest groups--Thonga, Ngoni, and Sotho--moved to Southern Africa where they established great kingdoms such as Zimbabwe, Rozwi, and the Zulu nation. Bantus encountered Europeans in the fifteenth century when Portuguese explorers and Christian missionaries came to Africa.

Kaula's objectivity is seriously undermined because she minimizes European involvement in the slave trade and states that Europeans went into "savage" parts of Central Africa. Similarly, in discussing the conquests of Zulu rulers like Shaka and the Boer trek into Natal, she advances the Boer perspective. By the end of the nineteenth century, Europeans were living in every part of Africa where Bantus lived; yet, Kaula does not question the wrong done to them. Instead, she focuses on the efforts of missionaries to bring education and improvements to the "primitive" Bantu lifestyle. The book ends with a brief survey of emerging Bantus in a postcolonial world. The segments on Rhodesia and South Africa are the most blatantly racist because of their many omissions and distortions of reality. Kaula states that when Bantus work in gold and diamond mines or as domestic servants, they do so willingly for higher wages and a better life. The complex social, economic, and political factors that control the lives of blacks are not mentioned. Also, there is no statistical data on the disparity between Bantus and whites.

064. Kerina, Jane. *African Crafts*. Illustrated by Tom Feelings. Diagrams by Marylyn Katzman. New York: Lion, 1970. 64p. Grades 4-8.

Western children are introduced to African craftsmanship through a variety of objects required for daily use. Simple and clear directions are provided for making calabash kitchenware, fly whisks, fans, and Nubian mats from East Africa; leather cushions, *grigri* amulets, and silver jewelry from North Africa; the *kora* (a musical instrument), wooden headdresses, royal stools, Akuaba fertility dolls, and textiles from West Africa; stone and terra cotta sculptures and Mangbetu waterpots from Central Africa; and beaded jewelry and wooden headrests from Southern Africa. In addition, the processes for making vegetable dyes and the popular game Mankala (also called Oware and

Ohoro) are outlined. Kerina gives the history and cultural context of each object and explains the many symbols and patterns that decorate it.

Katzman's diagrams support the written directions, while Feelings' illustrations indicate that creativity and visual beauty are an integral part of traditional African life.

065. Kroll, Virginia L. *Africa Brothers and Sisters*. Illustrated by Vanessa French. New York: Four Winds, 1993. N.p. Grades K-2.

Jesse and his father play a ritual game that engenders pride in their African heritage and a sense of identity with their African brothers and sisters. Through questions and answers they list the names and cultural contributions of twenty-one separate ethnic groups from all over Africa. As they repeat this litany, Jesse recognizes the influence of African traditions on his own life in America: the finely woven Zulu baskets his parents acquired on their honeymoon; the Wolof head scarves his mother wears; his skill at clay modeling is akin to Falasha pottery; and the colorful Asante cloth he wears to parties. French's illustrations not only capture the warm and loving relationship between father and son, but they also reflect the intertextual connection between African customs and their adaptation in America.

066. Lye, Keith. *Africa*. Today's World Series. London: Gloucester, 1987. 36p. Grades 5-7.

Individual chapters discuss the land and climate, plants and animals, cultures and peoples, recent history, and agriculture and economy of the five regions of the African continent. Focusing on the postcolonial period, Lye presents Africa as a fast-changing continent that has faced many problems. According to him, the slow growth of the per capita gross national product indicates that the continent does not have the means to benefit from its vast natural resources. African nations have united under various organizations such as the Arab League, Organization of African Unity, and Organization of Petroleum Exporting Countries in order to promote unity, provide assistance, raise living standards, defend each country's territory, and oppose colonialism and racialism. Each chapter is generously illustrated with photographs, political and physical maps, and flags of each country. A glossary, index, and list of facts on type of government, capital city, population, and land area provide ready access to information.

067. McCauley, Jane R. *Africa's Animal Giants*. Books for Young Explorers Series. Washington, D.C.: National Geographic Society, 1987. 34p. Preschool-Grade 2.

Through breathtaking full-color photographs and a simple text, this book introduces young children to the world's biggest, fastest, and tallest animals--elephant, lion, ostrich, rhinoceros, hippopotamus, Cape buffalo, giraffe, and gorilla--that have survived in the wild in Africa. McCauley discusses their natural environment, physical characteristics, food habits, care of the young, and survival techniques. She emphasizes the harmony that exists between these large animals and the smaller animals and their habitats.

The biggest dangers facing African wildlife, as a more detailed essay intended for adults states, are a growing human population and illegal hunting for tusks and horns. The gorilla, rhinoceros, and elephant are listed as the most endangered of the larger animals. A reading list for children ranging from ages eight to twelve is also included. Another book that is appropriate for preschool children is John Wallace Purcell's *African Animals* (Children's Press, 1982). In addition to covering the above material, it also discusses some of the smaller animals such as crocodiles, zebras, antelopes, and baboons.

068. Murphy, E. Jefferson. *Understanding Africa.* Illustrated by Louise E. Jefferson. New York: Crowell, 1969, 1978. 208p. Grades 7-12.

This is a superb introductory book that shatters the prevalent myths and stereotypes about Africa. Murphy examines the physical characteristics, languages, social groupings, colonialism, and modern nations of Africa over history. Africa is seen as a dynamic continent with a rich and lively history of achievements in skillful leadership and law-making, religion, the arts, metal work, mining, trade and communication, and military tactics. The contributions to world culture of the kingdoms and empires of Ghana, Mali, Aksum, Kush, Egypt, Sudan, Zimbabwe, and Songhay are cited as examples. Europeans, according to Murphy, chose to ignore the accounts of Arab travelers and Moorish scholars because they came mainly to the coastline, whereas these civilizations were flowering inland. Because of environmental limitations, especially in the Sahara Desert, Murphy acknowledges that Africa could not participate fully in the progress of science and technology that changed Europe.

The arrival of Europeans and colonization fixed people in given areas. The slave trade, in particular, led to political unrest, shift in the power base, virtual end to production of consumer items, and population depletion by seventy million due to capture, war, sickness, and death. Murphy also compares traditional slavery in Africa to the commercial ventures of Arab and European traders. Next, he discusses nationalist movements under the leadership of men like Kwame Nkrumah and Julius Nyerere who studied abroad and were inspired by European philosophers. Today, Africa is once again on the move in its attempt to build prosperous and stable nations.

In describing the workings of neocolonialism in Africa, Murphy states that Western powers maintained economic control by regulating African development through financial aid and insufficient foreign investment and by setting prices for African products and European manufactured goods. The West, thus, allowed Africa to develop only at a slow pace. However, Africans are determined to rely on themselves and set their own priorities as underlined by Pan-Africanism and the Organization of African Unity. Murphy is hopeful of Africa's future because the resources are substantial, the leaders are able, and the people are intelligent.

069. Murray, Jocelyn, ed. *Africa.* Cultural Atlas of the World Series. Alexandria, VA: Stonehenge, 1981, 1991. 240p. Grades 8-adult.

Written by an international team of expert Africanists, this cultural atlas of Africa provides an introduction to the continent as a whole. It dispels the various myths and misconceptions regarding the geography, peoples, religions, history and empires, and cultures of Africa. Every aspect of life--population distribution, languages, mineral resources, political organization, economy, and social institutions--is seen as operating within its specific geographical and historical context. Hence, Africans developed political systems ranging from empires to sacral kinships to age-based republics and village democracies, and social organizations from stratified slave-holding societies to completely classless communities. Of the numerous topics discussed, especially interesting are the individual essays on human evolution in Africa and the development of agriculture and productive economies; the kingdoms of Kush, Egypt, Zimbabwe, and Asante; Europe in Africa and the slave trade; African diaspora; debate on the source of the Nile; mapping of Africa; growth of cities; architecture and the arts, especially masked dances; education, literacy, and the role of missionary schools; and game parks and wildlife conservation. Despite the obvious diversity, the unity of African peoples is seen in religions based on veneration of ancestors, elevation of royal and heroic ancestors, and the idea of one God; circumcision of young people to mark their entrance into adulthood; and the unifying forces of Islam and Christianity.

In addition to the above general discussion, the book outlines the geography, history, political system, and economy of individual nations. Over three hundred photographs and ninety-six maps indicating the physical features and mineral, agricultural, and industrial resources of each country are also included. The bibliography, gazette, and index will aid the serious researcher.

070. Musgrove, Margaret. *Ashanti to Zulu: African Traditions.* Illustrated by Leo and Diane Dillon. New York: Dial, 1976. N.p. Grades K-3.

Winner of the 1976 Caldecott Medal, this unique alphabet book introduces readers to twenty-six African peoples. Each letter of the alphabet focuses on a specific custom that reflects the lifestyle and values of the culture being described. By using representative groups from all over Africa, Musgrove hints at the vastness and variety of the African continent. Musgrove's research is further apparent in the details she provides of each ethnic group. For instance, the *kente* cloth of the Asante, the origin of the crocodile legend of the Baule, the hairstyles of the Masai, the bridal procession of the Ndaka, and the veiled men of the Tuareg group. The magnificent earthtone paintings by the Dillons match the research and thoroughness of the text. The illustrators meticulously portray the diversity in facial features, clothing, housing, environment, and customs. In addition to accuracy of detail, the paintings extend the text by artistically including a man, a woman, a child, their living quarters, an artifact, and a local animal to provide a multitextured, vibrant experience of each culture. Both text and illustrations convey the distinct impression that the dignity and confidence of Africans stem from their respect for traditional rituals and beliefs. Although this book has been criticized for emphasizing only the exotic features of each culture, it is visually pleasing and informative.

071. Nabwire, Constance, and Bertha Vining Montgomery. *Cooking the African Way.* Photographs by Robert L. and Diane Wolfe. Easy Menu Ethnic Cookbooks Series. Minneapolis, MN: Lerner, 1988. 47p. Grades 4-6.
    East and West African cuisines are presented in their proper geographical, historical, social, economic, and cultural contexts. Complete traditional and modern menus from both regions include popular dishes such as Fufu, Egusi Soup, Jollof Rice, Groundnut Sauce, Luku, Akara, Greens with Coconut Milk, and Samosas. Although the recipes have been slightly modified to suit Western tastes, they represent the authentic cooking of East and West Africa. Easy-to-follow instructions, a list of culinary terms and utensils, and tips for careful cooking make this an ideal book for beginning cooks.

072. Onyefulu, Ifeoma. *A is for Africa.* Photographs by author. New York: Cobblehill Books, 1993. N.p. Grades K-2.
    Although the photographs were taken in Nigeria, this alphabet book introduces readers to what the people of Africa have in common: traditional village life, warm family ties, and hospitality. Both the diversity and universal characteristics of the continent are emphasized through various objects and customs such as offering kola nuts, fondness for jewelry and body painting, storytelling, and beating of drums for entertainment and for announcing special events. The book focuses on the rural and exotic aspects of traditional Africa; there are no urban images.

073. Paysan, Klaus. *Wild Animals of Africa.* Photographs by author. Sketches by Angela Paysan. Translated from the German *Wehrhaftes Wild in Afrika* by Jane Owen. Minneapolis, MN: Lerner, 1971. 107p. Grades 4-6.
    Paysan's detailed account of the physical characteristics, habits, natural surroundings, and hunting methods of thirteen African animals is enlivened by anecdotes of his experiences while photographing them. In discussing the elephant, rhinoceros, hippopotamus, horned buffalo, and crocodile, he emphasizes the symbiotic relationship between these predators and smaller animals. It is especially heartening, he says, that humans can finally observe the animals' behavior and protect them in national parks, instead of killing them out of fear and greed. Paysan's beautiful color photographs and his wife's humorous sketches accompany the informative text.

074. Rooney, Douglas David, and E. Halladay. *The Building of Modern Africa.* London: Harrap, 1966. 261p. Grades 8-12.
    Although outdated, this account of the building of modern Africa can

be read for its biased Western perspective. Far from considering tropical Africa of any economic importance to Europeans (Southern Africa being an exception), Rooney and Halladay believe that the scramble for Africa was precipitated solely by the complicated European diplomacy following the Franco-Prussian War of 1870-1871. Rivalries among the "great powers" were channelled into the "less dangerous" struggle for African colonies. The destiny of modern Africa is viewed as the work of many important figures who left their imprint on African history: the antislavery and philanthropic campaigns of David Livingstone; Lord Delamere, Julius Nyerere, and Haile Selassie in East Africa; King Leopold in the Belgian Congo; Lord Lugard and Kwame Nkrumah in West Africa; and Cecil Rhodes and Jan C. Smuts in South Africa. The rapid growth of African nationalism after 1945 is attributed to the European development of economic and commercial potentialities in Africa, the foundation of an educational system, and the colonial policy of "restraint and conservatism" in granting self-government to African states.

075. Ryden, Hope. *Wild Animals of Africa ABC*. Photographs by author. New York: Dutton, 1989. N.p. Preschool-Grade 1.
   From aardvark to unicornfish, xoxo, yellow-legged galago, and zebra, a variety of wild animals from the African continent represent the letters of the English alphabet. Color photographs of each animal in its natural environment introduce young readers to the varied African terrain of lush jungles, hot deserts, rivers and oceans, open grasslands, rocky cliffs, and underground dens. While the main text only names the animals, detailed information on the physical characteristics, habitats, food, and behavior is provided at the end.

076. Sabin, Francene. *Africa*. Illustrated by Allan Eitzen. Mahwah, NJ: Troll, 1985. 30p. Grades K-3.
   A sparse text introduces the contrasting landscapes, climates, peoples, religions, cultures, languages, and plant and animal life of the African continent. Despite the rich natural resources of the land, the author states that many of its people are poor. In modern times, Africa's mineral and oil resources have become its most important contribution to world trade. Sabin hopes that income from the sales will provide medical facilities, education, proper food, employment, and self-reliance to Africans.

077. Sanford, William R., and Carl R. Green. *The African Rhinos*. Edited by Howard Schroeder. Mankato, MN: Crestwood House, 1987. 47p. Grades 3-6.
   Color photographs and an anecdotal style take readers on an imaginary safari to Tanzania's Selous Game Reserve to see two species of rhino--the black rhino and the white rhino, although both are blackish-gray in color. Readers are introduced to their history, natural environment, physical characteristics, mating habits, care of the young, and differences.
   The agenda of the book, however, is to emphasize that rhinos are

an endangered species, with only nine thousand black rhinos and three thousand white rhinos alive today, including those in game parks and zoos. Believed to be the mythical unicorns, rhinos continue to be killed illegally for their horns for dagger handles and medicine. Even though the horn has no scientifically proven medicinal properties because it is made of keratin, the same as fingernails, it continues to be sold at exorbitant prices. In 1985, powdered rhino horn sold for $11,000 (U.S.) a kilo in China. The book ends on a hopeful note that the efforts of various African governments, wildlife organizations, and individuals like Tom Mantzel, who breed rhinos on Texan ranches, will prevent the total extinction of rhinos in Africa.

078. Stone, Lynn M. *African Buffalo*. African Animal Discovery Library Series. Vero Beach, FL: Rourke, 1990. 24p. Grades K-2.
A simple text and attractive color photographs introduce young children to the natural environment, physical characteristics, and habits of the two species of buffalo found in sub-Saharan Africa. Differences in size and color are attributed to habitat. Although the buffaloes' most dangerous predator is the lion, they are also shot for their horns and meat, and their wild lands are being used for people's homes and farms. At present, buffaloes exist in large numbers only in two East African nations, Kenya and Tanzania. In the future, wildlife parks maybe the buffaloes' only homes.
Other titles in the African Animal Discovery series include *Antelopes, Giraffes, Hippopotamus, Hyenas,* and *Zebras.*

079. Turnbull, Colin M. *The Peoples of Africa*. Illustrated by Richard M. Powers. Cleveland and New York: World, 1962. 127p. Grades 6-8.
A noted anthropologist, Turnbull examines the relationship between humans and their environment in sub-Saharan Africa. Three major economic lifestyles comprise the focal point of this discussion--the "Pygmy" and "Bushmen" hunters; the Shilluk, Nuer, Dinka, and Masai pastoralists; and the Gikuyu, Asante, Kongo, and Baganda cultivators. Turnbull analyzes how the family, social and political organizations, economies, and customs and beliefs of these peoples are determined by their environment. Despite differences, the three groups are governed by their common belief in the sanctity of the family, kinship ties, age-sets, and worship of ancestors and supernatural forces. In discussing customs that Westerners consider "strange," Turnbull is careful to place the customs in their proper contexts. Hence, he describes the Leopard Man Society as a secret cult that ensures law and order, individual rights, safety of tribe or nation, and accepted moral standards. The book concludes with the challenges facing these lifestyles in a postcolonial Africa.
Turnbull's *Tradition and Change in African Tribal Life* (World, 1966) offers a more detailed treatment of "tribal" life. In discussing childhood, adulthood, and old age, it focuses on the Mbuti, the Ik mountain farmers, the BaNdaka fishermen, and the !Kung desert dwellers. Both books trace the evolution and complexity of social and political institutions.

080. Wellman, Alice. *Africa's Animals: Creatures of a Struggling Land.*
New York: Putnam's, 1974. 191p. Grades 6-8.
This detailed, yet highly readable account of African wildlife is
organized in three segments that discuss history, natural ecosystem,
and conservation efforts. Part I traces the history of animals in Africa
from cave paintings, to the exotic animals of Queen Hatshepsut and
Ramses II, to the wholesale destruction of animals between 1500 and
1950 due to hunting, trade in fur and ivory, disease, drought, and
migration. Part II describes the adaptation of both large and small
animals to the dry thornbush, rain forest, grassy plains, swamps and
lakes, Rift Valley highlands, and open bush and woodland. Part III
outlines the twentieth century efforts to conserve Africa's animal
heritage in national parks and to guard it against poachers, increasing
human population, and industrialization. In fact, some of Africa's
endangered species have been shipped to Lion Country Safari in
California, a commercial enterprise committed to saving African
wildlife.

081. Wolter, Annette. *African Gray Parrots.* Drawings by Fritz W. Kohler.
Translated from the German *Der Graupapagei* by Rita and Robert Kimber.
New York: Barron's, 1987. 63p. Grades 6-12.
Although intended as a pet owner's manual, this book can be enjoyed
by the general reader as well. In addition to providing information on
the purchase, acclimation, care, diet, and diseases of the African Gray
Parrot, Wolter also discusses the bird's natural environment, habits,
intelligence, and personality. Because of the severe trauma it
experiences while being caught, transported, and kept in quarantine,
Wolter cautions that it may take the African Gray Parrot as long as
two years to be completely integrated in domestic surroundings.
Brilliant color photographs and drawings illustrate every aspect of the
well-organized text. A list of books and addresses of parrot and avian
societies are included for the serious researcher or pet owner.

082. Zaslavsky, Claudia. *Africa Counts: Number and Pattern in African
Culture.* Brooklyn, NY: Lawrence Hill Books, 1973. 328p. Grades 8-12.
This survey of sociomathematics in Africa shatters the stereotypical
notion of Africa as a "savage" and "dark" continent intellectually.
Based on current studies of numeration systems, field work, and
scholarly research of literature pertaining to the history, economics,
linguistics, archeology, anthropology, art, and oral tradition of
mathematics in Africa, Zaslavsky provides a detailed account of the
many applications and evolution of numbers and patterns in African
culture. A bone tool handle found at the fishing site of Ishango on
Lake Edwards in Zaire provides historical evidence that a numeration
system was known to the fishing or hunting folk of the area at least
between the period 9000 B.C. and 6500 B.C.
The systems of numeration discussed here range from the few
number words of some San peoples to the extensive numerical
vocabulary and quinary numeration system known to nations with a
history of commerce. A characteristic of African counting is a

standardized system of gestures that accompany, or even replace, the number words. Zaslavsky also describes the mystical beliefs, number symbolisms, and taboos and superstitions associated with counting and numbers. Suspension bridges built with tree trunks and creepers, standardization of weights and measures, and geometric patterns that recur in art and architecture prove the ability of Africans to observe and reproduce form and mathematical concepts. Games like Omweso and Wari, counting rhymes, riddles, and rhythms popular throughout Africa reveal a strong sensitivity to numbers. In fact, the American games Pitfall (Creative Playthings), Chuba (Milton Bradley), and Oh-Wah-Ree (3M Company) are based on African number games.

Detailed studies of the mathematical concepts of southwest Nigeria and East Africa, as reflected in their political structures, economies, and trade, are discussed in separate chapters. Zaslavsky concludes that the disruptions caused by the slave trade and colonial rule during the past five centuries had a disastrous effect upon the potential development of science and technology in Africa. Numerous drawings, photographs, charts, appendices, references, and notes support the text.

083. _____. *Count on Your Fingers African Style.*   Illustrated by Jerry Pinkney. New York: Crowell, 1980. 33p. Preschool-Grade 2.

The text invites readers to Kenya, Sierra Leone, and South Africa to demonstrate how different cultural groups have different finger signs for the same numbers. The marketplace is the scene selected for each country because it best embodies the necessity for counting and communicating with others. In an introductory note, Zaslavsky points out that since Africans speak numerous languages, and since even within a single country people from different cultural groups cannot understand each other, finger language bridges the linguistic barrier necessary for conducting business.

Far from indicating that this is a primitive or typically African way of counting, Zaslavsky's repeated references to readers' personal experiences with finger counting establish the universality of the practice. Children all over the world learn to count on their fingers because fingers make a handy "calculator" that gives concrete form to an otherwise abstract concept. The author is quick to point out that adult Africans can count and do difficult sums mentally.

The text is both engaging and informative; however, the brief section on finger games strikes a discordant note in a book that is otherwise focused on finger counting. Pinkney's line drawings capture the frantic activity of market day and the cultural differences among ethnic groups.

North Africa

TRADITIONAL LITERATURE

084. Climo, Shirley. *The Egyptian Cinderella.* Illustrated by Ruth Heller. New York: Crowell, 1989. N.p. Grades K-3.

The Egyptian version of the Cinderella story is based on facts. Pharaoh Amasis (570-526 B.C.) married a Greek slave girl named Rhodopis and made her a queen. The Roman historian Strabo (first century B.C.) also recorded the account of a Greek girl, Rhodopis, who was kidnapped by pirates and sold to a rich man on the island of Samoa. She was later taken to Egypt where she was purchased by a Greek man, Charaxos, who treated her with kindness. As this story captured the popular imagination, the traditional motif of the oppressed young girl being made to cook, clean, and mend came to be attached to it. In Climo's version, Rhodopis is tormented by three Egyptian servant girls who are jealous of her favored treatment by their master. Rhodopis' rose-red slipper, a gift from her master because she loved to dance, is taken by a falcon and dropped in Pharaoh Amasis' lap. The pharaoh takes this as a sign from Horus, the Sky God, and is determined to marry the owner of the slipper. Climo's leisurely narration and Heller's illustrations reveal Rhodopis' gentle and kind nature.

085. El-Shamy, Hasan M. *Folktales of Egypt.* Foreword by Richard M. Dorson. Chicago: University of Chicago Press, 1980. 347p. Grades 7-12.

Prior to the publication of this collection, the recorded folklore of the Arab world consisted mainly of songs, poetry, and epic romances, while the oral prose tale was virtually neglected. El-Shamy, who did fieldwork among Egyptian immigrants in Brooklyn and among the Nubian, Bedouin, and Berber groups in Egypt in 1969 and 1970, has selected and translated seventy tales for this pioneering study in English. The tales are divided into eight storytelling forms: fantasy, realistic and philosophical tales, religious stories, etiological belief narratives, legends of saints and culture heroes, local belief legends and personal memories, animal and formulae tales, and humorous narratives and jokes. Each story is prefaced by the particulars of the informant and the circumstances under which it was recorded. For instance, "The Magic Filly," a fairy tale narrated by a sixteen-year-old Bedouin, reflects the small repertoire of the narrator and his inexperience in giving fullness to the story through details and descriptions. It also captures the narrator's personal view of the relationship between a child and a jealous stepmother and rivalry among brothers-in-law (husbands whose wives are sisters) to win the recognition of the father-in-law, both popular themes in Arab folklore.

Each tale is analyzed for its major themes, structural elements, and motifs based on *Types of the Folktale* by Antti Aarne and Stith Thompson and *Motif Index of Folk Literature* by Stith Thompson. Furthermore, variants in sub-Saharan Africa, Arabia, and ancient Egypt are identified to seek the origin and trace the development of the tale according to its social, cultural, and emotional relevance. This collection indicates that the Sahara Desert, far from being a barrier, was a highway between the peoples of the north and sub-Saharan Africa. It also provides an understanding of Egyptian folk traditions and the relationship between mental health and "stress-reducing folk practices" such as dancing, games, joking, riddling, storytelling, chanting, verbal duels, and mock rituals.

For the serious student, the Foreword will provide an in-depth account of Egyptian folklore, research of Egyptologists, and discussion of Edward Lane's work, especially *Account of the Manners and Customs of the Modern Egyptian* (1836, 1973).

086. Gilstrap, Robert, and Irene Estabrook. *The Sultan's Fool and Other North African Tales.* Illustrated by Robert Greco. New York: Holt, 1958. 95p. Grades 3-5.

Set primarily in Libya, Algeria, Tunisia, and Morocco, the stories in this collection evoke the atmosphere of the Arabian Nights. There are tales of noodleheads, of wealthy merchants and Grand Viziers, and of ordinary people who match wits with powerful sultans. However, each individual is motivated by the universal desire for happiness, love, and material comfort. The book also includes two tales of trickster animals that are popular in sub-Saharan Africa.

The narrative style combines humor, interesting descriptions, and lively dialogue to hold readers' interest. Islamic values and beliefs are treated respectfully.

087. Green, Roger Lancelyn. *Tales of Ancient Egypt.* Illustrated by Elaine Raphael. New York: Walck, 1968. 216p. Grades 6-12.

Twenty stories provide an introduction to the mythology, religion, history, lifestyle, and culture of ancient Egypt. Green's retellings are based on oral tradition, hieroglyphics, carvings and paintings on the walls of ancient temples and tombs, writings on sandstone tablets and papyri, and stories preserved in the Greek versions of Herodotus and

Aelian. Beginning with the Tales of the Gods, Green narrates stories
from Egyptian mythology and history. This section includes the story
of Ra, the Sun God, who created the world and ruled Egypt as the
first pharaoh; Thoth, the god of wisdom, who ended the earthly rule
of Ra; Isis, goddess of creation and plenty, and her husband Osiris,
god of the underworld; and Horus, last of the god-pharaohs, who
fought the symbolic battles between good and evil with Set. The
accounts of the mortal pharaohs, beginning with Menes in 3200 B.C.,
relate the dealings of the gods with their human rulers in Egypt.
When Zoser neglected to honor the gods, he was humbled because
the Nile did not rise for seven years for its yearly inundation, causing
drought, starvation, deterioration of morals, and general discontent.
Other stories narrate the exploits of Queen Hatshepsut, Thutmose IV,
and Ramses the Great.

The second section, Tales of Magic, contains the stories of famous
magicians and how they resolved the difficult problems facing their
pharaohs. It narrates the exploits of Teta, who found and read the
book of Thoth; of Se-Osiris, who was the greatest magician Egypt
had ever known; and of Setna and Zazamankh, who attained
supernatural powers by virtue of their wisdom and learning. The third
section, Tales of Adventure, narrates legends of ordinary warriors,
sailors, and peasants who had achieved fame by virtue of their
courage, steadfastness, and intelligence. This segment also includes
the adventures of the cunning Treasure Thief, the Egyptian version of
the Cinderella story, and the story of Helen of Troy in Egypt.

This collection is a testimony to ancient Egypt's wealth, empire
building, rules of government, sophisticated religious and philosophic
ideas, scientific and artistic achievements, and seafaring and
shipbuilding skills. Green's leisurely narration provides background
descriptions and in-depth character delineation. In addition, he
provides a lucid interpretation of the historical, geographical,
religious, and cultural content of each story and places it in the
context of his general account of Egyptian history and civilization.

088. Haggard, H. Rider, and Andrew Lang.   *The World's Desire.*
Introduction by Lin Carter. New York: Ballantine, 1972. Originally
published in 1890. 239p. Grades 9-12.

This fantasy, an alternate to the Homeric plot, states that the gods
spirited Helen away from Paris and hid her in Egypt while a phantom
in her exact likeness took her place in Troy. Conceived as a sequel to
Homer's *Odyssey, The World's Desire* has all the mystical and
romantic supernaturalism that enthralled the readers of *She* by Rider
Haggard.

089. Hutton, Warwick. *Moses in the Bulrushes.* Illustrated by reteller. New
York: McElderry, 1986. N.p. Preschool-Grade 3.

This retelling of the Biblical story focuses on the birth and infancy of
Moses. It describes the intense love of a mother who courageously
defies the pharaoh's decree to save her son. It is also about the love
and humanity of the pharaoh's daughter, who overcomes fear and

racial prejudice to adopt a helpless baby. The illustrations control readers' involvement in the story by first distancing them with a formal frame, and then inviting them to share in the emotional drama through full-page and double-page pictures. The pastel watercolors enhance the soft and tender tone of the book.

090. Lattimore, Deborah Nourse. *The Winged Cat: A Tale of Ancient Egypt.* Illustrated by author. New York: HarperCollins, 1992. N.p. Grades K-3.

The Egyptian account of the netherworld and Judgment Day is illustrated through the story of Merit, a humble girl who serves in the temple of Bastet, the cat goddess. When Merit accuses Waha, the High Priest, of killing the temple cat, Bast, both journey to the netherworld in Horus' golden boat to be judged by the gods. While Waha goes with numerous spells from the *Book of the Dead* inscribed on *ushabtis* (small wooden figures), Merit only has the *ba,* or soul-spirit, of Bast to help her. Both cross the twelve gates of the netherworld and appear before the Hall of Judgment to have their hearts weighed against the feather of Truth. Wealth, position, and prestige do not help Waha and he is devoured by Ammit, while Thoth and Anubis find Merit innocent.

Lattimore's knowledge of Egyptian mythology, religious symbols, and hieroglyphics is further evident in her unique illustrations. In turning the pages of the book one gets the impression of unrolling an ancient papyrus manuscript. Details of each event in the story are intricately told through pictures, hieroglyphics, and English text.

091. Madhubuti, Safisha L. *The Story of Kwanzaa.* Illustrated by Murry N. DePillars. Chicago: Third World Press, 1989. 32p. Grades K-3.

The African American celebration of Kwanzaa (December 26 to January 1) is inspired by the ancient myths and harvest festivals of Africa. Central to the Kwanzaa story are the good examples set by Khnemu, god of the annual Nile flood and Egyptian leader who fashioned the first man on a potter's wheel, his female counterpart Sati, and their son Nubti. Like them, African Americans are enjoined to work hard in unity to feed, clothe, house, and defend themselves. Both text and illustrations emphasize the seven principles of Umoja (unity), Kujichagulia (self-determination), Ujima (work together), Ujamaa (sharing), Nia (purpose), Kuumaba (creativity), and Imani (faith) that enabled ancient African communities to survive and prosper, and which are equally relevant in the United States today. A Teacher's Guide and suggestions for introducing Kwanzaa to school children are included. Maulana Karenga's, *The African American Holiday of Kwanzaa: A Celebration of Family, Community & Culture* (University of Sankore Press, 1989), and Deborah Chocolate's *Kwanzaa* (Children's Press, 1990), are recommended for further information on the rituals and symbols of the festival.

092. Mike, Jan M. *Gift of the Nile.* Legends of the World Series. Illustrated by Charles Reasoner. Mahwah, NJ: Troll, 1993. 32p. Grades K-3.

This ancient legend of the Pharaoh Senefru, who is credited with building the first of the great pyramids, comes from a papyrus hieroglyphic that was written about 3,500 years ago. The story focuses on the pharaoh's possessive love for Mutemwia, a young girl at the royal palace who had won Senefru's favor with her charming music and wise counsel. When Mutemwia longs for nature and the freedom of her former life, Senefru refuses to grant her wish for fear of losing her forever. However, a pleasure ride on the Nile convinces him of Mutemwia's steadfastness, and he realizes that love and friendship are gifts of the heart that cannot be caged.

093. Price, Leontyne. *Aida*. Illustrated by Leo and Diane Dillon. Based on the opera by Giuseppe Verdi. San Diego: Harcourt Brace Jovanovich, 1990. N.p. Grades 3-5.

Based on an actual historical incident brought to light during an archeological excavation in Egypt, Verdi's *Aida* was written to commemorate the completion of the Suez Canal in 1869 and the opening of the Opera House in a redesigned Cairo. Price, a highly acclaimed operatic performer of *Aida,* convincingly portrays the inner self and dilemma of the protagonist through her retelling. The Ethiopian princess, Aida, who is captured by the invading Egyptian army and made to serve Princess Amneris, falls in love with Radames, the handsome captain of the Egyptian army. Radames also loves Aida and he plans to conquer Ethiopia so that his beloved can reign as queen. Their conflicting love for each other and loyalty to country is further complicated by Princess Amneris' love for Radames and her resulting jealousy and hurt pride. The lovers are eventually united in death.

This story of frustrated love raises interesting political, social, and moral questions. The conflicting emotions of loyalty to self, lover, parents, and country are eloquently captured in the illustrations as well. The brilliant artwork portrays the majesty of Egyptian culture and achievements through vibrant gold, red, and blue colors.

094. Schwartz, Howard, and Barbara Rush. *The Sabbath Lion: A Jewish Folktale from Algeria.* Illustrated by Stephen Fieser. New York: HarperCollins, 1992. N.p. Grades K-3.

Ten-year-old Yoseph's faith in the Sabbath laws is the subject of this popular Jewish folktale from North Africa. Yoseph risks his life to observe the Sabbath when he travels with a caravan across the Sahara to claim an inheritance left by his uncle in Cairo. The caravan leader refuses to keep his promise to stop for the Sabbath and leaves Yoseph alone in the desert. Yoseph performs the required rituals with devotion, and the Sabbath Queen, symbol of the spirit of Sabbath, sends a lion to protect and accompany Yoseph till he fulfills his mission and returns home safely. The illustrations portray the cultural setting of Algeria, the bravery of the young boy, and the vast loneliness of the desert.

FICTION

095. Alexander, Sue. *Nadia the Willful.* Illustrated by Lloyd Bloom. New York: Pantheon, 1983. N.p. Grades 1-3.

Nadia, who is called willful because of her stubbornness and flashing temper, loses the only person who understands her when her older brother Hamed is lost in the desert while seeking new grazing land. Yet, by decree of her father, sheik of their Bedouin clan, no one is allowed to mention Hamed's name in the camp. Nadia's behavior becomes intolerable because of her unexpressed grief and loneliness. When she teaches her siblings a game she had learned from Hamed, her pain is eased and she refuses to abide by the sheik's order. Hamed once again lives in their hearts as Nadia remembers his ready laughter and smile and the stories and games he had taught her. Eventually, she convinces her grief-stricken father of the cathartic influence of releasing one's pent-up emotions. Filled with peace, he renames her Nadia, the Wise.

This story introduces young children to death and coping with loss. Bloom's illustrations juxtapose the human drama against the stark expanse of the Sahara Desert, which is both harsh and arid as well as beautiful and nurturing.

096. Bradshaw, Gillian. *The Dragon and the Thief.* New York: Greenwillow, 1991. 154p. Grades 5-8.

Dragons, grave robbers, treasure-filled tombs, superstitions, oppressed slaves, and magicians comprise the exotic details and stereotypes of this fantasy set in ancient Egypt. The story's only redeeming factor is the personal growth of the ill-fated protagonist, Prohotep. When his every attempt to seek gainful employment ends in disaster, he decides to become a thief in the City of the Dead. Instead of finding the tomb of a rich nobleman, Prohotep finds the lair of Lady Hathor, the last dragon in Egypt. He becomes a hero and gains stature when he overcomes every obstacle to help Hathor escape to Nubia in Kush to look for fellow dragons.

The Dragon and the Thief is a "thriller" that children will enjoy and then forget about as it presents no lasting insights into life. The cliche-ridden, episodic plot reminds one of the adventures of Sinbad and Aladdin. The most destructive aspect of the book is the distorted view of ancient Egyptian culture. Egyptian gods are seen as capricious beings who use magic to control their followers. They bicker with one another and have to be bribed into compliance by devotees. It is the dragon--who is reminiscent of Chinese mythology --that represents transcendental powers, and not the several gods of Egyptian mythology. However, even the great possibilities that Hathor suggests are not adequately pursued. She is a "cranky" old maid who is concerned with her looks and unreasonably covetous about her treasure. Likewise, the great achievements of pharaonic civilization are reduced to cruel and corrupt officials and architectural feats that are the result of human exploitation and misery.

097. Byars, Betsy C. *The Dancing Camel.* Illustrated by Harold Berson. New York: Viking, 1965. 32p. Grades 2-4.

Set in Morocco, this whimsical tale evokes the charm and exotica of the Arabian Nights. The human interest is generated by Camilla, a camel who dances to express her joy and oneness with the desert. However, when Camilla is purchased by Abul the Tricky, she refuses to exploit her talents for money or vanity. Deemed a business failure, Abul returns Camilla to the leader of the caravan in exchange for a cheap ring with which he intends to dupe people. Berson's black-and-white illustrations capture the pride of Camilla, the greed of Abul, and the hustle and bustle of crowded bazaars.

098. Coatsworth, Elizabeth. *Bess and the Sphinx.* Illustrated by Bernice Loewenstein. New York: Macmillan; London: Collier-Macmillan, 1948, 1967. 88p. Grades 2-4.

This novel is remarkable for its autobiographical account of Coatsworth's trip to Egypt when she was a young child. Set at the turn of the century, the author considers Egypt a turning point in her life because it marks her transformation from an awkward child to a confident young girl. With the story of Moses as a reference point, young Bess makes a spiritual connection between the mysterious Sphinx and the myth of the holy family resting at its feet. On the surface, she wins recognition by being the first one to find a genuine Egyptian Osiris, but, on the inner level, Bess discovers her talent for creating exciting stories and reliving her travels in Egypt. It is at the foot of the Sphinx that the writer is born. Egyptian culture is treated superficially, emphasizing the exotica of archeological sites and the thrill of hunting for ancient artifacts.

099. Ellerby, Leona. *King Tut's Game Board.* Minneapolis, MN: Lerner, 1980. 120p. Grades 5-7.

Myth, pharaonic history and culture, Einstein's theory of relativity, science fiction, and travel are deftly integrated in this adventure story set in modern Egypt. When Justin is vacationing in Cairo with his parents, he is delighted to meet Nate, a boy his own age. As Nate expertly guides Justin through the national museum and the many architectural wonders of ancient Egypt, Justin senses that underlying Nate's intimate knowledge of the Eighteenth Dynasty is some vital secret. The ibis symbol in a game board found in King Tutankhamen's tomb leads the boys to Lake Nasser, the Valley of the Kings, and the Temple of Abu Simbel in search of the unidentified royal tomb of Aye, pharaoh from 1352 to 1348 B.C. Nate confesses that he and his father are time travelers from outerspace; they are descendants of the lost Atlantis who have come to Egypt to seek information on Aye, Nate's uncle, who immigrated to Egypt over three thousand years ago.

Nate's personal quest and Justin's sightseeing excursions are interwoven into their growing friendship and mutual trust. Their mission accomplished, Nate and his father return to Atlantis, leaving Justin with the credit of finding the tomb. However, Justin keeps

Nate's secret because disclosure of the superior technology of Atlanteans would disturb the balance of power and cause harm on earth. The factual information never once overpowers the emerging drama of this fast-paced adventure, because every historical detail, wall painting, and artifact is inextricably connected with Nate's mysterious background.

100. Goodenow, Earle. *The Last Camel*. Illustrated by author. New York: Walck, 1968. 30p. Grades K-2.

Phoum, a disagreeable and antisocial camel, overcomes his fears and psychological problems when he accidentally leads the caravan during a sandstorm. The illustrations create sympathy for Phoum by focusing on his shifting emotions and inner turmoil.

101. Guillot, Rene. *Riders of the Wind*. Illustrated by Richard Kennedy. Translated from the French, *Les Cavaliers du Vent* (Magnard, 1953), by Geo. H. Bell. London: Methuen, 1960. 190p. Grades 7-12.

Set in the mid-1600s, this adventure story recounts the exploits of a fifteen-year-old French orphan, Calvar. Owned by a ruthless ex-Captain, Calvar's intelligence and courage are exploited to steal from ships bringing goods from far-off places. A surreal atmosphere pervades the story once Calvar is bound for Africa on a merchant ship. Reincarnated as Gorgol and Oule, Calvar goes through the entire range of human experiences in his three lives: he is cheated, exploited, enslaved, beaten, and abandoned; and he is befriended and helped by the French, Moors, West Africans, and those of mixed races. Likewise, his attitude toward Africans shifts from superiority to respect to oneness. Matured by his experiences, Calvar returns to France to marry his beloved and head a successful shipping business. Through Calvar, Guillot universalizes the experiences of the entire continent of Africa. Philosophy, fantasy, harmony with nature, and legend blend to give depth and richness to this novel.

102. Harris, Rosemary. *The Moon in the Cloud*. New York: Macmillan, 1968. Originally published in Great Britain by Faber and Faber. 182p. Grades 5-7.

Myth, history, fantasy, and realism combine in this story of the Great Flood set in Israel and Egypt at the time of the Old Kingdom. The interest, however, focuses not on Noah and his family, but on the equally virtuous Reuben and his lovely wife, Thamar. The events concern Reuben's dangerous journey to Kemi (or Egypt) to capture two lions in order to win passage on Noah's ark. Egypt is depicted as a "dark" kingdom of superstition, magic, and idolatry; and the authority figures like priests, courtiers, and judges are seen as corrupt, cruel, and selfish. The characters in the story are one-dimensional, either all good or all bad except, perhaps, Tahlevi, the tomb robber. The only distinction of *The Moon in the Cloud,* winner of the 1968 Carnegie Medal, is Harris' engaging prose style which is both humorous and descriptive.

103. Heide, Florence Parry, and Judith Heide Gilliland. *The Day of Ahmed's Secret.* Illustrated by Ted Lewin. New York: Lothrop, Lee & Shepard, 1990. N.p. Grades K-3.

Young Ahmed nurtures a special secret all day as he delivers canisters of butane gas through the crowded streets of Cairo. While Ahmed is proud of being an earning member of the household, his real joy comes when he tells his family that he has learned to write his name. Both plot and illustrations introduce readers to the sights, sounds, and colors of Cairo. The city is a blend of modern buildings and ancient mosques and arches, camel caravans and buses and motor cars, and traditional and Western clothes. Ahmed senses a spiritual affinity with Cairo: his ability to write his name connects him to his ancient heritage and his hopes for the future.

104. Hostetler, Marian. *Fear in Algeria.* Illustrated by James Converse. Scottdale, PA and Kitchener, Canada: Herald, 1979. 126p. Grades 5-8.

Set around 1969, Hostetler, who served as a missionary and teacher in Algeria for nine years, fictionalizes her experiences through the adventures of a fourteen-year-old American girl. Zina's first person account conveys the young girl's enthusiasm for traveling to a foreign land, her initial reaction to the customs and peoples she encounters, and her genuine desire to learn as much as possible about Algeria. From the time she arrives in Algiers, Zina has a series of adventures from a raid on the Palmeraie, a Methodist camp (based on an actual incident in December 1969), to visiting Constantine and the Roman ruins at Djemila, to living in a Berber settlement, to seeing the Saharan towns of El Oued and Ghardaia. The episodic plot is unified by the constant fear of being followed and the persecution of foreign Christians who conduct missionary activities under the guise of teaching and social work. Eventually, Zina and her hosts are summarily expelled from Algeria on the unfounded charge of "subversive activities."

While Zina is open minded and appreciative of everything she sees in Algeria, the book leaves readers with the overwhelming impression of unfairness toward Christian missionaries and foreign employees and visitors. Algeria is portrayed as a police state that denies its citizens the freedom to worship and choose their own lifestyle. Hostetler's perspective is that of the outsider, and no attempt is made to understand the Algerian desire to pursue its own national identity without outside interference.

105. Lezra, Giggy. *Mechido, Aziza & Ahmed.* Illustrated by Nancy Seligsohn. New York: Atheneum, 1969. 110p. Grades 3-5.

Details of everyday life in modern Morocco are recreated through the individual stories of three children: Mechido, a bread boy who cannot stay out of trouble; Aziza, a pampered only daughter of a rich household; and Ahmed, a shy and withdrawn boy. Each story is centered around the protagonist's effort to resolve his or her basic conflict. Mechido resents being a bread boy as his skill rests in cabinet-making; Aziza rebels against the confining duties of a "lady" by occupying herself with gardening; and Ahmed overcomes his low self-esteem by saving the life of a donkey. Lezra places her characters in compromising situations that lead to self-knowledge and growth. The interesting plots, engaging characters, and lively prose make this a truly delightful book.

106. Lloyd, Norris. *The Village That Allah Forgot.*   Illustrated by Ed Piechocki. New York: Hastings House, 1973. 128p. Grades 4-6.

Set in the early years of Tunisia's freedom from French rule, the tiny village of Msalla feels betrayed by the unfulfilled promises of President Bourguiba. To ten-year-old Ali, the disappointment is a personal one symbolized by the sudden death of his father at the hands of the French in Bizerte. To regain his pride and independence, Ali sells flowers and eggs to passing motorists to help support his widowed mother and sickly sister. Progress comes in the form of a young student, Farhat, who teaches the boys and girls to read and write, narrates anecdotes from history, and explains the problems of independent Tunisia. Once Ali comes to regard his father as a hero who challenged the French troops, he is no longer embittered. With the help of the children, he builds a road to his village so that a school can eventually be opened. The future looks hopeful for Ali because he is able to make decent money by selling his drawings to tourists visiting the ancient Roman aqueducts. This is a touching story of a young boy's struggle to overcome external and inner obstacles in order to help himself, his family, and his community.

107. Marston, Elsa. *The Cliffs of Cairo.*   New York: Signet Vista/New American Library, 1981. 151p. Grades 6-8.

When sixteen-year-old Tabby, daughter of a technical expert stationed in Cairo, buys an ikon of Saint Jerome from an antique shop, she is pursued by two underground groups: a ring of international art thieves and a fundamentalist religious cult. Suspense and tension are heightened as the independent heroine stumbles into potentially dangerous situations when she visits the little-known Al Guyushi mosque, runs into the secret hideout of black-robed men, and surprises a thief in her family's apartment. The mystery is finally solved with the help of an Egyptian student. Both underground groups desire Tabby's ikon because a valuable carved wooden panel from the Fatimid dynasty (909-1171 A.D.) is hidden in it. The art thieves want to smuggle it out of the country, while the religious cult feels the carving depicts El Hakim, whom they worship as a savior who will restore Egypt to her former glory and rid the country of foreign influence.

Marston lends texture and depth to the mystery through descriptions of crowded bazaars and old historical buildings, details of Cairene lifestyle and attitudes, and an account of the factual and legendary history of Egypt. Above all, the protagonist, who resents adult supervision and guidance, learns how foolish and irresponsible her behavior has been. Yet, one also admires Tabby's knowledge of and enthusiasm for Egyptian history and culture.

108. Myers, Walter Dean. *Tales of a Dead King.* New York: Morrow, 1983. 89p. Grades 4-6.

This fast-paced mystery is set in Aswan, Egypt, where a famous archeologist, Dr. Leonhardt, is on the brink of discovering the tomb of King Akhenaton. Two American teenagers, John Robie and Karen Lacey, arrive in Aswan to assist with the excavations, but Dr. Leonhardt has disappeared without a clue to his whereabouts. The interest now focuses on the different reactions and personalities of the two characters. While both complain about the discomforts of the hotel and their frustrated expectations, Karen's keen mind can detect clues that suggest a cover-up. Their sleuthing leads them to a Nubian theater, a crowded bazaar, a felucca ride on the Nile, and a deserted Nubian village where Dr. Leonhardt--and eventually they--are held hostage. All ends well with their dramatic rescue.

It is refreshing to read a detective story with a female character who is the "brains" of the team. While John knows more about ancient Egyptian history and the discovery of King Tutankhamen's tomb, he is no match for Karen's quick thinking and ability to critically scrutinize every insignificant detail and draw logical conclusions. Details of the land, peoples, culture, and history are deftly integrated into the story.

109. Randin, Susan Lowry. *Captives in a Foreign Land.* Boston: Houghton Mifflin, 1984. 218p. Grades 6-9.

Six children--four boys and two girls--of American delegates to an international conference on nuclear disarmament are kidnapped by an Arab organization and taken to a secret hideout in North Africa, possibly Libya. On the surface, this appears to be a stereotypical plot of Arab terrorists employing violence to achieve unreasonable demands. Happily, this is a thought-provoking adventure story whose main themes are U.S. foreign policy and the consequences of the nuclear arms race, respect for cultural differences and commonalties among peoples, and sensitivity toward the Arab world. The story, however, can also be enjoyed for its exciting and suspenseful plot. As days pass into weeks, the children develop group dynamics and problem solving strategies. They observe their surroundings to gather information and formulate an escape plan.

The story achieves depth when all the characters change and grow. The hostages, who are treated relatively well, come to know their Arab captors as individuals. They learn about the importance of discipline and religion in daily life, Arab interpretation of the Bible, Islamic respect for women, and the hard physical labor that is required to cultivate the North African terrain. Common stereotypes are shattered as the Americans realize that Arabs are not cruel, and that they do not hate Jews because Jews and Arabs had lived together peacefully for centuries. All six children agree with the Arabs that the nuclear arms race is counterproductive and actually leads to a proliferation of global tension. For the first time, the protagonists are forced to see themselves as others view Americans: materialistic, lazy, overindulged, ignorant, and self-centered. This reflection and self-examination transforms each child: the brothers, Matt and Gib, place their jealousy in perspective and come to respect each other; Steven, a nervous and insecure child because of tension between his parents, gains self-confidence; Sidney, a Jew, recognizes the friendship, love for family, and camaraderie of his Arab captors; and Jessica and Martha, the only girls, display their intelligence to themselves and to the rest of the group. The Arabs, on their part, learn to respect the American children for their ability to work on the dike with the Bedouins and for their courage in facing captivity.

110. Sales, Francesc. *Ibrahim.* Illustrated by Eulalia Sariola. Translated from the Catalan by Marc Simont. New York: Lippincott, 1989. 31p. Grades K-2.

Ibrahim's entry into the adult world of the Marrakesh marketplace is marred by his longing for the freedom of the desert. He feels that duty to his parents has imprisoned him in the city. When a genie in Ibrahim's dream instructs him that freedom is a state of mind, he is no longer restless and unhappy. Ibrahim overcomes his physical confinement by imaginatively sharing the adventures of folktale heroes. Sariola's illustrations capture the colors and scenes of the crowded marketplace, as well as focusing on the inner world of Ibrahim.

111. Stinetorf, Louise A. *Musa the Shoemaker.* Illustrated by Harper Johnson. Philadelphia: Lippincott, 1959. 183p. Grades 5-7.

This charming story is set in the remote village of Villeperes in the Atlas Mountains of Algeria, which is renowned for the acrobatic abilities of its menfolk. From early childhood, every boy practices tumbling, tightrope walking, and swinging on the trapeze, so that he can bring honor to the village by joining a traveling circus--that is, everyone except Musa, who has a crippled foot. A simple operation in a city hospital cures Musa, but he does not win fame through acrobatics; instead, his skill as a shoemaker, especially of orthopedic shoes, wins him recognition when he designs a shoe for the lame princess.

Musa's journey to the city of Oran serves as a rite of passage that broadens his perspective and teaches him that there are other ways of earning fame--and money--for his village. Musa is a generous and caring individual who does not allow his personal disappointment to make him bitter and jealous. Details of village life, customs and beliefs, and desert travel are presented respectfully.

112. Stolz, Mary. *Zekmet the Stone Carver.* Illustrated by Deborah Nourse Lattimore. San Diego: Harcourt Brace Jovanovich, 1988. N.p. Grades K-3.

Central to this fictional account of Egyptian history is the irony that the Sphinx was not designed by an architect or engineer, but by a humble stone carver. When Pharaoh Khafre expresses his egocentric desire to make himself immortal, the vizier is challenged to present a suitable design. However, it is Zekmet, who works at the site of Khafre's pyramid, who conceives of the majestic Sphinx rising from the desolate desert. Lattimore's illustrations capture the glory of ancient Egypt and present an especially touching account of Zekmet's personal life. Both illustrations and text emphasize the contrast between Zekmet's poor dwellings and the pharaoh's extravagance, Zekmet's artistic nature and the vizier's total lack of ideas and creativity, and Zekmet's humility and happy personal life and the arrogance and sterile emotions of the pharaoh and his vizier.

113. Williams, Gregory. *Kermit and Cleopigtra.* Illustrated by Sue Venning. New York: Muppet Press/Random House, 1981. N.p. Grades K-3.
When the Muppets, Kermit and Bo, accidentally enter the Time Machine, they are warped to ancient Egypt just before their matinee performance. As the time travelers attempt to return to the present, Kermit becomes the object of Queen Cleopigtra's amorous advances. He runs away from his wedding to Cleopigtra, hides in a pyramid, and is ultimately rescued just as Cleopigtra is about to catch him. Upon returning to the present, Kermit is overwhelmed by Miss Piggy's affectionate embrace, whom he momentarily mistakes for Queen Cleopigtra because she is dressed like Cleopatra for her new Egyptian act.
The episodes in the Muppet Theater and ancient Egypt are cleverly structured and integrated. The irony arising from the duplication of events and characters in the two worlds is both funny and a telling commentary on Kermit's fear of emotional involvement. The dialogue is particularly lively and witty because of puns and double meanings. However, the bright illustrations of Egyptian clothing and jewelry, ancient monuments, and hieroglyphics are thoroughly exploited for their exotic appeal, bordering almost on the disrespectful.

BIOGRAPHY

114. Bennett, Olivia. *A Family in Egypt.* Photographs by Liba Taylor. Families the World Over Series. Minneapolis, MN: Lerner, 1985. Originally published in 1983 as *Village in Egypt* by A & C Black. 31p. Grades 2-4.
As is typical of this series, ten-year-old Ezzat's life provides a cursory view of the lifestyle, personal relationships, religion, and means of livelihood of a family in rural Egypt. The village economy is dependent both on the soil and the waters of the Nile as well as on transporting goods to the cities. On the one hand, Ezzat's is a typical extended family with three generations living under one roof, and, on the other hand, the younger generation represents the blending of modern and traditional in present-day Egypt. Because of a rapid increase in population and industrialization, there is less land for cultivation, making formal schooling essential to obtain jobs. Color photographs of Ezzat's family and their daily activities add a pleasing

visual dimension to the book. Facts about ancient and modern Egypt are also included.

115. Daly, Bridget, trans. and adapt. *Mokhtar of the Atlas Mountains*. My Village Series. Morristown, NJ: Silver Burdett, 1985. Translation of *Moktar et le Noyer Centenaire* by Elisabeth Thiebaut. English version originally published in 1984 by Macdonald. 47p. Grades 3-6.

Mokhtar's experiences provide a point of entry into the daily routine, family life, food and housing, social life, and customs of a Berber tribe in the High Atlas mountains of Morocco. Berber lifestyle is dictated by Islam, the seasons, and the needs of cattle and fields. Like devout Muslims all over the world, Mokhtar and his family observe the prescribed rituals and festivals, especially for L-Aid El-Kebir, when a sheep is slaughtered to commemorate Abraham's sacrifice of his son Issac. This is also the personal story of Mokhtar, who is an introspective child with a deep spiritual feeling for the family farms. His longing to travel and see the world is fulfilled when he is entrusted with an errand to the marketplace in Ayt-Tamllil. This trip gives Mokhtar the opportunity to witness the *fantasia* festival in which men display their horsemanship and warrior skills.

Numerous color photographs enable readers to visualize Mokhtar and his world; however, the relationship between the photographs and the text seems contrived because of the author's interpretations of the characters' thoughts and feelings. A glossary of terms and a list of important facts about the Berbers and Morocco are included.

116. _____. *Tarlift, Tuareg Boy*. My Village Series. Morristown, NJ: Silver Burdett, 1985. Translation of *Tarlift Fils de Touareg* by Anne Rochegude. English version originally published in 1984 by Macdonald. 47p. Grades 5-7.

The experiences of twelve-year-old Tarlift serve as a point of entry into the nomadic lifestyle of the Tuaregs who inhabit the Sahel countries of North Africa. An examination of the terrain, migratory patterns, desert camps, economy, social organization, and Islamic beliefs indicate that Tuareg culture is a direct response to the harsh conditions of the Sahara Desert. Interest in Tarlift's story centers around his inner conflict to give up his nomadic life for the promise of a settled life and a better future. He moves to his uncle's house in the village of Lere and begins his education in French. However, Tarlift feels confined by village life, and he returns to the freedom and open spaces of the desert.

The photographs, drawings, and text achieve the dual purpose of providing basic information on the Tuaregs, as well as portraying the human angle through the daily activities, joys and fears, and future hopes of Tarlift and his well-to-do family.

117. DeChancie, John. *Gamal Abdel Nasser*. World Leaders Past & Present Series. New York, New Haven and Philadelphia: Chelsea House, 1988. 111p. Grades 6-8.

President Nasser's political life is examined in the context of

Egyptian history. Separate chapters discuss Nasser's early childhood under British colonialism; the Egyptian nationalist movement and his role in the military coup by the Free Officers; his carefully orchestrated political moves to become president of Egypt; war in Suez; landownership and the social revolution; and stormy foreign policy. DeChancie portrays both the strengths and weaknesses of his subject. Despite President Nasser's undemocratic rule and the use of domestic surveillance to stifle opposition, he is credited with being the architect of an independent Egypt and for restoring Arab pride. Numerous photographs testify to the charm and magnetism of Nasser. Several quotations provide the personal philosophy of Nasser and the opinions of world leaders, historians, and authors.

118. Finke, Blythe Foote. *Anwar Sadat: Egyptian Ruler and Peace Maker.* Charlotteville, NY: SamHar Press, 1986. 32p. Grades 8-12.
As the title implies, this brief biography--or long essay--focuses only on the public life of Anwar Sadat from his anti-British revolutionary activities in the early 1940s to his assassination in 1981. Because of his achievements as politician, international strategist, and champion of peace in the Middle East, he is praised as a realist, hero, passionate nationalist, and a devout and noble man. However, the biography does not portray the inner man through revealing anecdotes and dialogue.

119. Kyle, Benjamin. *Muammar El-Qaddafi.* World Leaders Past & Present Series. New York, New Haven and Philadelphia: Chelsea House, 1987. 112p. Grades 7-12.
This thoroughly researched biography portrays Qaddafi as a controversial world leader who is at once highly intelligent, dedicated, and charismatic as well as dictatorial, undiplomatic, and fanatical. His keen political awareness and principles of government are traced to his simple Bedouin upbringing, faith in Islam, his relatives' resistance to Italian rule, and his pride in Arabic culture. By the age of twelve, despite his social drawbacks in the elitist atmosphere of his private school, he had organized a sophisticated revolutionary movement based on Islamic socialism. With Gamal Abdel Nasser, Napoleon Bonaparte, and Abraham Lincoln as role models, Qaddafi staged a successful coup against the Libyan ruler, King Idris I, and established a revolutionary government. As head of state, his aim was to preserve the political independence and cultural integrity of his country from Western influence. He reformed the domestic policy to effect a social revolution that ensured an equitable sharing of Libya's oil wealth and to enforce a strict Islamic lifestyle on individual citizens. On the international front, he pursued his dream of Arab unity and the annihilation of Israel. While Qaddafi raised the standard of living in Libya, his unpredictable behavior alienated both Western and Arabic nations; his only friends were terrorists and reactionary groups whom he supported and in whose terrorist acts and assassination attempts he was implicated.
Kyle discusses both the public achievements and failures of

Qaddafi, and the interference in Libyan affairs by the C.I.A. and the attempted assassination by the United States. There is no attempt to portray the private life, or to understand the motivations of Qaddafi. Supplementary quotations provide a multiplicity of perspectives on Qaddafi; however, the impression of a vengeful, hated, and isolated world leader remains.

120. Rosen, Deborah Nodler.   *Anwar el-Sadat: A Man of Peace*. Chicago: Children's Press, 1986. 152p. Grades 7-9.

Although heavily researched, this biography succeeds in conveying the "voice" and "presence" of President Anwar Sadat. In his own words, readers are told of the shaping influences in Sadat's life and his conclusion that to make progress one has to overcome the root cause or psychological barrier to every problem. Fortified with this philosophy of life, he became a risk-taker, a leader known for his bold, decisive actions. Sadat's private role in the revolutionary takeover of Farrouk's government, his disagreements with President Nasser over foreign policy and handling of the Israeli problem, his attack on Israel in the Yom Kippur War (October 1973), and his decision to negotiate with Israeli Prime Minister Menachim Begin were all dictated by this inner vision. He understood that fear and hatred prevented Arabs and Israelis from trusting each other; hence, the October 1973 war was intended to restore Arab pride and to prompt Israel to come to the negotiating table--a stance that antagonized the Arab world and Muslim fundamentalists and cost him his life.

Excerpts from President Sadat's autobiography, *In Search of Identity*, and the biography by his daughter Camelia Sadat, *Father and I*, reveal a loving father and sensitive man who despite the upheavals in his life and country tried to fulfill his family obligations. He also supported his wife in her struggle for women's rights. He is remembered as a shrewd statesman and diplomat, a courageous patriot, and a world leader who tried to dislodge hatred and prejudice. For these achievements, he received the Nobel Peace Prize.

121. Shivanandan, Mary. *Gamal Abdul Nasser: Modern Leader of Egypt*. Outstanding Personalities Series. Charlotteville, NY: SamHar Press, 1973. 32p. Grades 8-12.

The popularity of President Nasser is attributed to the fact that he was the first native ruler of independent Egypt since 525 B.C. As in the biography by DeChancie, Shivanandan traces the career of Nasser from his revolutionary activities as a student and army officer, to his rise to political power, to his role as architect of modern Egypt and Arab unity. Although sympathetic to Nasser, Shivanandan does not fail to point out his ruthless suppression of political opposition, expulsion of Jews after the Suez War, and severe restrictions on the press. In the final analysis, Nasser is seen as a complex leader who attracted both praise and blame.

The above material has not been made attractive or accessible for readers. The entire biography consists of page after page of solid text without any chapter divisions, headings and subheadings, or photographs of the subject.

122. Stewart, Judy. *A Family in Morocco.* Photographs by Jenny Matthews. Families the World Over Series. Minneapolis, MN: Lerner, 1986. Originally published in 1985 as *Moroccan Family* by A & C Black. 31p. Grades 2-4.

Insight into a Moroccan family living in Tangier is provided through the daily activities of twelve-year-old Malika Bakkali. Both color photographs and text emphasize the importance of a close-knit family as Malika helps with household chores, goes to school and does homework, watches TV and plays on the beach, and shares the family meal. Islam and religious education form a vital aspect of Malika's upbringing and preparation for adult life. Living in Tangier, a favorite tourist attraction, gives Malika a broad perspective on life, while a visit to Jbila, a mountain village about fifty miles from Tangier, connects her with her rural background. Salient facts about Morocco and Islam are included.

INFORMATIONAL BOOKS

123. Aliki. *Mummies Made in Egypt.* Illustrated by author. New York: HarperCollins, 1979. N.p. Grades 1-4.

A simple text and illustrations adapted from paintings and sculptures found in ancient Egyptian tombs introduce young readers to the technique of mummy-making, burial tombs, and pyramids. Although the complicated and expensive seventy-day procedure of embalming is explained and illustrated in a clear and straightforward manner, children will not find it disturbing or grisly. In addition, the book provides background information on the gods and goddesses of the dead, philosophy of the *ba* (soul) and *ka* (invisible twin of the dead person), funeral processions and rituals, journey to the underworld, and the *Book of the Dead.* This picture book presents ancient Egypt's achievements in science, medicine, philosophy, engineering, and art in a very positive manner.

124. Alotaibi, Muhammad. *Bedouins: The Nomads of the Desert.* Original Peoples Series. Vero Beach, FL: Rourke, 1989. Originally published in 1985 by Wayland. 48p. Grades 4-6.

The first impression created by this book is a negative one because of some glaring oversights in printing: there are six pages that have photographs but no text and two pages that are completely blank. Apart from this gross negligence in production, the text provides a clear analysis of the history and warfare, political organization, strict rules of conduct, and customs and beliefs of the Bedouins of North Africa and the Middle East. Adaptability to the scanty rainfall and sparse vegetation of the desert is reflected in the Bedouins' camel and goat herding economy, hunting, cultivation in oases and wadis, and clothing, food, and housing. However, Bedouin lifestyle, which had remained constant since the days of the Old Testament, says Alotaibi, has seen rapid changes in recent decades due to the discovery of oil. The high technology and profits of the oil industry have led to alternative employment opportunities, improved housing, education, and public health. Good quality roads and trucks have replaced the camel as transportation. Herds are often moved by trucks to better grazing areas and tube wells. However, the new method of land use known as *hema,* which allows unrestricted grazing in any area, has led to the problems associated with overgrazing. Since the benefits of the oil money are felt mainly by those living in the city, young Bedouins are leaving the desert in large numbers for the permanent settlements and progress of the towns.

125. Brill, Marlene Targ. *Algeria.* Enchantment of the World Series. Chicago: Children's Press, 1990. 127p. Grades 6-8.
    The second largest country in Africa, Algeria is seen as a land of contrasts that is desperately trying to evolve a single national identity. Brill's discussion of the land, history, government, economy, people, religion, and everyday life is both an objective analysis of facts and a sensitive portrayal of Algeria's desire to restore its Arab and national heritage. Algeria wants to stop the long history of changing its religion, language, and work to satisfy the oppressors from Carthage, Rome, Southern Europe, Arabia, Spain, and France. Efforts to fashion a sense of historic identity with Islam and the desire to become a modern industrialized nation have led to conflicting policies: the decision of President Houari Boumediene to focus on industry and oil and gas production rather than on agriculture; President Chadli Benjedid's liberal reforms of the 1980s focusing on agriculture and the creation of a multiparty system; concept of "official Islam" being considered a natural part of state reform and modernization as well as of the revival of fundamentalist beliefs; battle over women's rights and the family code under Quranic law; and teaching children Islam at home and in mosques and science and technology at school. Brill believes that the challenge of the future is to redirect traditional Islam toward keeping Algeria pointed in the modern direction.
    Maps, photographs, a detailed list of facts, and an index complement the text. Readers interested in the difficulties Algerian women confront in a traditional society may want to view *Desert Wind,* which won the 1982 Cannes Film Festival Award.

126. _____. *Libya.* Enchantment of the World Series. Chicago: Children's Press, 1987. 127p. Grades 6-8.
    An account of Libya's land and peoples, history and government, Islamic religion, economy and oil industry, and rural and urban lifestyles is a story of sharp contrasts. Historically and culturally, Libya is closely related to the other countries of the Maghrib and Barbary Coast--Morocco, Algeria, and Tunisia--in that it had Berber

origins and was subject to conquests by the Phoenicians, Greeks, Romans, Arabs, and Turks. Libya, however, was colonized by Italy and after World War II became an independent nation for the first time in centuries. An interesting account of the Barbary pirates and Barbary Wars to end piracy in the Mediterranean is also included. Modern Libya represents a blending of the old and the new. On the one hand, the fierce nationalism of the revolutionary government of Colonel Qaddafi marks Libya's break from Western influence and signals the introduction of a socialistic form of direct democracy, sharing the wealth gained from the new oil industry, and modern education for boys and girls. On the other hand, Qaddafi embraces a strict and fundamentalist Islam and celebrates their Arab ancestry to unite all Libyans and the Middle East against Western powers.

Numerous color photographs illustrate everyday life and customs in clothing, housing, farming techniques, role of women, and marriage ceremonies. They also portray the grandeur of Greek and Roman ruins and the modern cities of Tripoli, Banghazi, and Misratah. Additional information is provided by maps, mini-facts, and a list of important dates.

127. Browder, Atlantis Tye, with Anthony T. Browder. *My First Trip to Africa*. Illustrated by East Koast Graphics. Washington, D.C.: Institute of Karmic Guidance, 1991. 38p. Grades 2-4.

The eight-year-old author narrates the story of her first trip to Egypt and her pride in discovering her African heritage. As Atlantis Tye (named after Queen Tiye, mother of Pharaoh Akhenaton) visits Cairo, the Nile River and Aswan Dam, Saqqara, pyramids at Giza and the Valley of the Kings and Queens, temples at Luxor and Karnak, and Nubian villages, she provides all the pertinent information on Egyptian history, culture, and achievements in mathematics, engineering, architecture, and medicine. The author is particular about giving the original names of places, people, and objects before the Greeks changed them. For instance, Egypt was known as Kemet and the statue of the Sphinx was called Hor-em-aket. Readers are challenged to consider the importance of names and the subversive political tactic of changing African names. Upon returning to Washington, D.C., Atlantis Tye recognizes the Egyptian influence on things she sees: the Washington Monument reminds her of the obelisks in Kemet, the Lincoln Memorial of the temples of Abu-Simbel and Rameses II, the emblems on the dollar bill of Egyptian images and symbols, and some buildings on 16th Street of the Sphinx and step pyramid.

A Parent/Teacher Guide provides detailed suggestions for activities that will enable children to understand aspects of personal history, African history, and world history. The discussion questions, in particular, will stimulate critical thinking and broaden understanding of subjects mentioned in the text through topics like geography and the impact of exploration upon the lives of the "newly discovered," analyzing facts and comparing data on Cairo and Washington, D.C., significance of the seven Egyptian inventions, and similarities between Nubians and Native Americans. Photographs of the monuments visited by the authors, illustrations, maps, glossary of terms, and hieroglyphic alphabet are included.

128. Carpenter, Allan, and Bechir Chourou. *Tunisia.* Enchantment of Africa Series. Chicago: Children's Press, 1973. 93p. Grades 6-8.
Information on the land, peoples, history, government, economy, health and education, and social life of Tunisia is juxtaposed against the biographies and lifestyles of four children in modern Tunisia. The enchantment of Tunisia rests in its unique blend of Eastern and Western cultures and in its natural beauty as seen in coastal towns and historic cities like Tunis and Carthage. Photographs, maps, a list of important facts, and an index are included.

129. Caselli, Giovanni. *An Egyptian Craftsman.* Illustrated by Trevor Scobie. Everyday Life Series. London: Macdonald, 1986. 30p. Grades 2-4.
Both text and illustrations describe the life of a royal tomb painter and his family during the reign of Pharaoh Rameses II (1279-1212 B.C.). Readers' interest, however, is focused on Kaha, young son of the painter, and his dismay at his father's promotion to scribe because he will now be required to attend school. With Kaha as a point of entry, Caselli recreates the artisans' village, Deir el-Medina, on the west bank of the Nile near the Valley of the Kings. He describes the daily life and activities; structure of the houses; celebration of the Festival of Ophet, which marks the yearly inundation of the Nile; clothes and makeup; the many duties of a scribe, who is regarded as an important civil servant; and schoolwork for the sons of scribes. A picture glossary provides additional information on tools and equipment, the pyramid at Giza, and the furniture and houses of the workmen engaged in building the royal tombs.
Children interested in seeking further information on Egyptian archeology may refer to Judith Crosher's *Ancient Egypt* (1992), *Ancient Cities* (Macdonald, 1985), *A Closer Look At Ancient Egypt* (Archon, 1977), *Pyramid* (Collins, 1976), *The Egyptians* (Macdonald, 1975), *The First Civilizations* (Macdonald, 1983), and *In Search of Tutankhamun* (Macdonald, 1985).

130. Cross, Wilbur. *Egypt.* Enchantment of the World Series. Chicago: Children's Press, 1982. 128p. Grades 6-10.
The impact of environment on human settlement and the course of history is clearly illustrated in this detailed account of the geography, history, people and customs, economy, and lifestyle of modern Egypt. Geographically, the land and people are controlled by the power of the sun and the fertile waters of the Nile in a country which is 95 percent desert. Human ingenuity and technology were needed to harness the gifts of the land when the Suez Canal and the Aswan High Dam were built and when drilling for oil began in the Gulf of Suez and the Sinai Peninsula. The history of Egypt is traced from predynastic times (going back some thirteen thousand years) to pharaonic rule, to three thousand years of foreign domination by the

Greeks, Romans, Ottomans, Arabs, and Europeans, to independence and a Republican government. Present-day Egypt is described through chapters on life in a village and city (Cairo), rapid urbanization and the growth of satellite cities, and dependence of the economy on agriculture (especially cotton production), industry, and tourism. Modern Egyptians are facing the challenge of nation building through an aggressive plan of universal education, encouraging foreign investments, industrialization, and championing the cause of women.

The enchantment of Egypt to the world, however, is its artistic and scientific contributions which embody not only elements of beauty and imagination, but every facet of human experience. Cross' discussion of Egyptian metalwork, stonecutting and sculpture, art, paper-making, pottery, weaving, astronomy, and mathematics is evidence of the hardworking character and ingenuity of Egyptians. Although Egypt is changing today, its integrated concept of life as reflected in religion, work, family relationships, and social outlook is still cemented by deep traditions and customs. Maps, charts, photographs, and list of mini-facts and important dates enhance the above account.

131. Der Manuelian, Peter. *Hieroglyphs from A to Z: A Rhyming Book with Ancient Egyptian Stencils for Kids.* Illustrated by author and Suwin Chan. Boston: Museum of Fine Arts, 1991. N.p. Grades K-3.

Hieroglyphics representing the letters of the English alphabet--except V and X, for which the Egyptians had no letters--are depicted on individual pages. In addition, the picture of a word beginning with each letter and its spelling in hieroglyphics are also included. Appropriate information on history, religion, customs and beliefs, animals, and architecture accompany the illustrations.

The brightly colored borders and drawings reflect the richness, style, and symbolism of ancient Egyptian art. An essay discussing the origin and history of hieroglyphics, their usage, and the discovery of the Rosetta Stone which enabled Europeans to decipher the script is included. Also, there is a hieroglyphic chart, stencils, and instructions to enable children to write secret messages.

An excellent background book on hieroglyphics is *Egyptian Hieroglyphics: How to Read and Write Them* (Dover, 1989) by Stephane Rossini.

132. Diamond, Arthur. *Egypt: Gift of the Nile.* Discovering Our Heritage Series. New York: Dillon, 1992. 127p. Grades 4-6.

Based on extensive research, Diamond provides an objective discussion of Egypt's geography, history from prehistoric to modern times, form of government, peoples and culture, industry and farming, education, religion, and national celebrations. In addition, he briefly introduces children to Egypt's oral literature, folk beliefs, art and architecture, and sports and entertainment. Numerous color photographs and an engaging prose style enable Diamond to enliven the factual information by conveying the "feel" for life in Egypt. For instance, in discussing dating and marriage, role of women, housing, food habits, and overpopulation, he lists several anecdotal details that create the impression of having actually visited Egypt and met its hospitable people. A brief profile of Egyptian Americans, list of Embassies and Consulates in the United States and Canada, glossary of terms, bibliography, and index are included.

133. Feinstein, Stephen C. *Egypt in Pictures*. Revised Edition. Visual Geography Series. Minneapolis, MN: Lerner, 1988. 64p. Grades 5-7.
Photographs, maps, charts, and text provide an introduction to the geography, history, religion, culture, economy, and peoples and lifestyles of modern Egypt. The chapter on history and government is especially detailed as it summarizes the long history of Egypt from pharaonic times (3100 B.C.) to Greek and Roman rule, to conquests by various Muslim dynasties, to European colonization and independence. It clearly explains the diplomatic and military difficulties Egypt has experienced with Israel and Britain over the Suez Canal and the Sinai Peninsula, and it analyzes the leadership roles of Presidents Nasser, Anwar el-Sadat, and Hosni Mubarak in facing these problems and achieving lasting peace and stability in the Middle East. This account also focuses on the many challenges facing Egypt: overcrowding in Cairo, which has a population of fifteen million people; overpopulation in general and the tremendous burden it places on the land and natural resources; insufficient food production and the necessity of importing it; providing adequate medical and educational facilities for all; and an economy dependent on foreign trade and limited exports. Despite these challenges, Mubarak's government is concentrating on modernization and raising the standard of living for all Egyptians.

134. Fox, Mary Virginia. *Tunisia*. Enchantment of the World Series. Chicago: Children's Press, 1990. 123p. Grades 6-8.
Tunisia is presented as a land of many contrasts through a discussion of its varied geography of mountains, desert and sea; history from early Berber times, to rule by Phoenicians, Romans, Vandals, Byzantines, Arabs, and French, to independence under President Habib Bourguiba; vast array of cultural groups, religions, and lifestyles; economy and industry from primitive farming to modern shipping; housing from underground homes to high-rise buildings; and an absolute one-party government with socialistic ideals. Tunisia is indeed a blend of the traditional and the ultra modern. The informative text is enlivened by attractive photographs and anecdotes from history and literature such as Queen Dido's cleverness in winning Carthage, the Barbary Pirates, and Djerba as the enchanted land of the Lotus Eaters. The above information is easily accessible through well-organized chapters, a list of important facts, and an index.

135. Isnard, H. *Algeria*. Translated from the French by O. C. Warden. London: Nicholas Kaye, 1955. 233p. Grades 8-12.

Published before Algerian independence (which took place in 1962), this book provides a typically Eurocentric view of French colonialism in Africa. After giving a brief overview of the history and the two distinct natural regions--the densely populated Mediterranean and the scattered, nomadic population of the Steppe--Isnard focuses on giving a detailed tour of Algeria's major attractions, economic activities, and lifestyles. Thus, readers are introduced to cities like Algiers, Constantine, and Oran; to regions like the coast, Great and Lesser Kabylia mountain ranges, and the Sahel; and to the excavations at Tipasa. Everywhere, the author emphasizes the efforts of the European colonists to subdue the hostile land and natives to bring civilization and urbanization to Algeria. Descriptions of Roman ruins, dams, canals, roads, ports, and vineyards are testimonials to the economic development and exploitation of natural resources initiated by colonists. Isnard does, however, admit that Algeria was used as a supplier of agricultural products for France and as a place to settle its unemployed population. He concludes with the earnest wish that the French may continue in Algeria and that the European and native Algerian societies would learn to intermingle and develop a culture that synthesizes East and West. Perhaps, the 156 black-and-white photographs best portray the contrasting landscapes, the variety of peoples and lifestyles, and the contribution of Islamic, Roman, and European cultures to Algeria.

136. Kristensen, Preben, and Fiona Cameron. *We Live in Egypt*. Photographs by Preben Kristensen. New York: Bookwright, 1987. 60p. Grades 4-8.

Men and women from all walks of life provide insight into the living conditions of modern Egyptians. As archeologists and geologists, engineers and sailors, farmers and fishermen, carpet weavers and camel dealers, and shopkeepers and government officials tell the stories of their lives, the picture of Egypt that emerges is of a forward-looking nation which is trying to achieve the technological advancements of the twentieth century, as well as maintaining its past traditions. While the Aswan High Dam is important for a steady supply of water and electricity, while factories are needed for producing fertilizers and other products, and while the latest machinery is necessary for drilling oil, Egyptian pride in its ancient civilizations and culture is reflected in the art of the belly dancer, the designs in carpets, the styles of designer clothes in boutiques, the reenactment of ancient living conditions in the pharaonic village, and the scholarly inquiries at Al-Azhar, an Islamic University. Modern Egyptians value education as vital to their progress as individuals and as a nation. Both photographs and autobiographical sketches give a very positive image of Egyptian achievements of the last four decades. A list of facts gives basic information on the government, religion, languages, currency, population, housing, climate, agriculture and industry, and education of modern Egypt.

137. Lye, Keith. *Take a Trip to Egypt.* Take a Trip Series. London: Franklin Watts, 1983. 32p. Grades 1-3.

Attractive full-color photographs and a simplified text introduce beginning readers to Egypt's geography, ancient history and monuments, religion, and life in modern cities like Cairo. Egypt is presented as a progressive country that is raising its standard of living through free education for children from ages six to twelve, harnessing the Nile River at the Aswan High Dam, and rapid industrialization. The future of Egypt is seen as peaceful because of the 1979 Arab-Israeli treaty.

138. Meadowcroft, Enid La Monte. *The Gift of the River: A History of Ancient Egypt.* Illustrated by Katharine Dewey. New York: Crowell, 1937, 1965. 242p. Grades 4-6.

Ancient Egyptian history is surveyed from 6000 B.C. to 609 B.C. The discussion of each era or dynasty focuses around a key episode or individual who dominated it. Hence, in presenting the achievements of Pharaohs Menes, Khufu, Thutmose III, Tutankhamen, and Rameses, Harkhuf the explorer, and Queen Hatshepsut, Meadowcroft also provides details of government, religion, social and economic life, and arts and letters. The material is free from scholastic bias, ethical prejudgment, and personal animus. Meadowcroft's engaging style invites readers to view Egyptians as a people and as human beings, to explore their history, and to think deeply on some of the questions posed.

139. Messenger, Charles. *The Middle East.* Conflict in the 20th Century Series. London: Franklin Watts, 1988. Originally published in 1987 by Aladdin. 62p. Grades 8-12.

The Middle East is viewed as the most volatile and dangerous region of the world in modern times. A detailed examination of events from World War I to 1987 indicates the area was very important in strategic and economic terms for powers like the Soviet Union, United States, Britain, France, Turkey, and Germany to ignore it. The major causes of the conflict are identified as the demands for national self-determination against colonial powers and territorial disputes in the region after independence; the emergence of Israel and Arab opposition to its existence; the Palestinian Question; deep religious divisions between Jews and Arabs; and the religious split in the Muslim world. The situation has been made worse by the discovery and exploitation of oil, giving the region an added importance to the industrialized world. Egypt, as part of the Middle East, is deeply engaged in the politics of the region because of the strategic importance of the Suez Canal and the common goals of Arab unity. The role of Egyptian leaders like Nasser and Sadat in the Suez Canal Crisis of 1956, Six-Day War of 1967, Yom Kippur War of 1973, and the peace negotiations with Israel orchestrated by the United States is examined. Messenger concludes that the future looks bleak with the prospect of continued war and violence in the region because none of the tensions and problems that created the conflict has been solved.

140. Naden, Corinne J. *The Nile River.* A First Book. New York: Franklin Watts, 1972. 77p. Grades 5-7.

The Nile is a mysterious river that has shaped the lives and history of the peoples who live along its banks. After tracing the 4,150-mile journey of the Nile from its source in Lake Victoria to its mouth in the Mediterranean Sea, Naden narrates the many adventures in search of the source of the White Nile and its tributary the Blue Nile. The account of Herodotus (460 B.C.) and the map of Ptolemy (second century A.D.) were accepted as correct till two British explorers, Richard Burton and John Speke, proved them wrong. However, Burton and Speke sparked off the controversy whether Lake Victoria or Lake Tanganyika was the source. The Royal Geographical Society entrusted David Livingstone with the task of proving Speke's claim that Lake Victoria was the source--a task that was completed by Henry Morton Stanley when he came to East Africa in search of Livingstone. Next, Naden provides a brief history of the rich civilizations that flourished in Egypt from the ancient pharaohs to independence. In modern times, the role of the Nile as the bringer of water and fertility to an arid region has changed with the completion of the Aswan High Dam in 1970. Instead of the yearly inundation, the Nile's waters are stored in Lake Nasser to provide a steady supply of water throughout the year, and its energy is converted to electricity to power industries and raise the standard of living in Egypt and Sudan. The text is illustrated with numerous black-and-white photographs.

141. Nelson, Nina. *Tunisia.* New York: Hastings House, 1974. 183p. Grades 7-12.

The opening chapter is an interesting account of the history and culture of Tunisia, or Numidia as it was called earlier, from ancient times to the socialist government of Habib Bourguiba. The remaining chapters are geared more to the tourist visiting the major cities of Tunis and Kairouan and the island of Djerba. Nelson describes the climate, transportation, shopping, food, and religious, historical, and wildlife attractions. The anecdotal accounts of Nelson's trips to Tunisia and graphic descriptions of the beautiful seven-hundred-mile coastline convey her personal enjoyment of Tunisia's charm.

142. Pace, Mildred Mastin. *Wrapped for Eternity: The Story of the Egyptian Mummy.* Illustrated by Tom Huffman. New York: Dell, 1974. 192p. Grades 8-12.

This detailed account of mummy-lore is given almost entirely from the perspective of archeologists, scientists, doctors, and scholars. Beginning with the discovery of Queen Hetepheres' tomb, mother of Pharaoh Khufu, Pace engages readers' interest by recounting the experiences of numerous archeologists. Interspersed with these narratives is vital information on the historical, geographical, religious, and socioeconomic conditions that first gave rise to and later saw the end of the practice of mummification. Herodotus' fifth century B.C. account of mummy-making is examined for accuracy and a step-by-step description of the method provided. The remaining chapters focus on tombs and their plunderers from the ancient grave robbers to modern archeologists like Howard Carter, who discovered King Tutankhamen's tomb, to mummy unwrappers like Thomas J. Pettigrew, who gave public performances in mid-nineteenth century London, to the wanton destruction of mummies for medicinal purposes, paper making, and scientific research.

Next, Pace universalizes this study of mummies by discussing natural mummies in the dry hot and cold climates, where the royal Inca and Guanajuato mummies were found, and in the peat bogs of northwestern Europe and the British Isles, where the bodies of Iron Age men and women were preserved. Pace ends on a positive note by stating that much is still left to be discovered in Egypt. She fires the imagination of future archeologists by mentioning the on-going search with modern cosmic-ray detectors for hidden burial chambers in ancient monuments.

143. Percefull, Aaron W. *The Nile.* A First Book. London: Franklin Watts, 1984. 61p. Grades 5-7.

Like Naden (see # 140), Percefull also traces the course of the Nile, narrates the explorations in search of its source, and recounts the history of Egypt from ancient to modern times. However, this book provides a more detailed account of the dependence of ancient Egyptian economy and transportation on the Nile; the lifestyle and culture of ancient Egypt; varied uses and export of papyrus; French control of Egypt under Napoleon; and Colonel Charles Gordon's efforts to stop the slave trade in Sudan. In discussing the twentieth century efforts to exploit the resources of the Nile, Percefull analyzes the problems of high evaporation and seepage, waterlogging of fields, excessive salt content, coastal erosion, and loss of ancient temples and tombs--only fourteen including Abu Simbel could be saved--as a direct result of the Aswan High Dam. The dam is seen as a modern monument on the Nile, a symbol of Egypt's power and determination to control the river and enter the industrial age. Black-and-white illustrations and an index are included.

144. Perl, Lila. *Mummies, Tombs and Treasures: Secrets of Ancient Egypt.* Illustrated with Photographs. Drawings by Erika Weihs. New York: Clarion, 1987. 120p. Grades 6-8.

Information on Egyptian mummies and funeral rites is organized in seven chapters that discuss history, religious beliefs, process, tomb architecture, treasures, and tomb robbers. Belief in an afterlife and the necessity of providing an identifiable body to which the dead person's *ka,* or unseen twin, and *ba,* or spirit, could return stimulated research and experimentation in the art of preserving the body after death. Furthermore, Perl provides the historical and mythological background of this practice. For instance, the roles of the various gods like Osiris, Isis, Horus, Toth, and Anubis are explained in connection with rituals for the dead. The lengthy process of mummification is clearly and frankly discussed, while acknowledging the discomfort modern children may feel in reading these graphic details. The end of the age of pyramids is examined in the context of the beginning of foreign rule in Egypt and the shift of the capital to Tanis with its humid atmosphere and soggy soil. Interesting bits of information such as the discovery of King Tutankhamen's tomb, Europe's fascination with the medicinal properties of mummies, Rosetta Stone and decoding of the hieroglyphics, and socioeconomic conditions in ancient Egypt enhance each chapter. Charts, maps, drawings, and photographs of ancient monuments, treasures, and mummies support and extend the text.

145. Rothkopk, Carol Zeman. *The Opening of the Suez Canal.* A World Focus Book. New York: Franklin Watts, 1973. 85p. Grades 5-8.
    The story of the Suez Canal is narrated with all the drama, political intrigue, and excitement that accompanied the project. It is interesting to note that the idea of joining the Mediterranean and Red Seas was one that had been dreamed and partially realized before. An inscription on the Great Temple of Amon at Karnak suggests that such a canal was built in Pharaoh Sesostris I's time (1926 B.C.) and was still in use during the reign of Seti I (died 1290 B.C.). Herodotus provides an account of Pharaoh Necho (609-593 B.C.) who began construction of another canal, which was continued by Ptolemy II (285-246 B.C.). The Roman Emperor Trajan made this canal navigable again in 98 A.D. after years of disuse, but the Muslims closed the canal for strategic reasons in the eighth century. In modern times, Napoleon Bonaparte was the first to examine the possibility of a new canal linking East and West, but it was Ferdinand de Lesseps who fulfilled it.
    The story of the Suez Canal is clearly the story of de Lesseps' passion to build the canal from the time he arrived in Egypt in 1832 on a diplomatic assignment. His daring scheme created political, financial, and personal problems for him and his supporters in Egypt and France. When work on the canal began, he did not have enough money or the support of any government, and he had to use his diplomatic skills and indomitable pluck to convince Mohammed Said and Ismail Said of Egypt and Empress Eugenie of France. It is because of de Lesseps' courage, determination, and shrewdness that the Suez Canal was inaugurated in November 1869 with great fanfare and expense by Ismail Said; however, his dream of international ownership was not realized as the canal became the focus of conflict between Egypt and Britain in 1956 and repeatedly in the 1950s, 1960s, and 1970s between Egypt and Israel.

146. Siamon, Sharon and Jeff. *Egypt.* Children of Other Lands Series. Danbury, CT: Grolier, 1990. 48p. Grades K-3.
    Western children are provided a glimpse of what it is like to grow up in Egypt through a discussion of various facets of life. Whether they are being introduced to the geography, village and city life, food and clothing, school and play, family ties and household chores, or religion and festivities, the text first establishes commonalities before

describing how the situation may be different in Egypt. This book will appeal to young children as it asks relevant questions and uses informal diction and familiar examples and comparisons. Numerous color photographs of Egyptian boys and girls at home, at play, at the park, and on field trips further illustrate that modern Egypt is a blend of traditional and Western lifestyles. The overwhelming message is that children in Egypt are no different from children in the United States and that their lives and futures are just as happy and bright.

147. Soghikian, Juanita Will. *Lands, Peoples and Communities of the Middle East.* Illustrated by Penny Williams Yaqub. Middle East Gateway Series. Waverly, MA: Juanita W. Soghikian, 1980. 74p. Grades 3-5.
    This description of the Middle East as a distinct cultural region includes five countries of Northern Africa. First, the commonalities of the region are presented through a discussion of the Arabic language, Islam, arts and crafts, architecture, food and clothing, music and dance, games and sports, and the value placed on family and hospitality. Next, follows a description of the various landforms and topography and the resulting differences in economy and means of livelihood, natural resources, lifestyles, and customs of the twenty countries that comprise this region. In fact, variety in land and climate also accounts for differences within a country. Numerous illustrations, maps, charts, flags, and activities both introduce as well as review information.

148. Terzi, Marinella. *The Land of the Pharaohs.* The World Heritage Series. Translation of *Imperio de los Farones.* Chicago: Children's Press and UNESCO, 1992. 33p. Grades 6-8.
    Committed to protecting the cultural and natural wonders of the world, the World Heritage Convention, established in 1972 under the aegis of UNESCO, targeted three historic sites in Egypt for preservation. Through spectacular color photographs and a concise text, this publication introduces children to Memphis and the pyramids at Giza, Thebes and its necropolis, and the monuments of Nubia and Aswan in the context of ancient Egypt's historical, cultural, religious, and scientific achievements. Detailed background information on the photographs and brief insets on specific topics such as the principal gods and goddesses, the curse of King Tut [sic], and writing in hieroglyphics complement the text and testify to the rich heritage of Egypt.

149. von Haag, Michael. *Egypt: The Land and its People.* Countries Series. London: Macdonald, 1975. 61p. Grades 6-8.
    As is typical of this series, subtopics pertaining to a single country are discussed in double-page spreads. Photographs, drawings, charts, maps, and explanatory captions both clarify and extend the brief text. Central to the discussion of Egypt is the role of the Nile in determining past history and the modern task of finding new applications for the river after its energy was harnessed by the High Dam at Aswan. Subsequent sections discuss topics such as ancient

civilizations, Arab and Turkish conquerors, European colonization and the revolution of 1952, Islam and the Coptic Church, education and the emancipation of women, family life, customs and superstitions, shopping and travel, rural life, Cairo and industrial development, and Egypt's contribution to world knowledge. Additional reference pages list key facts, information on climate and vegetation, pharaonic gods, population growth, government, economy, and a glossary of places in Egypt. The fact that some of the information is outdated does not detract from the primary intention of conveying a multifaceted experience of life in Egypt.

150. Watts, Daud Malik, with Tony Browder. *Gifts of the Nile Valley.* Positive Image Education Series. Washington, D.C.: Afro-Vision, 1992. 20p. Grades 5-7.
The primary purpose of this series is to resolve the problem of self-hate created by negative stereotypes of Africans and African Americans by offering accurate lessons from black history. In keeping with this agenda, the geography, human origins, history, culture, religion, scientific achievements, and architecture of Egypt (Kemet) are examined with the specific aim of establishing that ancient Egypt was populated by or had direct contact with the African heartland. References to primary Egyptian, Greek, Roman, and Biblical sources, and the research of scholars like Cheik Anta Diop, Gerald Massey, and Yosef ben-Jochannan support the above claim. A list of Afrocentric historical publications is included for those interested in Kemetic studies.

151. Wilkins, Frances. *Let's Visit Egypt.* Let's Visit Series. Toronto: Burke, 1977, 1983. 96p. Grades 5-8.
Let's Visit Egypt surveys the land and people, history, religion and culture, rural and urban life, and modern challenges of Egypt. While information regarding current statistical data, oil deposits, and government leadership is outdated, the book provides a clear and detailed discussion of specific topics such as the treasure of King Tutankhamen, Islam and Coptic Christianity, Cairo and Alexandria, the Nile and the Aswan Dam, the deserts, the revolution of 1952, education, and the politics of the Suez Canal. Both text and photographs present Egypt as a country which is attempting to define its identity in the twentieth century by gaining knowledge of modern economics and technology from the rest of the world without in any way losing its traditions and glorious heritage.

152. _____. *Let's Visit North Africa.* Let's Visit Series. London: Burke, 1979, 1983. 96p. Grades 4-6.
This introductory book briefly discusses the land, history, peoples and their customs, Islam, and education of the five countries of North Africa. Separate sections on Morocco, Algeria, Libya, Tunisia, Egypt, and the Sahara Desert emphasize the great civilizations that flourished in this region before the birth of Christ and its glory when it was incorporated in the Arab empire in the eighth century.

Although its former prestige has passed, North Africa is seen as a land of contrasts where rich and poor, modern and traditional exist side by side.

153. _____. *Morocco*. Places and Peoples of the World Series. New York: Chelsea House, 1987. 96p. Grades 5-7.

Separate chapters introduce readers to the land, history, peoples, religion, living conditions, government, and economy of Morocco. Beginning with the various climatic regions and historical cities, Wilkins presents Morocco as a beautiful country with a rich and varied heritage. Historically, Morocco experienced the same fate as the other countries in the Maghrib area. The first known inhabitants, the fiercely proud and independent Berbers, were invaded and conquered by Romans (149 B.C.), Vandals (429 A.D.), and Arabs (680 A.D. onwards). By the fifteenth century, Spain and Portugal had driven out Muslims from Europe and had established a few small communities in Morocco. In the twentieth century, Morocco became a mere pawn in the hands of rival European powers, and by mutual consent of European nations it became a French protectorate by the Treaty of Fez in 1912. Ironically, exposure to European culture and education also spurred nationalistic feelings, and in 1955 Morocco became an independent nation.

Modern Morocco is a mingling of Moorish and Western cultures. Contrasts between traditional and modern ways can be seen in the government, which is a monarchy with an advisory council; in clothing and arts and crafts; in the Berber village dwellings and modern Arab cities with their beaches and high-rises and souks and medinas; and in education and changes in the role of women.

West Africa

TRADITIONAL LITERATURE

154. Aardema, Verna. *Anansi Finds a Fool.* Illustrated by Bryna Waldman. New York: Dial, 1992. N.p. Grades K-3.

To the satisfaction of all, especially his wife Aso, lazy Ananse is tricked into doing all the hard work when he plans to dupe someone into fishing for him. In addition to Aardema's delightful narration, this picture book has exquisite illustrations. Waldman individualizes the characters and faithfully portrays West African rural life, paying attention to details of clothing, housing, pottery, and jungle life.

155. _____. *Half-a-Ball-of-Kenki: An Ashanti Tale Retold.* Illustrated by Diane Stanley Zuromskis. New York and London: Frederick Warne, 1979. 31p. Grades K-3.

When Leopard and Fly go in search of brides, Leopard finds he is rudely treated and thrown out of each town, while Fly is welcomed. In a fit of jealousy, he ties Fly to a tree and challenges anyone to rescue him. Half-a-Ball-of-Kenki (corn mush) engages Leopard in a heroic fight and throws him in the fire, thus causing him permanent humiliation because of the spots from the fire. Aardema's humorous dialogue, repetitive refrains, and poetic diction make this an ideal read-aloud story. The illustrations echo the humor and humanity of the story, as well as manipulating readers' involvement by using frames to lend distance and objectivity and full-page illustrations for emotional engagement in the characters' experiences.

156. _____. *The Vingananee and the Tree Toad: A Liberian Tale.* Illustrated by Ellen Weiss. New York and London: Frederick Warne, 1983. N.p. Preschool-Grade 2.

Spider and his helpers live in a happy household, but the monster Vingananee comes each day to eat their stew. Rat, Buck Deer, and Lion in turn try to defeat the monster, but it is the tiny Tree Toad who quite by chance--or with divine help--kills the Vingananee. Aardema's text will entertain as well as generate discussion of big and small, strong and weak. The illustrations lend a humorous tone to the story as these very individualized characters, who dress and behave like humans, go about their daily chores.

157. _____. *Why Mosquitoes Buzz in People's Ears*. Illustrated by Leo and Diane Dillon. New York: Dial, 1975. N.p. Preschool-Grade 3.

Winner of the 1976 Caldecott Medal, this pourquoi tale from West Africa provides a humorous explanation for why mosquitoes buzz in people's ears. One day, when Mosquito tells a tall tale to Iguana, he causes a series of misunderstandings and mishaps that lead to the death of an owlet, and Mother Owl is too sorrowful to wake up the sun. King Lion holds a meeting of the jungle animals to determine why the night has lasted so long. Working backwards and accumulating detail upon detail, the crime is traced to Mosquito. Mosquito remains hidden, but to this day he whines in people's ears to find out if they are still angry with him. Leo and Diane Dillon's intricate illustrations also emphasize the humorous undertones of this very serious situation. The pictures are a combination of a series of cutouts with rubbed pastels, india ink, and watercolors applied with airbrush and splatter techniques.

158. Achebe, Chinua. *The Drum*. Illustrated by N. K. Mbugua. Junior Readers Series. Nairobi, Kenya: Heinemann, 1988. Originally published in 1977 by Fourth Dimension, Nigeria. 34p. Grades 2-4.

A master storyteller, Achebe makes the well-known folktale of the magical object that produces sumptuous food come alive with vivid descriptions, lively dialogue, brilliant characterization, and leisurely narration. During a prolonged drought, Tortoise receives a magical drum when his palm fruit accidentally rolls down to the land of the spirits and is eaten by a child-spirit. Tortoise uses his ability to feed the hungry animals to gain power and proclaim himself their king. When the drum breaks, the animals, who are only interested in the food, desert Tortoise. Tortoise goes back to the land of the spirits and very greedily selects the largest drum, which releases masked spirits that give him a severe beating. Undaunted, Tortoise returns to his compound and once again invites the animals to a feast and lets them get whipped for their ingratitude and rudeness.

The black-and-white illustrations, though lively, are not as attractive as the color pictures by Anne R. Nwokoye for the Fourth Dimension publication.

159. _____. *The Flute*. Illustrated by Boniface O. Ager. Nairobi, Kenya: Heinemann, 1988. Originally published in 1977 by Fourth Dimension, Nigeria. 27p. Grades K-3.

Disease and sickness come to the world when two stepbrothers react differently to the same situation. Both boys leave behind their flutes on their farm which borders the land of men and spirits. When the younger brother goes to retrieve his bamboo flute at night, he is courteous to the spirits, rejects their offers of more expensive flutes, and selects a small pot when offered a gift. The older brother, who is the exact opposite in nature, is rude, ungrateful, and greedy. The larger pot he brings home does not contain riches, but diseases like leprosy, smallpox, and yaws. The tale is told interestingly and without didacticism. The illustrations are unattractive.

160. Achebe, Chinua, and John Iroaganachi. *How the Leopard Got His Claws.* Illustrated by Adrienne Kennaway. Nairobi, Kenya: Heinemann, n.d. Originally published in 1972 by Nwamife, Nigeria. N.p. Grades K-3.

This pourquoi tale explains how disharmony and enmity shattered the peaceful jungle and the wise and gentle rule of Leopard. Dog, with his unfriendly ways and sharp teeth and claws, incited the animals to defy the authority of Leopard. Forced to get sharp teeth and claws from the blacksmith and a roaring voice from Thunder, Leopard returns to challenge and defeat Dog. The jungle paradise is destroyed forever; each animal now becomes a predator who hurts weaker ones. The dog leaves the jungle to live with the hunter, and in exchange he agrees to lead the hunter into the jungle to kill his fellow animals.

On the political and philosophic levels, this eloquently narrated folktale serves as a metaphor for the Biafra War and the human condition, because nothing but strife is caused among peoples and nations due to power and superior weapons. It also illustrates that fickleness and cowardice lead people to reject the good and follow the strong, though morally inferior person. Achebe ends on a hopeful note that if people would only cooperate, they could live without fear of enemies. The book is beautifully illustrated.

161. Adedeji, 'Remi. *Four Stories About the Tortoise.* Illustrated by Ade. Oloye. Junior African Literature Series. Ibadan, Nigeria: Onibonoje, 1973. 25p. Grades 2-4.

Four Nigerian tales about the tortoise represent familiar traits and motifs associated with the trickster figure. In this collection, the tortoise tricks an elephant, suffers loss of hair and pain when a scheme backfires, acknowledges his foolishness in trying to collect all the wisdom in the world for himself, and breaks his back while helping his friends. The stories are told in a pleasant narrative style.

162. Aidoo, Ama Ata. *The Eagle and the Chickens and Other Stories.* Accra, Ghana: Afram, 1989. 44p. Grades 2-4.

Two folktales and two realistic stories are written with an awareness of the personalities and desires of children in mind. Each story heightens the central conflict and allows the protagonist to develop a new understanding of self and the surrounding world. Aidoo's superior storytelling ability is evident in her descriptive narration, dramatic plots, and character delineation.

163. Anderson, David A. *The Origin of Life on Earth: An African Creation Myth.* Illustrated by Kathleen Atkins Wilson. Designed by Pete Traynor. Mt. Airy, MD: Sights Productions, 1991. N.p. Grades K-3.

According to Yoruba mythology, the world was created because of the restlessness of Obatala, a male deity. Olorun, the Supreme God, entrusts Obatala with creating earth and populating it with plants, animals, and humans. Wilson's illustrations capture the dignity of the myth, the sense of awe and mystery associated with the gods, and the liveliness and human quality of Obatala. Wilson, who is well known for her silhouettes, combines this style with the rich images of African art and culture.

164. Appiah, Peggy. *Tales of an Ashanti Father*. Illustrated by Mora Dickson. Boston: Beacon, 1989. Originally published in 1967 by Andre Deutsch, London. 156p. Grades 5-7.

Twenty-two folktales reflect the rich traditions, beliefs, and wisdom of the Asante of Ghana. Prominent among the stories are the adventures of the trickster Ananse. Difficult tasks are assigned to him by Nyame, the Sky God, and the village chiefs, winning him the title of wisest among God's creatures. With his intelligence and cunning, Ananse outwits pythons, wins a kingdom with a grain of corn, and obtains the prized possessions of Death. However, Ananse's cleverness also brings out his darker side: he is boastful, greedy, ill-mannered, and selfish. Sometimes he escapes punishment, as in "Kwaku Ananse and the Donkey"; more frequently, the moral order is maintained. In "How Kwaku Ananse Became Bald," he is caught for stealing; in "Why the Lizard Stretches His Neck," he is tricked by a lizard; and in "How Death Came to Mankind," he has to live with the guilt of bringing pain and suffering to human beings. But Ananse uses his gift of storytelling to talk himself out of the most embarrassing situations. Other stories represent Asante legends, fables, origin of customs, and animal traits. Appiah's retellings are enlivened by descriptions of people and places, underlying motivations of characters, leisurely narration, and lively dialogue. The black-and-white drawings lend visual artistry to the text.

Another engaging collection of Ananse stories is Joyce Cooper Arkhurst's *The Adventures of Spider: West African Folktales* (Little, Brown, 1964). Jerry Pinkney's humorous illustrations of the awkward situations Ananse gets himself into are especially appealing.

165. Bali, Esther. *Taroh Folktales*. Ibadan, Nigeria: Spectrum, 1990. 95p. Grades 4-6.

Fifteen folktales of the Taroh people of the Langtang area of Nigeria reflect the values and culture of this farming community. The tales strongly indicate the Taroh belief that harmony among supernatural beings, humans, and animals is essential for happiness. Hence, the stories recount why animals no longer live with people, the exploits of Izum, the trickster hare, and the greed of the hyena. However, emphasis is placed on family solidarity and peace in stories about jealous co-wives, wicked stepmothers, and importance of selecting a virtuous mate. Bali's graceful narrative style is hampered by unnecessary moralizing.

166. Beier, Ulli, comp. *Yoruba Myths.* Illustrated by Georgina Beier. Cambridge, England: Cambridge University Press, 1980. 82p. Grades 5-7.

Forty-one mythological tales introduce young readers to Yoruba religious beliefs. According to Beier's Introduction, the myths fall into four major categories: myths of creation and the principal gods and deities; folkloric tales in which the protagonists bear the names of gods; myths that serve a historical function; and stories of the Ifa oracle which were created for the purpose of assisting in the process of divination. Beier deliberately employs a sparse prose style to preserve the dignity and archaic mystery of these religious myths. The text is complemented by black-and-white motifs taken from Yoruba shrines and murals, beadwork, and religious objects. The Notes provide background information on the myths, religious practices, and cultural details.

167. Berry, Jack. *West African Folktales.* Edited and with an Introduction by Richard Spear. Evanston, IL: Northwestern University Press, 1991. 229p. Grades 6-8.

Collected and translated by Berry, a specialist in West African languages and culture, the tales in this volume are representative of the Akan, Yoruba, Ga, Twi, Sefroi, and Krio groups. Berry extracts the storyline from the storytelling environment and converts the tales into simple narratives. The operatic devices of West African spoken art such as appropriate voices, careful timing, digressions, opening and closing formulae, dynamic relationship with the audience, and songs have not been employed; instead, the literary techniques of choice of vocabulary, style, and metaphor which are more suited to reading have been utilized. In the Introduction, Richard Spear emphasizes that this conversion to Western literary folk traditions does not rob the original stories of their "simplicity, purposeful innocence, directness, and moral tone."

In keeping with the above objectives, a variety of stories follow one another as they would in an actual storytelling session. There are trickster tales, pourquoi tales, and tales of enchantment. Popular folk motifs such as the wicked stepmother, wisdom in supposedly foolish people, bridal contests, and the pineapple child are incorporated in their many variations. In addition to entertaining, these tales instruct readers on the virtues of kindness to animals, respect for elders, and loyalty between friends; and warn them of the ill-fortune that befalls the gluttonous, cruel, excessively proud, and foolish. Each story focuses on the swift movement of the plot; there is a minimum of description and character development. All explanatory and supplementary materials are placed in the Notes and Index sections.

168. Bryan, Ashley. *Beat the Story-Drum, Pum-Pum.* Illustrated by reteller. New York: Atheneum, 1987. 70p. Grades 3-6.

Bryan's adaptation of five Nigerian folktales from the Hausa, Bavanda, and southern Nigerian traditions retains the vigorous narrative quality of a story told to the accompaniment of a drum. There is a creation myth about how animals got their tails; two pourquoi stories explaining why frog and snake do not play together and why the bush cow and elephant fight; a cumulative tale of a hen outwitting the lazy frog; and a realistic story of a man who cannot keep a wife because of his bad habit of counting spoonfuls as food is served. Committed to keeping alive the African tradition of storytelling, Bryan's stories are best enjoyed if recited because of the oral techniques of repetition, rhythmic lines, rhyming words, onomatopoeic sounds, and crisp and lively dialogue. Bold and forceful woodcuts also echo the beat of the story-drum and Bryan's poetic prose.

169. Chocolate, Deborah M. Newton.   *Talk, Talk: An Ashanti Legend.* Illustrated by Dave Albers. Legends of the World Series. Mahwah, NJ: Troll, 1993. 32p. Grades 1-3.

Winner of the 1992 Parents' Choice Award, this cumulative tale narrates the exploits of four villagers who run to their chief because they have been frightened by animals, plants, and objects that talk to them. The underlying theme emphasizes the Asante belief that all god's creatures, even objects, have thoughts and feelings that human beings should be sensitive to. That humans are not in control, after all, is ironically depicted when the all-powerful chief chides the men for being foolish, till his own golden stool talks to him. The exaggerated fear of the villagers and the folkloric element are both captured by Albers' illustrations.

170. Courlander, Harold.   *The Hat-Shaking Dance and Other Ashanti Tales from Ghana.*   New York: Harcourt, Brace and World, 1957. 115p. Grades 3-5.

Prominent in this collection are some of the most popular stories of Ananse, the Asante folk hero. Through his wit and cunning, Ananse tricks and conquers animals much larger and more powerful than he. In "Anansi and the Elephant Go Hunting," Ananse devises a way to get food during a severe drought and famine. However, this story also reveals a darker aspect of Ananse's nature--that not all his deeds are morally justified. While his keen intellect and wisdom are to be admired, Ananse is often a victim of his excessive greed, pride, and insincerity. It is only fitting that this master trickster should be outwitted and shamed by someone equally intelligent like the turtle.

Anansesem, or the body of stories surrounding Ananse, teach valuable lessons by depicting human frailties through animal characters. Even when Ananse gets away with his tricks, the concepts of right and wrong and the rules of acceptable social behavior are strictly upheld. The Asante also employ these stories as a vehicle for understanding their environment: why elephants have smaller hind parts, why spiders are bald, and why spiders hide in rafters and dark corners. Far from being didactic and moralistic, Courlander's retellings are entertaining, humorous, and stylistically graceful. Children will enjoy the rhythmic prose, songs, and repetition of motifs.

171. _____. *Tales of Yoruba Gods and Heroes.* Illustrated by Larry Lurin. New York: Crown, 1973. 243p. Grades 6-12.

This collection of traditional stories provides an overview of Yoruba mythology, religious beliefs, and the relationship between humans, the forces of nature, and the various orishas, or deities. Beginning with a series of creation myths, Courlander narrates how orisha Obatala descended from the sky to found the sacred city of Ife. Other orishas came to live with the newly created beings to regulate human life on earth. To carry on their tasks, the gods were given various powers, which led to jealousy and intrigues in their interpersonal relationships and dealings with humans. The most fascinating god was Eshu who spread confusion and dissension, but who also proved to be a sincere and selfless friend. As life on earth became more complicated, differences among people developed and they left Ife to establish other cities and nations. The religious system of divining was developed to perceive the meanings and intentions of Olorun, the Sky God, and to determine what course of action to take.

There are also stories of heroes and heroines who distinguished themselves and were later deified. For instance, Moremi became a sacred personage after she saved Ife from Oyo attackers; Oshun became a river deity after being humiliated by a co-wife; and Oya became an orisha after she and her husband, orisha Shengo, were driven out of their kingdom. Of the warrior heroes, the legends of Timi and Gbonka of Oyo, Oranmiyan of Ife, Ogbe of Ibode, and Oko and Onugbo of the Idoma people are most popular. Collectively, these myths comment on the human condition in the midst of the various forces that surround them.

172. Courlander, Harold, and George Herzog. *The Cow-Tail Switch and Other West African Stories.* Illustrated by Madye Lee Chastain. New York: Holt, 1947. 143p. Grades 3-6.

The contemplative tone of these folktales offers an opportunity for discussion and philosophic enquiry. Some of the issues raised are the impact of time on one's material circumstances, the pride and arrogance that generally come with wealth, mental state during sleep, vagaries of social justice, and humans being responsible for their own fate. The title story, for instance, has the popular motif of deciding which son helped the most in bringing his dead father back to life: Is it the son who assembled the bones, the one who gave power of movement, the one who put blood in the veins, or the son who put breath in the body? Ultimately, the prize is given to the youngest son who asked for his father and prompted the search by his older brothers. Some of the other selections include pourquoi stories, trickster tales of Ananse, and humorous tales that employ play on words, tongue twisters, and exaggeration.

173. Courlander, Harold, and Ousmane Sako. *The Heart of the Ngoni: Heroes of the African Kingdom of Segu.* New York: Crown, 1982. 178p. Grades 7-12.

Based on the legends and heroic narratives of the Bambara and

Soninke peoples of Segu (now part of modern Mali), Courlander has reconstructed the glory of the Segu kingdom from its founding on the banks of the Upper Niger in the early seventeenth century to its disintegration nearly three centuries later under pressure from Muslim and French conquerors. Courlander's leisurely narrative style, which maintains tension and drama through dialogue, quick action, and songs, recounts the exploits of the principal kings, djelis (bards), and heroes.   The account includes a detailed recitation of the deeds of Biton Mamari Kulibali, Da Djera, Da Monzon, Ngola Diara, and the epic hero, Bakaridjan Kone. The Introduction discusses Bambara religious and philosophic beliefs, social structure, code of chivalry, and prestige and influence of the djeli.

174. Creel, J. Luke, and Bai Gai Kiahon. *Folk Tales of Liberia.* Illustrated by Carol Hoorn Fraser. Minneapolis, MN: T. S. Denison, 1960. 144p. Grades 5-8.

Sixteen tales of the Vai group of Liberia faithfully adhere to the plot, thought, mood, and purpose of the originals. The tale types and motifs represented here are common throughout Africa in varying versions. Animal trickster stories teach that excessive pride and greed deserve to be humbled, while the stories of people illustrate that only virtuous deeds and moderate behavior can lead to harmonious personal relationships. ''The Handsome Young Man'' is a particularly interesting story that comments on physical beauty and the arrogance and trouble it can lead to. Stories of jealous co-wives and sisters who are opposites in nature further demonstrate that ill-feelings prompt evil deeds. On the community level, tales like ''The Deserted Child'' and ''The Tribes that United'' state that a society built on equality, freedom, and friendship is stronger than one based on exploitation of slaves, warfare, and corruption. It is common sense, hard work, generosity, and patience that ensure happiness for the individual at home and in society.

The stories are elegantly told with an emphasis on the philosophic meaning rather than on the moral. Hence, in ''The Princess Turned Servant'' and ''The Princess and the Prisoner,'' the issue of secluding daughters in order to ensure their virtue and chastity is discussed in detail. The former states that innocence bred in ignorance and goodness without knowledge are worthless, while the latter illustrates that human nature cannot be suppressed indefinitely.

175. Dankwa-Smith, Hannah. *Some Popular Ananse Stories.* Illustrated by Alex. Odjidja, Jr. Accra, Ghana: Waterville, 1975. 113p. Grades 5-8.

Prominent among the twelve trickster stories from Ghana are those of Ananse, the indomitable spider who wins despite great odds. Moral right is seldom on the side of Ananse, except in ''How Ananse Outwitted Kokroko,'' where his daughter is ill-treated by the powerful King Kokroko. In story after story, Ananse's greed, selfishness, and survival instincts prompt him to cheat, and sometimes even kill, friends and opponents alike. Animal characteristics such as why the black ant has a bad smell, why the pig has a long nose, and why a dead snake exposes its stomach are also attributed to the tricks of Ananse. He gets his just rewards when he approaches the creator to exchange his wife for one without a mouth, so that he can eat all the food. The creator gives him one with a large stomach and a mouth hidden under the armpit. When even more food is being consumed than before, Ananse acknowledges defeat and returns to the creator for his original wife, Okodor. Ananse's behavior raises moral and philosophic questions on how far one should go in order to survive. Surprisingly, in the stories of human tricksters, justice is always on the side of the ''good'' characters. The book is poorly illustrated and produced.

176. Dee, Ruby. *Tower to Heaven.* Illustrated by Jennifer Bent. New York: Holt, 1991. N.p. Preschool-Grade 3.
    In this Ghanaian folktale, Onyankon, the Sky God, leaves earth to dwell in the heavens when Yaa, the wise old woman of the village, continually hits him with her pestle while chattering away about the joys and sorrows of villagers. When everyone misses the presence of the Sky God, Yaa decides to build a tower to heaven with mortars, but she is one mortar short. It is believed that Yaa is still waiting for one more mortar, while shouting at the god. Bent's brilliant color illustrations capture the humor of the story and portray Asante traditions.

177. _____. *Two Ways to Count to Ten: A Liberian Folktale.* Illustrated by Susan Meddaugh. New York: Holt, 1988. 32p. Grades K-2.
    In this beautifully illustrated folktale, Leopard, the wise king, holds a spear-throwing contest. Any animal who can throw the spear in the air and count to ten before it falls to the ground will be his successor and marry the princess. The animals boast of their prowess and leadership qualities, but not one can pass the test. When all seems lost, a small antelope accepts the challenge and counts to ten by twos, instead of by ones, and wins the contest. This folktale not only teaches young children to count, but it also tells them that intelligence and not physical strength wins the prize.

178. Ekwensi, Cyprian. *The Boa Suitor.* Illustrated by John Cottrell. Junior Readers Series. Nairobi, Kenya: Heinemann, 1990. Originally published in 1966. 56p. Grades 3-5.
    Prominent in this collection of sixteen stories are exploits of the trickster tortoise, village maidens looking for suitors, and women longing to have children. In addition, there are wonder tales, pourquoi tales, and moral tales that expose human foibles. *The Great Elephant Bird*, another set of folktales by Ekwensi, has all the representative tale types with an emphasis on stories of supernatural creatures and magical happenings. Ekwensi's vigorous narration, which includes songs and choric responses, focuses on the interesting plots and predicaments of the characters, instead of on the lessons to be learned.

179. _____. *The Rainmaker and Other Stories.* Illustrated by Prue Theobalds. African Reader's Library Series. Ibadan, Nigeria: African Universities Press, 1965. 78p. Grades 5-7.

Written in Ekwensi's typically economic style, this collection of folktales and short stories narrates incidents covering a wide range of experiences. There are stories about lost pets, apprehending smugglers, a little boy who can make rain, school bullies, and Ekwensi's favorite topic of the volatile nature of Hausa men and their vendettas over women, power, and wealth.

180. *Folk Stories from The Gambia.* Book 1. Banjul, The Gambia: Book Production and Material Resource Unit, Ministry of Education, 1985. 14p. Grades K-3.

Compiled at a Production Workshop, the four stories in this slim volume illustrate basic moral values and the art of living successfully in a community. Hence, Diamond rewards the hardworking man; Donkey is sad because of his antisocial habits; Hyena's greed is exposed; and Lion displays his honorable nature by keeping a promise. The engaging narrative style emphasizes the choices presented to each character, rather than the moral lessons.

181. Foston, Mike. *The Animal Story Book-2.* Stories and Songs from Sierra Leone. Freetown, Sierra Leone: People's Educational Association of Sierra Leone, 1985. 30p. Grades 1-3.

This collection of thirteen tales is part of an ongoing project of the People's Educational Association to collect and translate stories, songs, riddles, and proverbs from different areas of Sierra Leone. While the book is poorly produced, the stories are interestingly told with fast-moving plots, vigorous dialogue, and ensuing moral lessons. A majority are animal fables that uphold the virtues of unity, common sense, obedience to parents, and using one's wit. There are also three tales that provide explanations for why mosquitoes buzz in people's ears, why the tortoise's back is cracked, and why all animals are enemies. These tales are popular throughout Africa, and some like "The Old Man and His Children," "The Monkey and the Shark," and "The Leopard and the Monkey" can be found in the *Panchatantra,* a collection of fables from India.

182. Fuja, Abayomi. *Fourteen Hundred Cowries: Traditional Stories of the Yoruba.* Ibadan, Nigeria: University Press, 1986. 108p. Grades 4-8.

A variety of tales--such as stories of animals and people, trickster tales, fairy tales, and heroic legends--represent the rich oral heritage of the Yorubas. "The Twins" and "The Orphan Boy and the Magic Twigs" celebrate courage, an upright moral character, and the harmony that can exist between humans and nature. Fuja's leisurely narration makes liberal use of songs and dialogue to engage the interest of the reader, as well as creating an actual storytelling experience.

For additional examples of Yoruba folktales refer to *Olode the Hunter* (Harcourt, Brace & World, 1968), retold by Harold

Courlander with Ezekiel A. Eshugbayi. Prominent in this collection are stories of the Yoruba trickster hero, Ijapa the tortoise, who, like Ananse the spider, is both intelligent and an embodiment of evil forces and bad behavior.

183. Gerson, Mary Joan. *Why the Sky Is Far Away: A Nigerian Folktale.* Illustrated by Carla Golembe. Boston: Little, Brown, 1992. Text originally published in 1974. N.p. Preschool-Grade 2.
Reminiscent of the Biblical account of the expulsion of Adam and Eve from paradise, this Bini pourquoi tale explains why the sky is so far away. When the world was created, people could just reach up to the sky for all the food they needed, but human greed, wastefulness, and disregard for nature forces the sky to recede. People are compelled to grow their own food. Gerson sets the tale in the Bini kinship era of the sixteenth and eighteenth centuries in order to capture the achievements of West African civilizations. Golembe's use of bright colors, bold figures, and Nigerian motifs gives force and power to the myth.

184. Guy, Rosa, trans. and adapt. *Mother Crocodile.* Translated from the French "Maman-Caimon" by Birago Diop. Illustrated by John Steptoe. New York: Delacorte, 1981. N.p. Grades 2-4.
This Senegalese folktale is intended to teach respect for the wisdom of elders. When Dia, Mother Crocodile, snaps at Golo the Monkey, he spreads vicious rumors that she is crazy. Golo even convinces Dia's children that their mother is mad, especially because she tells stories of African wars and the exploitation by merchants, hunters, and slavers. The truth is that Mother Crocodile is wise and has learned from the experience of past generations. Her children come to respect her only when their lives are endangered by another war, and they are being hunted for their skins. This tale can also be read as a political allegory that universalizes the past history of Africa by warning nations to guard against war and human greed.

185. Hagher, Iyorwuese Harry. *Modern Kwagh-hir Stories for the Young.* Vol. 1. Illustrated by Daniel Nyikwagh. Ibadan, Nigeria: Y-Books, 1987. 44p. Grades 3-5.
Based on the oral tradition of the Tiv Kwaghlon and Kwagh-hir, eight stories are retold in a contemporary context and idiom. Mr. Hare, the trickster, is an enigmatic figure who outwits others to uphold justice and peace, but at times he becomes the victim of his own greed, excessive pride, and intelligence. Another trickster figure is Mr. Toad who defeats Mr. Elephant in a race through cooperation and resourcefulness. Intended to educate the young, each story ends with a moral lesson.

186. Haley, Gail E. *A Story, A Story.* Illustrated by reteller. New York: Atheneum, 1970. N.p. Grades K-3.
Winner of the 1971 Caldecott Medal, this folktale relates the origin of the Ananse stories. Once, all the stories belonged to Nyame, the Sky

God, but Ananse purchased them with a leopard, hornets, and Mmoatia, the fairy-whom-men-never-see. Hence, the cycle of Ananse stories, which celebrate the successful exploits of small, defenseless men or animals against great odds, scattered to the corners of the world. Haley's colorful woodcut illustrations and narrative style capture the culture and lifestyle of an African village.

A more detailed version of this Akan myth is *Spider and the Sky God* (Troll, 1993) by Deborah M. Newton Chocolate. Dave Albers' modern art offers interesting material for comparison of styles, cultural details, and interpretation.

187. Jablow, Alta, trans. and adapt. *Gassire's Lute: A West African Epic.* Illustrated by Leo and Diane Dillon. New York: Dutton, 1971. 47p. Grades 4-8.

Believed to be composed in its present form no later than the seventeenth century, this West African legend is translated and adapted from Leo Frobenius' German recording in 1909. *Gassire's Lute* is part of a still earlier and greater epic, the *Dausi*, now lost with only a few scattered fragments remaining, that chronicled the legendary history of the Soninke, especially the rise and fall of their city-state, Wagadu. The events of *Gassire's Lute,* which Jablow believes took place before the beginning of the Christian era, narrate the fall of Dierra, the first Wagadu, and celebrate the heroism of Gassire, son of the last Soninke king of the Fasa dynasty and founder of the bardic tradition or griot caste. Gassire's vanity and restlessness for fame are responsible for the downfall of his kingdom and his continual wars with the Boroma and Burdama, two Berber groups of the Sahara Desert. In fulfillment of a prophecy that he will gain immortality through the lute after suffering pain on the battlefield, Gassire leads his people and his sons into one battle after another, weakening Dierra and losing seven sons in his quest for fame. With the loss of Dierra and his personal suffering, his magical lute sings of what his heart and soul have felt keenly. Words outlast material accomplishments, and it is only through songs that immortality is achieved.

The Dillons' folk art and Jablow's evocative verse express Gassire's human yearnings and feelings. The epic, introductory essay, and glossary give information on historical events and cultural details like the caste system among the Soninke.

188. Johnevi, Eta. *Feed Me For Ever.* Tema, Ghana: Ghana Publishing Corporation, 1989. 52p. Grades 4-6.

Set at a time when human body parts lived separately, this rather long pourquoi tale explains why Hand was punished with feeding Mouth forever. The narrative is enriched by details of rural life and scenery, threat to crops from wild animals, necessity of medicine men in times of adversity, and importance of unity among people.

189. Keelson, M. B. *Story Time with the Animals.* Tema, Ghana: Ghana Publishing Corporation, 1974. 49p. Grades 2-4.

Kofi, a young boy who is kind to animals, joins his animal friends in a storytelling session where they narrate their personal experiences. Most of the stories center on human cruelty to animals; however, Kofi's story has an interesting twist. When an antelope is killed by Kofi's father, the animals send Mosquito to confiscate the gun. Kofi's father agrees, but cleverly offers Mosquito some palm-wine. Mosquito, who becomes addicted to wine, forgets his mission and stays on to drink peoples' blood when the wine is finished. Ever since then mosquitoes have fed on human blood.

190. Kimmel, Eric A. *Ananse and the Moss-Covered Rock.* Illustrated by Janet Stevens. New York: Holiday House, 1988. N.p. Grades K-2.

When Ananse finds a magical moss-covered rock, he uses its power to trick the larger animals out of their food. Little Bush Deer, who has witnessed all, outwits Ananse at his own game. Children will be amused by Stevens' portrayal of animal life, especially the depiction human material comforts.

191. Kuwabong, Dannabang. *Naa Kcnga: A collection of Dagaaba Folktales.* Accra, Ghana: Woeli Publishing Services, 1992. 81p. Grades 8-12.

Kuwabong recreates an actual storytelling session by organizing eleven Dagaaba folktales around the framework of village youth narrating stories night after night while shelling groundnuts. The villagers entertain themselves with humorous stories of the unfaithfulness and witchery of wives, the treachery of men, the cruelty of power-hungry chiefs, and their awe of supernatural powers, especially in times of drought. Without sounding moralistic, the stories also convey ancient group wisdom and cultural beliefs to the younger generation. The stories become part of living experience when juxtaposed against the playful banter and teasing of the villagers, interruptions in the storytelling and the task of shelling nuts, details of activities between stories, and comments on the stories in relation to their lives. The author-narrator's prose style captures the flavor of the Dagaaba language and the frank, sometimes coarse, conversation of the villagers.

192. Lantum, Daniel, ed. *Tales of Nso.* Illustrated by J. Jarvies. African Reader's Library Series. Lagos, Nigeria: African Universities Press, 1969. Originally published by the Nso Historical Society, Cameroon. 76p. Grades 5-7.

Collected by members of the Nso Historical Society, the twelve folktales in this volume are representative of the varied Nso tales of animals, hunters, ogres, princesses, and simple folk. Prominent among these tales are those of the trickster Wanyeto, sometimes seen as an anteater and sometimes as a cannibal man, and Kpuntir the rat-hunter. The lively narratives infuse songs, details of Nso rural life, and cultural beliefs to provide information as well as a storytelling experience.

193. Maddern, Eric. *The Fire Children: A West African Creation Tale.* Illustrated by Frane Lessac. New York: Dial, 1993. N.p. Grades K-3.

This Akan creation myth explains the origin of the earth, moon, stars, and, above all, the various peoples who inhabit the earth. When Nyame, the Sky God, creates the earth, two spirit people, Aso Yaa and Kwaku Ananse, accidentally fall to earth. To avoid loneliness, they form children out of clay, bake them in the fire, and then breathe life into them. However, as they bake a daily batch of clay figures, Nyame visits them for varying lengths of time, hence resulting in children of different shades and colors. Whether black, brown, white, yellow, red, or pink, the first parents love their children equally. Both the retelling and the illustrations--which use folk motifs and a flat dimension--emphasize global harmony and oneness.

194. Martin, Francesca. *The Honey Hunters.* Illustrated by reteller. Cambridge, MA: Candlewick, 1992. Originally published in 1992 by Walker Books, London. N.p. Preschool-Grade 2.

According to this Ngoni tale, the harmonious life of the forest is shattered when the honey bird tempts a boy and the larger animals to a honeycomb. In their greed to get the most honey, the animals quarrel among themselves till the boy commands them to stop. Once calm is restored, the honey bird continues to tempt everyone with his call. The illustrations capture the opulence of nature through rich details of the varied plant and animal life. Despite the permanent strife among animals, the illustrations continue to portray the forest as a peaceful paradise.

195. McDermott, Gerald. *Anansi the Spider: A Tale from the Ashanti.* Illustrated by reteller. New York: Holt, Rinehart and Winston, 1972. N.p. Preschool-Grade 2.

Adapted from his animated film version, McDermott very successfully conveys a sense of continual motion through bold geometric illustrations of the sequential phases of every incident in this tale. Ananse's life is saved by the combined effort of his six sons, each possessing a unique gift. When Ananse cannot decide who should be rewarded with the mysterious shining ball he finds in the forest, he asks the Sky God to hold it for him. Hence, this folktale also offers an explanation for why the moon shines in the sky at night.

196. _____. *Zomo the Rabbit: A Trickster Tale from West Africa.* Illustrated by reteller. San Diego: Harcourt Brace Jovanovich, 1992. N.p. Preschool-Grade 2.

Brightly colored modern art and a simple text combine in this delightful story of Zomo's desire to attain wisdom. He earns this gift by performing three impossible tasks--to get the scales of Big Fish, the milk of Wild Cow, and the tooth of Leopard. Zomo's wit and cunning enable him to trick the larger animals, and he is rewarded with the wisdom to be cautious.

197. Morgan, Kemi. *Legends from Yorubaland.* Ibadan, Nigeria: Spectrum, 1988. 100p. Grades 4-6.

    Based on the collections of several renowned scholars, this book provides a general overview of Yoruba folklore. There are creation myths, stories of the gods, legend of the founding of Ife, heroic tales, origin of festivals, a Cinderella story, trickster tales, and realistic tales intended to regulate human behavior. Morgan's engaging narratives excite the imagination and give explanations for Yoruba social and cultural beliefs.

198. Niane, Djibril Tamsi. *Sundiata: An Epic of Old Mali.* Translated from the French *Soundjata, ou l'Epopee Mandingue* by G.D. Pickett. Harlow, Essex, England: Longman, 1965. 96p. Grades 7-12.

    This retelling of Sundiata's heroic deeds is based on the words of Mamadou Kouyate, an obscure traditionist griot from the village of Djeliba Koro. In narrating the extraordinary events of Sundiata's birth, difficult childhood, exile, and triumphant return to his empire, Niane retains the conventions of an actual storytelling session. His richly poetic narrative style maintains the tension and drama of Sundiata's adventures and achieves objectivity and distance through the recitation of genealogies, inclusion of epithets and maxims, and editorial comments on the events. The text clearly conveys the role of the griot as the counsellor of kings; recorder of customs, traditions, and principles of government; depository of oaths sworn by ancestors; conserver of history; and teacher of wisdom. Older readers interested in a more detailed version of the Sundiata epic are referred to Camara Laye's *The Guardian of the Word* (Fontana/Collins, 1980), translated from the French by James Kirkup.

199. Nkoso, E. *How Ato Killed the Dragon.* Illustrated by Tanueh Borsah. Accra, Ghana: Adwinsa, 1983. 10p. Grades 2-4.

    Traditional fairy tale motifs combine with the symbols of Western civilization in this story from Ghana. The plot focuses on how Ato, a brave but ordinary-looking man, rescues an overprotected young girl, Ama, from the lair of a dragon. Although the misadventure is a result of Ama ignoring her parents' warning against talking to strangers, the moral does not mar the interest generated by the events.

200. Opare, Agyei. *The Cock, the Hen and the Chicks.* Illustrated by Alex Odjida. Accra, Ghana: Waterville, 1971. 16p. Grades K-2.

    This easy-to-read book will help beginners to improve their reading skills and acquire information on the physical characteristics of a rooster, hen, and chicks. In addition, the rudimentary storyline also depicts a nuclear family and the concept of time and growth.

201. Owusu-Nimoh, Mercy. *The Walking Calabash and Other Stories.* Tema, Ghana: Ghana Publishing Corporation, 1977. 71p. Grades 2-4.

    Six folktales and a modern story both instruct and entertain readers. There are stories that teach caution, leadership qualities, rewards of hard work, and the necessity of using cunning to outwit enemies.

Owusu-Nimoh's prose, which is an ideal blend of narration, description, and dramatic plot, holds the interest of readers. "The Adventures of a River" is an especially delightful story that describes the changing personality of a river as it journeys from its source in the hills to its delta near the sea.

202. Robinson, Adjai. *Singing Tales of Africa.* Illustrated by Christine Price. New York: Scribner's, 1974. 80p. Grades 3-6.

The reteller's experience as a storyteller on Radio Sierra Leone is reflected in his combination of narrative and song in seven folktales of the Krios and Yoruba groups. Readers/listeners are invited to participate by chanting songs and refrains and by imitating the sounds of animals and people. There are pourquoi tales that explain why the baboon has a shining seat and why there is death and sickness on earth; there are stories that explore the relationship between mothers and daughters; and there are realistic and wonder tales that teach the valuable lessons of respect for elders and obedience to parents. "Mother-in-Law, Today is Shake-head Day!" is interesting because of its references to the early contact between the Krios of Sierra Leone and Western civilization. Whatever the subject, Robinson's lively prose and Price's fluid woodcuts capture the informality, warmth, and excitement of an actual storytelling session.

203. Saro-Wiwa, Ken. *The Singing Anthill: Ogoni Folk Tales.*   London, Lagos and Port Harcourt: Saros, 1991. 142p. Grades 6-8.

Stories of Kuru, the trickster tortoise, embody not only the culture and wisdom of the Ogoni of Nigeria, but also the universal traits of human beings all over the world. The numerous exploits of Kuru reveal the difficulties of peasant life in the eastern delta of the Niger; importance of respect and equality for wives in a polygamous society; necessity of arranging suitable marriages for children; just punishment for crimes; and need to consult an oracle when problems are beyond human intelligence. The stories also embody the lessons of loyalty, honesty, wit and cunning, and fulfilling one's obligations, and warn against excessive greed, pride, fear, and gossip.

Saro-Wiwa holds the interest of readers by focusing on the plot rather than on character development. Crisp dialogues and accompanying songs add to the "oral" quality of the narration and make the tales highly suitable for storytelling.

204. Sierra, Judy. *The Elephant's Wrestling Match.* Illustrated by Brian Pinkney. New York: Dutton, 1992. N.p. Grades K-2.

In this folktale from Cameroon, the mighty elephant is humbled when he challenges the animals to a wrestling match. He defeats the leopard, crocodile, and rhinoceros, but it is the weak and tiny bat that drops him to the ground by entering his ear and causing pain. The tension, excitement, and quick movements are deftly captured in Pinkney's scratchboard drawings.

205. Tutuola, Amos. *Yoruba Folktales*. Illustrated by Kola Adesokan. Ibadan, Nigeria: Ibadan University Press, 1986. 58p. Grades 4-6.

Seven tales display the richness and variety of Yoruba folklore. There are stories of Ajantala the evil spirit, the desperation of a childless couple, problems of overindulging a child, magical transformations, jealousy among co-wives, and exploits of the cunning tortoise. Tutuola's vigorous narrative engages the interest of readers; however, Adesokan's line drawings lack grace and appeal.

206. Ugorji, Okechukwu K. *The Adventures of Torti: Tales from West Africa*. Illustrated by Brenda Pinkston. Trenton, NJ: Africa World Press, 1991. 66p. Grades 4-7.

Ten Igbo tales of the trickster tortoise have been linked together to give the collection organic unity. As clever Torti goes through his adventurous life, he both dupes and is fooled by other animals till he realizes that he does not have the sole monopoly on smartness and wisdom. Ugorji's style will appeal to Western children as he focuses on the humorous aspects of Torti's behavior, maintains the fast pace of the plots, and uses a modern, colloquial idiom.

207. Ukoli, N., and M. Olomu. *The Antelope That Hurried*. Benin City, Nigeria: Ethiope Publishing Corporation, 1975. 13p. Grades K-2.

Through the antics of a young antelope who just cannot sit still, this didactic story teaches children to listen to the advice of elders. The lively antelope is so excited about the dance in the forest that he starts dancing from morning and scoffs at his mother's and grandmother's warnings to wait till the evening. Just before the dance, he breaks a leg and has to miss all the fun.

208. Vormawor, Patience O. *Afua and the Magic Calabash*. Accra, Ghana: Adwinsa, 1983. 14p. Grades 2-4.

Some of the familiar motifs of the Cinderella story are present in this Ghanaian folktale of Afua, an orphan who is overworked and physically abused by an aunt. As in the European version, a supernatural being, Mother Tortoise, approaches the kind and virtuous Afua and rewards her with a magical calabash. With the help of the calabash, Afua is able to perform all her household chores and eat good food. Once the aunt discovers the calabash, she tries to first control it and then destroy it, but the calabash burns the wicked aunt to ashes. Afua is now cared for by a kindly old woman and, eventually, she marries the chief and lives happily ever after. Another Cinderella tale which employs the motif of the magical calabash is Obi Onyefulu's *Chinye* (Viking, 1994).

209. Wisniewski, David. *Sundiata: Lion King of Mali*. Illustrated by reteller. Photographs by Lee Salsbery. New York: Clarion, 1992. N.p. Grades K-3.

This picture book version of the Sundiata epic is based on *Sundiata: An Epic of Old Mali* by Niane (see entry # 198). Wisniewski retains the dignified tone of the original and conveys the courage and determination of the epic hero. The unique illustrations reflect painstaking research and artwork. Details of clothing, architecture, and lifestyle are based on the history and culture of Mali and on motifs from pottery and textile patterns. The illustrations consist of paper cutouts of each intricate detail, which are later assembled with foam tape and photo mountings. The completed pictures are then photographed, hence depicting light and shadow. Wisniewski's training as a puppeteer specializing in shadow puppetry is evident: he is able to present a full scene with depth, perspective, and multiplicity of action. A detailed Note recounts the history of Mali and the role of the griot in recording significant events and deeds of kings.

FICTION

210. Achebe, Chinua. *Chike and the River*. Junior Readers Series. Nairobi, Kenya: Heinemann, 1990. Originally published in 1966. 66p. Grades 4-6.
   Achebe's artistic and structural skills are evident in this simple story of an adolescent's growth and self-discovery. When eleven-year-old Chike is sent to Onitsha to study and improve his chances in life, he is both awed by the technological advancements of city life and dismayed by Onitsha's impersonal and self-serving values. His mother's warning not to go near the river Niger becomes the personal challenge that transforms him from a shy and withdrawn boy to one capable of achieving his true potential. To fulfill his quest, he undergoes many hardships to procure the shilling needed for the ferry ride, but, ultimately, he earns it quite easily by washing a car. While stranded on the other side of the river, he stumbles on a band of thieves and bravely reports it to the police. Overnight, he becomes a hero and is offered a scholarship to continue his studies. The Niger symbolizes the inner obstacles he had to overcome in order to broaden his horizons.

211. Adedeji, 'Remi. *The Fat Woman*. Illustrated by Ade. Oloye. Junior African Literature Series. Ibadan, Nigeria: Onibonoje, 1973. 7p. Grades 1-3.

212. _____. *Papa Ojo and His Family*. Illustrated by Ade. Oloye. Junior African Literature Series. Ibadan, Nigeria: Onibonoje, 1973. 9p. Grades 1-3.
   Both books have the repetitive style and stilted, choppy sentences sometimes associated with easy-to-read books; however, the vocabulary is too difficult to qualify these books for beginners. The plot and subject matter are equally uninteresting. *Papa Ojo and His Family* describes the weekly routine of the family members, while *The Fat Woman* recounts the efforts of a woman to lose weight. The latter book, in particular, is objectionable because it promotes the stereotype that obese women are lazy and slothful. The illustrations, although accurate, are unattractive.

213. Alexander, Lloyd. *The Fortune-Tellers*. Illustrated by Trina Schart Hyman. New York: Dutton, 1992. N.p. Grades K-3.

A young carpenter who is dissatisfied with his trade goes to a visiting fortuneteller to find out what the future holds for him. The enigmatic predictions that he will be rich if he can earn a lot of money and that he will have a happy life if he can avoid misery satisfy the carpenter. As luck would have it, the fortuneteller mysteriously disappears from his balcony, and the carpenter is mistaken for him. The carpenter is blessed with riches and happiness because he uses his wit and presence of mind to fulfill the role thrust upon him. The misadventures of the old fortuneteller, in contrast, are hilarious as he falls from the balcony onto a passing bullock cart that takes him to the jungle. This story will generate an interesting discussion of fate and the role of fortunetellers in people's lives.

Hyman's colorful illustrations are based on her many trips to Cameroon. Each picture captures the vibrant and pulsating life of a village, which includes details of natural scenery, people and animals.

214. Anane, F. K. *Kofi Mensah*. Illustrated by Owusu Banahene. Accra: Ghana Publishing House, 1968. 60p. Grades 3-5.

This didactic story is intended to inspire young boys with the dream of success through education and hard work. Set in the early years of Ghana's independence, the story catalogs the major events in the life of Kofi Mensah from babyhood till he gets a good job as a junior assistant in a business concern. Kofi's childhood in rural Berekum is filled with fun and play as well as hard work at school and on his parents' coco farms. The author provides a detailed description of the joyous Kwafie festival of the Asante when the spirits of the dead chiefs are invoked, the royal stools are purified, and the current chief is honored. Kofi's carefree life at home ends when he enrolls in a senior school in the city, because at that time rural areas did not have secondary schools. He has to adjust to living in the home of a trader with two wives and performing household chores to pay for his board and lodging. However, he continues to work diligently and is rewarded with success. While respect for traditions and ancestors is important, this story promotes the agenda that village youth must get a Western education in order to progress.

215. Anno, S. W. *We Went Hunting*. Accra, Ghana: Waterville, 1970. 25p. Grades 3-5.

This simple story describes the early morning hunting trip of three eleven-year-old boys. The narrative pauses to provide details of village life, hunting gear, and the importance of hunting as a supplement to agricultural economy. Graphic descriptions of killing small animals, especially the rodents who enter homes, may disturb Western readers. However, the text makes it clear that mice in homes are unwanted pests and that the only way one can eat meat is by killing animals. As hunters, the boys are taught not to torture animals, but to learn compassion--and practical sense--by not killing the very young.

216. Appiah, Peggy. *Gift of the Mmoatia.* Illustrated by Nii O. Quao. Tema, Ghana: Ghana Publishing Corporation, 1972. 110p. Grades 3-5.
    The themes of international goodwill and universality of experiences overpower the plot and characters of this novel set in Kumasi, Ghana, and the English town of Oakenton. The lives of two protagonists, Anne Marie Brooke and Abena Mensah, illustrate that their family relationships, childhood joys and fears, and basic values and beliefs are the same regardless of cultural differences. Both the Ghanaian and British grandmothers in the story believe in supernatural creatures like the mmoatia and fairies, and the girls' faith in these beings is central to resolving the crises that face the two families. While there are no great dramatic scenes or characters, this is a simple story of friendship, faith, and racial harmony.

217. Asare, Meshack, illus. *I Am Kofi.* Accra-Tema, Ghana: Ghana Publishing Corporation, 1971. 15p. Preschool-Grade 2.

218. _____. *Mansa Helps at Home.* Accra-Tema, Ghana: Ghana Publishing Corporation, 1973. 15p. Preschool-Grade 2.
    These brightly illustrated easy-to-read books describe the lives of a brother and sister at home. As Kofi and Mansa recount the chores they perform at home, it becomes clear that each is being trained for his or her specific role. While Kofi fetches water, runs errands, and helps his father on the farm, Mansa cooks, cleans, and cares for the baby. Surprisingly, despite the emphasis on education in postcolonial Africa, there is no mention of school in either of the books.

219. _____. *Tawia Goes to Sea.* Illustrated by author. Accra, Ghana: Ghana Publishing Corporation, 1970. N.p. Grades K-3.
    With this story of a young boy's longing to go to sea, Asare won international recognition for the high quality of his picture books. Tawia's determination to become a fisherman finds expression in fantasy play with a toy boat he makes from a coconut frond. His uncle is so impressed that he takes Tawia fishing the next day. The illustrations capture both the changing emotions of Tawia as well as the hectic activity on the beach.

220. Asiedu, Michael. *Fifi and His Dog.* Tema, Ghana: Ghana Publishing Corporation, 1977. 25p. Grades 3-5.
    While the book has no storyline apart from cataloging the habits and role of Fifi's pet dog, it does, however, provide a rare glimpse into the life of a well-to-do urban family living in Accra.

221. Beier, Ulli. *The Stolen Images.* Cambridge, England: Cambridge University Press, 1976. 55p. Grades 5-7.
    The didactic content of this short novel completely overpowers the plot and characters. It condemns Nigeria's neocolonial school curriculum and missionary education for teaching young Nigerians to despise their religion as backward and superstitious. As the novel opens, Olu guiltily succumbs to the mystery, excitement, and lively

celebrations of the Sango festival despite the warnings of his Christian teacher. His idea of right and wrong, good and bad, truth and superstition are further shaken when he meets a sophisticated journalist from Lagos who offers him another perspective--that of awe and respect for his traditions. With this new insight, Olu comes to despise the crass materialism and utter lack of respect for his beliefs displayed by the white antique dealer who wants to buy the holy idols. The images are no longer primitive and grotesque to Olu; he sees them as exquisite pieces of art. When the images are stolen from the shrine, Olu goes to Lagos to seek the help of the journalist. The antique smuggler is apprehended by the authorities, and Olu is acclaimed a hero. This episode prompts Olu and his classmates to accept Sango, the legendary hero who was later deified. Olu takes a job in the Sango theater so that he can make others aware of his rich cultural heritage. Leaving school temporarily is not considered a big loss because initiation into one's culture is just as important as book knowledge. Photographs and drawings of Sango festivities and artwork illustrate the story.

222. Berry, Erick. *Juma of the Hills: A Story of West Africa.* Illustrated by author. New York: Harcourt, Brace: 1932. 260p. Grades 6-8.
    Set before the colonial era, this fast-paced novel recreates the world of slave raids, the opulence of the Hausa kingdom, and the Emir's efforts to end slavery. The narrative focuses on the adventures of the plucky heroine, Juma, who escapes from her Fulani captors; is rescued by a Hausa trader; and, finally, is installed in the Emir's palace in Katsina. Berry exploits the exotic atmosphere of Islamic and Hausa culture by including episodes of harem life, snake charmers, horsemanship, festival of Ramadan, and praise drumming. Juma's story ends happily when she returns to her village on a diplomatic mission to end slavery. The overwhelming impression created of the Hausa kingdom is one of decadent hedonism, arbitrary justice, and nonchalant political control by the Emir. Slavery, however, is not dreaded by all. Two of Juma's fellow captives actually assist in the slave raid and long for the social opportunities of Katsina.

223. Bess, Clayton. *Story for a Black Night.* Oakland, CA: Parnassus; Boston: Houghton Mifflin, 1982. 84p. Grades 6-8.
    The rhythmic force of the ''pidgin'' English, the references to the majesty and beauty of nature, and the deep emotions evoked by the simple story surround the novel with an epic aura. On a dark, stormy night when electricity is cut off, a Liberian father tells his son the story of another black night when he learned firsthand of good and evil--not as the Christian missionaries and animistic religions taught it, but from the heart and love of his mother. That night, his Ma gave refuge to some strangers in the middle of the night. Early next morning, the strange woman and grandmother disappeared, leaving behind a baby with smallpox. Rejecting the advice of her mother to let the baby die, Ma's maternal instinct prompted her to care for the baby. The family was ostracized by the villagers--even by Ma's sister

Musu--and they were left alone as everyone got smallpox. The stranger's baby recovered, while Ma's baby died, and Ma was horribly disfigured. The tragedy taught them the true meaning of beauty, family love, selflessness, and good and evil.

Ma's actions are contrasted with the choices made by Musu, who drove the strangers to her sister's house; by the villagers, who showed no heart to the strangers or to the unsuspecting Ma and her family by sending the disease their way; and by the mother and grandmother, who left the sick baby in a stranger's hut. Lest one condemns them, the story confronts each reader with the choices the characters had to make. How would you have reacted if a total stranger had left a baby with smallpox at your doorstep? Would you have cared for it and risked disease and death for yourself and your children? Would you have abandoned your baby or grown-up daughter if she had a deadly disease? The story raises other philosophic and legal issues as well. Once the family is cured of smallpox, the grandmother returns to demand the baby, but Ma claims the baby as her own and offers the body of her dead daughter instead. The whole village thinks it morally just that the old woman should die of loneliness and guilt for first abandoning her grandchild and then her own daughter.

224. Burroughs, Edgar Rice. *Tarzan of the Apes*. New York: Ballantine, 1983. Originally published in 1912 by Frank A. Munsey. 245p. Grades 9-adult.

First in a series of books on Tarzan, the son of an English aristocrat who was raised by gorillas in the jungles of West Africa, *Tarzan of the Apes* reflects its author's familiarity with the popular theories on evolution and heredity. Although raised by a tribe of apes, Tarzan soon displays his biological superiority to them. By the age of ten, though no match in size and strength, he recognizes he is apart from his tribe by virtue of his power of reasoning and moral superiority. Tarzan's evolution from ape-child to polished Victorian gentleman illustrates that heredity is stronger than environment. He is attracted to books and letters, and he teaches himself to read and write English through picture books, primers, and dictionaries when he has never even heard the English language being spoken. He instinctively makes tools and sliding knots, wears clothes and takes cold baths, evolves sophisticated ideas on religion, and acquires gentlemanly behavior. We see him journeying through the various "stages" of human evolution in a matter of four or five years. Tarzan's moral superiority is exemplified by juxtaposing two scenes of cannibalism-- one by the ape tribe of Kerchak and the other by the human tribe of Mbongi. The details of the rituals are almost exact, emphasizing that developmentally Africans are no different from apes. But when Tarzan starts to eat a man that he has killed, for that is the law of the jungle, his genetic refinement cautions him. Eventually, Tarzan dominates both the apes and Africans by virtue of his superior intellect. Tarzan's adventures had so powerful a hold on readers' imaginations that the stereotypes they popularized persist till today.

225. Chukwuka, J. I. N. *Zandi and the Wonderful Pillow.* Illustrated by Norma Burgin. African Junior Library Series. Lagos, Nigeria: African Universities Press, 1977. 48p. Grades 2-5.

Reality and fantasy merge as the cruel custom of throwing humpbacked babies in the Evil Forest to die is ended. When Zandi is born with a humpback, his parents keep his presence a secret from the chief and villagers till he is sixteen. Zandi's only companions are the folktales his parents have nourished him on and a human skull that he finds in the dry riverbed. The inevitable happens and, according to custom, he is left in the Evil Forest. Like the trickster tortoise of his favorite tales, Zandi survives by stealing, tricking, and using his intelligence. When the Queen of Spirits takes him to the underworld to be sacrificed, his lucky skull helps him to escape on the Queen's magic pillow. The pillow takes him home and provides him with a big house and riches, but Zandi does not ask the pillow to remove his hump. The village elders are impressed by Zandi's ability to escape from the forest and the prosperity he has brought to the entire village. Practical concern for the common good of the village leads the elders to reevaluate the validity of their ancient traditions. They accept that physical handicaps do not indicate an evil soul and that humpbacks can also be self-sufficient and productive.

226. Clifford, Mary Louise. *Salah of Sierra Leone.* Illustrated by Elzia Moon. New York: Crowell, 1975. 184p. Grades 6-8.

This historical novel recreates the political turmoil, ethnic rivalries, and partisan politics that characterized the first decade of Sierra Leonean independence. The focal point, however, is the friendship of two teenage boys, Salah and Luke, which is tested severely because of their differing backgrounds. Salah Lansaissay is a Mende whose sergeant father supports the corrupt prime minister, Albert Margai, of the Sierra Leone People's Party, while Luke Taylor is a Freetown Creole whose family supports Siaka Stevens and the multiparty system. As Salah socializes with the "enemy," he learns firsthand that the stereotypes about Creoles are unfounded. While the Taylors' Western lifestyle is quite different from his traditional rural upbringing, Salah finds them warm and considerate. As the elections draw near, both friends become embroiled in the political situation: Salah warns Mr. Taylor of the army's plan to install Albert Margai as prime minister, even if Siaka Stevens of the opposition party wins; and Luke causes panic and the death of a child when he and a companion light some firecrackers in a crowded political rally. When Salah returns to his ancestral village, he is questioned by the secret Poro Council about his responsibility for his father's arrest. Both friends realize that they must face their difficult situations in order to earn respect and peace of mind. Their friendship symbolizes crossing barriers--Creole versus Mende, Christianity versus traditional religion, urban versus rural--for the sake of building a strong nation. Details of Sierra Leonean history, account of the founding of Freetown with freed slaves between 1787 and 1860, and descriptions of Freetown are deftly integrated into the story to add depth and meaning.

227. Cousins, Linda. *Huggy Bean and the Origin of the Magic Kente Cloth*. Illustrated by Chris Hall. New York: Gumbs and Thomas, 1986. 21p. Grades 1-3.

As she travels through time and place to the Ghana of King Tutu's time, Huggy Bean discovers the glory of ancient Ghana and the significance of the magic kente cloth that has been in her family for generations. Her guide explains the symbolic meaning of the kente designs and narrates the story of the first kente woven by Nana Tah who copied the work of a black and yellow spider making his web. Huggy also learns that she is descended from a great queen mother who said the magic kente cloth would stay in the family as long as it was used for good. As Huggy returns to her world, King Osei Tutu advises her to spread love and goodness, to listen and learn from the wisdom of elders, and to be proud of her African ancestors. The only jarring note is in the illustrations of Huggy who, though she has brown skin, has obviously European features.

228. Ekwensi, Cyprian. *An African Night's Entertainment*. Illustrated by Bruce Onobrakpeya. African Reader's Library Series. Lagos, Nigeria: African Universities Press, 1971. Originally published in 1962. 94p. Grades 6-10.

Wealth, power, social status, and a burning desire to fulfill his wishes lead Mallam Shehu to unfairly win Zainobe, the betrothed of Mallam Abu Bakir. Abu Bakir, hardly a sympathetic character, undergoes years of hardship and, eventually, avenges this insult by using a magical potion that causes Shehu's son, Kyauta, to become a criminal character. Kyauta becomes the agent of Abu Bakir's revenge when he unwittingly kills his father during a robbery. This error breaks the spell, and it is now Kyauta's turn to wreck vengeance on Abu Bakir.

Readers are held captive by the continual action, sensational and violent episodes, and vigorous dialogue. Ekwensi deftly manipulates the perspective by making it difficult to determine who is the protagonist and who the antagonist. The story structure--the frame of a village storyteller challenging his listeners to stay awake throughout the narration--perhaps justifies the paucity of descriptive details and lack of in-depth character delineation.

229. _____. *The Drummer Boy*. Illustrated by George Mogaka. Junior Readers Series. Nairobi, Kenya: Heinemann, 1991. Originally published in 1960. 87p. Grades 4-6.

Believed to be the first book written especially for Nigerian children, *The Drummer Boy* is a picaresque novel that traces the wanderings of Akin, a blind beggar boy abandoned by his parents. A series of episodes narrate his experiences with people who treat him kindly, exploit him, and force him into criminal company, but Akin remains patient, long-suffering, and forgiving. While Ekwensi does create social awareness for the needs and abilities of the handicapped, he does not fully explore the potential of the story. For instance, Akin remains a wooden figure whose character is not developed in psychological depth. It is unclear why Akin resists attempts to place him in a welfare home. Is he afraid of losing his freedom, or has the early rejection by parents made him suspicious of emotional involvement? In the end, he is "controlled" by society, and his gift of enchanting listeners with his music is used to inspire boys in a reformatory to good behavior.

230. _____. *Juju Rock*. Illustrated by Bruce Onobrakpeya. African Reader's Library Series. London: Ginn, 1971. Originally published in 1966 by African Universities Press. 109p. Grades 5-7.

Based on popular British adventure novels, this is the story of a curious student, Rikku, who is lured into a dangerous search for a secret gold mine. With the help of some villagers near Juju Rock, Rikku apprehends the crooks and rescues his white benefactor. This fast-paced adventure employs the stereotypes of the evil secret society, criminal Europeans looking for gold, superstitions and "strange" rituals, wild animals, and an ape-like African. The plot is advanced more by sensationalism and chance rather than by the critical thinking abilities of the young sleuth.

231. _____. *The Motherless Baby*. Junior Readers Series. Nairobi, Kenya: Heinemann, 1990. Originally published in 1980. 96p. Grades 6-12.

Teenage pregnancy, the growing independence of youth in modern Nigeria, and the influence of Western culture are the major themes of this novel. Ngozi, a Westernized young girl, lives independently in the city to pursue her schooling. Her "fast" life and involvement with a popular rock musician lead to her pregnancy. Because of societal norms, fear of parents, and thoughts of her own future, she is forced to abandon her baby. Sobered and matured, she completes her education, gets a job in a bank, and marries well. However, she can never forget her past and is haunted with guilt feelings for her son Pedro and, ironically, is unable to conceive. Ostracized and taunted for being childless, Ngozi secretly goes to a spiritualist who, for a large fee, promises her success. After the birth of her second son, she is forced to steal money from the bank to pay her debt. Tormented by visions and sickness, Ngozi dies a broken woman.

Pedro's story runs parallel to Ngozi's. He is adopted by a loving couple, but there is trouble when he turns out to be the next in succession to a tribal chief. His adoptive parents refuse to give him up and win the custody suit. Despite the love showered on him, Pedro becomes a delinquent, drops out of school, and leaves home to drive taxis. After a serious car accident, he abandons his irresponsible ways and plans to become a doctor.

Both plot and characterization are manipulated to advance the moral theme of *The Motherless Baby*. Long passages condemning Ngozi's pregnancy, her fascination with Western music and culture, and teenage disrespect toward elders are intended to prevent adolescents from going astray. Ngozi's prolonged suffering and inability to conceive are repayment for her sins, which can only end with her death. In contrast, the motives and inner turmoil of Pedro are not explained, and his transformation from a happy and well-adjusted child to a rebellious, disobedient teenager is abrupt. More interesting than this account of youth in Nigeria is the clash between traditional and modern values. Ngozi leaves her modern ways and Christianity to find comfort in traditional medicine and religion. Ogbuka, the medicine man, although materialistic and conniving, has genuine spiritual powers as proven by Ngozi's pregnancy and the mysterious circumstances of his death. Pedro's succession to the leadership of his tribe introduces readers to the validity of tribal law. While the village elders lose the custody suit, they do not abandon their claim on Pedro. They patiently conduct investigations and wait for the opportune moment. After Ngozi's death, they follow all the tribal rituals to have her union with the wayward musician sanctified before Pedro can be installed as their chief. Pedro unites the two opposites of traditions and modernity by introducing modern medicine to the village and fulfilling his traditional role.

232. _____. *The Passport of Mallam Ilia.*   Cambridge, England: Cambridge University Press, 1960. 80p. Grades 6-8.
    Set in the Hausa region of Nigeria in the early 1900s, this is yet another story of lifelong revenge over a beautiful woman. However, unlike *An African Night's Entertainment,* this story ends with the protagonist's mature realization that the teachings of Islam are superior to revenge. When Mallam Ilia wins Zarah in the deadly game of Shanchi, he makes an enemy of another suitor, Mallam Usuman, and the two men relentlessly pursue each other for over forty years. Ekwensi's episodic plot and sparse narrative style trace their adventures till the final chance encounter in a train, where they cause each other's deaths.
    Despite the charge of sensationalism and violence by critics, Ekwensi's works have an undeniable haunting quality that attracts readers. Also, he expresses human nature both in stories of social realism and romantic adventure. Characters and places from earlier novels like *Juju Rock* and *The Drummer Boy* are mentioned in this story, giving his works an organic unity and a sense of depth and verisimilitude that the individual novels appear to lack.

233. Emecheta, Buchi. *The Moonlight Bride.* New York: Braziller, 1983. Originally published in 1980 by Oxford University Press in association with University Press, Ibadan, Nigeria. 77p. Grades 6-9.
    Seen from the perspective of a twelve-year-old girl, this delightful story reveals the importance of a new bride to a rural community in modern Nigeria. Ever since Ngbeke finds out from her best friend and cousin, Ogoli, that a bride is to arrive in their village on the next full moon night, she is curious about the identities of the bride and groom and the reason for the secrecy. She gets the impression that the bride is much sought after and will bring honor to them. The groom turns out to be Chiyei, the village lazy man, whose stump foot and drunken ways have disgraced the village of Odanta. The marriage preparations proceed with gusto, but no one knows till the wedding night that the bride is the highly loved and regarded albino daughter

of a neighboring chief. The clanspeople of Odanta immediately accept her for who she is and make a praise song in honor of her radiance and call her ''Alatriki'' (electricity).

This simple story gives new meaning to the word beauty. Both bride and groom are physically marred through no fault of theirs, but while one possesses the inner beauty of good behavior and a good heart, the other allows his handicap to serve as an excuse for his shiftless ways. Emecheta also describes the harmonious organization of a village comprising of over five hundred relatives whose individual needs are second to the welfare of the entire clan. Emphasis on the pride and strength of the group, respect for the authority of elders, and responsibility for one's expected role ensures the continuance and prosperity of the village. Emecheta sensitively portrays the feelings of co-wives and their children, especially daughters, through the different attitudes of Ogoli and Ngbeke. As the favorite daughter of a senior wife, Ogoli upholds the traditional attitude toward women, while Ngbeke, as the daughter of a ''middle'' wife, is sensitive to implied insults against women and her mother's inferior status.

234. _____. *The Wrestling Match*. New York: Braziller, 1983. Originally published in 1980 by Oxford University Press in association with University Press, Ibadan, Nigeria. 74p. Grades 6-8.

Modern village life with its pastoral beauty and simple pleasures of weekly markets and seasonal festivities is juxtaposed against the very real problems of growing up and the lack of technological advancements. Through the story of sixteen-year-old Okei and his age-mates, Emecheta explores the problems of adolescents born during the Biafra Civil War (1964-1967). Okei and his friends express their resentment toward society through laziness, rude behavior, and acts of nuisance. Their situation is further complicated by their schooling, which sets them above their farming families, yet is not advanced enough to procure them jobs in the city. Okei's uncle schemes with the village elders to provide a source of conflict among these youngsters in order to snap them out of their self-centeredness. A disparaging remark by boys from a neighboring village leads to a wrestling match to settle the dispute. As leader of his group, Okei works hard and responsibly to ensure victory; he even approaches his uncle for training in wrestling. The ''friendly'' match ends in a free fight between the youth of both villages, and it is the elders who prevent the situation from ending in disaster.

As the complex plot unfolds and the central characters unwittingly reveal their stubbornness and false pride, the theme of maturity is developed. The wrestling match serves as a coming of age ritual which provides the characters with experience, knowledge, and self-confidence to assume their future social roles. In addition, Emecheta provides insight into Okei's psychological state of mind: He is a good person whose antisocial behavior is an attempt to cover his hurt and suffering over the death of his parents in the Civil War; his inability to accept his loss; and his guilt at having survived.

Okei's predicament, however, is a universal one. Village youth all over Africa and the world are confronted with conflicts between traditions and modernity, education and illiteracy, and youth and age.

235. Etokakpan, Essien. *The Force of Superstition.* Illustrated by E. O. Oguntonade. Adventures in Africa Series. Ibadan, Nigeria: University Press, in association with Oxford University Press, 1970. 94p. Grades 6-8.

Two stories--one set in the precolonial era and the other in colonial times--are juxtaposed to comment on the radical changes that the Ibibio community of Nigeria experienced with the passing away of its traditions. "The Story of Umo and Amasa" demonstrates family solidarity, respect for gods and rituals, and harmony within the community and among neighbors, while in "The Murder of Obong Ebio," with the coming of Europeans, communal values are replaced by selfishness, power, exploitation, and materialism. Etokakpan succeeds in presenting the objectivity of the modern reader and the emotional experiences of the characters. The fictional element is enhanced by songs, dialogue, descriptions, and extensive passages outlining the history, culture, and beliefs of the Ibibio.

236. Gerson, Mary Joan. *Omoteji's Baby Brother.* Illustrated by Elzia Moon. New York: Walck, 1974. 40p. Grades K-2.

Omoteji feels grown-up and responsible because he can help his mother at the vegetable stand, but the day his baby brother is born, he becomes an outsider. No one needs his services; he is in everyone's way. In his loneliness, he composes a poem expressing his feelings for the new baby and chants it at the baby's naming ceremony. All the guests praise him, and his parents are proud. Once again, Omoteji's self-esteem and confidence are restored.

Western readers will easily identify with this Nigerian boy's predicament and fears. Like children everywhere, Omoteji goes to school, plays with friends, and needs to be reassured of his parents' love. Both text and illustrations are free of the stereotypes of African poverty, even though Omoteji's father is a weaver and his mother a vegetable vendor.

237. Graham, Lorenz. *I, Momolu.* Illustrated by John Biggers. New York: Crowell, 1966. 226p. Grades 5-7.

Set in the newly created country of Liberia, the conflict arises from the imposition of Western civilization on the local villagers. This clash of two opposing lifestyles is seen from the perspective of Momolu, son of Flumbo, a respected member of his tribe. The Liberians are in control of the government and army, and they use military force to establish themselves: they build roads, introduce Western technology and medicine, and promote Christianity. The simple "bush" people are duly awed by American culture, and they acknowledge the inefficacy of their traditions and rituals. When Momolu and his father visit Cape Roberts, they are impressed by the progress they witness. Flumbo overcomes his suspicion of the outsiders and allows his son to be initiated into the church.

As a missionary in Liberia, Graham's agenda is clearly reflected in these words: "He [Momolu] learns the God palaver. By and by he will be what we call civilized. He will live with the Liberians. He will wear their clothes, and someday he will live in a house of iron and have for his wife a woman who will wear shoes." Graham, who has written with feeling about the plight of African Americans in a series of novels, assumes an Eurocentric stance toward African culture and religion.

238. Grifalconi, Ann. *Flyaway Girl*. Illustrated by author. Boston: Little, Brown, 1992. N.p. Grades 1-4.

The transition from the freedom of childhood to the responsibilities of growing up can be traumatic for a girl. Luckily for Nsia, her wise and sensitive mother makes the shift an easy and natural one for her playful daughter. When Nsia is sent to gather light and dark reeds from the banks of the Niger for the Ceremony of Beginnings, she is helped by the ancestral spirits. Instead of playing while the reeds dry, Nsia thinks and thinks for the first time. This experience serves as her initiation into maturity and connects her with her cultural and family heritage.

Grifalconi's creative artwork is a collage of photographs of animals and humans, cutouts, decorative motifs, and paintings of landscapes.

239. _____. *The Village of Round and Square Houses*. Illustrated by author. Boston: Little, Brown, 1986. N.p. Grades K-3.

This Caldecott Honor book describes Osa's happy childhood in the village of Tos, at the foot of Naka Mountain in Cameroon. An evening meal in the women's round hut provides Grifalconi with an opportunity to portray the respect children have for elders, the warm feelings shared by family members, and a lifestyle rich in traditional beliefs. The focal point of this picture book is the myth that explains why women live in round houses and men in square houses. The harmony of the village is ensured because of the separate roles of and boundaries between men, women, and children; yet, they also come together for mutual support and need.

Osa's story is continued in *Darkness and the Butterfly* (Little, Brown, 1987), which focuses on the universal theme of a child's fear of the dark. Grifalconi's evocative text conveys Osa's exuberance during the day and fears at night, and her ultimate triumph over her "monsters" when she discovers her inner "light" with the help of a wise woman and a tiny yellow butterfly. The latest book, *Osa's Pride* (Little, Brown, 1990), deals with another childhood problem--Osa's hurt and loneliness because her father is missing in war. However, Osa's feelings are manifested in foolish pride (which takes readers by surprise because of a lack of preparation by the author). Instead of chiding and scolding Osa, wise Gran'ma Tika uses a colorful story cloth of another proud girl to mirror Osa's behavior. Through this vicarious experience, Osa faces the truth and gains a new awareness of herself. Grifalconi's impressionistic artwork captures the changing moods of Osa, the warmth and concern of her elders, and the details of the rural setting.

240. Guillot, Rene. *The White Shadow*. Translated from the French by Brian Rhys. Illustrated by Faith Jaques. London: Oxford University Press, 1959. 222p. Grades 8-12.

Set against the exotic atmosphere of tribal rituals and magical jujus, thrill of the hunt and bagging trophies, and French colonialism in West Africa is Guillot's philosophy of the harmony between the jungle and primitive man. This theme, which Guillot has explored from various angles in *Sirga, Queen of the African Bush* (Criterion, 1959), *Oworo* (Oxford UP), and *Kpo the Leopard* (Oxford UP), takes on a more complex and mystical tone in *The White Shadow*. This adventure dramatizes the quest for friendship and love when a French game official brings his daughter, Frances, to Lobi Land. There are the obvious visible friendships of Frances, her father, and their associates; and then there are the invisible, mirage-like bonds between Frances and her African sister Yagbo, between the Customs Officer and his shipmate from a previous life, between the cat Malkin and the photograph of Frances' mother, and between the enigmatic Bruce and the lioness. It is in the savage and untamed environment of the African jungle that white colonials discover their kinship with nature, its creatures, and their spiritual selves. Guillot's descriptive prose, powerful characterization, and intricate plot heighten the dramatic tension between fantasy and realism.

241. Hanson, J. O. de Graft. *The People from the Sea*. Tema, Ghana: Ghana Publishing Corporation, 1988. 89p. Grades 4-6.

When Kofu and his sister visit the coastal town of Moree, they are embroiled in the mystery surrounding a robbery. The priest, an accomplice, uses the legend of the founding of the Asebu community to keep people in their homes while the stolen goods are being smuggled out. However, Kofu's curiosity helps him to discover the thieves and report them to the authorities. Details of the legend are deftly incorporated to lend suspense and depth to the story.

242. Hostetler, Marian. *African Adventure*. Illustrated by Esther Rose Graber. Scottdale, PA and Kitchener, ONT: Herald, 1976. 124p. Grades 5-7.

Set in Chad, this do-gooder, missionary novel focuses on the activities of Christian organizations in combatting the world food crisis. The book is demeaning to Chadians because of the constant comparisons between the plenty of the United States and the hot, dirty, and impoverished surroundings of Chad. Statements like, "In America we spend enough on pet food in one year to feed one-third of the world's hungry!" appear frequently. Ironically, the protagonist, Denise Carter, and her family do not accomplish anything substantial to justify even the money spent on their airfare. For eighteen months, they study Arabic, visit an agricultural official, and observe the long line of patients awaiting treatment. Their only concrete task is to help in the distribution of food to fifty of the poorest--two packets of instant breakfast per person once every other day. The relief efforts of the Chadian government are not mentioned. Instead, President Timbabel's government is portrayed as unconcerned with human rights and the religious freedom of Chadian Christians. The experiences of Denise also lead to a debate on the ideologies of two rival church organizations: one wants to save heathen souls by bringing the Gospel to them before they die, while the other wants to nourish their physical bodies without forcing them to convert.

Stripped of its missionary content, *African Adventure* is a charming story of a young girl who finds herself in unfamiliar circumstances. Hostetler successfully captures Denise's fear and discomfort and her sensitivity to racial slurs in addressing the male household help as "boy." There is excitement in her story caused by the chaotic political situation: Denise survives a plane crash, forceable removal to a Yondo youth camp, and capture by rebels. Denise's idealism is constantly rebuffed with statements to the effect that unfairness is a fact of life and that the church is there to make things better. Sensitized to the needs of others, Denise arrives at some visionary insight, but nothing specific is stated.

243. Ike, Chukwuemeka.   *The Potter's Wheel.*   Fontana African Fiction Series. London: Fontana/Collins, 1974. 223p. Grades 7-12.

This superbly crafted and elegantly written novel narrates the experiences of a hopelessly spoilt eight-year-old boy. In-depth character delineation reveals that Obu's lazy, despotic, and selfish behavior is a result of his mother's pampering. The only hardship this privileged child has ever known is the bullying of his friend Samuel; however, physical and verbal abuse, hunger, exploitation, and hard work become his constant companions when his father sends him to live with a strict teacher and his tyrannical wife. When Obu returns home for Christmas, he realizes that his mother's preferential treatment is only a gentler form of oppression that will ultimately lead to an irresponsible and unproductive future. In order to achieve his full potential, he returns to the hated school. Igbo words, customs, details of family life, and conditions in Nigeria during World War II are intricately woven into Obu's experiences.

244. Iroh, Eddie.   *Without a Silver Spoon.*   Ibadan, Nigeria: Spectrum, 1981. 112p. Grades 4-6.

Recipient of the International Board on Books for Young People Certificate of Honour, *Without a Silver Spoon* is a thought-provoking novel about an honest and hardworking rural boy who is falsely accused of stealing money from his classmate. Ure's name is cleared when his schoolteacher plans a sting operation to catch the real culprit. Although the plot is stereotypical, the author's sensitive delineation of Ure's character, descriptions of his humble but happy family life, and importance of traditional values and wisdom lend meaning, depth, and distinction to this story. The message of the book is that every child needs to be trusted completely to be good, but first he or she must earn that trust.

245. Itayemi, Phebean, and Mabel Dove-Danquah. *The Torn Veil and Other Stories*. Illustrated by Gay Galsworthy. Evans Africa Library Series. London: Evans, 1975. Originally published in 1947 by Lutherworth Press, London. 44p. Grades 8-12.

Set in colonial times, four stories focus on the conflict between modernity and traditions in a changing society. In "Payment," traditions are denounced in the form of a charlatan medicine man who is caught cheating a client. The remaining three are consciousness raising stories on the status of women. In each story, the victimized female is victorious against lechery, fickleness, or sexual abuse. In "Anticipation," a chief pays a hundred pounds as bride price for a girl he sees at his anniversary celebrations. When the girl dutifully appears before the chief, she reveals to him that she is already part of his large harem, and that he had paid only fifty pounds for her earlier. Similarly, in "The Torn Veil," an upwardly mobile professional decides that his uneducated wife is no longer socially acceptable. When he informs her of his decision to remarry, he is surprised by her anger and hurt. She leaves him, only to reappear as a ghost on his wedding night to lead him to death. "Nothing So Sweet" is the story of a middle-aged man who marries a girl of seventeen whom he has been courting with gifts of money and food from the time she was two. As a child, Subowa felt uncomfortable when she was fondled and made to sit on Eso's lap, and she grew up hating him. Despite the violent treatment, Subowa avoids consummating the marriage and escapes to the home of two European missionaries who promise to help her.

All four stories are didactic in tone, and the characters and plots are manipulated to denounce everything traditional and non-Western as backward. While the bartering and abuse of women is not acceptable, the authors do not fully explain the customs and social norms surrounding the marriage issue.

246. Lofting, Hugh. *Doctor Doolittle's Post Office*. New York: Stokes, 1923. 359p. Grades 4-6.

What purports to be a charming animal fantasy set in West Africa is, in reality, a racist book denouncing Africans and their institutions, especially their ability to govern. King Koko of Fantippo lacks the administrative skills and personal qualities of an effective ruler; instead, he is childish in his love of trinkets, indolent as he sits at the palace door sucking a lollipop, and gullible in his superstitious beliefs. When he introduces postal service to his kingdom, he is unable to grasp the concept; his motivation is simply to see his "serene and beautiful face" on all the stamps. The stamps are issued, put on letters, and thrown in mailboxes, but no one collects or delivers them as he expects that to happen magically. In this state of disorder, Doctor Doolittle arrives with his animals and in a very short time improves the postal service and communications, shipping and commerce, educational system, and general prosperity not only of Fantippo but of the neighboring kingdom of Chief Nyam-Nyam as well. Doctor Doolittle organizes the domestic mail to be run by

Fantippans and the foreign mail by swallows and other birds; however, as Fantippans prove incapable, the birds have to take care of city deliveries also. Slavery is blamed on African rulers who sell their prisoners-of-war at great profit to "certain bad men" who take them to other lands. The fact that these men are white is not mentioned; rather, the British government is praised for abolishing the slave trade.

247. _____. *The Story of Doctor Doolittle*.   Illustrated by author. New York: Stokes, 1920. 180p. Grades 4-6.

While serving as a lieutenant in the Irish Guards during World War I, Lofting wrote illustrated letters to his children about animal characters because he had become conscious of the important role that animals played in the war. These letters later became *The Story of Doctor Doolittle,* which narrates the exploits of a gentle and kindly, albeit eccentric, country doctor who loves animals more than the opportunity to make money for himself. In this first of twelve animal fantasies, Doctor Doolittle travels with his pets to Africa to save the monkeys who are dying from a "horrible" epidemic. In fulfilling this mission, Doolittle and his pets are captured twice by the king of Jolliginki because he fears that Doolittle has come to exploit the riches of Africa. The first time, the king is easily duped by Polynesia into freeing the captives, but the second time Polynesia enlists the help of Prince Bumpo, who lives in the make-believe world of fairy tales. He wants to marry Sleeping Beauty, but she rejects him because she wants to be kissed only by a handsome white prince. Polynesia promises that Doctor Doolittle will turn Bumpo's face white if Bumpo will help them leave Africa. Both parties fulfill their bargains, and Doolittle returns to England with his unusual two-headed animal, the pushmi-pullyu, which makes him rich.

Doctor Doolittle's African adventures are continued in *The Voyages of Doctor Doolittle,* which won the 1923 Newbery Medal, *Doctor Doolittle's Circus, Doctor Doolittle and the Green Canary, Doctor Doolittle and the Secret Lake, Doctor Doolittle's Garden,* and *Doctor Doolittle in the Moon.* In all these creations, there is an air of white supremacy. Africans are portrayed as naive, ignorant, gullible, and incapable of handling their affairs. Verbal abuse and ridicule are hurled freely at them by both Europeans and animals. They are called "superstitious," "savages," "heathen idolaters," "poor pagans," and "terribly afraid of anything they cannot understand." Lofting's illustrations convey the quaint humor of his prose, as well as stereotyping Africans as lethargic and ludicrous, with grotesque physical features that appear more ape-like than human.

248. Mendez, Phil. *The Black Snowman*. Illustrated by Carole Byard. New York: Scholastic, 1989. N.p. Grades 1-3.

Nothing short of fantasy can cure Jacob, an inner city youth, of his self-hatred and rage at being black and poor. When his younger brother drapes a discarded magic kente cloth--which had come with the slaves--on a snowman he has made with dirty, slushy snow, the black snowman comes to life. The snowman infuses courage and self-pride in Jacob by reminding him of the great civilizations and warriors of Africa. The transformation in Jacob is evident when the snowman helps him to rescue his brother from a burning building. Byard's illustrations reflect Jacob's somber mood and the surrealistic atmosphere of the story.

249. Meniru, Teresa E. *The Drums of Joy.* Macmillan Winners Series. Lagos and Ibadan, Nigeria: Macmillan, 1982. 91p. Grades 5-7.

250. _____. *Footsteps in the Dark.* Macmillan Winners Series. Lagos and Ibadan, Nigeria: Macmillan, 1982. 97p. Grades 5-7.
Gathered around their parents and grandparents, three children hear stories of the bravery and intelligence of an Igbo girl and boy. *The Drums of Joy* recounts the story of Nnenne, who was kidnapped from her village and later rescued by a priest and educated in a mission school, while *Footsteps in the Dark* narrates Uche's misadventures with a gang of thieves. The protagonists' desire to return home to their families and to make the most of their experiences and opportunities lends unity and tension to the episodic plots. Uche's story, however, is more complex as he has to face the moral issues of theft and deception. Meniru delicately balances the listeners' interest in the storytelling and the surprise ending that Nnenne and Uche are none other than the children's parents. Details of daily life and the warm relationships among family members add depth and counterpoint to the storytelling sessions.

251. _____. *Unoma.* Illustrated by Gay Galsworthy. London and Ibadan: Evans, 1976. 58p. Grades 4-6.
When the village treasurer is tricked out of money because he cannot read and write, he is determined to educate his children. He ignores traditional ideas that girls do not need education by sending his first born, Unoma, to school. The episodic plot takes the lively Unoma from one misadventure to another: she is wrongly accused of stealing the school fees; she is chased by an evil village elder; and she is punished by the masqueraders for intruding upon their secret rituals. In each episode, Unoma's impatient and impulsive personality gets her into trouble, but her honesty, sense of responsibility, and intelligence earn her the respect of peers and elders alike. Meniru's narrative style is sparse and economical, and it rarely delves beneath the surface to provide a multifaceted portrait of characters and events. The tensions caused by traditional religion versus Christianity, status of women, and changing values in modern Nigeria are not explored in depth. It is the theme of progress and education for girls that overpowers the story.

252. Mwangi, Meja. *Kill Me Quick.* African Writers Series. London: Heinemann, 1973. 151p. Grades 9-12.
Written with humor and excruciating frankness, *Kill Me Quick* takes

readers to the backstreets and shantytowns of a big city in modern Nigeria. Meja Mwangi, who comes to the city after getting his Secondary School Certificate, is initiated into the life of the backstreets by the more experienced Maina. When both are unable to procure jobs despite their education, they settle into living out of dustbins and from there onto petty theft, crime, and prison. If education is the hope of village youth, then it is certainly a false hope: Meja and Maina lack the skills, experience, and further specialization necessary to compete for jobs in the cities. Ironically, they can never return to their villages because they have not fulfilled the expectations and sacrifices of their parents.

However, this is not a bitter recounting of the frustrations of unemployment, poverty, and daily survival. There is fun, excitement, friendship, kindness, and success of sorts in their lives. The protagonists live by the philosophy that in life there is always a foreman or overseer who will try to cheat you. Although they stumble into crime, they are good characters who have done everything in their power to avoid crime and danger. The personalities of the two youths transcend every obstacle set before them.

253. Ntrakwah, Abena. *My Brother Yao.* Illustrated by Fred Okore. Accra, Ghana: Adwinsa, 1986. 13p. Preschool-Grade 2.

Little Abena assists her mother in the care of her seven-month-old baby brother. While she experiences some jealousy because of his incessant demands, Abena realizes Yao's physical needs have to be met. She is proud of her brother, and especially of the praise she earns for helping her mother. This is one of the few children's books that depicts a well-to-do urban family in Africa. However, the line drawings are unattractive and the book is poorly produced.

254. Nwakoby, Martina. *A Lucky Chance.* Winners Series. Ibadan, Nigeria: Macmillan, 1980. 65p. Grades 4-6.

Winner of the 1978 Macmillan Nigeria Children's Literature Competition, this novel narrates the hardships and disappointments of a poor, though dearly loved village boy. When Chisa's rich uncle invites him to study in the city, both Chisa and his parents think the move will provide him with endless opportunities for advancement. Unfortunately, the family and community values Chisa is accustomed to are replaced by the acquisitiveness and self-centeredness of urban life. Chisa is exploited and treated like a servant by his mean aunt and his indulged cousins. The better he does in school, the worse become the taunts and pranks against him. However, Chisa's diligence pays off when he wins a scholarship to secondary school, and he is no longer economically dependent on his uncle. The inner feelings of Chisa are sensitively portrayed as he struggles to keep up with schoolwork, complete his arduous tasks at home, and satisfy his human yearning for companionship.

255. Nwapa, Flora, and Obiora Moneke. *Journey to Space and Other Stories.* Enugu, Nigeria: Flora Nwapa Books, 1980. 55p. Grades 3-5.

A science fiction story, two pourquoi tales, and a realistic story teach lessons in good behavior, human exploitation of plant life, and introduction of farming to Womo village. The title story, a science fiction adventure, is disappointing because it lacks internal logic. There is no reasonable explanation for the children's adventure into space in the elevator of their apartment building. The events are arbitrarily contrived to teach a moral lesson. The book is poorly edited and produced.

256. Nzekwu, Onuora, and Michael Crowder. *Eze Goes to School.* Illustrated by Adebayo Ajayi. African Reader's Library Series. Ibadan, Nigeria: African Universities Press, 1963. 91p. Grades 2-5.

Set during World War II, this novel focuses on the theme of education for boys and girls as the only road to progress for Nigerian villages. Eze Adi is the only child from his hamlet to attend school, but this dubious honor is won at great cost. With his father's untimely death, Eze's jealous relatives squander all the money and food on the funeral, and there is nothing left for school fees. Mr. Okafor, the teacher, pleads with the village elders to support Eze, but they feel education is unnecessary on a farm. With hard work and help from Mr. Okafor and the chief, Eze continues to excel at school. It is only when the soldiers return home from war that the farmers realize their backwardness. One soldier, who takes a lively interest in Eze, appeals to the farmers' sense of community pride to establish a scholarship fund and village improvement committee. At last, Eze is able to continue his studies, and other children from the hamlet also begin school.

The story also challenges traditional views on the status of women. After her husband's death, Eze's mother is treated disrespectfully by her male relatives who take charge of her husband's property and condemn her for insisting on Eze's education. Eze learns to respect his very intelligent classmate, the girl Chinwe. He is no longer ashamed to let a girl outdo him in studies, just as he is not ashamed of his mother's courage and determination. Yet, the old ways are not abandoned. The hamlet can advance only if it unites according to tribal law, with the elders cooperating to make decisions for the benefit of all.

257. Odejide, 'Biola. *Ropoto Finds a Home.* Ibadan, Nigeria: Y-Books, 1987. 25p. Grades 2-4.

When Grandma Otitoju visits her family in Ibadan, she comes loaded with gifts for her grandchildren. The lovely white kitten, Ropoto, that she gets for her youngest grandchild, Dipo, is the source of conflict in the story. Dipo's mother simply cannot live in the same house with a cat because, according to legend, one of her remote ancestors was a tiger. Mama finally gives in to the tactful suggestion of Grandma that perhaps the taboo is not valid now that they live in the city, and to the children's argument that they are Daddy's children also and they need a cat to chase the rats. Ropoto's cat-nature is tested when he is placed in the attic with the rats. When he kills and eats his first rat and returns victorious on Mama's lap, he is accepted. This simple story has endearing characters whose motives and feelings are skillfully drawn. Children will especially respond to Dipo's need for a friend or a pet he can care for. The legend of the quarrel between the tiger and cat, however, is not explained adequately. Is the author trying to imply that traditions finally give way to modernity and practical concerns?

258. Okojie, Olufunke. *The Boy Doctor.* Illustrated by Thea Dupays. Ibadan, Nigeria: University Press, 1986. Originally published in 1964 by Oxford University Press. 58p. Grades 4-6.

Oziegbe's story provides insight into the life of a chief with many wives and children; the separate roles of each member of the family; and rural occupations and recreations. The focal interest centers around the oracle's pronouncement that Oziegbe will become a doctor. He is apprenticed to a traditional doctor, but Oziegbe does not have the aptitude for remembering herbs, making medicines, and foretelling the future. However, when he enrolls in a school and assists in the clinic, he is interested in studying Western medicine. The reason why Oziegbe rejects traditional medicine for the lengthy schooling required to become a medical doctor is not stated.

259. Okoro, Anezi. *One Week, One Trouble.* Illustrated by Charles Ohu. African Reader's Library Series. Ibadan, Nigeria: African Universities Press, 1972. 112p. Grades 5-7.

This action-filled story of the misadventures of Wilson Tagbo is set in a British-style boarding school, a legacy of Nigeria's colonial past. From his very first week at St. Marks, a prestigious secondary school, Willie becomes notorious as the pupil who is constantly in trouble. From filling a pillow with soap, to eating "illegal" roasted yams for breakfast, to riding a bull and inhaling laughing gas, every week of the first term finds him breaking some cardinal rule. Some of his scrapes are deliberate, while others are a result of his desire to succeed and do the right thing. Okoro's lively prose conveys the hilarity of Willie's predicaments, as well as maintaining an ironic tension between the poor opinion the schoolteachers and prefects have of Willie and the high regard with which he is viewed at home by family and village community (his younger sister is the only one who recognizes his mischievous nature). The ultimate irony is that the school feels it cannot dismiss him because of his brilliant academic performance. Happily, this story does not end with a didactic message as does a similar story by Cyprian Ekwensi, *Trouble in Form Six* (Cambridge UP, 1966).

260. Okoye, Ifeoma. *Only Bread for Eze.* Illustrated by Emmanuel Okereke. Enugu, Nigeria: Fourth Dimension, 1980. 16p. Preschool-Grade 2.

This is one of a series of books on Eze, an only child who wants to manipulate and control his environment. In this story, Eze balks at the food served to him and wants only bread. The more his mother cajoles him to try garri and soup, yams and plantains, or rice and stew, the more adamant Eze becomes. Finally, his father insists that Eze will get nothing but bread for breakfast, lunch, and dinner. Eze soon tires of bread and longs for the delicious preparations of his mother. This story could lead to a lively discussion of fussy eaters and the fine line between encouraging a child to eat everything and contributing to his eating problem. Men and women are portrayed in stereotypical roles, and disapproval of the mother's indulgence and lack of firmness are implied.

261. _____. *Village Boy!*   Macmillan Winners Series. Ibadan, Nigeria: Macmillan, 1980. 101p. Grades 4-6.
Rural progress is achieved when Joseph Iba overcomes financial problems at home and social and learning difficulties at school to continue his secondary education in the city. Joseph is honest, courageous, and hardworking, qualities that earn him respect and enable him to face obstacles posed by his inadequate educational background, his mother's illness, and accusation of stealing. While at first it may appear that he is headed for failure, his mother's vision and determination, the villagers' help, and private lessons build Joseph's self-confidence and provide him with the necessary skills to succeed. The message to rural boys seeking an education is clear: work hard, be good, and disregard the cruel taunts of snobbish city boys.

262. Okri, Ben. *Flowers and Shadows.*   Longman African Classics Series. Harlow, Essex, England: Longman, 1980. 208p. Grades 9-12.
Against the background of corruption, disorder, power, and money in modern Lagos, a sensitive nineteen-year-old youth, Jeffia Okwe, is harshly initiated into adult realities. Two sayings that echo throughout the novel--"Sins of the father visit the son" and "People are like little flowers existing in the shadows"--assume many shades of meaning in connection with Jeffia's experiences and the overall structure of the novel. Characters, events, themes, cultural details, and images are superbly crafted to effect Jeffia's transformation from a happy, protected child of well-to-do parents to a self-supporting young man who has just witnessed the shattering of his secure life. During the transitional stage between high school and university, Jeffia is relentlessly confronted with the long, dark shadows of his father's past: His mother's deep sorrow and ill-health; his father's preoccupation with his business empire; evidence of the lives wrecked by his father's ruthlessness and illegal business practices; his best friend's death as a result of civil irresponsibility; and government corruption at all levels. Yet, Jeffia also witnesses his mother's sweetness and love and Cynthia's--an innocent victim of his father's deception--resilience and personal philosophy of putting the painful shadows to rest in order to await a happier future.
Despite the somber tone, *Flowers and Shadows* is a hopeful novel of cleansing and regeneration. The evil empire created over decades by Jeffia's father disintegrates upon his accidental death, and the wrongs begin to be righted. Jeffia refuses to be drawn into the power

politics and hedonistic culture of the Westernized elite of Lagos; instead, he seeks the contemplative and aesthetic order of his mother and the human comfort and quiet courage of Cynthia. Jeffia's maturation is complete when he realizes that he, too, is an instrument of change when he meets the street urchin to whom he had paid two naira at the beginning of the book to prevent further cruelty to a dog. This small gesture had transformed the boy's exploitative ways, and he was trying to better himself through education and hard work.

Okri explores the inner world of a sensitive and lonely young adult in even greater psychological depth in *The Landscapes Within* (Longman, 1981).

263. Onadipe, Kola (Nathaniel Kolawole).   *The Adventures of Souza.* Illustrated by Adebayo Ajayi. African Reader's Library Series. Ibadan, Nigeria: African Universities Press, 1963. 80p. Grades 5-7.

This is a delightful first person account of Souza's childhood in Makele Village. With total frankness, Onadipe narrates the many adventures that Souza shared with his three best friends--a hunting accident, bee stings while gathering honey, the secret cult accident, moonlight raid on the pastor's fruit trees, running away from home, enlisting a magician's services to do well in school, and taking revenge on village children. If Souza appears to be an unruly character, one is also impressed by the fact that this mischievous and energetic boy does not allow the severe physical punishments to destroy his love of adventure and his inner sense of moral order. The author conveys a definite feeling of nostalgia for traditional village life and customs.

264. _____. *Koku Baboni.* Illustrated by Frances Effiong. African Junior Library Series. Ibadan, Nigeria: African Universities Press, 1965. 79p. Grades 3-5.

The social agenda of denouncing the practice of killing twins at birth overpowers the plot and characterization. Adia, a childless widow, is prompted by a mysterious lady who appears in her dreams to rescue an abandoned baby. Both Adia and the child, named Koku Baboni, are portrayed as ideal, albeit wooden characters; they are kind, loving, and generous to all. When Koku Baboni's compassionate nature leads him to his biological mother, the entire village acknowledges that twins are not evil, and the custom of killing twin babies is ended.

265. _____. *The Magic Land of the Shadows.* Illustrated by Bruce Onobrakpeya. African Junior Library Series. Lagos, Nigeria: African Universities Press, 1970. 63p. Grades 2-4.

Ajua, a modern Cinderella who is treated cruelly by her stepmother, is given magical powers by a kindly shadow from Magic Land to stop the abuse. However, when the stepmother goes to Magic Land to get wealth and beauty, her wicked nature earns her ugliness ("as black as the bottom of a cooking pot") and dirty rags, and she is driven out of the village. Ajua lives happily with her father and stepsister; wealth does not make her arrogant toward others.

266. _____. *A Pot of Gold.*   Natona Junior Series. Ijebu-Ode, Nigeria: Natona, 1986. 55p. Grades 2-4.
>   This didactic story condemns the false social and materialistic values of the rich. Lola, a rich girl, is forbidden by her mother to meet Jumai, a poor girl. However, Lola's and Jumai's good nature and friendship overcome these barriers. The author employs stereotypical characters and coincidences to advance his social message and expose the inner psychological motives of Lola's mother. Regrettably, Onadipe's prose style for younger readers is characterized by short, choppy sentences that lack descriptive details and aesthetic grace.

267. _____. *Sugar Girl.* Illustrated by Charles Ohu. African Junior Library Series. Ibadan, Nigeria: African Universities Press, 1964. 72p. Grades 2-4.
>   Sugar Girl, so named because of her obedient, hardworking, and cheerful nature, undergoes much suffering when she is lost in the forest while gathering firewood for her handicapped parents. She returns home after being given shelter by Ayawa, an old woman thought to be a witch, a kindly family, and a prince. Once again, Onadipe's favorite theme of social reform is raised when the villagers' cruelty and inhumanity to Ayawa is condemned

268. Opong, Sarah F. *Sam and His Blue Train.*   Accra, Ghana: Sedco, 1988. 15p. Preschool-Grade 3.
>   Reminiscent of "The Little Engine That Could," this story is about an outdated steam train and its aging driver who intend to serve the public as long as they are functional. The story is cleverly offered at two levels: For the preschooler, the illustrations and captions on the versos tell a simple story; while the slightly older child will enjoy the details of the journey from Accra to Kumasi on the rectos. The text also explains the operation of a steam engine as compared to diesel-powered trains. However, the book suffers from a major artistic flaw because of an inconsistent point-of-view. Both illustrations and third person narration present the train as an object; however, sometimes the train converses with the driver on the difficulties of his job and falls asleep in his bed as though he is a person.

269. *The Race.* Illustrated by Campbell Kennedy. Leopard Readers Series. London: Collins, 1980. 32p. Grades 2-4.
>   Amina and Bello, two newcomers to the school, easily defeat the best athletes at table tennis, hurdles, high jump, and track. At the forthcoming Sports Day, all hopes rest on Oludele to beat Bello in at least one event. In the meantime, Oludele and Bello spend so much time practicing together that Oludele comes to know Bello, who is very different from the boastful and aggressive Amina. On Sports Day, Oludele vindicates his honor by winning the hundred meters, but he is also fortunate to have found a worthy opponent in the sensitive and gentle Bello. This simple story beautifully describes the feelings and motivations of the characters. Readers will easily identify with the characters' competitive spirit and their hostile thoughts toward a talented outsider.

270. Segun, Mabel D. *Youth Day Parade*. Illustrated by DUCA. Ibadan, Nairobi, Kampala and Accra: DUCA, 1984. 22p. Grades 3-5.

Tunde is unsure of his abilities when the Headmaster appoints him organizer of the school's contingent in the Youth Day Parade. The support of his parents, teachers, and classmates strengthens Tunde's confidence in himself. As a leader, he has everyone involved, but obstacles appear in the form of low attendance at rehearsals, lack of marching ability, and laziness. Disappointed and afraid of poor performance, Tunde decides to cancel their school's participation. The reaction of committee members who have worked hard makes him realize that leadership means doing the best one can under the circumstances and recognizing that while some have not fulfilled their responsibilities, others have excelled. This story is intended to build character and leadership skills in youth.

271. Sikuade, Yemi. *Ehanna and Friends*. Macmillan Winners Series. Ibadan, Nigeria: Macmillan, 1978. 72p. Grades 5-7.

The mischievous pranks of Ehanna and his gang cause exasperation for the villagers. However, when the gang members and their female rival, Dupe, become victims of a real crime, the villagers acknowledge the harmless nature of the gang's behavior. The children are kidnapped by modern-day slave catchers and sold as cheap labor across the border in Benin. Ehanna and Dupe use their intelligence and combined resources to outwit the criminals, and they return home as heroes. Happily, Ehanna's exuberance is not destroyed by the experience and he is back to his old tricks. The juxtaposition of the two types of gangs provides material for discussion of antisocial behavior.

272. Singer, Caroline, and Cyrus LeRoy Baldridge. *Boomba Lives in Africa*. Illustrated by Cyrus LeRoy Baldridge. New York: Holiday House, 1935. N.p. Grades 3-5.

Boomba, the son of a hunter, tries to save his pet gazelle's life by using his father's gun to shoot a leopard. While he is praised for ridding the village of the leopard, he is scolded for disobedience and risking his life when the gazelle was not in any danger. Around this central episode, the book provides a detailed sociological account of Sierra Leoneans (the exact cultural group is not mentioned), their lifestyle, customs, village organization, and beliefs. On the one hand, the authors are anxious to point out that Africans had prosperous cities and technological and industrial achievements before European colonization, and, on the other hand, their reporter-like descriptions of the anatomy, clothing, and habits of these "brown" people is dehumanizing. Emphasis on exotic cultural features, exaggerated emotions of the characters, and statements that Africans lost their land because nations are stronger than tribes, somehow detracts from the very human and interesting story of Boomba.

273. Solaru, Lanna. *The Prize*. Rainbow Series Supplementary Readers. Ibadan, Nigeria: University Press, 1991. 23p. Grades 2-4.

This is an inspiring story of a young boy who puts duty to family above his personal needs. When his father is sick, Ade willingly walks to his uncle's house in the neighboring village to collect chickens for market day. He does not inform his parents that he was to receive a prize at school that day. Upon returning home late that evening, Ade is rewarded both for his sense of family responsibility and for hard work at school.

While Ade is praised for being a perfect little boy, what makes the story truly touching is Ade's humanity: his forgetfulness and daydreaming enroute to his uncle's house; his need to eat first before catching the chickens; and his near drowning of the chickens. Solaru's prose style is wordy, and the black-and-white illustrations are unattractive (the artist's name is not mentioned).

274. Steptoe, John. *Birthday*. New York: Holt, Rinehart and Winston, 1972. 32p. Grades K-2.
Javaka's eighth birthday calls for a celebration in the farming community of Yoruba. As the firstborn of this town, Javaka is conscious of his personal joy as well as the promise of communal happiness, prosperity, and harmony that his birthday symbolizes. The artwork is appealing, especially the mirror images of Javaka which belie his reflective nature. At first, hearing Black English in an African town sounds incongruent, but as the feast continues, it indicates the capacity of the land to absorb and welcome all.

275. Tutuola, Amos. *The Brave African Huntress*.   Illustrated by Ben Enwonwu. New York: Grove, 1958. 150p. Grades 9-12.
Adebisi, the brave African huntress, breaks the taboo against women inheriting the hunting profession by entering the dreaded jungle to search for her four older brothers who were lost there before her birth. Both Tutuola's prose and Enwonwu's black-and-white illustrations create a surreal atmosphere as this brave girl boldly enters the primeval jungle with its treacherous animals, supernatural creatures, and forbidding environment. Armed with her father's weapons, a variety of jujus and herbs, and her remarkable skill and courage, Adebisi overcomes all obstacles. She destroys the Pygmies and their town and frees the thousands of hunters and warriors imprisoned there. As leader of the freed captives, she returns home with the gift of her four brothers for her family and with the riches of the jungle--gold dust, silver, copper, brass, antimony--for her community.

The episodic plot allows Tutuola the opportunity to collect a vast array of folktales, cultural rituals, and folk wisdom into an organic whole. Each chapter is prefaced by a traditional Yoruba proverb that provides the thematic focus of the event being narrated, as well as marking a stage in Adebisi's personal development. On the one hand, this heroic exploit symbolizes the efforts of early Africans to appropriate the minerals of the land for their use and technical development, while on the other hand mention of guns and gunpowder belies a European presence, a subject which Tutuola refuses to entertain in his works. Tutuola disregards the conventions of the English language to fashion a vivid and robust prose style that conveys the flavor of the Yoruba idiom.

276. _____. *Feather Woman of the Jungle*. London: Faber and Faber, 1962. 132p. Grades 7-10.

Set in precolonial Nigeria, this collection of Igbo folklore is organized around the storyframe of a newly appointed village chief who narrates his past adventures over a period of ten days. Beginning with his first adventure at the age of fifteen, the protagonist's quests are aimed specifically at accumulating wealth--since he hates farming--for his poverty-stricken parents. As soon as he sets off on his six journeys, the hero immediately changes from a lazy son to one who is willing to face the most severe physical hardships, punishments, and risks. Each adventure poses a different challenge that tests his singleness of purpose, intelligence, patience, courage, and moral character. He returns to his parents and village permanently when he has earned enough riches to last the remainder of their lives. The stories also provide justification for the hero's personal qualifications as chief and his right to the wealth for which he endured so much. Tutuola's narration is rich in details of animal and plant life, rural and urban cultures of traditional Nigeria, fabulous riches of ancient kingdoms, religious beliefs and social customs, and, above all, awareness of the world beyond the village of Abeokuta, which is the focal point of the stories.

277. _____. *Simbi and the Satyr of the Dark Jungle*. London: Faber and Faber, 1955. 136p. Grades 6-10.

Simbi, the female protagonist, embarks on an epic journey when she senses that something vital is missing from her life and she wants to experience Poverty and Punishment. Defying the advice of her mother and village elders that such experiences are not desirable, Simbi deliberately sets off on the Path of Death just outside her village. At the crossroads, she is captured by Dogo, the kidnapper of innocent children, and sold as a slave. Thus begins her initiation into poverty, punishment, illness, cruelty, and death. She is forced to work hard as a slave; she is nearly sacrificed to the gods in the City of Sinners; she escapes from the town of multicolored people; and, finally, she confronts the terrible Satyr of the Dark Jungle. She endures excruciating physical and emotional pain when beaten repeatedly and forced to sacrifice her two babies, but her experiences also reveal her courage and intelligence, leadership skills, and ability to endure. Because of the unique manner in which she is rescued from each adventure, she develops an optimistic philosophy that no matter how bad the situation, she will overcome. Her greatest triumph comes when she destroys the Satyr and traverses back along the Path of Death to her village. On the outskirts, she once again meets Dogo, the slave catcher; she defeats him and extracts the promise that he will never return.

Although Simbi states that the moral of her story is that she should have obeyed her mother, she is nevertheless a wiser character in the end because of her harsh experiences. On one level, this is an interesting fantasy of the victory of good over evil, with its fairy tale element of magical objects, transformations, and supernatural beings; on the allegorical level, the various characters, settings, and adventures symbolize the duality of life and the enslavement of Africans by foreigners. Tutuola's distinctive prose style matches these powerful themes and gains in eloquence and force as Simbi goes through her heroic adventures.

278. Whyte, James Ebo. *The Dancing Jaromi*. Illustrated by B. O. Idowu. Ibadan, Nairobi, Kampala and Dodoma: DUCA, 1985. N.p. Grades 1-3.
    Ato steals Kofi's favorite joromi (shirt) because his feelings are hurt when Kofi and his friends taunt him and refuse to let him join their games. Without moralizing or authorial intrusion, Whyte conveys that Ato's behavior is inappropriate. The joromi turns out to be magical, and when Ato wears it he is forced to dance and jump. Exhausted, he is glad when Kofi removes it. Kofi, on his part, realizes that his insensitive treatment of Ato was the motivation for the theft. This story raises interesting philosophic questions: Should Ato have been punished further? Will the ready forgiveness encourage Ato to steal again? The color illustrations superbly portray details of Ghanaian life and capture the mood and action of the story.

279. Williams, Akinyele. *Dele's Travels and Sallah in Ilorian*. Illustrated by J. F. Adenuga. Adventures in Africa Series. Ibadan, Nigeria: University Press, 1979. Originally published in 1974 by Oxford University Press. 76p. Grades 4-6.
    Dele and Adisa, two Nigerian boys from relatively well-off middle class homes, learn of different peoples, places, and customs through their travels. Dele's travels to the rural northwest and the southwestern coastal regions teach him ecology, cultural anthropology, and scientific principles. He comes to respect the simple, ''illiterate'' country folk for their knowledge and application of science in daily activities. Adisa, in contrast, visits Ilorian and attends the Islamic celebration of Id el Kebir and learns about the beliefs and lifestyle of Nigerian Muslims. Both Dele and Adisa become broad-minded because of their experiences and recognize the cultural diversity of their country.
    Both stories have the definite agenda of promoting travel as a supplement to formal classroom education and multicultural understanding as a means of overcoming narrow regionalism. The episodic plot, prescriptive style and tone, and didactic themes take precedence over artistic concerns.

280. Wimbush, Dorothy. *The Land of the Crocodile's Teeth*. Illustrated by Laszlo Acs. Adventures in Africa Series. Ibadan, Nigeria: University Press, 1979. Originally published in 1968 by Oxford University Press. 64p. Grades 5-7.
    Two adventure stories are juxtaposed to comment on traditional beliefs in supernatural beings. In ''The Land of the Crocodile's

Teeth,'' two youngsters learn to respect ancient myths and taboos, while in ''Hassan and the Spirits,'' the protagonist overcomes his fear of spirits to apprehend thieves. Both stories are written in an engaging style that balances narration, description, and dialogue.

281. Wiredu, Anokye. *The Adventures of Dabodabo Akosua.* Illustrated by Tanueh Borsah. Accra, Ghana: Adwinsa, 1981. 16p. Grades 2-4.

Elements of fantasy and folklore merge in the adventures of Dabodabo Akosua, a beautiful black duck who is dissatisfied with her appearance. She leaves home because she wants to be a white swan. Although she is admired for her looks by all, with the help of Ananse the spider her black feathers are painted white. Now she has to face the ridicule and abuse of her former admirers. Disappointed and humiliated, she returns to the warm welcome of her family. On the personal level, Dabodabo learns the importance of being proud of who she is. She realizes that self-hatred only prevented her from achieving her full potential. On the political level, this story obviously intends to infuse racial and color pride in African children in order to counteract the experiences of the colonial era. However, the repeated jibes that white is ugly are unnecessary to the theme, and they encourage reverse discrimination.

POETRY

282. Achebe, Chinua.   *Beware, Soul Brother: Poems.*   Enugu, Nigeria: Nwamife, 1972. 68p. Grades 9-12.

Winner of the 1972 Commonwealth Poetry Prize, *Beware, Soul Brother* is Achebe's first collection of poems. Written during the Nigerian crisis and civil war, the twenty-nine poems reveal the writer's agony at witnessing the pain and tragedy of war; the confusion of values in a changing postcolonial society; and the ironies of international politics. Achebe's simple diction and imagery, reflecting both traditional and modern Nigeria, respond eloquently to these powerful themes. In ''Christmas in Biafra (1969),'' he describes an emaciated child in these words:

> Her
> Infant son flat like a dead lizard
> on her shoulders his arms and legs
> Cauterized by famine was a miracle
> of its own kind.

Despite the desolation and suffering of war, Achebe envisages a hopeful future because of his faith in traditional beliefs and the wisdom of the ancestors.

282a. Mezu, Rose Uregbulam. *Songs of the Hearth*. Owerri, Nigeria: Black
Academy Press, 1993. 64p. Grades 6-adult.

With her family home in Akwuosa as the focal point, Mezu arranges
her intensely personal poems in a circular, almost womblike structure.
She pays tribute to and celebrates her husband's virtues and the
unique personalities of her children. The metaphor of the hearth and
family togetherness is expansive enough to embrace her several
worlds in Nigeria and the United States; her concern for the ecology
of the earth; her fear of the "dark, menacing clouds" of war, hunger,
and power that loom over society worldwide; and her faith and solace
in God. In her concern for the rights of children and the
downtrodden, Mezu takes a strong feministic stance that women and
daughters should assume their rightful place in society.

283. Tadjo, Veronique.   *Lord of the Dance: An African Retelling*.
Illustrated by author. New York: Lippincott, 1988. Originally published in
1988 by A. C. Black, London. N.p. Grades K-3.

Inspired by the hymn, "The Lord of the Dance," that the author had
heard at a wedding, Tadjo adapts the theme to the Senufo tradition of
carving sacred wooden masks to symbolize various emotions and the
spirits of nature. The Lord of the Dance is conceived as a mask that
leads celebrations and processions accompanied by music and
singing. From the time of creation, the mask has danced with the
heavenly bodies, with the plants and animals on earth, and with the
villagers during sowing and harvest seasons and in times of sorrow
and happiness. The mask also represents past traditions and continuity
in a modern and changing Africa. The old beliefs--or masks--are
discarded by people living in industrialized cities, but the longing for
their roots, for a sense of mystery and awe in creation, is still there.
For those who seek him, the Lord of the Dance still lives in the
colors of the rainbow, sound of thunder, breath of wind, and cities
and villages. The mask is the physical symbol of the invisible,
eternal, all-pervading spirit of nature.

This simple poem is almost a prayer to the transcendental spirit of
God, and it reminds one of the Hindu belief in Lord Shiva's cosmic
dance. Tadjo's illustrations are also inspired by Senufo tribal art,
except that she replaces the traditional brown vegetable ink with
bright colors to express the joyous mood of the poem.

284. Vatsa, Mamman J.   *Children's Stories and Riddles in Verse*.
Illustrated by Adelfo M. Suzuki. Enugu, Nigeria: Fourth Dimension, 1978.
55p. Grades K-2.

Narrative and descriptive poems and riddles and proverbs in verse
reflect the traditional wisdom of a people close to nature. In addition
to the folkloric content, this collection also voices the hopes of
postcolonial Nigerians: the importance of formal education, the need
for doctors, and the responsibility of young Nigerians toward building
a strong nation. The poems are simply written and attractively
illustrated for younger children.

285. _____. *Stinger the Scorpion.* Illustrated by Ann Nwokoye. Enugu, Nigeria: Fourth Dimension, 1979. 15p. Grades K-3.

This illustrated poem describes the physical features and habits of a scorpion. While Scorpion's physical beauty is admired, his habit of stinging is considered antisocial. Yet, Scorpion has the last word as he praises the power his sting gives him despite his small size. The poem does not have a pleasing rhythm, but the imagery is clever. Scorpion is variously described as a "load of kola nuts tied with rope in a raffia bag" and "effective like a live electric wire." The colorful pictures will influence readers' attitudes toward Scorpion because they portray him as a likeable family man.

DRAMA

286. Henshaw, James Ene. *This Is Our Chance: Plays from West Africa.* London: Hodder and Stoughton, 1956. 95p. Grades 7-12.

Three short plays focus on the conflict between traditions and modernity and personal and social needs. In "This Is Our Chance," two kings acknowledge that their rivalry is counterproductive in a changing political and social climate. In contrast, "The Jewels of the Shrine" and "A Man of Character" respectively emphasize the importance of traditional duties toward elders and the strength of character required to reject bribes, regardless of the situation. All three plays are intended to infuse values in modern youth. The plot, characters, and dialogue are handled with skill.

287. Olagoke, D. Olu. *The Incorruptible Judge.* Plays for African School Series. London: Evans, 1962. 48p. Grades 7-10.

The didactic theme of corrupt government officials is the driving force of this play and the plot and characters merely its agents. When a fresh graduate applies for a job, he is asked to pay a bribe of five pounds before he can be hired. Rather than pay the money, Ajala makes a police report. The guilty man unsuccessfully attempts to use his money and connections to influence the judge. His punishment is intended to serve as an example to other offenders. The play serves the social purpose of denouncing bribery and corruption, but as a piece of literature it lacks artistic grace. There are no character revealing dialogues, manipulation of plot, or profound imagery.

288. Sarpong, Peter K. *The One Honest Man.* Accra, Ghana: Sedco, 1983. 36p. Grades 8-12.

There are no great dramatic scenes or characters in this tragedy; instead, the play is an intense debate on the issue of corrupt leadership. Set in precolonial times, the discussion focuses on the future of the kingdom of Hiayeya when two of the three kingmakers accept bribes and the promise of powerful governmental positions to appoint Yaw Anto as the next king. However, the third kingmaker, Kofi Bekoe, opposes the arrangement by continuing to support a more worthy candidate. Once Yaw Anto is duly enthroned, Kofi Bekoe's honesty and loyalty prompt Yaw Anto to banish his two flatterers from the kingdom, and he tries to convince Kofi Bekoe to serve as his advisor. Bekoe refuses because he realizes that this is just Yaw Anto's method of controlling him. He, too, is exiled, but he remains incorruptible. Eventually, Yaw Anto abdicates and goes into self-imposed exile because he realizes that a leader who is not governed by justice, honesty, and good conscience is harmful to the state and displeasing to the ancestors.

BIOGRAPHY AND AUTOBIOGRAPHY

289. Akinlade, E. K.   *Ajayi the Bishop.*   What Great Men Do Series. Ibadan, Nigeria: Onibonoje, 1973. 22p. Grades 3-5.

This short biography recounts the experiences of Ajayi--better known by his Christian name, Samuel Crowther--from his capture by slave raiders, to his rescue by a British patrol on April 7, 1822, to his appointment as the first African bishop in the English church. Hard work enabled Ajayi to distinguish himself throughout his career. The first chapter, which narrates the events leading to the capture, is interestingly developed for plot and character, but the remainder of the book simply summarizes the story of Ajayi. The short, choppy sentences and stilted vocabulary further make this an unattractive book.

290. _____.   *Oluyole the Basorun.*   What Great Men Do Series. Ibadan, Nigeria: Onibonoje, 1973. 51p. Grades 4-6.

Brief biographical sketches highlight four significant episodes from West African history and one from Ethiopian history. Akinlade recounts King Oluyole's wisdom in settling disputes; young King William Dappa Pepple's success in stopping the slave trade in Bonny; El Kanemi's schemes to save Bornu from the Fulani threat; and the pivotal role of Tinubu, a wise and highly respected woman trader and diplomat, in stopping the slave trade with the help of the British. Likewise, King Menelik of Ethiopia is praised for defeating the Italians in 1895 and introducing modern reforms. While the dialogue format is ineffective and stilted, the content of this book is a testimony to the bravery, wisdom, and leadership qualities of Africans.

291. Barker, Carol.   *A Family in Nigeria.*   Families the World Over Series. Revised edition of *Village in Nigeria.* Minneapolis, MN: Lerner, 1985. 31p. Grades 1-3.

With the life of twelve-year-old Thaddeus as a point of entry, Barker provides an insider's view of a Yoruba family from Aye-Ekan, a small village in Southern Nigeria. Thaddeus' father, Chief Afolayan, his six wives, and their children lived in a compound which they shared with his uncle and uncle's family. Although there were forty-four people in the family, harmony and mutual respect characterized their relationships whether they were farming, cooking, raising children, selling produce at the market, weaving, making pots, or praying. Their lifestyle was a happy blend of traditional and modern in all areas: herbal medicine and Health Centers, traditional upbringing and formal education in a Roman Catholic school, and Yoruba religious beliefs and Christianity. Three of Chief Afolayan's wives and nearly half his children were Christian, while the others followed Yoruba gods and goddesses. Belonging to a rural community did not limit Thaddeus' opportunities and choices, as he hoped to go to the University of Lagos to become either a doctor or an engineer. Color photographs of Thaddeus and his family testify to the closeness, joy, and security shared by this Nigerian family. Information on Nigeria's growing oil industry, the famous Yoruba wood sculptures, and basic facts on Nigeria are also included.

292. _____. *An Oba of Benin.* Illustrated by author. Carol Barker's Worlds of Yesterday Series. Reading, MA: Addison-Wesley, 1977. Originally published in 1976 by Macdonald and Jane. N.p. Grades 1-3.

Focusing on the reign of Oba Esigie who came to power around 1504 A.D., Barker's text and illustrations bring to life the civilization of Benin at the height of its glory. Through the training and experiences of a fictional crown prince, Ewedo, readers learn of the lifestyle, political power, and achievements of Benin. The story is set at a crucial period when the Portuguese, having heard of the fame of Benin, came to trade in ivory, metals, pepper, slaves, jewels, and cloth. The Portuguese, on their part, established a Christian mission school and church in 1514 and supplied the Bini with guns in their wars of expansion with neighboring kingdoms. This appealing picture book combines the study of African history with aesthetic enjoyment. Rendered in the style of the famous Benin bronzes, the illustrations of palace buildings, temples, ceremonial processions, war preparations, leopard hunts, village life, clothing, and arts and crafts testify to the wealth and prestige of this kingdom.

293. Diallo, Nafissatou. *A Dakar Childhood.* Translated from the French *De Tilene au Plateau: Une Enfance Dakaroise* by Dorothy S. Blair. Harlow, Essex, England: Longman, 1982. 134p. Grades 9-12.

A Senegalese wife, mother, and working woman narrates the story of her growing up in Dakar from the 1940s to the 1960s and the changes her extended family underwent in just one generation. At times nostalgic, emotional, and humorous, Diallo describes the happy and full life that she shared with her grandfather, grandmothers, father and his wives, aunts and uncles, brothers and sisters, and cousins and guests. Together, they celebrated religious festivals, marriages, and births. Events concerning individual members--such as admission to school and visits to dressmakers and jewelers--were also given due consideration by elders. This account is also the very personal story of a rather mischievous and spirited young girl who was continuously in trouble because of her strict Islamic upbringing. Rules about family honor, modest behavior, and feminine purity interfered with her independent nature as she secretly ate mangoes with the money intended for the Islamic teacher, joined her cousins and school friends in various escapades, teased lepers, and met clandestinely with boyfriends. Although she was severely punished by her father on a number of occasions, Diallo was grateful for the discipline, strong values, and sense of dignity that were instilled in her. Diallo's loving relationship with the paternal grandmother who raised her is particularly touching. Grandmother's loving care tempered the strict rules with indulgence and provided a safe outlet for the young girl's zest for life.

As Diallo describes her passage from childhood to adolescence to the deepening emotions of young womanhood, readers become aware of the many changes that had crept into her family. While the author is generally silent on the social and political turmoil that marked the end of colonialism and the beginning of a new era, her family home subtly reflected the new environment: the large family was divided into two homes; the rules of conduct were relaxed and daughters could choose their own spouses; Diallo, as the first girl in the family to receive formal education, trained to be a midwife and child welfare worker; and family festivities included Western music and dancing.

294. Fritz, Jean. *The Animals of Doctor Schweitzer.* Illustrated by Douglas Howland. New York: Coward-McCann, 1958. N.p. Grades 2-5.

By narrating the stories of the many animals that were given shelter at the hospital, Fritz presents Dr. Albert Schweitzer's reverence for all life. While the stories and illustrations of the animals are endearing, West Africa and its people are stereotyped. Schweitzer's hospital on the banks of the Ogowe River is presented as a haven of love and civilization in the midst of wilderness and fear. It is implied that Africans lacked gentleness toward animals, and that it was the reward money that prompted them to take orphaned animals to the Great Doctor's compound.

295. Humphrey, Sally. *A Family in Liberia.* Minneapolis, MN: Lerner, 1987. 31p. Grades 2-5.

Through the experiences of ten-year-old Kamu, this book introduces readers to the social customs and family life of Mobuta, a village in Liberia. Kamu was a contented child whose time was occupied at school, at home with his extended family, and at play with his friends. Interspersed with Kamu's daily activities is information on housing, clothing, eating habits, village economy and farming, and polyandry. When Kamu accompanied his cousin to Monrovia, the capital, he was fascinated by the sights and sounds of the city. Despite the plentiful food in the village, most Liberian youth, like his cousin, wanted to move to the city. Kamu, however, hoped to become a famous weaver like his father. Beautiful color photographs illustrate the various aspects of Kamu's life. A brief history of Liberia, list of important facts, and maps accompany the text.

296. Jacobsen, Peter Otto, and Preben Sejer Kristensen. *A Family in West Africa*. Families Around the World Series. New York: Bookwright, 1985. Originally published in 1985 by Wayland. 32p. Grades 3-5.
As the authors journey from The Gambia to a remote village in Senegal to interview Chief Mamat Drammeh, they focus on rural and traditional life without balancing the account with the many changes that have taken place in recent decades. Both text and color photographs describe the chief's polygamous family, living conditions, food habits, centuries-old farming techniques, and importance of Islam. Along with the poverty and difficulties, the authors also emphasize the villagers' happy lives, ready hospitality, and dignity.

297. Laye, Camara. *The African Child*. Translated from the French *L' Enfant Noir* by James Kirkup. London: Collins, 1959. Originally published in English in 1955 under the title *The Dark Child*. 159p. Grades 7-12.
With his evocative prose and direct simplicity, Camara Laye recreates his early life in French Guinea from his childhood recollections to his departure for France as a young adult. Camara's telling dialogues and detailed narration of a few carefully selected episodes provide a clear picture of his family life in Kouroussa and Tindican; the distinct personalities of his mother and father; and schooling at Camille-Guy College and the Technical College. He reveals the development of his inner life with equal frankness from his awareness of the guardian snake of his race, to his mother's supernatural powers, to the mysterious manhood ceremonies, to his love for Marie. Camara's frank and intimate portrait of life under French rule reveals that it was possible to honor and uphold one's rich traditions and take advantage of Western education and training.

298. Omoregie, S. B. *Emotan and the Kings of Benin*. Makers of African History Series. Harlow, Essex, England: Longman, 1972. 51p. Grades 3-5.
This biography narrates the story of the Nigerian heroine Emotan (1360-1440 A.D.), who lived during a turbulent period in the history of Benin. Although a poor and childless market woman, Emotan's courage and sacrifice saved the life of Oba Ewuare, one of the greatest rulers of Benin. Upon her death, Ewuare issued a decree which deified her and people paid homage at her shrine. Even five hundred years later, Emotan's memory is kept alive in monuments, rituals associated with funerals and title-taking ceremonies of chiefs, and stories and songs praising her deeds. The biographer provides the necessary cultural and historical details in order to place this legendary figure in her proper social and historical context.

299. Powell, Erica. *Kwame Nkrumah of the New Africa*. Illustrated by Carabine. London: Nelson, 1961. 68p. Grades 3-5.

Adapted from the autobiography of Kwame Nkrumah titled *Ghana,* Powell traces the early childhood, education, and political career of this leader of modern Ghana. Powell's swift narration and engaging dialogue make this an interesting story which highlights important episodes and shaping influences on the life of Nkrumah.

300. Segbawu, Kwami. *Osei Bonsu: Warrior King of Asante.* Makers of African History Series. London: Longman, 1977. 59p. Grades 4-6.

The fast-moving plot captures the momentous historical events, continual warfare between the Asante and Fante, and treaties and betrayals by Europeans during the nineteenth century. Under the able leadership of Osei Bonsu, first as prince and then as Asantehene, the Asante attempted to preserve their unity and sovereignty to trade on equal terms with the British and Dutch. Throughout his dramatic career, Osei Bonsu displayed courage on the battlefield, wisdom and intelligence in domestic affairs, and a fervent desire for peace on the international front.

301. Segun, Mabel. *My Father's Daughter.* Illustrated by Prue Theobalds. Nairobi, Kenya: East African Publishing House, 1965. 80p. Grades 5-7.

A well-known writer and scholar, Segun recalls her early childhood in a Nigerian village where her father served as pastor. Whether at home or at the mission school, her life was dominated by the overpowering personality of her father who symbolized Christian values and Western civilization. In recollecting her experiences, Segun skillfully blends both the child's perspective and the mature woman's understanding as she recounts her attempts at farming, fear of vaccinations, exploits at school, escape from the Egungun dancers, and compassion for a young woman being forced into marriage because of the bride price. The account ends with the sudden death of her father when she was eight; she felt that he had bequeathed to her his legacy of strict discipline, human understanding, and untiring service.

302. Syme, Ronald. *Nigerian Pioneer: The Story of Mary Slessor.* Illustrated by Jacqueline Tomes. New York: Morrow, 1964. 189p. Grades 6-8.

The career of Mary Mitchell Slessor (1848-1915) symbolizes the fervent missionary zeal of Christians in West Africa in the nineteenth century. At the age of twenty-eight, Slessor left her hard and monotonous life in Scotland aboard a slaver, S.S. Ethiopia, with the determination to bring law and order to the "heathens" of the Calabar Coast. For several years she taught at a mission school in Duke Town, but her pioneering zeal beckoned her to the interior whose "fierce" and "savage" people, she was warned, lived by bloodshed, drunkenness, murder, human sacrifice, and slavery. Undaunted, she got permission to move into "cannibal" country, where she taught school, set up a mission church, gave medical treatment, and negotiated disputes in intertribal fights. Despite her failing health, she was reluctant to give up her work. She died in

1915 surrounded by her adopted African children and the work she loved. Slessor's courage, singleness of purpose, and selflessness are remarkable; yet, her ethnocentric attitude toward Africans is unmistakable. Even the biographer's tone and diction reflect a biased, colonial perspective.

303. Tamuno, Tekena N. *Herbert Macaulay, Nigerian Patriot.* African Historical Biographies Series. London: Heinemann, 1975. 48p. Grades 5-7.
This biography outlines the contributions of Herbert Macaulay (1864-1946) to Nigeria's long struggle for freedom from British rule. However, the biography does not narrate events in chronological sequence, but discusses various aspects of Macaulay's life and work in individual chapters: Birth and Education, Private Life, Journalist and Critic of Government, Defender of the House of Dosumu, and Founder of the National Democratic Party. As the grandson of the famous Bishop Crowther, it was expected that Herbert would also become a missionary; instead, he was the first Nigerian to get a civil engineering degree and a certificate in Music from England. Known as "the Gandhi of West Africa" and "the Musical Wizard of Kirsten Hall," Macaulay's thirteen years in the colonial civil service taught him that even qualified Africans were looked upon as inferior to whites. He devoted the remainder of his life to fighting for the emancipation of Nigerians through peaceful agitation and not through armed conflicts. The biography also reveals his complex personality: he respected his Yoruba traditions just as much as his Christian background; and he was constantly in debt due to his generosity to beggars and such.

304. Wiredu, Anokye. *Nii Ayi Bontey.* Illustrated by S. Frank Odoi. Accra-Tema, Ghana: Ghana Publishing Corporation, 1972. 54p. Grades 4-6.
Elements of legend and myth combine with facts of history in this account of Prince Ayi Bontey's mysterious birth, kidnapping, early youth in the home of a herdsman, and return to his kingdom. The reunion with his parents, the king and queen of Gas, was marred by the impending execution of his surrogate parent. However, a recognition ring saved the herdsman's life and the plot to kill the baby prince was exposed. The swiftly moving biography engages readers' attention by focusing on the welfare of the prince.

305. _____. *Queen Amina.* Illustrated by S. Frank Odoi. Accra-Tema, Ghana: Ghana Publishing Corporation, 1972. 29p. Grades 3-5.
A lively plot and well-developed characters narrate the dramatic story of Queen Amina, favorite wife of King Tinko Ali of the Muslim kingdom of Kong, in present-day Cote d'Ivoire. The jealousy and treachery of the co-wife Salamantu led to the king's order for Amina's execution, but the executioners took pity on their queen and secretly transported her to another part of the country. Amina gave birth to a lovely daughter, Fatima, and remained in hiding till the death of Queen Salamantu. When King Ali ordered all marriageable girls to appear at the palace so that he could select a new queen,

Amina and Fatima both went to the capital. King Ali chose Princess Fatima, but, at the time of marriage, Amina was presented as the bride, and she was reinstated as queen. The many folktale motifs--sparing the life of the condemned one, showing a garment soaked in an animal's blood as proof of the execution, gathering eligible girls for a bridal contest, and mistaken identity--lend a legendary quality to this fictional biography. The illustrations are unattractive and, at times, inaccurate.

306. Wurie, Ahmadu, and Elizabeth Hirst. *Rassin.* London: University of London Press, 1968. 114p. Grades 6-8.
> Coauthored by a grandson of the subject, this biography of Alimamy Rassin, chief of Mafondu from 1857 to 1890, is based entirely on oral tradition and interviews with family members and clansmen. The story of Rassin's life also provides information on the migration of the Bundukas from Senegal to Sierra Leone and their subsequent rise to power. Although their initial aim was to serve as Islamic missionaries and middlemen for French traders, the Bundukas, under the leadership of Ali Hafsa, Alimamy Ahmadu, and Alimamy Rassin, established an era of peace and prosperity in Sierra Leone. Rassin was successful in putting an end to the incessant warfare between the neighboring chiefdoms of Port Loko, Temne, Limba, Dibia, and Safroko through peaceful negotiations. Increased farming replaced slave trading as a means of economic security. Depth of thought and the benevolent principles of Islam gave Rassin the determination and wisdom to carry out his bold plans. The above account retains the freshness of an oral recitation because of its emphasis on the characters who shaped events and lively dialogues and descriptions.

INFORMATIONAL BOOKS

307. Abanga, Doreen. *Affa.* Illustrated by Fiona Arkorful. Tema, Ghana: Ghana Publishing Corporation, 1978. 33p. Grades 1-3.
> This is a well-produced hardcover book that provides insight into a farming community of northeastern Ghana (the exact ethnic group is not mentioned) through the life of a young boy, Affa. The account begins with the construction of houses, organization of the compound, extended family, and roles of men, women, and children. Next, both text and illustrations catalog the animals, plants, and trees that Affa is most likely to see while playing outside or grazing the herd during school holidays. Details of crops and vegetables, implements, crafts like weaving, pottery, and basketmaking, and market day explain the main economic activities of this self-sufficient community. However, life is not all hard work because there is time for music, song and dance, and storytelling when everyone gathers in the bright

moonlight. The book ends with a folktale on the importance of loyalty and unity in a small community.

308. Agyemang, Fred. *Accused in the Gold Coast.* Tema, Ghana: Ghana Publishing Corporation, 1972. 98p. Grades 9-12.
Based on extensive and painstaking research, Agyemang recreates the political atmosphere, trading activities, and lifestyle of nineteenth century Europeans on the west coast of Africa, popularly known as the "White Man's Grave." The account focuses on the public and private lives of four British officials who regulated the activities of the Royal African Company and the Company of Merchants. All four individuals were accused and tried of serious crimes which, as Agyemang discloses, were never conclusively proven. George Maclean, president of the Committee of Merchants of the Gold Coast, was accused of his wife's sudden death; Kenneth Mackenzie, commandant of Fort Nassau, was tried for murder and notorious behavior in the British rivalry against the Dutch; investigation of the ill-treatment and death of Henry Meredith, commandant of the British trading fort at Winneba; and Doctor Knowles was accused of shooting his wife. Agyemang reports the mystery surrounding the above unsolved cases, as well as portraying the turbulent political, economic, and social atmosphere that influenced the lives of the early Europeans on the west coast.

309. Allen, Chris. "Benin." In *Benin, The Congo, Burkina Faso: Economics, Politics and Society.* Marxist Regimes Series. London and New York: Pinter, 1989. 1-144p. Grades 9-adult.
High school students interested in doing research are referred to this book on the political history, government, economy, domestic and foreign policy, and social institutions of the Marxist regime of Benin (formerly Dahomey).

310. Amoaku, Joe. *The Sparkling Gem.* London and Basingstoke: Macmillan; Accra, Ghana: Unimax, 1989. 14p. Grades 2-4.
A young girl's curiosity about her mother's sparkling diamond jewelry leads to an informative account of how diamonds are formed, mined, cut and polished, and utilized. In the relaxed atmosphere of the family's living room, Mary and her friends ask relevant questions and are encouraged to think for themselves. Despite the childish comments of one girl on the pain the diamond has to endure, Mary's mother maintains a scientific outlook in her explanations. While the girls' desire for expensive diamonds is stereotypical, they are also inspired to read further about diamonds and to compose a poem on the beauty of this gem.

311. Bailey, Donna, and Anna Sproule. *Nigeria.* Where We Live Series. Austin, TX: Steck-Vaughn, 1990. Originally published in 1989 by Macmillan. 32p. Grades 1-3.
This is a rather disjointed description of Kano, a large city in Northern Nigeria. Color photographs, drawings, and sketchy text

focus on the exotic features of Kano--walls made of mud bricks, camels and modern transportation, dye pits, pottery, roadside food vendors, mosques and Friday prayers, and the Emir at the Sallah festivities. The above account provides no understanding of the extended family, significance of the Sallah festival, influence of Islam on the daily lives of people, and the chief economic activities of Kano.

312. Barnett, Jeanie M. *Ghana.* Places and Peoples of the World Series. New York: Chelsea House, 1988. 104p. Grades 5-7.
A discussion of Ghana's geography, history, government, economy, health and education, peoples and lifestyles, and arts and crafts acknowledges the impact of European colonialism and the challenges facing Ghana in postcolonial times. However, as the first African nation south of the Sahara to win independence, Ghana continues to inspire other African states. Maps, photographs, list of salient facts, glossary, and index are included.

313. Bleeker, Sonia. *The Ashanti of Ghana.* Illustrated by Edith G. Singer. New York: Morrow, 1966. 160p. Grades 6-8.
The Asante way of life is presented with an understanding of its customs, beliefs, and hardworking and independent people. Based on the accounts of early Europeans who visited the capital of Kumasi, Bleeker provides a detailed account of the pomp and splendor of Asante civilization; well-organized political and social systems; economy based on farming, hunting, fishing, mining, and trading; complex family relationships based on patriarchy, matriarchy, and the high status of women; and slave trade prior to the coming of the Europeans. Bleeker also provides information on talking drums and communication; creation myth and the origin of the golden stool; rituals associated with ancestor worship, initiation of girls, and marriage; and arts and crafts, especially gold work and weaving of the kente cloth. The author believes that the destiny of the Asante was determined by the superior quality and large quantities of gold deposits. The Guinea Coast became a hub of competition for Portuguese, British, Dutch, French, and Danish traders who exchanged European manufactured goods for gold, slaves, and ivory. Eventually, the coastal trade led to explorations into the interior for gold deposits and colonization by the British. The account concludes with independence in 1957 and the Asante adaptation to new conditions: a two-party political system; economic activity centering on cocoa farming; clash between traditional inheritance laws and ownership of cocoa fields; and breakup of close family ties due to rapid industrialization and urbanization. While the above account is interesting and presented with insight, Bleeker emphasizes the exotic, or the differences between Asante and Western cultures.

314. _____. *The Ibo of Biafra.* Illustrated by Edith G. Singer. New York: Morrow, 1969. 157p. Grades 5-7.

This is the least substantive of Dr. Bleeker's sociological studies of various African groups. This discussion of the Igbo culture of Nigeria focuses on the traditional lifestyle, religion and beliefs, economic activities, democratic government, family life and child rearing, high status of women, rituals associated with initiation, marriage and death, and the arts, especially mask-making. A brief concluding chapter analyzes the many adjustments the Igbo have been forced to make in the twentieth century. The account ends with the 1967 clash between the Nigerian government and the Igbo people who declared their independence to form a new nation.

315. Boyd, Herb. *The Former Portuguese Colonies.* A First Book Series. London: Franklin Watts, 1981. 62p. Grades 5-7.
Individual chapters provide a brief discussion of the land, peoples, history (mainly colonial), rise of nationalism and independence, and modern conditions in the former Portuguese colonies of Angola, Mozambique, Guinea-Bissau, Cape Verde, Sao Tome, and Principe in Southern and West Africa. Boyd points out that unlike the other European nations, Portugal's economic well-being was directly tied to its African colonies, hence its reluctance to grant them independence till the mid-1970s. Photographs, maps, and a reading list are included.

316. Carpenter, Allan, and James W. Hughes. *Chad.* Enchantment of Africa Series. Chicago: Children's Press, 1976. 94p. Grades 5-8.
Both text and photographs introduce the geography, history, peoples and lifestyles, government and economy, and education and medical services of Chad. While Chadians are proud of the achievements of the Sao civilization and the Kanem-Bornu empire, life since independence in 1960 has been difficult. A large desert region and the prolonged drought of the late 1960s resulted in a shattered economy, challenged the young Republic under President Francois Tombalbaye, and destroyed the environment. The book, however, presents a balanced picture of modern Chad's problems and its efforts to modernize technology and raise the standard of living.

317. Carpenter, Allan, and Janice E. Baker. *Niger.* Enchantment of Africa Series. Chicago: Children's Press, 1976. 95p. Grades 6-8.
This is a brief discussion of the land, natural resources, peoples, history, government, and economy of Niger. As is typical of the series, the information is made more interesting through a narrative account of an episode from Tuareg history, achievements of the Songhay and Kanem-Bornu empires, and brief biographies of four modern children. The photographs are poor in quality.

318. Carpenter, Allan, and Thomas O'Toole. *Guinea.* Enchantment of Africa Series. Chicago: Children's Press, 1976. 95p. Grades 6-8.
The authors provide an objective discussion of the land, natural resources, peoples, history (especially of Sundiata and the Mali empire), colonization and independence, and modern government and economy of Guinea. The photographs are unappealing.

319. Chu, Daniel, and Elliott Skinner. *A Glorious Age in Africa: The Story of Three Great African Empires.* Illustrated by Moneta Barnett. Garden City, NY: Doubleday, 1965. 120p. Grades 5-8.

The story of three highly developed and fabulously rich West African empires has been pieced together from the evidence of explorers, historians, archeologists, scientists, and a restudy of old manuscripts. The authors meticulously trace the rise and fall of the ancient kingdoms of Ghana, Mali, and Songhay, beginning with the spread of Islam in northwest Africa by Arab and Berber invaders to their eventual downfall in the fifteenth century. The power of these kingdoms was founded on iron weapons, gold mines of Wangara, fertile fields, and control of the trans-Saharan caravan trade route that moved the two most prized commodities, gold and salt. In addition, the authors also discuss principal historical events and personages such as Sundiata, Mansa Musa, Sunni Ali Ber, and Askia Muhammad; the highly complex political, economic, and social structure; and the religious beliefs and customs of the people. These empires also symbolized the advancement of human knowledge when the arts, philosophy, mathematics, and medicine flourished in many parts of the Muslim or Muslim-influenced world. Some of the most famous and highly respected universities were established in the commercial towns of Timbuktu, Jenne, and Gao. In short, the fame and influence of Ghana, Mali, and Songhay helped to shape the direction of events not only in Africa but in Europe and Asia as well.

The above information is readily accessible through well-organized chapters and subtopics. Barnett's pleasing illustrations will enable readers to visualize the golden age of West African civilizations.

320. Collin, Charlotte. *Games Children Play in The Gambia.* Banjul, The Gambia: Book Production and Material Resources Unit, 1985. 48p. Grades 3-6.

A pioneer in the field of Gambian children's games, Collin has collected forty rural games representing nineteen separate ethnic groups, including the Mandinka, Fula, Wolof, and Jola. The games are organized in five chapters according to category: Circle Games, Ball and Jumping Games, Animal Games, Hide and Seek, Blindfold and Running Games, and Mixed Games. The games--some are easily recognizable ones like blindfold, tug-of-war, and hopscotch--are presented in their sociological setting when a group of village boys and girls meets at the *bantaba* (the focal point of the community) on five consecutive evenings. The author emphasizes the specific cultural aspects of the games through the daily activities and conversations of the children. The universal qualities are reflected through the songs (given both in the vernacular and in English), dances, and rhythmic dialogue that accompany the games. Information on the ethnic origin of and the place from which each game was recorded is provided at the end of each chapter. This is a good resource book for children and adults alike. Crude line drawings accompany the text.

321. *Cote d' Ivoire in Pictures.* Visual Geography Series. Minneapolis, MN: Lerner, 1988. Revised edition of *The Ivory Coast in Pictures* by Sterling. 64p. Grades 5-7.

Named after the flourishing ivory trade of the late nineteenth and early twentieth centuries, Cote d'Ivoire is presented as an example of a developing nation that has achieved substantial growth because of economic strategies which encourage both foreign investment and expanded internal production, especially in agriculture. Discussion of the geography indicates that Ivorians had no significant advantages in raw materials and resources over their neighbors till the off-shore petroleum explorations in the 1970s. President Felix Houphouet-Boigny's strong leadership and unquestioned power led the nation from the independence struggle to freedom in 1960 to economic prosperity. However, readers are cautioned that Houphouet-Boigny's refusal to chose a successor, despite his advancing years, portends a difficult transition. His greatest opposition is from student organizations that are critical of the one-party system, capitalism, and the belief that a strong economy is more important than political goals. Furthermore, there is financial inequality because the wealth is being enjoyed mainly by Europeans (50,000 French people became permanent residents after independence) who fill top management positions in business and industry. Other problems that have begun to surface in the cities as a result of rapid urbanization and a high rate of population growth are overcrowding, unemployment, crime, poor housing, and stress on the traditional family. Cote d' Ivoire's privileged economic position has also attracted Lebanese businesses and unskilled workers from other African countries, hence adding to the diversity of the population. The sixty ethnic groups belonging to four main cultures--the Agni and Baule of the Atlantic East, the Atlantic West, Senufo of the Voltaic Group, and Manding--have begun to develop a sense of national identity and unity only since 1960.

Maps, charts, and photographs testify to the country's remarkable achievements in industry, agriculture, transportation, petroleum production, hydroelectric power, and arts and crafts. The only drawback of the book is the sparse discussion of the early history of Cote d' Ivoire.

322. Craz, Albert. *Getting to Know Liberia.* Illustrated by Don Lambo. New York: Coward-McCann, 1958. 64p. Grades 3-5.

Written in an appealing narrative style, this informational book draws parallels between the ideals, history, political structure, and civilizations of Liberia and the United States. Viewed entirely from the perspective of the colonizers, the rights and protests of native Liberians are summarily dismissed. The pioneering freed slaves are praised for establishing, with American assistance, a new country based on American political, economic, educational, and cultural values. In contrast, native "bush" peoples with their village economy and traditional culture are presented as primitive. While "tribal" religions, festivities, coming of age rituals, and arts and crafts are described respectfully, they are clearly seen as less desirable than the advancements offered by Western Liberians.

Another Eurocentric book that is readily available in libraries is Camille Mirepoix's *Liberia in Pictures* (Sterling, 1973). The English-speaking Christian settlers are likened to the early white colonists who endured great suffering in a strange land of hostile natives and wild animals. The chapter on history devotes only two or three sentences to the social organization and customs of indigenous peoples before the advent of the settlers. There is embedded racism when Africans are referred to as "aboriginal population" and "extremely primitive" and when the text states that with the introduction of Western education, "ritualistic cruelty no longer exists and the barbarous acts of old tribal groups have become simply legends." Photographs of Monrovia, urban life, and modern industry testify to the advancements of the Americanized Liberians, while photographs of native African peoples endorse the stereotype of their backwardness and lack of progress.

323. Foy, Colm. *Cape Verde: Politics, Economics and Society.* Marxist Regimes Series. London and New York: Pinter, 1988. 199p. Grades 9-adult.
An examination of Cape Verde's geography, history, political structure, economy, domestic institutions, and foreign policy focuses on its having undergone a revolution without bloodshed, civil unrest, or economic chaos. The success of this desert island's Marxist government is attributed to its hardworking citizens, wise leaders, and political theories of Amilcar Cabral.

324. Freville, Nicholas. *Let's Visit Nigeria.* Let's Visit Series. London: Burke, 1985. Originally published in 1968. 95p. Grades 4-6.
Nigeria is presented as one of the most important and progressive countries in modern Africa. While its financial and civil strife problems are acknowledged, Freville gives a positive account of Nigeria's struggle for freedom, republican government and tribal laws, natural resources and industry, ethnic groups, town and village life, and education and the arts. Attractive photographs portray a balanced view of the various facets of Nigerian life.

325. *Ghana in Pictures.* Visual Geography Series. Minneapolis, MN: Lerner, 1988. Revised edition of *Ghana in Pictures* by Sterling. 64p. Grades 5-8.
This is an objective examination of the land, history, government, people, and economy of Ghana. Emphasis, however, is placed on why Ghana, which in the 1950s and 1960s was regarded as a model of orderly resistance to colonialism and economic dependence on foreign powers, has now fallen into serious political and economic decline. Once the seat of the great empires of Ghana, Mali, and Songhay, Ghana is now characterized by political instability as seen in the eight governments that have changed since independence in 1957. The problem, which started with Nkrumah's dictatorial regime and unwise spending, has worsened with government corruption, lack

of strong leadership, and mounting despair and unrest. Likewise, severe droughts in the 1970s and 1980s, mismanagement of assets, and a changed international economic environment have resulted in high unemployment, inflation, poverty, rising food and import prices, and low price of cocoa, Ghana's major export. Despite the rich natural resources and skilled labor, the future is seen as bleak, unless Ghana can improve its technical and practical training and have an honest and intelligent leadership.

326. Hathaway, Jim. *Cameroon in Pictures*. Visual Geography Series. Minneapolis, MN: Lerner, 1989. Revised edition of *Cameroon in Pictures* by Sterling. 64p. Grades 4-7.

The text traces the impressive history of Cameroon from the Sao civilization in the fifth century B.C., to the Kanem-Bornu empire which flourished from the ninth to the nineteenth centuries, to the European slave trade and colonization by Germany, France, and Britain. Cameroon won independence in 1960 and is the only African country that uses both French and English as its official languages. Cameroon has enjoyed one of the strongest economies and one-party political systems under Presidents Ahmadou Ahidjo and Paul Biya. The present government is also attempting to unite the two hundred ethnic groups, especially English-speaking and French-speaking Cameroonians, and the various ethnic and traditional laws at the local level provided they do not contradict the national law.

While the text states that Cameroon exports more than it imports, that Cameroonians have a higher average yearly income than most Africans, and that 67 percent of all school-going children attend school because of free public education and financial aid for private schooling, the photographs emphasize only the poverty, hardships, and poor diet. Likewise, both text and illustrations focus on rural life and the need for development. There are only two photographs of children in school and seven in an industrial or urban setting, even though 42 percent of the population lives in cities. With a few exceptions, the photographs are generally unattractive.

327. Hintz, Martin. *Ghana*. Enchantment of the World Series. Chicago: Children's Press, 1987. 127p. Grades 6-8.

The text is perhaps the least interesting in the Enchantment of the World Series. It follows the usual format of examining the country's geography, history, government, industry, economy, people, religions, social life, and culture. Unlike the other books in the series, the individual chapters are not extended by brief insets on relevant topics. Hintz' style, however, is engaging and it provides an interesting account of the Asante ceremony honoring ancestors, status of women, and the importance of sports, art, and literature in modern Ghana. The brilliant color photographs, in particular, portray Ghana as a subtle mixture of traditional and modern.

328. Hope, Constance Morris. *Liberia*. New York: Chelsea House, 1987. 92p. Grades 5-7.

This discussion of Liberia's geography, economy and industry, history and government, educational policies and health care, and peoples and culture frankly acknowledges the influence of Americo-Liberians. Hope states that the founding of Liberia by black Americans was no different from the colonization of Africa by the British, Dutch, and French. Americo-Liberians repressed and enslaved the native African peoples, exploited their territory and resources, and imposed legislation restricting where they could live and work. It was not till President Tubman's rule in 1944 that Africans were welcomed into the mainstream of Liberian affairs. In 1980, a group of African soldiers staged a coup d'etat and overthrew the Americo-Liberian government. In 1985, the Second Republic was inaugurated under General Samuel K. Doe. Today, Liberians hope to unify their country with the best of traditional and American cultures.

Another balanced account is presented by Allan Carpenter and Harrison Owen in *Liberia* (Children's Press, 1973). Based on existing data, they present a brief history of the Kru, Vai, Kisi, Gola, Loma, and Kpelle cultural groups prior to the coming of black settlers from America. The perspective of native Liberians to the occupation and exploitation of their land and their lack of representation in the government is presented objectively. Both text and photographs present a positive account of traditional culture as embodied in animism, the Poro and Sande secret societies, arts and crafts, and music and dancing.

329. Jenness, Aylette. *Along the Niger River: An African Way of Life.* Photographs by author. New York: Crowell, 1974. 135p. Grades 6-12.

With revealing photographs and a text based on her firsthand experiences, Jenness introduces young readers to the river Niger, its landscape, peoples, and former civilizations of Mali, Ghana, and Songhay. This sociological study, however, focuses on the northern town of Yelwa and its surrounding countryside where Jenness spent much of her time. She finds the area a perfect example of multicultural harmony despite the diverse customs and lifestyles of its mixed Kamberi, Gungawa, Fulani, Sarkawa, and Kyedyawa population; economic specialization in farming, herding, hunting, fishing, or individual crafts based on ethnic group; and religions varying from traditional African to Islam to Christianity. The flourishing marketplace of Yelwa is the microcosm of this cultural independence and cooperation: It represents peaceful bartering of goods, pride in their unique cultures, and tolerance of great social differences. Jenness believes Yelwa will continue to prosper in the future as it has adapted to Western technology and outside influences without sacrificing its diversity.

330. Kwofie, Paulina, Patrick Adu-Bempah, and Bennette Armah Hanson. *A Visit to the Hospital.* Illustrated by authors. Kumasi, Ghana: Book Industry Section, University of Science and Technology, 1990. 27p. Grades K-3.

The routine in the Out-Patients Department of a hospital is seen through the eyes of a young child. As her brother Kojo is treated for a wound and a dislocated bone, Aba and her parents visit several departments in the hospital: OPO desk, waiting room, consulting room, x-ray room, operating theater, injection room, dispensary, laboratory, and baby clinic. The names and functions of instruments, commonly used terms, and stages in Kojo's treatment are explained to the children in a noncondescending manner. Excellent line drawings help readers to visualize the visit to the hospital. The only negative feature is the book's sex role stereotyping--nurses are always women, while doctors, technicians, and pharmacists are men. A glossary of medical terms used in the book is included.

331. Lear, Aaron. *Burkina Faso.* Edgemont, PA: Chelsea House, 1986. 95p. Grades 5-7.

This informational book discusses the land, peoples, history, government, and economy of Burkina Faso, formerly known as Upper Volta. The account, however, emphasizes the recent problems of political instability, food shortages, trade deficits, frequent droughts, hunger and malnutrition, inadequate medical care, and 98 percent illiteracy. The military rule of Captain Thomas Sankara is committed to eliminating these problems at all levels. While the author terms Burkina Faso a land of contrasts where ancient and "primitive" and modern coexist, the illustrations emphasize only the rural, exotic, and underdeveloped aspects of the economy. Likewise, the photographs accompanying the chapter on recent history bear no relationship to the text; the chapter abounds in colorful (albeit very attractive) photographs of a variety of ritual masks and ceremonial dancers.

332. Lopes, Carlos. *Guinea-Bissau: From Liberation Struggle to Independent Statehood.* Translated by Michael Wolfers. Boulder, Colorado: Westview/London and New Jersey: Zed Books, 1987. 194p. Grades 10-adult.

The aim of this meticulously researched and highly scientific book is to understand the problems of Guinea-Bissau's transition from a Portuguese colony to independent statehood. The country's political conditions, social structure, and economic activity are examined in the light of various political ideologies like Marxism, dependency theory, political-sociology, and philosophy of Amilcar Cabral. Lopes offers a global vision by including the experiences of comparable nations, especially in Africa. He states that the failures of the new African countries cannot be blamed on imperialism, colonization, and neocolonialism because such a stance attributes a passive role to the leaders of the new states and offers a simplistic interpretation of the problems.

333. Lutz, William. *Senegal.* Places and Peoples of the World Series. New York: Chelsea House, 1988. 104p. Grades 6-8.

Senegal is seen as a country that has kept a low profile in world news because it does not attract attention for conflicts, racial prejudice, disease, famine, and extremist governments. Instead, it is a resilient nation that has put its past experiences to advantage. Historically, its strategic location made it a meeting place for traders from South and West Africa; a stopping place for European voyages around Africa to Asia and South America; and a crossroad for the slave trade. Senegal also became the center of kingdoms like Tekrur, Wolof, and French West Africa. Today, Senegal is a cosmopolitan nation with a multiethnic population--mainly Wolof, Serer, and Fulani--that has forged a national identity and a spirit of cooperation for itself. The moderate governments of Presidents Leopold Sedar Senghor and Abdou Diouf ensure political freedom through a multiparty democratic system. Senegal also maintains close relationships with France and the Organization for African Unity. Senegal's major problems are high population growth, unpredictable weather and frequent droughts, economic dependence on the peanut harvest, 10 percent literacy despite its modern educational system, and inadequate health and social benefits for 80 percent of the population. President Diouf's policies attempt to deal with these problems by improving and diversifying agricultural production and irrigation, encouraging foreign trade and investment, and raising the standard of living. This informational book has interesting segments on Goree, an island which was a major collection and shipping point for the transatlantic slave market; organization and physical plan of a Wolof village; the capital city of Dakar; and the role of the griot in society. Photographs, glossary, index, maps, and list of facts and important dates are included.

Another book that examines the land, history, government, people, and economy of Senegal is the revised edition of *Senegal in Pictures* (Lerner, 1989). While the basic information is the same, this book gives more details on Senegal's history prior to the arrival of Europeans. It mentions the large and powerful empires of Ghana, Almoravids, Mali, and Wolof, which included regions of Senegal, from the fifth to the sixteenth centuries. However, the segment on Islam--which 90 percent of the population follows--mistakenly calls Islam a "belief system based on the holy writings of the Koran as interpreted by the prophet Muhammad." In actuality, Prophet Muhammad founded the religion and the Quran, which was compiled after his death, included his teachings and precepts. As the title indicates, each chapter is profusely illustrated with attractive black-and-white and color photographs.

334. Lye, Keith. *Take a Trip to Nigeria.* Take a Trip Series. London: Franklin Watts, 1983. 32p. Grades K-2.
Color photographs and a sketchy text provide information on the government, major cities, economy, agriculture and industry, religion and festivals, ethnic groups, and art of modern Nigeria.

335. Milsome, John. *Sierra Leone.* New York: Chelsea House, 1988. 95p. Grades 5-7.
Brief chapters survey the country's varied geography, history from cave dwellers at Yengema to the mid-1980s, government, economy,

mining and industry, rural and urban lifestyles, and religion and culture. In discussing the abolition movement in Britain and the selection of Sierra Leone as the ideal home for freed slaves, called Creoles, from Britain, Jamaica, and later Canada, Milsome views the arising political problems from the perspective of the local peoples. Their resistance is understandable because their territories were suddenly appropriated and controlled by strangers. Milsome also presents the Sierra Leonean perspective in wanting to change to a one-party government because the first decade after independence in 1961 was marked by partisan politics along ethnic lines. The challenges facing modern Sierra Leone focus on providing technical training for agriculture, reducing cost of mining diamonds and other natural deposits, expanding trade, and improving educational and living standards.

The book's content, tone, and diction also attempt to attract the tourist by providing information on appropriate clothing, hotels, prominent beaches and tourist attractions, wildlife sanctuaries, and arts and crafts. Frequent use of terms like "tribe" and "bush" displays lack of sensitivity to African pride. *Sierra Leone* does not have the reference tools that are typical of the Places and Peoples Series. Also, lack of subheadings within chapters makes it difficult to access information easily; however, an index is included. Attractive black-and-white and color photographs illustrate the text.

336. O'Toole, Thomas. *Mali in Pictures.* Visual Geography Series. Minneapolis, MN: Lerner, 1990. 64p. Grades 5-8.

Mali is portrayed as a country that at one time was the center of several important African realms and developed civilizations, but in modern times is one of the world's ten poorest nations due to its semi-arid land, severe droughts, and drop in export income. Mali's impressive history boasts of a series of three strong and prosperous trading empires--Ghana empire (around 300 A.D.), Mali empire (1200s), and Songhay empire (mid-1300s)--that controlled the Saharan commercial routes leading to the Mediterranean and Asian markets. Cities like Gao, Timbuktu, and Djenne were centers of trade and Islamic learning and culture. Mali's decline began in the 1800s when Europeans, particularly the French, subdued the Islamic realms to establish a colonial empire. Mali achieved independence from the French in 1960, and since then it has been governed by a one-party system with a mixed military-civilian regime under Presidents Modibo Keita and Moussa Traore. Economic challenges dominate Mali's future because only a strengthened economy can lead to improved health care, educational facilities, and nutrition.

337. Perl, Lila. *Ghana and Ivory Coast: Spotlight on West Africa.* New York: Morrow, 1975. 160p. Grades 8-12.

Perl spotlights two of the most successful nations in West Africa--Ghana and Cote d'Ivorie--in order to discuss the postcolonial era. She first focuses on the similarities in land, climate, ethnic peoples, agriculture, civilization, natural resources, and European trade and colonialism. However, the differences between the two countries are evident in the ideological paths taken in economic development. In Ghana, especially under President Kwame Nkrumah, liberation meant an openly expressed antagonism toward Western capitalist values. In contrast, Cote d'Ivoire achieved a remarkably smooth economic growth and a high degree of national prosperity by encouraging widespread foreign economic activity, especially in the area of industrial development. In Ghana, there has been development without growth, whereas in Cote d'Ivoire there has been economic growth without development of adequate health, educational, social, cultural, and housing opportunities for all citizens.

Although the above information is outdated, Perl correctly assesses the West African situation: There have been deep cultural, political, and economic inroads of foreign origin whose effects are still being felt and dealt with today. First, multiparty systems are not conducive to African traditions because they are often the voices of regionalism and divisiveness that threaten and destroy national unity. She believes some military regimes have been more benevolent and democratic than majority-elected governments. Second, establishing national borders by longitude and latitude has separated groups and families in terms of citizenship, language, religion, laws, and educational opportunities. Another unfortunate impact of externally imposed boundaries is balkanization, or the breaking up of large territories into numerous small and often hostile states (for example, The Gambia). Third, fierce nationalism has prompted West African nations to maintain closer ties with former colonial masters and other Western nations than with their African neighbors. This tendency is aggravated by language and communication barriers. For colonial nations the greatest advantage in withdrawing administratively and politically from the region has been release from responsibility for internal development, while still enjoying broad economic advantages. Next, as in former colonies in Asia, there has been the development of an elite African Administrative and Civil Service class whose lifestyle is patterned after that of the colonials. Finally, the educational system, which was designed during the colonial period, does not help the general population to advance. Perl views the West African situation as a mass of contradictions: intermingling of traditional and modern, politically free but economically fettered, nationalism versus unity, and great wealth versus widespread poverty and ignorance. She believes that the greatest hope rests in economic cooperation among West African countries. Photographs, maps, bibliography, and index are included.

338. Pern, Stephen, and the Editors of Time-Life Books. *Masked Dancers of West Africa: The Dogon.* Photographs by Bryan Alexander. Peoples of the World Series. Amsterdam: Time-Life Books, 1982. 168p. Grades 8-12.

Pern and Alexander spent several months in Tireli, an isolated village situated on the steep rocky slope at the foot of the Bandiagara Cliffs, recording their impressions of the land, culture, religion, economy, and political organization of the Dogon. As honorary "kinsmen," they visited family members, attended market day and beer-drinking parties, sat in on village meetings, participated in sacrifices and boisterous festivals for rain, planted crops after the first rain, and accompanied funeral processions. The only activity that was denied to them was burial of the dead, although they were allowed to visit ancient burial sites in crevices in the cliffs.

On the surface, Tireli's agricultural lifestyle seems to be a necessary response to the environment, but Pern's sensitive first person account quickly reveals that the Dogon group has evolved a sophisticated egalitarian culture. He explains the complicated family structure that divides the village into two parts and six wards; rules by which the sparse farm land is allocated; political control based on consensus reached by male elders; and judicial system that emphasizes acceptance of guilt rather than punishment. Marriage, birth of children, initiation rites, funerals, and roles of men and women are prescribed with equal rigidity, and everyone is pressured to conform. Women are second-class citizens whose main function is to reproduce, raise children, and do household and planting chores. Men dominate in the area of religion also, which is based on the mythology of a supreme creator, lesser gods or spirits, and numerous legends and epics of historical characters. To find solutions to their spiritual, physical, and social problems, the Dogon people approach shamans, healers, and diviners who read the footprints of foxes to foretell the future. The spirits of the dead are propitiated through elaborate masked dances performed by boys and young men to console the dead for their loss of life. Every aspect of Dogon life is aimed at strengthening family and community bonds and establishing harmony with the land, gods, and ancestors.

The text is complemented and extended by Alexander's brilliant color photographs and photo essays on the landscape, fertility rites, market day, arts and crafts, making a granary, day in the life of a young boy, and masked dances.

339. Price, Christine. *Dancing Masks of Africa.* Illustrated by author. New York: Scribner's 1975. N.p. Grades K-3.

This picture book provides information on the symbolic role of masks in West African traditions. Accompanied by singing and the music of drums, gongs, flutes, and xylophones, masked male dancers mystically assume the powers of their animal and spiritual deities to ensure happiness and prosperity for the individual and universal peace for the community. These religious beliefs unite hunters and kings, farmers and fishermen, men and women, and city dwellers and villagers. The dancing of the masks also represents the blessings conferred by Oloka, the protector of animals; Orangun, the bringer of rain; Antelope Spirit, the patron of planting and harvests; spirits who provide safety from danger, sickness, and pain; and spirits who expel evil and ensure law and order. In short, masks dance to celebrate the symbiotic relationship between the forces of nature and the destiny of people.

The excitement and drama of a celebration are further captured by the poetic text. Through repetition, alliteration, and assonance, an internal rhythm is created that reflects the stamping of feet, beating of drums, and swishing and swirling of the dancing masks. While the pictures of masks are lively and dynamic, the illustrations of men, women, and children are static and unappealing. The notes on the masks explain the purpose and intrinsic value of the masks. Drawings of masks from various countries of West Africa are also included.

340. Stride, G.T., and Caroline Ifeka. *Peoples and Empires of West Africa: West Africa in History 1000-1800.* London: Nelson, 1971. 373p. Grades 8-12.

African students are introduced to their cultural heritage through a study of the peoples, government, religions, and cultures of various West African empires. A discussion of kingdoms such as Gambia, Ghana, Mali, Songhay, Hausa and Niger delta city states, Bambara, Akan states, Dahomey, and Benin demonstrates the dynamic and purposeful past of West Africa, which was dependent neither on European influence nor on European personnel. It was notable rulers and chiefs like Sundiata, Mansa Musa, Osei Tutu, Dunama II, Sunni Ali, and Askia Muhammad who controlled the destiny of West Africa. The arrival of the Portuguese in the fifteenth century is attributed to the desire for economic wealth, political power, and religious fervor. However, it is clearly pointed out that Portuguese settlements and forts on the coasts were established with the consent of local rulers for the purpose of organized trade. The transatlantic slave trade was also firmly controlled by African chiefs and headmen who supplied the slaves in exchange for European consumer goods and controlled the inland routes and markets. Slaves were procured through kidnapping, as captives in wars, as penalty for crimes, and as recompense for family debts. The authors point out that slavery as understood and practiced by Europeans was different in concept from slavery in Africa. Although the legal position of slaves was the same as in Europe, the customary situation was significantly different. Slaves were members of their masters' families; they received comparable treatment with the free members of the community; they were workers with rights unless guilty of serious misconduct; and they could rise to positions of eminence in their masters' households or in their communities. The abolition of slavery by Europeans is attributed to a mixture of humanitarian, political, and economic motives.

The above material is presented analytically and the available evidence is weighed and evaluated. The account includes folk traditions and oral history because the authors believe that future historians will have to study this material and indicate its value and limitations. The discursive prose engages the reader actively by posing challenging questions and exploring hypothetical possibilities and solutions. For instance, had there been no slave trade, or the loss of a strong and healthy manpower, West Africa could have cultivated virgin land, increased food production, and increased economic wealth by manufacturing its own consumer goods.

341. Sutherland, Efua. *Playtime in Africa.* Photographs by Willis E. Bell. New York: Atheneum, 1962. Originally published in Ghana. 58p. Grades K-3.

Sutherland's poetic text and Bell's warm and candid photographs capture boys and girls at play in Ghana. Whether rich or poor, urban or rural these children lead happy and fulfilling lives. They engage in group games like hide-and-seek, skipping and jumping, soccer, ouware, and marbles; and they play alone with dolls, share secrets with friends, fish, draw and mould clay figures, and construct trucks out of discarded materials. Ghanaian children enjoy nature in all its moods: they play in the rain, swim in the sea, and hide in the dry leaves tossed by the harmattan. Like children everywhere, African children express their capacity to enjoy life, develop their creative skills, and prepare for their future adult roles through play.

342. Synge, Richard. *Nigeria: The Land and its Peoples.* Countries Series. London: Macdonald, 1975. 61p. Grades 6-8.

While the factual information is not current, the book's format allows Nigeria's richness and variety to be presented in an interesting manner. Double-page spreads discuss topics such as history, geography, cultural diversity, family life, fashions, sports and recreation, religions, education, food, and arts and crafts. First, each topic is presented briefly, and then it is extended by maps, charts, photographs, drawings, cartoons, and explanatory captions. Additional information is provided in a reference section on human and physical geography; salient facts of history, economy, and the arts; glossary; index; and physical and political maps.

343. Watts, Daud Malik. *The 100,000 Horsemen of West Africa.* Positive Image Education Series. Washington, D.C: Afro-Vision, 1992. 20p. Grades 6-12.

In keeping with the mission statement of this series, Watts infuses pride in African history through an examination of the equestrian traditions of West Africa. Although horses were used in West Africa for over a thousand years, Watts focuses his research only on the training and horsemanship, uses of horses, and cavalry equipment of the past 150 years. Based on historical records, photographs and sketches, and eyewitness accounts of European explorers, dating as far back as 1805, Watts provides an interesting account of the impact of horses on the history, European colonization, slave trade, economy, and culture of West Africa. There were an estimated 100,000 cavalry horses in the Bornu, Hausaland, plateaus, Niger Bend, and Guinea savannah regions of West Africa. Watts ends by hinting at the impact of these equestrian skills on America.

344. Wilkins, Frances. *Let's Visit The Gambia.* London: Burke, 1985. 94p. Grades 5-7.

The Gambia is presented as a classic example of exploitative European policies which created artificial barriers between and within African nations. Consisting of only a narrow strip of land--4,000 square miles in all--The Gambia, a former British colony, is entirely surrounded by Senegal, a former French colony. A discussion of the tiny nation's geography, early history and slave trade, economic dependence on a single crop (groundnuts), Islam, education, and peoples is further proof of its isolation from immediate neighbors. The only hope for The Gambia is seen in forming a federation with Senegal for their mutual economic prosperity, trade, foreign policy, and political and cultural unity.

345. Winslow, Zachery. *Togo*. Places and Peoples of the World Series. New York: Chelsea House, 1988. 96p. Grades 5-7.

An examination of the geography, history, government, peoples, art and culture, and economy of Togo leads to a discussion of the emergence of one of West Africa's smallest nations into a regional leader in international and economic affairs. Togo has been nicknamed "Little Africa" because it is seen as a microcosm of the continent. With its forty-three ethnic groups, emphasis on family, strong belief in animism and reincarnation, and blend of cultural heritage and modern lifestyles, it has achieved what all African nations desire--national unity, political stability, and modernity without losing traditions. Togo's achievements are largely due to the efforts of its charismatic and determined president, Etienne Eyadema, who introduced strategies to promote national unity, survival of ethnic traditions, a multicultural school system that includes the two major Ewe and Kabye languages in its curriculum, new technologies in agriculture and industry, foreign investment, and improved transportation and communication. In 1979, Togolese voters supported a new constitution which created a parliamentary system of government with a democratically elected president and National Assembly. Women hold great political power because hereditary titles were handed down from mothers to sons in ancient Togo. The village of Sarakawa is unique because women control all municipal and religious activities. In recent years, women have assumed economic power as well, especially in Lome, the capital, where business-women--called "Nanas-Benz" because they drive Mercedes-Benz automobiles--dominate the main market and are sought by President Eyadema for their support. Winslow also outlines the major problems facing Togo: hostilities with Benin over political dissidents and with Ghana over division of Ewe territories; low agricultural production; elitist education; weak economy; and inadequate health care.

346. Yemitan, Oladipo. *Happy Times in Iju*. Ibadan, Nigeria: University Press, 1983. 40p. Grades 3-5.

Two city children, Musa and Lola, learn about rural life when they visit a village during vacations. By participating in the daily activities of their relatives, they are introduced to village organization, communal activities, subsistence farming, cattle raising, and market day. They also eat different foods, wash clothes at the stream, and assist in dyeing cloth and planting vegetables. They realize that unlike urban life, village life is characterized by self-sufficiency.

East Africa

TRADITIONAL LITERATURE

347. Aardema, Verna. *Bimwili and the Zimwi: A Tale from Zanzibar.* Illustrated by Susan Meddaugh. New York: Dial, 1985. N.p. Grades K-3.

Bimwili's adventure warns little children against strangers and wandering off alone after beautiful objects. On her first visit to the sea, Bimwili finds a lovely shell with the sound of the sea in it, but she forgets it on the beach. When she returns for it, she is kidnapped by the Zimwi, a supernatural creature. Trapped in his drum, she is made to sing from village to village in exchange for food and shelter. One day, Bimwili recognizes her mother's voice, and through her song she informs her family of her presence. Bimwili is rescued, and the Zimwi transforms himself and returns to the beach--perhaps, to wait for his next victim.

348. _____. *Bringing the Rain to Kapiti Plain.* Illustrated by Beatriz Vidal. New York: Dial, 1981. N.p. Preschool-Grade 2.

Based on Sir Claud Hollis' recording of the tale in *The Nandi: Their Language and Folklore* (1909), Aardema narrates this cumulative tale as a nursery rhyme using the familiar rhythm of "The House that Jack Built." The tale explains how rain was brought to Kapiti Plain in Kenya during a severe drought. Ki-pat, a herder of cows, shoots an arrow into the rain cloud that shadows the plain but does not shed its moisture. The arrow pierces the cloud and releases thunder and rain, hence bringing green grass, wild animals, and prosperity back to the region. Ki-pat's own life is blessed with a wife and son, who carries his father's tradition of bringing rain when black clouds loom over Kapiti Plain. The serious tone and distance created by the illustrations are balanced by the lively rhythm and cumulative refrain which invite children to participate in the recitation.

349. _____. *Rabbit Makes a Monkey of Lion.* Illustrated by Jerry Pinkney. New York: Pied Piper, 1989. N.p. Grades K-3.

Once again, Aardema's graceful narrative style reflects the African art of storytelling in this Swahili trickster tale. With Rabbit in the lead, the tiny animals of the forest make a fool of Lion by repeatedly stealing his honey. When the exasperated lion concedes that rabbits are just too hard to catch, Rabbit wisely acknowledges that he should not invade Lion's domain. Pinkney's illustrations not only portray the lush East African landscape, but they also capture the emotions of the characters and heighten the drama of the story.

350. _____. *What's So Funny, Ketu?* Illustrated by Marc Brown. Adapted from *Otwe* by Verna Aardema. New York: Dial, 1982. N.p. Preschool-Grade 3.

A retelling of "The Man and The Snake," in *Nuer Customs and Folklore* (Oxford UP, 1931), this folktale narrates the humorous exploits of Ketu, who is given the gift of understanding the thoughts of animals by a snake. The only condition placed on Ketu is that he must not reveal his secret to anyone, or he will die. Ketu's uncontrollable laughter when he hears the funny thoughts of the mosquito who wants to enter the hut to bite his family, the rat who schemes to steal butter, and the cow who is determined not to give milk for Ketu's baby gets him into trouble with Nyaloti, his wife. When the rat jumps on her, the cow kicks the bowl, and the baby cries because of Ketu's laughter, Nyaloti's feelings are hurt. She accuses her husband of making fun of her and approaches the chief to arbitrate the case. While Nyaloti's mounting frustration and anger are understandable, it is Ketu's sense of fun and sensitivity to animals that win him readers' sympathy. Fear of losing his wife and child prompt Ketu to reveal his secret. He drops dead, but the magical snake revives Ketu because Ketu was goaded by the curiosity of others into betraying the secret. The humor and liveliness of the story are reflected in Brown's illustrations, especially in the fluid movements and exaggerated expressions of both human and animal characters. Aardema's descriptive reproductions of human and animal sounds make this an excellent read-aloud book.

351. _____. *Who's in Rabbit's House?* Illustrated by Leo and Diane Dillon. New York: Dial, 1969, 1977. N.p. Grades K-3.

Tiny caterpillar plays a practical joke by taking over Rabbit's house by claiming to be The Long One, destroyer of trees and elephants. Rabbit is too scared to enter his house. Jackal, Leopard, Elephant, and Rhinoceros offer to help by destroying the house with the intruder in it, but Rabbit, who loves his home and neat yard, does not want it ruined. It is the trickster Frog who scares the caterpillar by saying he is the hissing cobra who is going to creep under the door to blind him. The frightened caterpillar comes out and the other animals laugh at his predicament; however, the last laugh belongs to the frog because all the animals have been fooled.

In addition to the delightful humor of this Masai folktale, the book can be enjoyed for its unique artwork. The illustrations extend the text by presenting the folktale as a masked performance by Masai villagers for their neighbors. As the play gets underway, the perspective changes and readers become the audience. Continual movement is expressed through a series of frames of a single action. The illustrations provide an authentic depiction of Masai clothing, houses, hairstyles, and countryside. This book was listed as American Library Association Notable Children's Book, 1977; School Library Journal Best Books of the Year, 1977; A Children's Book of the Year, Child Study Association, 1977; and Learning, The Year's Ten Best, 1977.

352. Beneath the Rainbow: A Collection of Children's Stories and Poems from Kenya. Volume 1. Nairobi, Kenya: Jacaranda, 1992. 47p. Grades K-3.
    This collection of three traditional tales by Valerie Cuthbert and Kariuki Gakuo and three nature poems by Sam Mbure is an example of Jacaranda's distinctive books for children. The folktales are narrated in a lively modern style, and the color illustrations by the resident artists are both attractive and aesthetically pleasing.

353. Bere, Rennie. *Crocodile's Eggs for Supper and Other Animal Tales from Northern Uganda.* Illustrated by John Paige. London: Andre Deutsch, 1973. 104p. Grades 3-6.
    A variety of animal tales embody the wisdom, beliefs, and lifestyle of the Acholi of Northern Uganda and Southern Sudan. While the tales are lively and entertaining, the reteller's explanatory essay--based on thirty years' experience in Uganda--reflects a Western perspective toward Acholi culture, religious beliefs and rituals, and worldview.

354. Bible, Charles. *Hamdaani: A Traditional Tale from Zanzibar.* Illustrated by adaptor. New York: Holt, Rinehart and Winston, 1977. N.p. Grades K-3.
    When a magical gazelle gives the beggar Hamdaani great wealth and happiness, he is distressed by the ingratitude and arrogance he receives in return. Hamdaani is punished by being transported back to the dust heap where he used to scratch for food. Bible's illustrations evoke the Arabic atmosphere and culture of ancient Zanzibar.

355. Bozylinsky, Hannah Heritage. *Lala Salama: An African Lullaby.* Illustrated by reteller. New York: Philomel, 1993. N.p. Preschool-Grade 1.
    A young goatherd sings this popular Swahili lullaby as he returns home at dusk. As he bids peace and rest to the many animals he encounters on the way, he displays his harmony with nature. Bozylinsky's English translation, which deftly integrates the Swahili version, retains the rhythmic and incantational element of the song. The simple text and clear lines of the gouache illustrations will appeal to the very young child.

356. Bracey, Dorothy, and Peter Lieta. *Hare Is Bad.* Illustrated by Terry Hirst. Nairobi, Kenya: Longman, 1975. 30p. Grades K-2.

This easy reader narrates the exploits of trickster Hare who steals garden produce from Elephant, Zebra, and Monkey. Despite the controlled vocabulary and short sentences, the text is lively and witty. The color illustrations extend the text and emphasize the humorous situations, especially when the larger animals are gullible enough to be duped twice.

357. Courlander, Harold, and Wolf Leslau. *The Fire on the Mountain and Other Ethiopian Stories.* Illustrated by Robert W. Kane. New York: Holt, 1950. 141p. Grades 3-5.

Recorded by Courlander and Leslau, the twenty-four tales in this volume represent the folklore of the Amhara, Gurage, Tigrai, and Hamasein areas of Eritrea. These tales absorbed African, Jewish, Arabic, Indian, Christian, Islamic, and European influences as they were carried back and forth in the migrations of cattle herders, camel caravans, and traders. The Notes discuss the origin of each tale; its variants in Africa, the Middle East, and India; and its typically Ethiopian elements. Regardless of origin, each story is uniquely Ethiopian because of the names of people and places, details of geography and landscape, and local customs and lifestyles. The themes of both the animal and human stories, however, are universal: There are stories of litigation and justice; there are noodlehead tales of the foolish; there are humorous tales which poke fun at human pretensions and foibles; there are trickster tales of the hare and monkey and the legendary figure, Abunawas; and, finally, there are philosophic tales which reflect the Ethiopians' love for their country and their pride in thwarting invaders through the centuries.

358. Davis, Douglas F. *The Lion's Tail.* Illustrated by Ronald Himler. New York: Atheneum, 1980. N.p. Grades K-3.

This elegantly told creation myth explains that the great god Ngai gave the divine gift of cattle to the Masai to relieve their hunger. However, this gift creates enmity with the lion-people of the Serengeti Plain who claim a right to hunt all animals. The Masai and the lion-people challenge each other, but with divine inspiration the Masai build thorn fences to protect their cattle and outwit the lion-people. Himler's black-and-white framed illustrations lend distance and dignity to this most sacred of Masai myths.

359. Gakuo, Kariuki. *Nyumba Ya Mumbi: The Gikuyu Creation Myth.* Illustrated By Mwaura Ndekere. African Art and Literature Series. Nairobi, Kenya: Jacaranda, 1992. 36p. Grades K-3.

Brilliant artwork, an evocative text, and excellent production standards combine to make this an outstanding picture book. This creation myth explains the genesis of the Gikuyu community of Kenya and the formation of its nine clans. Gakuo's poetic diction, rhythmic prose, and dignified tone elevate the myth to the level of a religious text. Likewise, Ndekere's paintings capture the mystery of creation and the beauty of nature, especially of Mount Kirinyago, the abode of Mugai the Supreme God.

360. Gichuru, Stephen. *The Fly Whisk and Other Stories.* Illustrated by Adrienne Moore. Phoenix Young Readers Library. Nairobi, Kenya: Phoenix, 1967, 1988. 71p. Grades 3-5.

Ten delightful Masai folktales from the Rift Valley region of Tanzania and Kenya narrate the exploits of the trickster hare and hyena, Gautafan the giant, supernatural women who eat men, and humble warriors. Whether the story is about justice or trickery, Gichuru's delightful retelling focuses not on the moral, but on the engaging plot and humorous situations.

361. Grimble, Rosemary. *The Thief Catcher and Other Stories from Ethiopia.* Illustrated by reteller. London: Andre Deutsch, 1974. 100p. Grades 4-6.

The ten tales in this very readable volume are based on the 1914 collection of J. I. Eadie, a British Army officer stationed in Ethiopia. The illustrations are inspired by the work of John Martin Bernatz, the official artist for the British mission to Ethiopia from 1841 to 1843. The tales reflect the variety and richness of Ethiopian folklore from legends of Saint Tekla Haymanot, to stories of jesters, master thieves, and thief catchers, to tales of common sense and wisdom.

362. Hadithi, Mwenye. *Hot Hippo.* Illustrated by Adrienne Kennaway. Boston: Little, Brown, 1986. N.p. Preschool-Grade 2.

This pourquoi tale explains why Hippo is unhappy living on dry land and how he convinces God Ngai to permit him to live in the water. Both text and illustrations focus on Hippo's feelings and the humorous predicaments he gets into. Other books in this series that focuses on animal traits are *Greedy Zebra!, Crafty Chameleon, Tricky Tortoise,* and *Lend Me Your Wings.* In *Crafty Chameleon* (Little, Brown, 1987), Hadithi narrates how the clever chameleon punishes the crocodile and leopard for constantly abusing him with their brute strength. Kennaway's illustrations stress the feelings and frustrations of the harassed chameleon and his eventual triumph.

363. Kabira, Wanjiku Mukabi, and Karega Mutahi. *Gikuyu Oral Literature.* Nairobi, Kenya: Heinemann, 1988. 167p. Grades 10-12.

This book is both a collection of Gikuyan oral literature as well as a scholarly analysis of its structure, functions, and cultural and historical background. Recorded from live performances in the districts of Kiambuu, Murang'a, and Nyeri, the researchers have made a concerted effort to duplicate through the written medium the skills and techniques that accompany a performance. Qualities essential to a good performance are the artist's familiarity with and knowledge of cultural details, rich vocabulary, good memory, good voice, ability to dramatize various roles, and sensitivity to the mood and participation of the audience. Gikuyan oral literature is organized into five genres--narratives (ogre narratives and true narratives), songs and dances, poetry, proverbs, and riddles. An in-depth discussion is provided through numerous examples of narratives, songs, proverbs, and riddles in both Gikuyu and English translations.

364. King, Bridget. *Nyalgondho wuod-Ombare and the Lost Woman from Lake Victoria.* Illustrated by Joel Oswaggo. African Art and Literature Series. Nairobi, Kenya: Jacaranda, 1991. 30p. Grades K-2.

Both illustrations and text lend dignity to this Luo legend of the mysterious woman from Lake Victoria who showers riches and happiness on a poor fisherman. However, when the man's pride in his newly acquired wealth makes him ill-treat the woman, she returns to the lake with all his material possessions. It is human weakness that is responsible for one's ill-luck or fate, the story emphasizes. A well-known artist in Kenya, Oswaggo's original paintings infuse a sense of awe and wonder into the story.

365. Knutson, Barbara. *How the Guinea Fowl Got Her Spots: A Swahili Tale of Friendship.* Illustrated by reteller. Minneapolis, MN: Carolrhoda, 1990. N.p. Preschool-Grade 2.

This East African pourquoi tale not only explains the physical characteristics of the guinea fowl, but it also celebrates true friendship. One day Guinea Fowl saves Cow's life when they are foraging for food on the green hills. In appreciation for Guinea Fowl's bravery in distracting Lion, Cow splatters Guinea Fowl's glossy black feathers with milk so that Lion will not be able to take revenge.

The watercolor and ink illustrations add a pleasing visual dimension to the story. Knutson follows the scratching process to duplicate traditional African designs which were originally scratched into wood, gourds, or metals.

366. Mann, Kenny. *"I Am Not Afraid!"* Illustrated by Richard Leonard and Alfredo Alcala. Bank Street Ready-to-Read Series. New York: Bantam, 1993. 31p. Grades K-2.

Young Leys is full of fear when he attempts to take water from the river and dead branches from the tree. His brave older brother, who is initiating him into the life of a Masai cattle herder, teaches him both respect for the gifts of nature and courage and confidence in one's ability to survive. The illustrations, although bold and colorful, fail to capture Masai facial features with authenticity. The characters look like Europeans with brown skins and thick red lips.

367. Mollel, Tololwa Marti. *The Orphan Boy.* Illustrated by Paul Morin. New York: Clarion, 1990. 32p. Grades K-3.

This Masai myth explains why the planet Venus is called Kileken, or the Orphan Boy. When a lonely old man is gazing at the stars, he is startled by the presence of a boy who says he is Kileken, an orphan in search of a home. The old man welcomes him as a son and soon comes to appreciate and depend on his hard work and thoughtful ways. When the cows thrive in the parched countryside, the old man is curious to discover the secret of this mysterious boy. When the source of his power is discovered, Kileken explodes into a blinding star and rises into the sky as the planet Venus. Like the orphan boy who was up at dawn to herd the cattle and who returned to the compound at night for the evening milking, Kileken appears in the east at dawn as the morning star and in the west at nightfall as the evening star.

This simple, evocative story emphasizes the human emotions of loneliness, joy, satisfaction, love, despair, trust, and curiosity. It also captures the joyful relationship that can exist between young and old, the debilitating effects of old age, and the energy and vigor of youth. All these themes and moods are portrayed through Morin's brilliant color paintings and black-and-white drawings. Although the story ends unhappily, the last portrait of the old man gazing at the star-studded evening sky is consoling because he has a special relationship with one particular star.

368. _____. *The Princess Who Lost Her Hair.* Illustrated by Charles Reasoner. Legends of the World Series. Mahwah, NJ: Troll, 1993. 32p. Grades 1-3.

The importance of every living creature to the Akamba of East Africa is embodied in the story of a princess who is so proud of her lovely hair that she will not part with even a few strands to oblige a bird. The bird's curse makes her long hair disappear and a terrible drought descends on the kingdom. When neither the wise men nor the magicians can reverse the doom, Muoma, a beggar boy, embarks on a heroic journey to seek the bird. He is rewarded with the seed of the Tree That Grows Hair because he is generous to every living thing he encounters. By planting the seed and tending the tiny sapling, Muoma instills respect for nature in the princess. The princess' hair reappears and fertility returns to the land.

369. _____. *Rhinos for Lunch and Elephants for Supper!* Illustrated by Barbara Spurll. New York: Clarion, 1991. N.p. Grades K-2.

Mollel offers another delightful version of the Masai folktale narrated in entry #351. Barbara Spurll's illustrations, in particular, convey a subtle sense of humor as the "clever" hare and fox and "strong" leopard, rhinoceros, and elephant are outwitted by the tiny caterpillar and frog. Spurll's graceful lines represent the fear of the larger animals as they flee from the booming, threatening voice issuing from Hare's cave. Frog, whose nap has been disturbed by the chaos, stands firmly on the ground and is determined to resolve the mystery so that he can go back to sleep.

370. Mukunyi, Dickson. *The Pet Snake and Other Stories.* Illustrated by Beryl Moore. Nairobi, Kenya: Phoenix, 1968, 1988. 39p. Grades K-3.

The simple text and lively dialogue will hold the interest of youngsters as they read about friendship, loyalty, greed, and caution, or about the trickster squirrel and the wicked hyena. There are also two stories of orphans who find happiness and wealth and a pourquoi myth that explains why hens do not live in the forest. Another collection of folktales in this series is *The Lonely Black Pig* by Anne Matindi which illustrates the virtues of hard work, listening to elders, friendship, and sharing.

371. Mwalimu. *Awful Aardvark*.   Illustrated by Adrienne Kennaway.
Boston: Little, Brown, 1989. Originally published in 1989 by Hodder and
Stoughton. N.p. Preschool-Grade 2.
    Aardvark's snoring disturbs the jungle animals, so they try to oust
    him from the smooth branch he sleeps on. When the lion, rhinoceros,
    and monkeys fail, it is the tiny termites who eat up the roots of the
    tree. All ends well because now Aardvark sleeps during the day and
    eats termites at night. The illustrations focus on the tension between
    the plight of the animals and the self-centered Aardvark who is
    oblivious to the plot against him.

372. Ndung'u, Frederick. *Beautiful Nyakio and Other Stories*.   Illustrated
by Adrienne Moore. Nairobi, Kenya: Phoenix, 1968, 1987. 30p. Grades 3-5.
    Two animal tales and three realistic stories represent the varied
    folklore of Kenya. These traditional stories focus on the pursuit of
    happiness, survival, and respect for the property and rights of others.
    Whether the stories are about animals or humans, once the above
    aims are infringed upon, cleverness has to be employed to outwit
    enemies. For instance, when Nyakio, the most beautiful woman in the
    village, is tricked into marrying the ugliest man, her lover exchanges
    the bride and runs off with Nyakio. The stories are narrated simply,
    yet interest is maintained through a fast-paced plot, lively dialogue,
    and minimum of description.

373. Odaga, Asenath Bole. *The Hare's Blanket*.   Illustrated by Adrienne
Moore. Village and Town Readers. Kisumu, Kenya: Lake Publishers &
Enterprises, 1967, 1989. 28p. Grades K-3.
    Four short folktales narrate the exploits of the trickster hare. This
    pragmatic character is in turn wise, clever, and deceptive, but no
    matter what the situation, he always manages to win. Odaga's simple
    prose provides just enough dialogue and description to make the
    scene and characters come to life.

374. _____. *Yesterday's Today: The Study of Oral Literature*.   Kisumu,
Kenya: Lake Publishers & Enterprises, 1984. 147p. Grades 8-12.
    Intended as a textbook, this collection of Kenyan oral literature will
    prove both entertaining and informative to the general reader. The
    book is divided into four sections: oral narratives; proverbs, riddles,
    and tongue twisters; songs and dances; and a section containing an
    additional twenty-one narratives and suggestions for material collec-
    tion. Each item is accompanied by useful information on tale type, its
    role in society, and review exercises and discussion topics. This book
    is especially valuable for the English translations it provides of
    traditional songs, lullabies, and chants--a neglected area in African
    children's literature.
    A pioneer in the field of recording and translating into English
    Kenya's fast-disappearing oral literature, Odaga personally collected
    these stories from different parts of the country. She is also the
    collector and translator of the twenty-six Luo tales published in *Thu
    Tinda!* (Uzima Press, 1980).

375. Onyango-Ogutu, Benedict, and Adrian A. Roscoe. *Keep My Words.* Oral Literature Library. Nairobi, Kenya: Heinemann, 1974. 159p. Grades 6-12.

Thirty-six folktales represent the oral literature of the Luo, the second largest ethnic group in Kenya. The tales range from creation and pourquoi myths to stories that regulate social and moral behavior. Among the most thought-provoking stories are "Opondo's Strange Children," which demonstrates the rewards of not abandoning an abnormal baby; "A Noble Woman," which celebrates the intelligent wife and mother who ingeniously feeds her family during a severe drought; and "Kijenje's Best Friend" and "Orphans," which accept suicide as a means of coping with the loss of a dear one. Through the character of Opul, or hyena, the stories warn readers against being too trusting. To recreate an actual storytelling experience, the collectors have included songs, a vital element of Luo folktales, not only to highlight the main events and themes, but also to engage the audience emotionally and intellectually.

A detailed scholarly essay discusses Luo culture, history, and traditional religion and the techniques and rituals of storytelling. It also points out how Luo traditions are being incorporated in modern verse and short stories.

376. Soi, Elijah K. *The Peacock and the Snake.* Illustrated by Beryl Moore. Phoenix Young Readers Library. Nairobi, Kenya: Phoenix, 1976, 1988. 30p. Grades 2-4.

Seven folktales popular among the Kipsigis of East Africa teach moral lessons to the young. Sacrifice and loyalty to friends and family are virtues to be emulated, while cheating, stealing, and laziness are to be denounced. This collection also contains one pourquoi story of how the Kipsigis first started to eat cooked food. Each story is gracefully written with attention to details and character delineation.

377. Williams, Sheron. *And in the Beginning. . .* Illustrated by Robert Roth. New York: Atheneum, 1992. N.p. Grades K-3.

In this myth, Mahtmi designs the first man, Kwanza, in his own image from the dark, rich soil of Mount Kilimanjaro and the gifts of hair, eyes, and pearls from the other beings of the world. But Kwanza gets tired of his paradise and goes to explore other parts of the world. In his loneliness, Mahtmi creates more beings from the red soil of Georgia, from the sandy beaches of Normandy, and so on. When Kwanza returns from his travels, he is jealous of the new men and women enjoying the comfort of Mahtmi's presence, and he wants a special sign to convince him that he is physically as beautiful as the others. Mahtmi sets him apart from every other creature by giving him tightly curled hair as a token of his love.

The Kwanzaa myth is becoming increasingly widespread in the United States as it fosters racial pride in African Americans. Williams' narrative style, use of black diction, and references to contemporary places and concepts provide relevance to the story.

FICTION

378. Anderson, Joy. *Juma and the Magic Jinn*. Illustrated by Charles Mikolaycak. New York: Lothrop, Lee & Shepard, 1986. N.p. Grades K-3.

Text and illustrations evoke the exotic atmosphere of Arabic culture through the experiences of a modern child who lives on Luma Island off the Kenyan coast. When the artistic Juma is chided for not paying attention to his school work, he calls the Jinn and wishes to be in a place where he cannot learn anything and where he already knows everything. However, both options prove dissatisfactory. Finally, he asks to be in a place where everything is new and where there are still things to learn. Juma finds himself back in his home in Luma. Suddenly, life holds new magic and excitement for Juma, and he celebrates the sound of the sea, the sights of the bazaar, and the taste of ginger-spiced coffee through his poems and paintings.

379. Ballantyne, Robert Michael. *Black Ivory: A Tale of Adventure Among the Slavers of East Africa.* Chicago: Afro-Am Press, 1969. Originally published in 1873 by Nelson. 416p. Grades 8-12.

Based on historical facts and the accounts of missionaries and travelers, *Black Ivory* exposes the operation of the illegal slave trade on the east coast of Africa by Arab dealers, the Sultan of Zanzibar, and Portuguese officials. The adventures of two Britishers, Harold Seadrift and Disco Lillihammer, offer Ballantyne the opportunity to describe graphically the cruel methods employed: inciting wars between rival groups, looting and plundering villages, wholesale murders and merciless whippings, and starvation and torture on the long trek to the coast. The British navy is presented as the angel of mercy for intercepting Arab dhows and freeing the slaves. Interspersed with these scenes of the slave trade is the thrill of exploration into the interior of Africa--hunting, exotic animals and plants, customs of unknown peoples, and challenges of travel and disease. The emotional interest, however, is focused on the curiosity of the protagonists and the fate of the lovely slave, Azinte.

While the theme of *Black Ivory* reflects a strong sense of social purpose, the speech and attitudes of the protagonists belie the author's feelings of superiority. Ballantyne's imperialistic stance is further evident when he insists that the only solution rests in influencing the British government to declare domestic slavery illegal; to establish British consulates and settlements; and to send the Bible and missionaries to the uncivilized, childlike Africans.

380. Bickerstaffe, Derek. *Maefiti and the Drug Smugglers.* Illustrated by Chris Higson. London: Evans, 1981. 63p. Grades 5-7.

Set on the remote island of Mala in Uganda, this is the exciting story of Maefiti's success in stopping the drug smuggling operation being conducted from his village. The tension and suspense are maintained through swift action and detailed descriptions of the setting and Maefiti's solo airplane flight to get help.

Another novel on this popular subject is Rosemary Uwemedimo's *Akpan and the Smugglers* (African Universities Press, 1965) about a village youth who single-handedly exposes a ring of smugglers involved in contraband goods. The protagonist's family life, his sense of outrage when his father is falsely accused, and his courage and intelligence in solving the mystery are sensitively portrayed.

381. Bradley, Duane. *Meeting with a Stranger*. Illustrated by E. Harper Johnson. Philadelphia and New York: Lippincott, 1964. 128p. Grades 5-7.
A young Ethiopian boy, Teffera, helps an entire village overcome its suspicion of Western civilization when he tests the American *ferangi*, or stranger. While respect for Ethiopian history and culture are an integral part of the story, Mr. Jones is undoubtedly a do-gooder who cheerfully endures opposition and sabotage in order to teach the reluctant villagers how to breed healthier flocks. Once he passes Teffera's test, Sam Jones is praised for his good intentions and expertise. It is ironic, however, that Ethiopians, who have been raising sheep for generations, are depicted as lacking the most rudimentary knowledge about sheep.

382. Bustani, Juma. *Adventure in Mombasa*.   Junior Readers Series. Nairobi, Kenya: Heinemann, 1988. 73p. Grades 4-6.

383. _____. *Adventure in Nakuru*.   Junior Readers Series. Nairobi, Kenya: Heinemann, 1988. 66p. Grades 4-6.
Both adventures involve three characters--a Kenyan boy and girl and a British teenager--who accidentally stumble upon criminals. In *Adventure in Mombasa* they help undercover police to catch a gang of drug smugglers, while in *Adventure in Nakuru* they stop the illegal dumping of toxic waste in lakes and rivers. Bustani's prose maintains the drama and tension of the plot, as well as describing the Kenyan setting to make the stories believable. The interracial friendship displays teamwork, mutual regard, and sensitivity.

384. Chahilu, Bernard P. *The Herdsman's Daughter*. Nairobi, Kenya: East African Publishing House, 1974. 283p. Grades 8-12.
Set in the turbulent times preceding independence, this novel provides a very graphic and realistic portrait of the confusion of values that Kenyans underwent in the 1960s. The conflict centers on the emotional and psychological development of fifteen-year-old Rebecca Embenzi and her struggle to get an education. With the help of her school teacher and the village chief, Embenzi's father reluctantly agrees to pay for her secondary education; he is forced to adapt to the changing times, especially since his daughter's academic achievements bring him much honor. However, this is not a didactic novel that extols the virtues of education and the backwardness of villagers. The uneducated herdsman has pride, wisdom, and knowledge; he relies on Abalvhya legends, folktales, and beliefs to transmit values to his daughter, which she scorns and considers irrelevant.
This multidimensional and complicated novel goes on to narrate

the consequences of the heroine's rejection of traditions. Embenzi's story ends tragically because, although she has attained book knowledge, she sadly lacks knowledge of human nature. Once she begins to teach at the new harambee school in her village, the headmaster exploits her innocence and beauty to arrange a sexual encounter with an influential politician in exchange for a favor. Her good reputation is ruined and she leaves the village a sober individual who has come to respect the wisdom of her parents.

385. Dinneen, Betty. *Lion Yellow*. Illustrated by Charles Robinson. New York: Walck, 1975. 169p. Grades 5-8.
Set in the Mbuyu Game Park near Mount Kilimanjaro in Kenya, the story centers around the efforts of Ben Thorne, the British Game Warden, to save the wildlife preserve from the Masai herdsmen who claim it is their legal grazing grounds. The Thorne children, Robin and David, are also confronted with the reality of having to leave Kenya, their home, now that it has gained independence. Mr Likimani, Minister of Lands in the new government, comes from Nairobi to decide the fate of the game park and the future of the Thorne family in Kenya. Mbuyu Park assumes a variety of symbolic meanings: The animals born in captivity represent the ecology of "natural" Africa thriving in a controlled environment; the initiation of the playful black-maned lion, Black Prince, into the adult life of the park is paralleled with David's giving up of his Lion Boy persona to face the challenges of boarding school; and, finally, Mr. Likimani's confrontation with a lioness serves as a vicarious Masai manhood test of courage and strength--a test he could not face as an adolescent --and symbolizes his personal growth and the political maturation of Kenya as a sovereign nation. Mr. Likimani's career also implies that in independent Kenya the Masai need to dispense with their traditional lifestyle and seek Western education and political careers to maintain their former power and influence. There appears to be no compromise between the old and the new.

386. _____. *A Lurk of Leopards*. Illustrated by Charles Robinson. New York: Walck, 1972. 215p. Grades 6-8.
This is the story of eleven-year-old Karen, a white girl in Nairobi, and a leopardess who lurks around Karen's house. The leopardess is eventually put to sleep and her two cubs are raised by Karen. Although the book does not display any negative stereotypes about Africa, there are some vital omissions. The plot does not have a single Kenyan character who is vital to the story (the houseboy and gardener appear fleetingly), and there is no reference to Kenyan culture and lifestyle. Only the exotic wildlife is worthy of notice and preservation. This is a "charming" account of an innocent girl's love of wildlife, but one wonders about its authenticity. Do leopards really lurk under little girls' windows in a modern city like Nairobi?

387. Feelings, Muriel L. *Zamani Goes to Market*. Illustrated by Tom Feelings. New York: Seabury, 1970. 32p. Grades K-3.

The love and care of an African family are touchingly depicted when Zamani makes his first trip to the market. He is proud to be an earning member of the family, and he accordingly behaves maturely when he buys a necklace for his mother, instead of the *kanzu* (shirt-type garment) he had been longing for. His father surprises him with one. Both text and illustrations are unbiased in their depiction of African life.

388. Goetz, Lee Garrett. *A Camel in the Sea.* Illustrated by Paul Galdone. New York: McGraw-Hill, 1966. 60p. Grades 3-5.
    Mohamed, a Somalian adolescent, feels lonesome when he has to stop playing with his sister and helping his mother in the house in order to prepare for the adult world of male responsibilities. When his village of Mogadishu is ravaged by locusts and a prolonged drought, Mohamed has the opportunity to prove his worth and make a good friend. The village elder warns that the rains will not come until a camel can be led into the sea. Mohamed accomplishes this impossible task when he befriends the baby camel whose mother is being forcibly--albeit unsuccessfully--dragged into the ocean. Mohamed wins the camel's confidence and patiently leads him into the water. The clouds bring the life-giving rain and Mohamed is declared a hero.
    Both Goetz' text and Galdone's illustrations give a positive depiction of everyday life in a Somalian village. Life is regulated by the dictates of Islam, the seasons, and the tasks prescribed to men, women, girls, and boys. Western children will respond to the universal themes of friendship and the need to accomplish a difficult task.

389. Kabarungi, P. *Katsi and His Cattle.* Illustrated by Yerusa Azikuru. Crested Crane Books for Children. Kampala, Uganda: Uganda Publishing House, 1972. N.p. Grades K-2.
    During school holidays, young boys like Katsi spend their time tending the family's cattle. Katsi wakes up early to milk the cows and takes the herd to graze the green grass till evening. However, his day is not all work because he enjoys the company of other boys like himself. They play, sing songs, and eat lunch together. Katsi exudes a sense of pride and well-being in his rural lifestyle.

390. Kawegere, Fortunatus. *Inspector Rajabu Investigates and Other Stories.* Phoenix Young Readers Library. Nairobi, Kenya: Phoenix, 1968, 1988. 30p. Grades 4-6.
    The three short stories by this Tanzanian author are intended to be thought provoking and to stimulate critical thinking. The element of suspense and the clue to the mystery in the lead story are weak. The remaining stories, however, examine human conduct in the context of a changing East African society. "The Courage of Her Convictions" denounces parental control in selecting marriage partners and the giving and accepting of bride price, while "The Thin End of the Wedge" is about official corruption and the misappropriation of

funds. Both stories are didactic in tone, and the characters and action are directed solely by the theme.

391. Keable, Robert. *The Adventures of Paul Kangai.* London: Universities' Mission to Central Africa, 1918. 145p. Grades 6-8.

Set in 1875, the story of Kangai, a slave boy, illustrates the cruelty of the Arab slave trade and the activities of the Universities' Mission to Central Africa. Both the Christian mission and the British Navy collaborate to rescue and rehabilitate the slaves. Kangai, who is captured from his village in Nyasaland and sold to an Arab slaver, is admitted to the mission school in Zanzibar. Kangai's story, which spans over forty years of his life, reflects the book's agenda: the superiority of Christianity and Western civilization over the violence and enmity of Africa. Kangai learns to denounce both Islam and his traditional religion and culture, and he marvels at how the British can unite Africans, Arabs, and Indians in the mission's Boy Scout Camp. Photographs of the British Consulate, Christ Church Cathedral, and other places in Zanzibar provide the historical basis of the story.

392. Kennaway, Adrienne. *Little Elephant's Walk.* Illustrated by author. New York: Perlman, 1992. Originally published in 1991 by Orchard Books. N.p. Preschool-Grade 2.

As Little Elephant strolls through the plains and jungles of East Africa with his mother, he meets forty-two animals that inhabit the region. The illustrations of Little Elephant are especially warm and endearing as he displays a child's curiosity and caution. Young readers will identify with Little Elephant as he bends down to observe the shrew, gets out of the rhinoceros' path, rests on a termite mound at midday, splashes himself with cool water, and hides from the spines of a porcupine. As Little Elephant heads home at night, he sees animals like the aardwolf, springhaas, and aardvark who sleep during the day and wake up only at night to hunt for food. There is a lively quality to the text and illustrations as the everyday actions and motivations of the various animals, birds, and insects are explained.

393. Kroll, Virginia. *Masai and I.* Illustrated by Nancy Carpenter. New York: Four Winds, 1992. N.p. Grades K-2.

Details of traditional Masai life blend in present-day America as a young African American girl imagines she is Masai after studying East Africa in school. Carpenter's illustrations allow readers to simultaneously view similar activities performed under two very different cultural conditions. Images of American life flow into scenes of Masai life just as smoothly as the text shifts from the external world of Linda's reality to the inner world of her imagination. While Linda passes no judgments on either lifestyle, the illustrations reveal her fascination with Masai life and the freedom it offers.

Wood-Hoopoe Willie (Charlesbridge, 1992) is yet another picture book by Kroll that reveals the African roots of an African American boy. Willie, whose behavior is considered antisocial because he is constantly tapping, rapping, and clinking to some inner rhythm, discovers that he is actually reproducing the sounds of African musical instruments. It is at the Kwanzaa celebration that his kinship with African sounds is acknowledged by all. Katherine Roundtree's illustrations reflect pride in Africa as she blends African scenes with Willie's life in America.

394. Kulet, Henry R. ole. *To Become a Man.* Nairobi, Kenya: Longman, 1972. 141p. Grades 8-10.

In this thought-provoking novel, a Masai youth is caught in the midst of a society in transition. Through the conflict between Leshao and his father over Leshao's future, Kulet explores the choices the protagonist has to make between traditions and modernity. On the one hand is education in a missionary school and the prospect of a job in town, and on the other hand is the Masai concept of manhood and fulfilling one's traditional role as a moran (warrior). To prove that he is not a coward, Leshao willingly participates in the circumcision rituals and training of a moran. He wins fame by killing a lion, but refuses to accompany his age-mates in a cattle raid. Instead, he leaves his ancestral village to seek employment and riches in the city. Ironically, this dream of a better life, for which he has sacrificed his good name and the hopes of his father, is equally evasive; there are too many unemployed youth in the city, especially those lacking a school certificate. Moreover, city folk lack the hospitality, grace, and manners that are essential to Masai culture. Disappointed, he returns to his manyatta (a residence for morans) to once again prove his manhood by joining a cattle raid. Unfortunately, the police ambush the morans, and Leshao, who is the sole survivor of his sixty age-mates, is sentenced to fourteen years in prison.

Leshao's experiences raise important questions about manhood, bravery, and pride. The author presents both sides of the picture fairly--the world of progress and formal education and the fast-disappearing Masai lifestyle. Both worlds have their strengths and weaknesses, but the close-knit culture of the Masai people is becoming irrelevant in modern Kenya. Cattle raiding is seen as thievery by the laws of the country, and the role of morans is accomplished by soldiers. However, there is a touch of nostalgia in Kulet's descriptions of Masai social structure, customs, and beliefs. Kulet is also the author of *Is It Possible,* another novel of a young Masai boy who is regulated by the Western educational system while living within the confines of his traditional culture.

395. Levitin, Sonia. *The Return.* New York: Atheneum, 1987. 213p. Grades 6-8.

As in the Biblical story of the deliverance of Jews from Egypt, this novel is based on the exodus of some eight thousand Ethiopian Jews under Operation Moses, a secret airlift to Israel conducted between November 1984 and January 1985. All the elements of a heroic epic are present in this modern-day story: oppression of Jews under the revolutionary communist regime; a mysterious savior who leads them to the Promised Land; dreams and prophecies; historical connection with Queen Sheba's visit to King Solomon in Jerusalem; drought and famine; secret meetings to plan the escape; and the disciplined lives of black Jews who live by the Commandments. *The Return* is also the realistic story of a young teenager, Desta, who matures from a dependent girl to a self-reliant and sacrificing individual. As Desta and her brother and sister undertake the long, arduous journey from their mountain village to the rescue camp in Sudan, Desta's faith, physical endurance, and courage are tested repeatedly. The novel ends with their arrival in Israel--her brother was killed in the attempt--and the beginning of a life of freedom.

For a fictional account of the early experiences of Ethiopian Jews in Israel, refer to *Falasha No More: An Ethiopian Jewish Child Comes Home* (Steimatzky/Shapolsky, 1986) by Arlene Kushner. In this story, Avraham is happy to escape oppression, but he is equally determined to maintain his Ethiopian culture as he adjusts to his new life.

396. Lundgren, Gunilla.   *Malcolm's Village*.   Photographs by Lars Jacobsson. Illustrated by Militta Wellner. Toronto: Annick, 1985. Originally published in 1983 under the title *Tradet Som Aldrig Dog* by Verbum Forlag, Sweden. 37p. Grades 1-4.

This thought-provoking book explores the mystery of death and afterlife through the experiences of a seven-year-old Swedish boy. Malcolm's life in a village near Mount Kilimanjaro also provides insight into the lifestyle, traditions, and inner life of East Africans. His special relationship with Grandma introduces the young child to the villagers' affinity with Kilimanjaro. When Grandma dies, Malcolm places his grief in the context of the many folktales she used to narrate about the harmony of nature. Photographs, folktales, and funeral rituals symbolize that Grandma is a part of the eternal cycle of birth-death-rebirth, as well as living in the memories of family and friends.

397. Maillu, David G.   *Kisalu and His Fruit Garden*.   Junior Readers Series. Nairobi, Kenya: Heinemann, 1989. 41p. Grades 3-5.

Six short stories focus on controversial issues which are presented through vigorous plots and characters who fulfill their assigned roles. The consequences of misdemeanors are inexorable fate: the wicked wife who attempts to poison her mother-in-law kills her own children by accident and is sent to prison; the pampered son becomes a criminal and is to be hanged; and the wife who threatens to disclose her husband's secret is punished and made to appear ridiculous. Although placed in modern settings, these stories uphold folkloric themes of victory of good over evil, using intelligence and wit to win a just cause, respect for elders, and loyalty to family.

398. _____. *The Poor Child*. Illustrated by N. K. Mbugua. Junior Readers Series. Nairobi, Kenya: Heinemann, 1988. 55p. Grades 4-6.

Set in a village in present-day Kenya, this Cinderella story recounts the physical abuse, hard work, and neglect that young Mwende suffers at the hands of her stepmother. When the abuse reaches unbearable limits, Mwende takes charge of the situation by secretly writing to her father in Nairobi and running away from home to be with him. She faces tremendous obstacles en route because she has no money, cannot speak Swahili, and is ignorant of city life. She is helped by three "guardian angels": a gentleman who pays her fare to Nairobi; a kindly lady, Rhoda, who rescues her in Nairobi and takes her home, but eventually wants to retain her as a servant; and a couple that helps her escape from Rhoda's house. She is reunited with her father who has divorced the "wicked" stepmother.

As in the fairy tale, the characters are flat and one-dimensional; the good are all good and the bad, except for Rhoda, are without any redeeming qualities. The plot also moves swiftly from episode to episode, but there are some interesting twists to the traditional version. Mwende does not wait for a Prince Charming to rescue her; she takes charge of her destiny and is determined to continue with her education despite the financial temptation offered by Rhoda. The book ends on a happy note with Mwende back in school and a wonderful new stepmother to look after her. The setting provides information on Kenyan village and city life, especially the importance given to education. Young readers may be disturbed by descriptions of child and wife beating. Older children, however, could discuss the serious issues of child abuse, jealousy among stepchildren, favoritism by parents, and child-raising practices.

399. *Mcheshi Goes to the Market-Mcheshi Aenda Sokoni.*   Illustrated by Nicholas Sironka, Judy Wanjiku Mathenge, James Okello, and Martin Otieno. Nairobi, Kenya: Jacaranda, 1991. 23p. Preschool-Grade 2.
A variety of artistic styles capture the colorful crowds, excitement, and constant activity of market day. As Mcheshi goes shopping with her mother, she visits the tailor, shoemaker, fruit vendor, chicken seller, and egg seller. All aspects of this picture book--illustrations, production, layout of English and Swahili texts, and paper quality --are superior.

400. Mwangi, Meja. *Jimi the Dog.*   Illustrated by Kirui Koske. Anchor Readers Series. Nairobi, Kenya: Longman, 1990. 62p. Grades 4-6.
Set in colonial times, this is the simple story of a young boy's transformation from a dependent to a self-reliant character. When his stern older brother, Hari, presents him with a scrawny village mongrel who is full of fleas, Kariuki is delighted to have a pet he can love and care for. Surrounded by harshness and physical abuse from the Britisher on whose farm they live and work, from his brother and father at home, and from the headmaster at the mission school, Kariuki wants to offer Jimi, his dog, the best possible life he can. Ironically, Kariuki's single-minded effort only gets him into trouble at home, at school, and in the village.

Mwangi's subtle humor and ironic undertone expose both Kariuki's exaggerated affection for his dog and the love and concern lurking beneath the external hardness of Hari and his father. Through his experiences with Jimi, Kariuki learns the difficult lesson that only determination and endurance can lead to success.

401. _____. *Little White Man.* Illustrated by Kirui Koske. Anchor Readers Series. Nairobi, Kenya: Longman, 1990. 110p. Grades 5-8.

Kariuki's story is continued in this more serious novel set against the background of the Mau Mau Movement of the early 1950s. Older and wiser now, Kariuki has developed a distinct philosophy to explain why freedom, equality, and peace continue to evade him. His world--village, church, school, and family hut--is arranged hierarchically with the white Bwana Ruin on top, followed by the village men, women and girls, and everyone else. At the very bottom are the uncircumcised boys and village mongrels who have no rights whatsoever. Kariuki develops his own survival skills by escaping to his hiding place in the forest, while the adults deal with the beatings and abuse they receive at the hands of Bwana and Memsahib Ruin by releasing their pent-up anger and bitterness on those beneath them--on Kariuki, for instance.

Into this well-ordered world come two disturbing influences that change Kariuki's life forever: the Mau Mau men in the forest who want their land and political freedom from the white colonists, and Nigel, the grandson of the Ruins who is on vacation from England. Kariuki and Nigel become instant friends, ignoring the warnings of elders that the relationship will only lead to trouble. If Nigel knows about the outside world, Kariuki initiates his white friend into the pleasures of hunting and the life of a Kenyan boy. The two are unaffected by the racism--and violence--that surrounds them. Even the traumatic episode of Nigel's and Kariuki's capture by the Mau Mau men only strengthens their friendship. The rebel leaders are unsure about what to do with the boys, as their main goal was to use Nigel as a bargaining tool to win back their farm. Hari, who is also a member of the group, secretly frees the boys and is in turn killed by the white soldiers. In a powerfully ironic scene, Bwana Ruin tries to compel Nigel into stating that Hari was one of the kidnappers, but Nigel insists that Hari was the one who freed them. With Hari's death, Kariuki loses his best friend, the one who taught him everything. Although he learns of Nigel's strength and honesty, the innocence of childhood and the safety of the forest have been ruined forever.

Mwangi's powerful prose and ironic stance once again reveal the duality of human beings: both whites and Kenyans are kind and loving in their personal lives, but the colonial situation introduces violence in their interpersonal relationships. Likewise, the Mau Mau men are seen as freedom fighters, and not as cruel and vicious brutes who are out to kill all whites. Like Kariuki, they use all available tools and methods to win freedom and equality. Hope and transformation, the novel seems to imply, rest with children like Kariuki and Nigel who are not corrupted by the violence and hierarchy that govern their lives.

402. Nagenda, Musa, pseud. *Dogs of Fear*. Illustrated by Catherine Gombe. London, Nairobi, Ibadan, Lusaka: Heinemann, 1971. 94p. Grades 5-7.

This novel should, perhaps, be read in conjunction with Nagenda's *Mukasa* (Macmillan, 1973), which describes a village boy's successful first year at school. *Dogs of Fear,* in contrast, is a sensitive portrayal of the inner turmoil of the young protagonist, Kabana. Like so many children in a postcolonial society, Kabana is confused by the contradictory demands and values of his Westernized education and traditional lifestyle. The story focuses on Kabana's crucial thirteenth year when he has to undergo the initiation rites during his Easter break. One unfortunate event after another convinces his father that the mission school has made Kabana a coward, hence unfit for "tribal" life. When the wild dogs attack his herd of goats repeatedly, Kabana is determined to prove his worth. Using the stored knowledge from his childhood, he follows the dogs to their lair and defeats them. His bravery and sense of responsibility earn him the respect of his father and the entire village. Kabana learns that book knowledge and the practical lessons of traditional life can be reconciled. Nagenda's highly descriptive narrative style, revealing dialogue, and sensitive characterization enable him to draw readers into the events and experiences of his characters.

403. Ngugi wa Thiong'o. *Njamba Nene and the Flying Bus.* Translated from the Gikuyu by Wangui wa Goro. Illustrated by Emmanuel Kariuki. Nairobi, Kenya: Heinemann, 1986. 34p. Grades 5-7.

Set during the Kenyan struggle for independence, this is the first in a series of adventure stories about Njamba Nene, a puny looking boy whose name means "big hero." History, heroic myth, and fantasy intertwine with Njamba Nene's realistic experiences to emphasize the theme of patriotism. The protagonist, who is abused because of his poverty and adherence to traditional Gikuyu values, goes on a field trip with his classmates when their bus begins to fly and then crashes into Kagerangoro Mountain (meaning "measure for endurance"). Njamba Nene assumes leadership of the group because of his knowledge of the geography, plants, and animals of his country. He leads his friends safely through the Depression of Tears, Valley of Laughter, River of Life, and Valley of Death. They are eventually rescued from the white hunters by the freedom fighters. The political allegory is unmistakable. Each character, event, and setting assumes symbolic significance: The persecution of the hero represents the exploitation of Kenya; the school teacher represents the Western education that is imposed on Kenyans at the expense of their own culture; and the author's scathing commentary on Kenyans who support the British is a condemnation of unpatriotic behavior.

404. ____. *Njamba Nene's Pistol*. Translated from the Gikuyu by Wangui wa Goro. Illustrated by Emmanuel Kariuki. Nairobi, Kenya: Heinemann, 1986. 33p. Grades 5-7.

Thrown out of school because of his "subversive" actions, Njamba Nene seeks employment in Limuru, where he is perpetually hungry and exploited by his employer. He finds nourishment for his soul when he is initiated into the secret society of freedom fighters. He once again achieves heroic status when he is caught by the police while on a difficult assignment, but his courage and intelligence enable him to take charge of the British officer and his Kenyan followers. As in the previous adventure, Ngugi wa Thiong'o's narrative is characterized by a fast-paced plot, stereotypical characters, and sparse prose. The emphasis of the allegory is on the evils of colonialism and the bravery of the Mau Mau guerillas. The adventures of Njamba Nene are continued in *Njamba Nene and the Cruel Colonial Chief*.

405. Odaga, Asenath Bole. *The Angry Flames*. Illustrated by Adrienne Moore. Village and Town Readers Series. Kisumu, Kenya: Lake Publishers & Enterprises, 1968, 1989. 48p. Grades 4-6.

Jachia, a plucky Yapin girl, is tricked into the forest and offered as a sacrifice to the angry gods because of a prolonged drought and famine. As the angry flames approach her, Jachia manages to escape, but her retreating oppressor, Nyalowo, dies instead. Afraid to return to her village, Jachia takes refuge with the Kwacha clan, enemies of the Yapin, by pretending to be a boy. As the years pass and Jachia begins to mature physically, she suffers much ridicule from her age-mates as she struggles to hide her secret and her growing love for Kembo, the chief's nephew. When the secret is finally discovered, she is forgiven for deceiving the entire clan. Jachia and Kembo's marriage also ends the rivalry between the two groups.

This brief story provides enough material for in-depth study and philosophical discussion. Jachia is a strong female character who is not afraid to exert her personal autonomy, regardless of the consequences. Her loneliness and suffering, however, project her as a human being with feelings. The political roles of the two chiefs can lead to a discussion of the tough decisions that have to be made to ensure the welfare and consensus of the entire group. Interestingly, the debate on human sacrifice is kept deliberately vague. There are voices of dissent against the sacrifice among the Yapin and Kwacha; yet, once Nyalowo dies, the drought does end and the village prospers.

406. _____. *The Diamond Ring*. Illustrated by Adrienne Moore. Village and Town Readers Series. Kisumu, Kenya: Lake Publishers & Enterprises, 1968. 52p. Grades 2-4.

The episodic plot takes young Rapemo on a heroic journey through dangerous forests where he meets dwarves, receives magic ash from the wizard, discovers a mysterious city, and is given a diamond ring by the chief's daughter. However, these events are not organically related to the theme and the development of the protagonist. They are simply exotic details and events that have been attached to Rapemo's adventures. It is Rapemo's courage, survival skills, and intelligence that earn him the respect of the villagers.

407. _____. *Jande's Ambition.*   Illustrated by Adrienne Moore. Papyrus Junior Library English Readers. Kisumu, Kenya: Lake Publishers & Enterprises, 1966, 1988. 67p. Grades 3-5.
> The author's first published work, *Jande's Ambition* illustrates the importance attached to boys' education, while girls are married off in exchange for a handsome dowry. A champion of equal opportunities for girls, Odaga has created a strong female character who works hard to fulfill her ambition of becoming a school teacher.

408. _____. *Munde and His Friends.*   Village and Town Readers Series. Kisumu, Kenya: Lake Publishers & Enterprises, 1987. 28p. Grades 1-3.

409. _____. *Munde Goes to the Market.*   Illustrated by Inner Vision Communication. Village and Town Readers Series. Kisumu, Kenya: Lake Publishers & Enterprises, 1987. 18p. Grades 1-3.
> Both books focus on the daily activities of Munde, a happy twelve-year-old village youth. Munde leads a balanced life with homework and chores on the farm before and after school, fun and play with friends and pets, and market day during holidays. Munde's hardworking character and his family's success illustrate rural development in Kenya. The concept of *harambee,* or progress through cooperation, is emphasized on the farm as well as at school.
> Since the books are intended as supplementary readers, the controlled vocabulary and sentence structure make the prose rather stilted. Likewise, the black-and-white illustrations, though accurate, lack aesthetic appeal.

410. _____. *My Home.*   Illustrated by Phoebe Okulu. Village and Town Readers Series. Kisumu, Kenya: Lake Publishers & Enterprises, 1983. 17p. Grades K-1.
> This easy reader is intended for children learning English as a second language. The short sentences name objects in the home, farm, and family compound; and name the activities of children at play, at lessons, and at work. The concepts of time, numbers, spatial relationships, and extended family are also introduced.

411. _____. *The Secret of the Monkey Rock.*   Illustrated by William Agutu. Papyrus Library Series. Kisumu, Kenya: Lake Publishers & Enterprises, 1966, 1989. 31p. Grades 4-6.
> In this fantasy, a young village girl is invited to an underworld utopia where equality, magic, immense wealth, and immortality go hand-in-hand with technological advancement, education and research, and a humane judicial system. The "real" world is so full of gossip, poverty, jealousy, and selfishness that when the protagonist and her entire family disappear into this utopia forever, readers are happy for them. The basic structure of this ideal kingdom is so like our world that Odaga seems to imply that it can be created on earth.

412. _____. *The Storm.*   Illustrated by John Owuor. Papyrus Library Series. Kisumu, Kenya: Lake Publishers & Enterprises, 1985. 83p. Grades 4-6.

Munde's visit to his grandparents in Yimbo provides the ideal framework for introducing Kenyan children to the myths, folktales, and historical legends associated with the region. For example, on the way to Yimbo, Munde's uncle narrates the story of the rock formation called Kit Mikaye, and when they are stranded on Mageta Island during a storm, he describes how the island was used for slave trading and imprisoning the Mau Mau fighters. Munde also learns about the modern-day fishing and agricultural uses of the island and the myth of the deluge when the village of Simbi was totally submerged underwater. While Munde's linear narrative is contrived, the novel demonstrates how a people's beliefs, values, folklore, and history can be passed down to the younger generation in an entertaining and natural manner.

413. _____. *Sweets and Sugar Cane*. Illustrated by Beryl Moore. Town and Village Readers Series. Kisumu, Kenya: Lake Publishers & Enterprises, 1988. 24p. Grades K-3.
Through the experiences of Karibu and Peri, readers are provided insight into village life in modern Kenya. The children's happy life is characterized by school and household and farming chores. Like their older siblings--a brother who works in an office in Nairobi and a sister who is studying to become a doctor--their prospects for the future are bright. A visit to Nairobi connects them with the wider urban life of trains, airplanes, and crowded streets. The story lacks an interesting plot and in-depth characterization; it simply catalogs the lifestyle and opportunities available to rural children.

414. Oludhe-MacGoye, Marjorie. *Growing Up at Lina School.* Junior Readers Series. Nairobi, Kenya: Heinemann, 1971, 1988. 55p. Grades 5-7.
A popular subgenre of school stories, this boarding school story recounts the experiences of a young girl, Grace, who has just returned to Kenya after several years in Europe. The atmosphere and daily routine of the school allow Grace to adjust to Kenyan customs and lifestyle and to make new friends. Several dramatic episodes--a plane crash in which a teacher's fiance was traveling, news of a parent's death, inability to pay school fees, break-in by thieves--make the students regard teachers as human beings, increase awareness of the problems of others, and foster true friendships. In fact, so much takes place during the course of an academic year that Grace and her friends become caring, responsible, and mature young women.

415. Stevenson, William. *The Bushbabies*. Illustrated by Victor Ambrus. Boston: Houghton Mifflin, 1965. 278p. Grades 7-10.
This story is an eloquent expression of the Canadian author's love for the wildlife and natural landscape of Kenya. The three stories of the bushbaby, a tiny tarsier, Jackie Rhodes, and Headman Tembo, assistant to Jackie's father in the wildlife preserve, run parallel to each other. Now that Kenya is free, Jackie is shocked at the prospect of leaving the country that she loves and the bushbaby whom she has nursed since birth. When the Rhodes are ready to board ship, Jackie

loses the permit to take the bushbaby out of the country. Rather than abandon it near the harbor, she enlists Tembo's help to take the bushbaby to its natural habitat near Mount Kilimanjaro. Their adventures reveal the young girl's respect for Tembo, who symbolizes the idealized natural man through his knowledge of nature, his sense of freedom, and his lack of attachment to material things. Tembo, who had been made to feel "savage" by whites because of his lack of book learning, grows in self-esteem as he complements Jackie's education with his practical experience of survival in the bush. While all the dangers of the wild are present--tigers, leopards, wild elephants, crocodiles, pythons, and forest fires--they are not used to stereotype the African environment; rather, they stress the natural balance between humans and nature. *The Bushbabies* clearly states that Africa needs a little scientific know-how, while the Western world needs the knowledge of nature to lead a truly harmonious life.

416. Van Stockum, Hilda. *Mogo's Flute.*   Illustrated by Robin Jacques. New York: Viking, 1966. 88p. Grades 3-5.
    This is a charming story of a puny Gikuyu boy, Mogo, who has supposedly been cursed with ill-health by the spirits. Feeling sorry for himself, Mogo lives in his mother's hut, plays the flute, and whines for attention all day long. His sister Njoki, who has faith in his ability to make something of himself, dares him to visit Mundo-Mugo, the wiseman who takes care of spiritual matters in their Kenyan village. With his combination of psychic powers and practical wisdom, Mundo-Mugo instructs Mogo to stop using the flute as an escape and to share his responsibilities as a member of the village. Mogo begins to participate by planting and selling vegetables and herding goats. He even finds a practical use for his flute when he is able to call the scattered cattle during a thunderstorm. He realizes that he does not need to go on a lion hunt to prove his manhood, but that his ability to conduct himself properly and earn a livelihood constitute adulthood. He sees a balance between work and entertainment, between his personal needs and the collective good of the community.

417. Ward, Leila. *I Am Eyes-Ni Macho.*   Illustrated by Nonny Hogrogian. New York: Greenwillow, 1978. N.p. Preschool-K.
    Brightly colored illustrations and a simple poetic text depict the varied flora and fauna of Kenya through the eyes of a little girl. From the time she wakes up in the morning, she is awed by the majesty of creation: sunflowers and skies, grasses and giraffes, stars and starlings, and crabs and corals. The black-and-white drawings on the left-hand pages show the child marvelling at her world during the course of the day, while the colorful right-hand pages focus on those aspects of nature that she is naming. Hers is a world of beauty, family love, and carefree childhood.

POETRY

418. Karega, Muthoni, Helen Mwanzi, and Kithaka wa Mberia, eds. *The River Without Frogs*. Illustrated by Robert Mbui. Nairobi, Kenya: Phoenix, 1989. 118p. Grades 4-7.
This entertaining anthology of poems, stories, and plays has selections in English and Swahili. Intended to promote the agenda of the International Year of the Child, this book addresses various issues related to child survival and development. The works include an oral narrative, modern fiction, nature poems, and the dramatization of a popular trickster tale.

419. Luvai, Arthur, Wanjiku Kabira, and Barrack Muluka, eds. *Tender Memories*. Nairobi, Kenya: Heinemann, 1987. 103p. Grades 9-12.
This collection of poems and short stories commemorates the tenth anniversary of the International Year of the Child. It is intended to make adult readers--although the entries are suited to adolescents also--aware of their common duty to humanity through responsible behavior toward the children under their care. The first person accounts very sensitively, and with excruciating frankness, address such issues as child abuse, war, famine, bride price and forced marriages, psychological problems, and poverty.

420. Mbure, Sam. *Lots of Wonders*. Illustrated by Robert Mbui. Phoenix Young Readers Library. Nairobi, Kenya: Phoenix, 1990. 42p. Grades K-3.
Twenty-nine nature poems satisfy a young child's curiosity about the wonders of creation. There is inherent humor in the tongue-in-cheek manner in which the fly, frog, spider, and yam narrate experiences and present their philosophic view of life. Whether he is voicing a donkey's complaint that technology has not eased his burden, the roach's lament at being associated with the rooster, or the frog's wonder at discovering the wide world outside his hole, Mbure most definitely draws on the experiences of the sophisticated urban child who is familiar with telephones, bodyguards, nutrition, and satellites. The musical quality of the poems--rhyming verses, internal beat, repetition, assonance, and consonance--will appeal to young children. While the illustrations emphasize the humor of the text, they are generally not well executed.

421. Serwadda, W. Moses. *Songs and Stories from Uganda*. Transcribed and edited by Hewitt Pantaleoni. Illustrated by Leo and Diane Dillon. New York: Crowell, 1974. 81p. Grades K-3.
Thirteen traditional songs in Luganda are eloquent testimony to the intrinsic role of music and song in the daily lives of the Baganda of Southern Uganda. Some of the songs are intended as lullabies and work songs, while others accompany traditional stories and popular games and dances. Each song is prefaced by explanatory material on the culture and a guide to pronunciation. The musical scores and phonetic spellings of the Luganda words will enable English-speaking

children to sing these songs. English translations of the songs are also included. The woodcut illustrations by the Dillons enhance the folkloric quality of the songs and stories.

422. Sunkuli, Leteipa Ole, ed.   *Sing Me a Song.*   Illustrated by George Mogaka. Nairobi, Kenya: Heinemann, 1992. 41p. Grades 3-6.

This collection of poems by well-known Kenyan authors like Sam Mbure and Barrack Muluka is intended to sharpen children's enjoyment of poetry. While the musical quality of the poems is ideal for singing and recitation, the content will make readers aware of their world. There are poems about animals, nature, love for siblings, respect for grandparents, materialism, politics, social evils, racial discrimination, and love of country. The poems are patterned after Western models, while the vast fund of traditional themes, symbols, poetic forms, and idioms remains untapped.

DRAMA

423. Odaga, Asenath Bole.   *Simbi Nyaima.*   Kisumu, Kenya: Lake Publishers & Enterprises, 1982. 30p. Grades 6-10.

Based on a popular Luo legend, this play explains the origin of Lake Simbi Nyaima in Kenya. The story can also be considered a flood myth because the wrath of the supreme power and the ancestors descends on the prosperous, but evil villagers of Simbi who tempt fate and bring about their own disaster. On the night of the deluge, an old woman, a messenger from the ancestors, is cruelly treated by all except Buoro. In return for her hospitality and kindness, Buoro and her children are saved when Simbi is submerged forever.

As a play, *Simbi Nyaima* lacks great dramatic scenes, and the characters are mouthpieces for narrating the story. The play illustrates the importance attached to the traditional values of respect and kindness toward others, hospitality to strangers, democratic communal rule, and restraint against plundering the property of others.

424. Wandago, Albert. *Duogo.*   Nairobi, Kenya: Alwan Communications, 1985. 77p. Grades 8-12.

In this thought-provoking play, traditional religion and medicine are pitted against Christianity and Western medicine. Pastor Yohana condemns his traditions as superstition and magic and refuses to allow a traditional doctor to heal his dying daughter. When she is buried contrary to traditional norms, her spirit haunts his wife, and Yohana secretly gives her a second burial. However, the church he was so afraid of turns out to be flexible enough to research traditional cures and spiritual phenomena. The play does not have great dramatic scenes or characters; the theme of integrating African traditions with Western culture overpowers both plot and characterization.

BIOGRAPHY AND AUTOBIOGRAPHY

425. Archer, Jules. *African Firebrand: Kenyatta of Kenya.* New York: Messner, 1969. 192p. Grades 8-12.

Beginning with a detailed account of Kenyatta's traditional childhood in the village of Ichaweri, Archer narrates how Kenyatta witnessed the systematic destruction of Gikuyu "tribal" culture under colonial rule. His early introduction to Western education and Christianity created both a conflict in the sensitive youth and provided him with the means to understand and combat British rule. He strongly believed that missionaries--although they accomplished a lot--turned youth against their heritage by denouncing their gods and ceremonies, polygamy, coming-of-age rites, and "tribal" oaths. The colonial officials, on their part, exploited the land, resources, and people of Kenya. Once Jomo Kenyatta realized that his people would get back their land and political control only by ending colonial rule, he dedicated his life to the struggle for freedom. During his years in London, he acquired a university education and Western manners to be on equal terms with the settlers and British politicians. The more the British refused to correct social injustices in Kenya, the more inevitable, Kenyatta warned, they made violent protest. The Mau Mau Movement against white settlers and their African followers was proof of Kenyatta's prediction. Although imprisoned for inciting the Mau Mau "rebellions," Kenyatta's experience, courage, and charisma made him a legend in the eyes of his countrymen. Upon his release after nine years, Kenyatta was again in the forefront of the political scene. As President of an independent nation, he wielded the Swahili slogans of *uhuru* (freedom), *ujamaa* (national familyhood), and *harambee* (pulling together) to unite the diverse segments of the population.

426. Forsberg, Vera. *Gennet Lives in Ethiopia.* Children of the World Books. Photographs by Anna Riwkin-Brick. New York: Macmillan, 1968. Originally published in 1967 by Svenskt Djuptryck, Sweden. N.p. Grades K-3.

As is typical of this series, a number of diverse photographs are unified by a text that focuses readers' interest on a dramatic incident in a child's life. In this story, Gennet, who lived in a village in Ethiopia, rushed to get a doctor because her baby brother was bitten by a snake. Both text and photographs leisurely describe the people and animals she saw on the way--monkeys, flamingoes, cattle, witch doctor's hut, children near the baobab tree, and spice vendor--hence losing the urgency of the situation. As a reward, she went to the market to buy a yellow dress. This is more a description of the exotic aspects of Ethiopian life, rural economy, and natural landscape than Gennet's story.

427. Friedman, Juliann. *Jomo Kenyatta.* Wayland History Makers Series. London: Wayland, 1975. 88p. Grades 7-10.

Like Archer (entry # 425), Friedman parallels Kenyatta's life (1894-1978) with the story of Kenya from colonial times to its struggle for independence from Britain. Written objectively, *Jomo Kenyatta* is basically concerned with providing a factual account of the subject's evolution from an uneducated herdsman to the leader of his nation. However, readers do get to know the inner man through his actions and words and the opinions of others. Jomo Kenyatta's life also provides an example of the changes and struggles various ethnic groups had to endure and master in their quest for freedom. Friedman describes how the Gikuyu learned to take advantage of Western culture, particularly education, in order to participate in the economic and political destiny of their nation.

The author's vast research is apparent in the many quotations from books, journals, speeches, and newspapers. In addition, numerous photographs and a list of the major characters, events, and dates supplement the text. A list of books for further reading is also included.

428. Graham, Shirley. *Julius K. Nyerere: Teacher of Africa.* New York: Messner, 1975. 187p. Grades 6-12.

The theme of this biography is Nyerere's love for Tanzania and his determination to liberate his people from British rule in a nonviolent manner. The first half of the book moves from Nyerere's early life in his native village of Butiama, where his father was chief of the Zanake people, to young adulthood and gaining an education. Even as a youth Nyerere was dedicated enough to put aside personal fears and doubts when he left his family and village to study. Graham's fast-moving narration, powerful descriptions of settings, and invented dialogue lend force and immediacy to the story. The second half of the biography covers Nyerere's adult life as teacher, activist against colonial rule, and first elected president of Tanzania. This section is a factual account of the political history of Tanzania and the public career of Nyerere as a visionary leader whose concern for the welfare of his people was embodied in his political philosophy of *Ujamaa,* or working together as traditional societies had done. Hence, when political instability characterized the experience of other newly independent African nations, Tanzania was able to advance because of President Nyerere's single-mindedness to serve his country with loyalty and honesty. Through this biography, Graham presents a very positive picture of Africa as a continent rich in natural resources, traditional culture, and hardworking, friendly, and dignified people.

429. Grant, Neil. *David Livingstone.* Illustrated by Will Nickless. Discovery Books Series. London: Franklin Watts, 1974. 71p. Grades 3-5.

The action-filled plot traces Livingstone's career as a missionary-explorer in Africa from 1840 until his death in 1873. Since most biographies of Livingstone focus on his search for the source of the Nile, it may surprise young readers to learn that it was in South Africa that Livingstone first developed his ideas on serving Africans and exploring territories hitherto unknown to Europeans. The narrative highlights the dangers and excitement of Livingstone's adventures: attack by a lion, tramping through swamps, canoeing on the Zambezi, witnessing the massacre of an entire village, evidence of the slave trade, and the "discovery" of various lakes. While Grant emphasizes Livingstone's love for the land and people of the continent, he also perpetuates the stereotype of Africa as the "dark" continent with a wild and hostile environment, warlike tribes, backward societies, and diseases and death. Grant believes that Livingstone's lifelong mission in Africa was only partially successful. Although the Sultan of Zanzibar signed a treaty to end the slave trade on the east coast, ironically, Livingstone's explorations led to the political control and economic exploitation of Africans by Europeans --something that went against Livingstone's doctrine of a British colony in East Africa.

The True Story of David Livingstone (Children's Press, 1964) by Richard Arnold is a more detailed and well-researched biography for middle school children. Arnold states that Livingstone became a legend in his own life as one of the greatest explorers of all times and a second Saint Paul. Livingstone's campaign against slavery and the color ban, and his insistence that Africans be regarded as potential customers and consumers rather than as cheap labor, rank him as a progressive thinker and humanitarian.

430. Griffin, Michael. *A Family in Kenya.* Photographs by Liba Taylor. Families the World Over Series. Minneapolis, MN: Lerner, 1988. Originally published in 1987 as *Salaama in Kenya* by A & C Black. 31p. Grades 2-4.

An insight into both urban and rural life in modern Kenya can be gained from visiting eleven-year-old Salaama's family. Salaama and her brother Philip lived near Mombasa with their father because of better schooling, while their mother and younger siblings lived on the family's farm. While their roots were in the farm, family members were willing to make sacrifices for a better future. Each individual fulfilled his or her appointed tasks, whether it was tending the farm, grinding corn, working in an office, housework, or attending school. In addition to their regular chores, Salaama's mother made thatch tiles and her father ran an evening tea stall and sold farm produce to earn extra money. Family togetherness, security, and love are eloquently conveyed through photographs of reunions during holidays. Information on Kenya's wildlife and a list of facts are included.

431. Huxley, Elspeth. *The Flame Trees of Thika: Memories of an African Childhood.* New York: Morrow, 1959. 288p. Grades 8-12.

A well-known British author, Mrs. Huxley narrates the story of her eventful childhood in Kenya from 1913 to World War I. Although written from the perspective of a mature adult, the painstakingly detailed narrative succeeds in conveying the experiences of the six-year-old girl who had left her familiar world to share her father's dream of making a fortune in British East Africa. While riches evaded their coffee plantation, the young girl's sense of fun, curiosity, and interest in animals and people are clearly conveyed. Also unmistakable is the tone of British superiority reflected in accounts of her family's difficulties with the land, Gikuyu labor, and servants; the self-righteous attitude of European settlers; and the lack of understanding of Africans and their culture. The author's mother summed it up best when she said, "We must have a sticky passage ourselves, but when we've knocked a bit of civilization into them, all this dirt and disease and superstition will go and they'll live like decent people for the first time in their history."

432. Japuonjo, Roeland. *Mzee Nyachote*. Illustrated by Adrienne Moore. Phoenix Young Readers Library. Nairobi, Kenya: Phoenix, 1967, 1987. 56p. Grades 3-5.

Various episodes from the life of Mzee Nyachote, a respected elder and teacher who was born in 1902 in the Nyanza region of Kenya, are narrated in this short biography. From a mischievous prankster, Nyachote developed into a just and kind teacher and headmaster of a mission school. In a society where respect and discipline were strictly enforced, Nyachote's childhood experiences and sense of fun gave him a unique understanding of children. Whenever his students behaved irresponsibly, Nyachote employed innovative means to punish them. He never shamed or insulted a child's pride, but empowered him to do the right thing. As an elder, Nyachote retained his sense of humor and wit in the advice he gave to members of his community. Whether he was apprehending a thief or tricking a lion while hunting, he resembled the cunning trickster--the intelligent little person who could take on big challenges. This inspiring and delightful biography demonstrates the heroism and greatness that ordinary people are capable of.

433. Johnson, Osa Helen. *Osa Johnson's Jungle Friends*. Philadelphia: Lippincott, 1939. 200p. Grades 5-7.

Personal anecdotes and information on the habits of wild animals merge in Johnson's account of her life and safaris in East Africa. As animal collectors and naturalists, Osa and her husband Martin shared exciting adventures while capturing, photographing, and housebreaking their pet elephant, chimpanzee, porcupine, aardvark, cheetahs, baboon, and Gibbon ape. While much dignity and affection have been bestowed on these animal friends, Johnson's references to her African servants are far from flattering. She refers to them as "the black boys," "the cook boys," "our lazy cook," and "black native boy." Interspersed with these animal stories is Johnson's meeting with a young Somali girl. Ironically, Johnson speaks of this "friend" in the same tone and descriptive style as she does of her animal friends. Osa writes that she restrained her natural impulse to hug and kiss the girl and her brother because "such a display of emotion would be an affront to their savage dignity."

The endearing antics of some of these animals have been narrated in greater detail in books like *Jungle Pets, Jungle Babies, Pantaloons, Snowball,* and *Tarnish, The True Story of a Lion Cub*.

434. Laird, Elizabeth, with Abba Aregawi Wolde Gabriel. *The Miracle Child: A Story from Ethiopia.* Illustrations photographed by Angelo Hornak. New York: Holt, Rinehart and Winston, 1985. 32p. Grades 2-5.

One of the oldest Christian countries in the world, Ethiopia's oral literature celebrates not only Biblical characters but Ethiopian saints and their miraculous lives as well. This picture book narrates the extraordinary story of Tekla Haymanot, a beloved saint who lived in the thirteenth century and founded the monastery at Debra Libanos. Both text and illustrations, which are photographed from an eighteenth century illuminated manuscript, focus on the supernatural aspects of his birth and life, his miracles, and his compassionate nature. Saint Tekla Haymanot's soul was received by Jesus in Paradise after seven years of continual prayer and penance. The captions accompanying the illustrations provide information on the artistic style, symbols, and cultural details.

Another book by Laird that records the Christian heritage of Ethiopia is *The Road to Bethlehem* (Holt, 1987). Interspersed with the traditional Gospel narrative of the birth of Jesus are legends that were popular in the ancient world such as the travels of the Holy Family in Egypt, account of the Virgin Mary's life, story of the two thieves, and the story of the pearl. As in *The Miracle Child,* the illustrations for this nativity story have been taken from two-hundred-year-old handpainted manuscripts.

435. Lema, Anza A. *Horombo: The Chief Who United His People.* Makers of African History Series. London: Longman, 1976. 48p. Grades 3-5.

Based almost entirely on legends, songs, and ruins of old forts, this biography reconstructs the life and career of Horombo (1762-1802), chief of the Chagga who lived on the slopes of Mount Kilimanjaro in Tanzania. The various subgroups of the Chagga had always preferred to live in small chiefdoms--perhaps due to the nature of the terrain--which made them vulnerable to attacks by stronger groups. Horombo, who became chief of the Keni group at the age of eighteen, set himself the difficult task of uniting the Chagga in order to make them strong and independent. Through bravery on the battlefield, intelligent leadership, and a trained and disciplined army, he successfully defeated the mighty Masai warriors and made the Chaggas accept him as their Paramount Chief. He built a prosperous empire based on shared power, diplomacy, law and order, and an efficient intelligence service. Unfortunately, due to the jealousy of a chief, he was killed in battle at the age of forty, and the empire he had worked so hard to build quickly disintegrated. However, Tanzanians are still inspired by his brave deeds and his vision of cooperation and unity to ensure a prosperous and secure future.

436. Lindgren, Astrid. *Sia Lives on Kilimanjaro.* Children of the World Books. Photographs by Anna Riwkin-Brick. New York: Macmillan, 1959. N.p. Grades K-3.

Black-and-white photographs of eight-year-old Sia, a Chagga girl who lived on Mount Kilimanjaro, portray the young girl's family, her rural lifestyle, her daily chores, and a Chagga feast. Lindgren unifies the diverse photographs by imposing an engaging storyline about Sia's desire to attend the feast and meet King Marealle. Although there are no negative statements, the emphasis of the book is most definitely on the rural and exotic, rather than on the universal aspects of Sia's life and experiences.

437. Margolies, Barbara A. *Rehema's Journey: A Visit in Tanzania.* Photographs by author. New York: Scholastic, 1990. N.p. Grades K-3.

Nine-year-old Rehema's story of her first journey away from home is also intended as a discovery of Tanzania for readers. Photographs and text first introduce Rehema's home and family in the Pare Mountains and the simple dignity of their lives. Next, readers share the young girl's excitement and apprehension at leaving home, seeing both familiar and new sights along the way, and being overwhelmed by the noise and crowds of Arusha City, where she attended her first church confirmation ceremony. The highlight of the trip, however, was a visit to the wildlife sanctuary in the Ngorongoro Crater, where her father worked as a tourist guide. Margolies' attractive color photographs convey the beauty of the vast crater and the wealth of animal life that it supports. Rehema learned of the danger to animals, especially to the endangered rhinoceros, posed by poachers. She was also made aware of her multiethnic society when she met a Waarusha boy and girl and some Masai warriors, or morans. The journey gave Rehema a special appreciation for her country, her home, and her father's job.

438. Negash, Askale. *Haile Selassie.* World Leaders Past and Present. New York: Chelsea House, 1989. 111p. Grades 7-9.

The life and achievements of Haile Selassie I, Emperor of Ethiopia, are discussed in the context of Ethiopian and world history. Son of the powerful governor of Harer province, the young Tafari Makonnen was educated and groomed by his father to someday succeed to the throne. At the age of thirteen, he was appointed administrative head of a small region of the province. Tafari proceeded to use his education, skill in intrigue and diplomacy, and, at times, unscrupulous methods to be crowned emperor in 1932. In reviewing his forty-four-year reign, Negash discusses Haile Selassie's contradictions: While his charismatic personality won him the respect and allegiance of his people and a divine status by his Jamaican followers, the Rastafarians, he was condemned for his love of pomp and self-glorification; and while he modernized Ethiopia by introducing technology and reforms in government, the prison system, education, and foreign policy, he sacrificed leadership and social welfare by holding on autocratically to the throne. Ironically, the educational reforms that he initiated led to student protests for more reforms. Eventually, the human suffering of the drought and famine led to his ouster by the military regime of Mengistu Mariam in 1974.

Photographs, quotations, and accounts of journalists, historians, and world leaders show evidence of a well-researched biography.

439. Noronha, Francis. *Kipchoge of Kenya.* Nakuru, Kenya: Elimu, 1970. 157p. Grades 7-12.

The eventful career of track star Kipchoge Keino is traced from his humble childhood as a cattle herder in the Nandi Reserve, to the beginning of his running career as a trainee for the Kenya Police, to international competition and fame. Endowed with an amazing stamina and an easy loping stride, Kipchoge's ability was first discovered in his village school. Lacking a qualified coach, Kipchoge established his own workout program and in 1962 had his first taste of international competition in the Commonwealth Games held in Australia. Although he did not win a race, he observed the training programs and tactical strategies of other athletes and modified his own training to build up speed. He practiced hard, and with the 1964 Tokyo Olympics he gained international listing and numerous invitations to compete abroad. Thus began his career of setting new personal records and breaking world records, especially at the 1968 Mexico Olympics where he won the gold medal in the 1,500-metre race.

Noronha has enlivened the second-by-second account of races by providing details of Kipchoge's state of mind and physical condition, track conditions, and the strengths and weaknesses of his opponents. The biographer is also able to convey a sense of his subject's personality and how it impacted on his running. Because of his calm temperament, religious beliefs, and obvious enjoyment of the sport, Kipchoge was able to face each race with an equanimity which was the envy of his rivals. Above all, this biography symbolizes the national pride of Kenya and the potential of its athletes. The text is complemented by photographs and appendices outlining the life and track record of Kipchoge from 1962 to 1970.

440. Stewart, Judy. *A Family in Sudan.* Photographs by Jenny Matthews. Beans Series. London: A & C Black, 1987. 25p. Grades 3-5.

Insight into the life of an Arabic-speaking family in Sudan is provided through Dawalbeit, who lived in the village of Labadu. A description of the daily routine in the family compound, in the fields, on market day, in school, and during travel by camel and lorry provides information on social life and customs. The well-being of Dawalbeit's family was subject to environmental conditions--rains and destructive desert winds. The drought and famine of the 1980s forced some members of the family to seek work in Khartoum and a neighboring town; resulted in the death of nearly all of their livestock; and led to sickness and death. Once the rains came, their subsistence agriculture brought joy and plenty. Both text and color photographs emphasize the contentment and security of a polygamous family for children: all work and material comforts are shared, there are plenty of playmates, and there is always an adult around who is willing to give individual attention.

441. Weber, Valerie, and Tom Pelnar, eds. *Tanzania.* Photographs by Haruko Nakamura. Children of the World Series. Milwaukee, WI: Gareth

Stevens, 1989. Originally published in 1988 in a shortened form by Kaisei-sha Publishing, Tokyo. 64p. Grades 4-6.

Village life in contemporary Tanzania is explored through the experiences of twelve-year-old Rajabu who lived at the foot of Mount Kilimanjaro. Text and photographs portray various facets of Rajabu's life at home, at school, at work, and at play. This book also contains a fairly detailed reference section on the land, peoples and culture, history and government, economy, religion, tourism and wildlife, and arts and crafts of Tanzania. In addition to providing background information, this section will enable readers to gain a better understanding of Rajabu's life. For instance, the guiding principles of President Nyerere's government--uhuru, umoja, and ujamaa--can be seen as operating on the family, community, and national levels. To encourage individual research and critical thinking, this section also lists a number of projects and activities for children. Maps, an index, and a reading list are included for further study.

442. Wepman, Dennis. *Jomo Kenyatta*. World Leaders Past & Present Series. New York: Chelsea House, 1985. 112p. Grades 7-12.

As in the Archer and Friedman biographies (see # 425 and 427), Jomo Kenyatta's entire life is seen in relation to the beginning and end of colonial rule in Kenya. Throughout the biography, Wepman portrays how Kenyatta's Gikuyu roots, Western education, dedication and courage, and charisma took him to the forefront of the freedom struggle and into the position of president of independent Kenya. Kenyatta is credited with leaving behind a rich, peaceful nation that was probably the most stable and democratic in Africa.

As is typical of this series, each chapter is complemented by quotations, photographs, and explanatory captions on the history, politics, economy, and society of Kenya and Africa. A chronology, reading list, and index are included.

INFORMATIONAL BOOKS

443. Abebe, Daniel. *Ethiopia in Pictures*. Revised edition. Visual Geography Series. Minneapolis, MN: Lerner, 1988. 64p. Grades 5-8.

Ethiopia is portrayed as a nation attempting to emerge as a modern state while preserving its ancient traditions. Abebe describes the topography, wildlife, natural resources, peoples and lifestyles, and economy. The rich history of Ethiopia is traced from the Sabean immigration from Southern Arabia between 2000 and 1000 B.C. to modern times. What follows is a detailed and coherent account of the formation of the Solomonic dynasty in 980 B.C. by Menelik I, son of Maqeda, Queen of Sheba, and King Solomon; achievements of the Aksumite kingdom (4 A.D. to 7 A.D.) and the introduction of Coptic Christianity; Muslim conquests and conversion to Islam; achievements of the Zagwe dynasty; contact with Portugal and defeat of Muslim power; Menelik II and Italian attempts at colonization; and defeat of Haile Selassie and monarchy by a military declaration in 1974.

Ethiopia in Pictures also provides an objective view of the current socialist communist government through an analysis of its political machinery and reforms in the areas of land distribution, nationalized industries, education, medical services, and tourism. While the current problems--chronic drought and famine, mismanagement of resources, civil unrest, low literacy and life expectancy--are overwhelming, Abebe believes that Ethiopia has great economic, social, and political potential to transform itself into a stable and economically self-sufficient nation. Attractive color and black-and-white photographs testify to the beauty of the land, the grandeur of ancient and medieval civilizations, and the country's attempts to resolve its problems. Both urban and rural life are represented fairly.

444. Bailey, Donna, and Anna Sproule. *Kenya.* Where We Live Series. Austin, TX: Steck-Vaughn, 1991. 32p. Grades K-3.

Both text and photographs present a rather sketchy account of urban and rural life, major ethnic groups, national holidays, and animal parks of Kenya. The only distinguishing feature of this book is the beautiful color photography.

445. Bleeker, Sonia. *The Masai: Herders of East Africa.* Illustrated by Kisa N. Sasaki. New York: Morrow, 1963. 155p. Grades 6-8.

In her typical narrative style, Bleeker examines the history, environment, lifestyle, and beliefs of the Masai, a nomadic pastoral people who live in the Great Rift Valley of Kenya and Tanzania. The account begins with a description of their physical features, origin and migration, and almost sacred bond with their distinctive cattle. Bleeker, however, focuses on Masai social and political organization; cattle economy; status and function within the community according to sex and age-sets; religious beliefs; customs related to house building, clothing and personal ornamentation, and food; and rituals associated with puberty rites for girls and boys, initiation as warriors, and induction as community elders in middle age. Concern for the health and care of their cattle also led to the knowledge of mending broken bones, surgery, and treating a variety of wounds and ailments on humans. The many nights spent outdoors while grazing cattle also led to an interest in observing the movements of the planets and other heavenly bodies. The above account is enhanced by pertinent references to scientific investigations, early European exploration, and Masai legends. While the statistics are outdated, the author rightly concludes that Masais will have to face the changes brought on by independence, industrialization, modern medicine, formal education, and the fight to retain their grasslands.

446. Burch, Joann J. *Kenya: Africa's Untamed Wilderness.* Discovering Our Heritage Series. New York: Dillon, 1992. 127p. Grades 4-6.

This is an objective account of the land and wildlife, history and government, family life and customs, education and recreation, and agriculture and exports of modern Kenya. If Presidents Jomo Kenyatta and Daniel arap Moi are criticized for ignoring the democratic system of checks and balances, they are also praised for giving Kenya a stable government, prosperous economy, and bold measures for conserving wildlife. Harambee is seen as the cornerstone of Kenyan policy in trying to achieve progress and national cohesion. Hence, while ethnic groups like the Gikuyu, Luyha, Luo, Turkana, Samburu, Masai, Rendille, European, Asian, and Arab retain their distinctive cultures, they are encouraged to regard themselves as Kenyans. Both photographs and text portray traditional and urban lifestyles to provide a balanced view of the changes occurring in Kenya today.

Other topics discussed are exploitation and native reserves under British rule; fossils of protohumans found by anthropologists Louis and Mary Leakey and their son Richard in the Great Rift Valley, especially at Lake Turkana; Arab slave trade; nationalistic struggle and the Mau Mau Movement; achievements of athletes like Kipchoge Keino, Douglas Wakiihuri, and Joseph Kibor; and the views of immigrants and Kenyan students in the United States. A list of facts, addresses of the Kenyan Embassy and offices in the United States and Canada, glossary, Swahili words, and bibliography are included.

447. Carpenter, Allan, and James W. Hughes. *Tanzania*. Enchantment of Africa Series. Chicago: Children's Press, 1973. 95p. Grades 5-7.
The authors introduce Tanzania's geography, natural resources, history from Arab and European settlements to independence, peoples and lifestyles, economy and industry, and governmental reforms. The above information is enlivened by separate chapters on the Leakeys' archeological research in Olduvai Gorge and their discovery of Zinjanthropus, a near-human primate believed to be 1.5 million years old; and brief biographies of four children from Zanzibar, Tabora, Ngorongoro Crater, and Moshi. The enchantment of Tanzania rests in its high concentration of wild animals that can be viewed in reserves like Serengeti National Park, Lake Manyare Park, and Ngorongoro Crater; former Arab strongholds like Dar es Salaam and Zanzibar; and the highest point in Africa, Mount Kilimanjaro.

448. Creed, Alexander. *Uganda*. Places and Peoples of the World Series. New York: Chelsea House, 1988. 96p. Grades 5-7.
A discussion of Uganda's land, history, economy, and people focuses on the decades of ethnic rivalries, foreign domination, and dictatorial regimes that have prevented the country from advancing despite its rich natural resources. Creed perpetuates the stereotype that when European explorers came to East Africa in the 1800s to search for the source of the Nile, Uganda was governed by several unruly tribes that fought with each other. The impact of slavery by both Arab and European traders on the economic, social, and political life of Uganda is not even mentioned. He does, however, state that once Uganda

became a British protectorate in 1894, British policy favoring the Buganda kingdom increased the tension and internal strife. Regrettably, Creed does not discuss precolonial history; he also fails to elaborate on the achievements of the Buganda kingdom, which had an advanced society where people lived in beautiful five-story houses. Focusing on the political turmoil after independence from Britain in 1962, Creed discusses the military coup under Idi Amin, whose dictatorial regime was marked by suspension of constitutional rights, mass killings, and civil rights violations. Seventy-three thousand Asian residents and citizens, mainly Indian, were deported simply because they were a successful minority who either controlled the majority of the country's commerce and trade or were trained as doctors and teachers. (These events are portrayed in a 1991 movie, *Mississippi Masala*.) With Amin ousted in 1979, four successive governments have attempted to run the country. Today, Yoweri Museveni's government is working toward a recovery by improving health care, updating the outmoded educational system established by missionaries, invigorating the economy, and improving transportation and communication.

449. East Africa Publishing House. *The Work of the District Commissioner*. Our Nation Series. Nairobi, Kenya: East Africa Publishing House, 1973. 11p. Grades 4-6.

This book outlines the various roles of the District Commissioner, a civil servant within a province who fulfills the important task of carrying out governmental policies at the district level. The District Commissioner entertains dignitaries and presides at ceremonial occasions; maintains law and order; listens to complaints and problems; and chairs committees that plan the future trade and development for the district. While this position is clearly a remnant of colonial times, it is interesting to note that modern Kenya has incorporated traditional chiefs and elders under the District Commissioner. Far from being a dull recounting of information, the text speaks directly to young readers by anticipating their questions and providing concrete examples that they can relate to.

450. Edmonds, I.G. *Ethiopia: Land of the Conquering Lion of Judah*. Photographs by author. New York: Holt, Rinehart and Winston, 1975. 222p. Grades 7-12.

Edmonds narrates the history of Ethiopia from the legendary conquest of Moses, a prince of Egypt, in 1300 B.C. to the military takeover of Haile Selassie's regime under Mengistu Mariam in 1974. Edmonds deftly integrates the impact of geography, differences among the various factions, and religious persecution of Jews, Coptic Christians, and Jesuits on the events of history. Ethiopia is unique among African nations as being a free and independent nation since 1300 B.C., except for a brief period (1936-1941) when it was under Italy. Included in this survey are accounts of the introduction of Christianity in 326 A.D. by a young boy from Tyre; the Crusaders' search for the legendary Prester John; exploits of King Lalibela and the cruelty of "mad" King Tewodros II; famous queens like Gudit, Mentewab, and Taitu; political involvement of explorers like James Bruce and Henry M. Stanley; and Menelik II's defeat of Italy.

451. Feelings, Muriel. *Jambo Means Hello: Swahili Alphabet Book.* Illustrated by Tom Feelings. New York: Dial, 1974. N.p. Grades K-3.
    Spoken in Eastern Africa and parts of Central and Southern Africa, Swahili serves as a contact language for a large segment of the continent. Children are introduced to twenty-four words--the sounds Q and Z are not present in Swahili--that represent objects, animals, festivals, relationships, and concepts. Both text and illustrations go beyond the word being introduced to provide an understanding of the people and environment which created the language. Hence, details of culture, clothing, rural life, body gestures, codes of behavior, and flora and fauna are meticulously described. Tom Feelings' black-and-white artwork gracefully portrays the movements and expressions of the characters.

452. _____. *Moja Means One: Swahili Counting Book.* Illustrated by Tom Feelings. New York: Pied Piper Books, 1976. Originally published in 1971 by Dial. N.p. Preschool-Grade 1.
    Winner of numerous prestigious awards such as the Caldecott Honor Book (1972), American Library Association Notable Children's Book (1971), and School Library Journal's Best Books of the Year (1971), *Moja Means One* focuses not so much on the objects being counted as on introducing African American children to their African heritage. The Swahili numbers from one through ten portray various aspects of rural life in East Africa--clothing, musical instruments, animals, market day, coffee plants, and Mankala, a popular counting game. Tom Feelings' illustrations extend the text by conveying the beauty and serenity of the landscape, the self-sufficient village economy, and the inherent respect for traditions as expressed through storytelling, lifestyle, and cultural details.

453. Geography Department. *Kenya in Pictures.* Revised edition. Visual Geography Series. Minneapolis, MN: Lerner, 1988. 64p. Grades 5-7.
    This new edition provides a fair and objective discussion of Kenya's land, peoples, history, government, and economy. It states that Kenya as an independent nation has successfully avoided major ethnic conflicts and has maintained a relatively efficient administration. The future outlook is positive because of improvements in educational standards and enrollment, living standards, health facilities, housing, and economic activity, especially tourism. The text is illustrated with photographs, maps, and charts.

454. _____. *Madagascar in Pictures.* Revised edition. Visual Geography Series. Minneapolis, MN: Lerner, 1988. 84p. Grades 5-7.
    An examination of the land, peoples, religion and culture, history and government, and economy and industry portrays Madagascar as a country of contrasts. Once a part of the African continent,

Madagascar broke free more than 100 million years ago, and it remained uninhabited till travelers from Indonesia and Malaysia migrated in large canoes--some via East Africa--more than 1,500 years ago. In due course, Arab traders, Islamic missionaries, Africans, and European missionaries left their distinct cultural stamp on the island. Prior to colonization by the French, the Malagasy were governed by several kingdoms that vied for power and total control. Prominent among the many powerful Merina monarchs were Queen Ranavalona I, Rasoherina, and Ranavalona III. Madagascar won its independence in 1960, and in 1975 a military coup under Admiral Ratsiraka's leadership led to the establishment of a democratic republic with strong socialist and communistic tendencies. The outlook for Madagascar is seen as bleak and discouraging because of the problems of poverty, continual food shortages, underdevelopment, rigid state control, and a massive foreign debt. The above information is presented in an objective manner, and the numerous photographs fairly portray all aspects of Malagasy life.

455. Godbeer, Deardre. *Somalia*. New York: Chelsea House, 1988. 95p. Grades 6-8.

While this book is outdated with respect to the severe drought of the 1990s and the complete breakdown of the government and infrastructure, its compassionate analysis of Somalian history, geography, peoples, economy, culture, religion, and wildlife provides an understanding of the current situation. Since independence in 1960, Somalia has faced serious problems of war, famine, and refugees, which are a direct result of European colonization and natural disasters. With its strategic location on the horn of Africa, Somalia was a prized territory over which the Italian, French, and British fought. With independence, Somalia suffered loss of territory and continual war with Ethiopia due to an arbitrary demarcation of national boundaries. After the revolution in 1969, President Siyad Barre's socialist government mobilized Somalian resources and foreign aid to launch an aggressive program of education, agricultural development, and social welfare. However, devastating droughts from 1978 to 1981 and again in 1987 plunged the country in a cycle of poverty, illiteracy, food shortages, malnutrition, and disease. With the help of the World Bank and numerous international relief organizations, Somalians were given medical aid, agricultural training and technical help, and assistance with industrial development. On the positive side, Somalians are presented as a resilient people with an aesthetic gift for oral poetic composition. In addition, Islam's vital role in unifying a diverse ethnic population and arming it with a strong moral character is emphasized.

456. Haskins, Jim. *Count Your Way Through Africa*. Illustrated by Barbara Knutson. Minneapolis, MN: Carolrhoda, 1989. N.p. Grades K-3.

This Swahili counting book does not portray objects from East Africa where the language is spoken; instead, it introduces readers to the varied topography, history, and culture of Africa. Both text and illustrations go beyond the objects being counted to give a detailed account of such topics as the ivory and gold that attracted both traders and settlers; the ruins of the ancient civilization at Great Zimbabwe; the African roots of the banjo and jazz music; animals native to Africa; and the artistry of everyday objects like combs. Information on the lifestyle of the people of the Kalahari Desert, significance of initiation rites and scars, and creative expressions through poetry, dance, and music indicate how Africans adjusted to their environment and evolved numerous rich and varied cultures. There is no mention of changes that have taken place in modern Africa.

457. Khalfan, Zulf M., and Mohamed Amin. *We Live in Kenya*. We Live In Series. New York: Bookwright, 1984. 60p. Grades 6-12.

Twenty-six first person interviews with people from various occupations and ethnic groups provide valuable information on life in contemporary Kenya. Both photographs and text go beyond the individual to give an insider's look at the living conditions, beliefs, factual details, and professional opportunities of the group being represented. Hence, readers learn about tea and coffee plantations from a picker and a farm manager; religious freedom from a Roman Catholic priest and a Muslim Imam; opportunities for women from a member of parliament, bank manager, and student; wildlife conservation from a park warden and safari guide; art from a Lamu poet, curator, sculptor, and curio seller; health care from a herbalist and medical doctor; and education from school and college students. Whether urban or rural, black African or Asian, European or Arabic, all feel an immense pride in their heritage and their contribution to the economy and solidarity of Kenya. While the problems facing modern Kenya--high infant mortality, inadequate medical care, and widespread illiteracy--are not ignored, the overwhelming impression these portraits create is of pride in themselves and their country. Swahili, which is a blend of Bantu, Arabic, Asian, Chinese, and European languages, best symbolizes the spirit of harambee that Kenyans feel as a nation. A list of facts, glossary, and index accompany the text.

458. Kleeberg, Irene Cummings. *Ethiopia*. A First Book. London: Franklin Watts, 1986. 63p. Grades 4-7.

This book was prompted by the severe problems of drought, starvation, war, and disease in Ethiopia in the early 1980s. The immediate causes are continuous failure of rainfall, expanding Sahara Desert and soil erosion, overpopulation, and counterproductive farming methods like overgrazing and overcultivation; however, Kleeberg examines the land, people, languages, religion, and history to arrive at a truer understanding of the situation. The present crisis, she emphasizes, could have been averted if the socialist government of Colonel Mariam had carried out the reforms it had promised; instead, power is still centralized, the gap between rich and poor is as vast as ever. There is widespread corruption among officials; there is hoarding and selling of donated food; there is lack of adequate infrastructure; and there is little attention paid to education and social welfare. Despite the assistance by international relief organizations, the situation in Ethiopia is seen as truly tragic and hopeless unless the government decides to face its problems and plans for long-term solutions. This book provides an outsider's view of Ethiopia.

459. Lye, Keith. *Ethiopia.* Take a Trip Series. London: Franklin Watts, 1986. 32p. Grades 2-4.

A simple text and color photographs provide a brief introduction to the land, people, religion, history, and economy of Ethiopia. Emphasis is placed on the contemporary problems of drought and hunger, civil wars and unrest, and lack of farming education.

460. _____. *Kenya.* Take a Trip Series. London: Franklin Watts, 1985. 32p. Grades 1-3.

As is typical of this series, young children are provided with sketchy information on Kenya's landscape, ethnic groups, religion, history and government, and archeological discovery of the bones of protohumans at Lake Turkana by the Leakeys. The color photographs that illustrate the text are attractive and testify to the beauty of the country. A brief list of facts about Kenya is also included.

461. Mack, John. *Madagascar: Island of the Ancestors.* London: British Museum Publishers, 1986. 96p. Grades 8-12.

A joint venture by the British Museum and Musee d' Art et d'Archeologie, this publication discusses the history, peoples, culture, and arts of Madagascar. With the aid of the most recent archeological, historical, and ethnographic research, especially in the remoter central and eastern rain forest regions, Mack unravels the complex fabric of Malagasy culture. He discusses its African and Asian origins; historical developments that led to the incorporation of Islamic, European, and Christian features; and the resultant material objects and cultural institutions arising from this intermix.

A major portion of the book is devoted to traditions--meaning ways of the ancestors--which regulate Malagasy life. This is believed to be the first in-depth study of the tombs and cenotaphs, shrouds, coffins, and funerary memorials that explain the process of burial. In addition, the significance of funeral rituals, reburials, and constant invoking of the ancestors is respectfully explained to reveal the relationship of the living with the dead. The lengthy process of burial achieves the cultural transition from being merely human to becoming a revered ancestor. This concept of the ancestors encompasses and expresses all that is considered morally desirable and appropriate in social relations. An extensive bibliography will assist the serious researcher to further study this little-known island. Maps, photographs, and drawings both illustrate and extend the text.

462. Maren, Michael. *The Land and People of Kenya.* Portraits of the Nations Series. New York: Lippincott, 1989. 191p. Grades 7-12.

Based on his experiences as a Peace Corps teacher in a village and his five years as an aid worker, journalist, and consultant, Maren provides a lively insider's account of modern Kenya. While individual chapters discuss broad topics such as land, peoples, early history, colonialism and independence, education, arts and culture, and safari and wildlife, within each chapter a multifaceted view of the topic is presented through visual aids and a variety of supplementary essays. For instance, the chapter on ethnic groups, which discusses the Gikuyu, Luo, Masai, Somali, and Kalenjin, has two insets on terminology and traditional age-groups. Each essay, along with its accompanying photographs and detailed captions, supports and extends the main text. Each chapter emphasizes that Kenya is a nation in transition whose citizens are evolving new attitudes to respond to the recent changes. Male circumcision rites are now conducted in modern hospitals and the authority of the elders in the age-group system has been replaced by the government. While many believe that something of value has been lost, Maren states that the changes have not been entirely negative: women's rights have benefitted from the decline in female circumcision and all babies are now cared for.

Whatever the subject under discussion may be--the origin of humanity and the work of the Leakeys, ancient kingdoms, slave trade, missionaries and explorers, Africanization under Jomo Kenyatta and Moi, repressive measures against writer Ngugi wa Thiong'o, sports and Kipchoge Keino, tourism, or Pan-Africanism and Organization of African Unity--Maren's objective approach is quick to point out Eurocentric thinking as well as lack of democratic rights. He dispels the myths and inaccuracies associated with the Mau Mau Movement by citing that the guerrilla fighters suffered the heaviest losses. Between 1952 and 1957, only thirty-two Europeans were killed in the violence along with 1,819 Africans considered loyal to the British, but more than eleven thousand Mau Mau fighters died. Maren concludes that the driving force behind many aspects of Kenya's history, politics, economy, religion, and culture is the Kenyans' attachment to their land as it represents their roots and links with the past.

463. McCulla, Patricia E. *Tanzania.* Places and Peoples of the World Series. New York: Chelsea House, 1989. 112p. Grades 5-7.
A well-organized and objective text introduces readers to Tanzania's land, history, government, peoples and lifestyles, industry and economy, and education. Tanzania is presented as one of the most important countries in Africa because its leaders, especially Julius Nyerere, have sought unique solutions to the problems of ethnic division, poverty, and limited political rights. They have worked hard to forge a democratic, humane, and just society by adopting a socialist economy and a one-party political system. However, present-day Tanzania is still not self-reliant and its goals of social progress have not been fully realized. A list of important facts, a glossary, and numerous photographs supplement the text.

464. Perl, Lila. *East Africa: Kenya, Tanzania, Uganda.* New York: Morrow, 1973. 160p. Grades 7-10.

East Africa's geography, history, peoples, and traditions are discussed from the perspective of its being the gateway to traders, slavers, missionaries, explorers, and empire builders whose impact and disruptive influences can still be encountered in the present. Individual chapters provide an in-depth study of conditions in postcolonial Kenya, Tanzania, and Uganda. There is also discussion of special topics such as excavations at Olduvai Gorge; Asian influence in East Africa; conditions leading to the expulsion of Asians, especially Indians, from Uganda in 1972; and exploitation and destruction of wildlife.

Contemporary East Africa is presented as a complex community of three alike yet dissimilar nations that are united linguistically by Swahili; politically by the concepts of harambee, ujamaa, and uhuru and a unique brand of one-party democracy; culturally by the mixing of many influences from Asia, Europe, and the Middle East; and by the common goal of achieving political stability, economic development, and social welfare. Maps and photographs support and supplement the informative text.

465. Reuben, Joel, and Howard Carstens. *Tanzania in Pictures.* Visual Geography Series. New York: Sterling, 1973. 62p. Grades 5-7.

Tanzania is seen as a unique nation in East Africa. While it shares a similar geography and history with Uganda and Kenya, it differs markedly in its policies after independence in 1961. Politically, Tanzania is committed to African socialism and a one-party democracy based on the principles of group cooperation and a better standard of living for all. Its foreign policy is one of dynamic neutrality--that is, it has relations with both the former Soviet Union and Communist China and Western powers. Tanzania plays a leading role in affairs of the continent. It was the first to condemn apartheid in South Africa and refused to join the British Commonwealth if apartheid was not denounced and economic sanctions not imposed. Tanzania also serves as a haven for exiles and freedom units from all over Africa. Culturally, Tanzania has taken the lead in preserving Swahili, a language whose roots are in Arabic and Bantu.

Other topics discussed in *Tanzania in Pictures* are the birth of human civilization at Olduvai Gorge; migrations by Hamites and Bantus; Arab rule and Portuguese coastal control; explorations by European missionaries like David Livingstone; the lifestyles of peoples like the Chaggas and Masai; government and social services; economy and agriculture; exports and tourism; and wildlife preserves at Serengeti, Lake Manyana, and Ngorongoro Crater. The black-and-white photographs are not very attractive by today's standards.

466. Roddis, Ingrid and Miles. *Let's Visit Sudan.* Let's Visit Series. London: Burke, 1985. 96p. Grades 5-7.

The authors deftly link the impact of geography and history on the civil strife and political and economic problems facing modern

Sudan. The text also provides a fairly detailed account of ancient history, beginning with King Piankhy's invasion of Egypt in 750 B.C. and the Meroitic civilization (590 B.C.). Other topics discussed are Islam and other religions, peoples and social customs, city and rural life, education, and transportation.

467. Ross-Larson, Bruce C. *Kenya's Nomads.* Edited by Paul J. Deegan. Photographs by author. Mankato, MN: Amecus Street, 1972. 46p. Grades 4-6.

In discussing the nomadic lifestyle, social organization, and economy of the Samburu group of Northern Kenya, Ross-Larson stresses their reluctance to cooperate with the modern methods of herding, formal education, health care, and political system. The size, location, and duration of Samburu settlements is dependent on their continual search for water, grazing land, and an area free of predators. Since cattle are the basis of their wealth and economy, their daily activities focus on the care, milking, watering, and grazing of cattle. Even the shape and layout of settlements and individual farm units have the cattle in mind. Samburu social organization is based on strong family relationships and dependency on the community for protection. Each member has a specific role: Elders, men over 30 or 35, make all the decisions and settle disputes, while women have an inferior domestic role. Women do, however, own property in the form of cattle presented to them by their husbands at the time of marriage. After circumcision, a young girl is eligible for marriage to an elder. The marriage is arranged by her male relatives and she must adapt to co-wives. The lifestyle of warriors is complex and strictly regulated as they progress from one age-group to the next. They can marry and become elders after giving their most productive years to the service of the community.

While Ross-Larson's text has a definite Eurocentric tone, as a professional photographer his black-and-white photographs are artistic and sensitive in their portrayal of Samburu customs, daily activities, and ceremonies.

468. Shachtman, Tom. *Growing Up Masai.* Photographs by Donn Renn. New York: Macmillan, 1981. N.p. Grades K-3.

Through the experiences of a young boy and his sister, the poetic text and attractive black-and-white photographs depict the daily activities in a Masai settlement. Although many Masai have moved to cities, this book focuses on their traditional, pastoral lifestyle. More than any other ethnic group in East Africa, Masai are determined to preserve their unique identity. The central unit of their social structure is the polygamous family and kinship groups, with the elders governing and settling disputes, adolescent boys and young men guarding against enemies and dangerous animals, young boys herding, and girls and women in charge of the home, milking cattle, and building and repairing the huts. Moving from one stage of life to the next is marked by communal tests and rituals. Masai clothing, food, and entertainment reflect their harmony with the environment.

469. Ssemakula, P. *They Obeyed the True King: The Story of the Uganda Martyrs.*   Witnesses to the Gospel Series. N.p., Uganda: Saint Paul's Publications, 1983. 43p. Grades 6-8.

A bloody chapter from the history of the Buganda kingdom in the late 1800s is narrated in this book. As a result of Henry Morton Stanley's visit to the court of Mutesa I in 1875, there was an influx of Catholic and Protestant missionaries to the kingdom. However, while Mutesa I initially welcomed the missionaries, his son Mwanga persecuted the converts when he became the *kabaka* (ruler) in 1884. Ssemakula's straightforward, terse prose narrates the chilling events leading up to the May 27, 1886 burning of thirty-seven young men and boys who served as pages to Mwanga. The story of their persecution, long journey to the execution site, inhumane cruelty and torture, and glorious death takes on mythic proportions as it is likened to the martyrdom of Jesus Christ. The narrative does not include an objective discussion of possible political and nationalistic motivations of the *kabaka;* instead, his behavior is attributed to an irrational and evil character. Once the Christian pages refused to satisfy Mwanga's homosexual tendencies, he misused his absolute power by executing his Christian courtiers. The book ends by extolling the virtues of the martyrs and listing the twenty-two Catholic martyrs as patron saints.

470. Stevens, Rita. *Madagascar.* Places and Peoples of the World Series. New York: Chelsea House, 1988. 111p. Grades 5-7.

Although the political information is outdated, all the basic information on Madagascar that is presented in the Visual Geography Series (entry # 454) is covered here as well, except in a style and format more appealing to young readers. Stevens sparks readers' curiosity and interest by describing the many rare trees, plants, fish, and birds that exist--or existed--in Madagascar only. There is a captivating account of the cruel and bloodthirsty Ranavalona I, who in her thirty-three-year reign executed more than 100,000 subjects and brought about the deaths of an additional one million in various building projects. Ranavalona I, however, is not recognized for her nationalistic feelings in attempting to reverse the Europeanization policy and Christianization of her predecessors. Maps, a list of facts, a glossary, and an index make the information readily accessible to researchers.

471. Stewart, Gail B. *Ethiopia.* Places in the News Series. New York: Crestwood House, 1991. 48p. Grades 2-4.

The history, government, economy, and social conditions of Ethiopia are examined almost entirely from the perspective of the continual droughts and famine that have ravaged the country for the past twenty years. Emperor Haile Selassie's long reign and Mengistu Mariam's communist government have been blamed for the deaths of thousands of Ethiopians and the poverty of the country. Fighting among ethnic groups and the demand for independence by the Eritreans, Somalis, and Tigreans have further shaped government policy. For political reasons, food supplies and money donated by other countries are deliberately withheld from the rebel areas, which are also the areas worst hit by the drought. Power is still in the hands of wealthy landowners who have taken advantage of the situation by buying land from hungry farmers and profiting from donated grain. While this is a negative portrait of the Ethiopian government, the tone is compassionate toward the victims of drought. Stewart is also critical of Israel for supplying weapons to Mariam's regime--when even the Soviet Union and Cuba stopped doing so--because it will only prolong the strife. The account ends on a note of hopelessness because victims and relief workers are merely pawns in the hands of politicians.

472. *Sudan in Pictures.*   Visual Geography Series. Minneapolis, MN: Lerner, 1988. Revised edition of *The Sudan in Pictures* by Salah Khogali Ismail, Sterling Publishing. 64p. Grades 6-8.
    An examination of the land, people, history, government, and economy stresses that Sudan is a combination of two distinct cultures--Arab and African--that have not blended into a peaceful whole. The desert-like north is populated mainly by Arabic-speaking, Nubian, and Beja nomadic groups, while the forests, grasslands, and swamplands of the south are inhabited by the Nilotic ethnic groups. While the early history of the Kush and Nubian kingdoms was influenced by developments in Egypt and the Roman empire, the isolated south came under European Christian influence in the eighteenth and nineteenth centuries. While the north is Islamic, traditional African religions and the social and cultural heritage of black Africa prevail in the south. Even after independence in 1956, the division persists: The country is divided into the urbanized, market-based economy of the north and the pastoral, agricultural economy of the south, and the Muslim-educated, Arab-speaking elite of the north and the Christian-educated, English-speaking people of the south. Despite the progress seen in Khartoum, modern Sudan is presented as a nation struggling to survive the problems of civil war and political unrest, slow economic development and financial instability, high illiteracy, and poor diet and health caused mainly by the prolonged famine of the 1980s. New photographs, maps, charts, and captions make this a more appealing book than others in this series.

473. Yoshida, Toshi.   *Elephant Crossing.*   Translated by Susan Matsui. Illustrated by author. New York: Philomel Books, 1989. Originally published in 1984 as *Omoide* by Fukutake, Tokyo. N.p. Preschool-Grade 1.

474. _____. *Young Lions.*   Translated by Susan Matsui. Illustrated by author. New York: Philomel Books, 1989. Originally published in 1982 as *Hajimete no Kari* by Fukutake, Tokyo. N.p. Preschool-Grade 1.
    Both picture books introduce young readers to the wild animals that inhabit the open grasslands of East Africa. Elephants, zebras, giraffes, gnus, and Thompson gazelles share the same feeding grounds since each eats its own particular kinds of plants. Even carnivores like lions and cheetahs are essential to maintain the ecological balance. The

populations of impalas and other grass-eating animals, for instance, would become too numerous for the environment to support if it weren't for the meat-eating animals. The experiences of an elephant herd and three lion cubs learning to hunt focus attention on the natural dangers these animals face in their daily lives. However, an ultimately safe and nurturing world is presented to children as the elephants and cubs reach safety. There is no mention of humans in this idyllic world.

Yoshida's illustrations are distinctive because of their endearing portrayal of animals, descriptions of the grasslands, and the speed and movement of the animals, especially during a chase.

Central Africa

TRADITIONAL LITERATURE

475. Aardema, Verna. *Sebugugugu, the Glutton: A Bantu Tale from Rwanda.* Illustrated by Nancy L. Clouse. Grand Rapids, MI: William B. Eerdmans. Trenton, NJ: Africa World Press, 1993. N.p. Grades K-2.
   This folktale warns against disobedience and inordinate greed. Sebugugugu, a poor villager, repeatedly invokes Imana, the Creator, for food. He is given a fruit-bearing vine, a rock with mealie porridge and honey dripping from it, and a herd of cattle, but in his greed to get more he disregards the instructions of Imana. Eventually, he loses everything, including his wife and children. Clouse's earthtone collages deftly employ smooth, flowing lines to represent natural unity, and jagged lines for Sebugugugu's inner dissatisfaction and disharmony with the environment. The tale is ideal for reading aloud as it includes refrains that will delight the young listener.

476. _____. *Traveling to Tondo: A Tale of the Nkundo of Zaire.* Illustrated by Will Hillenbrand. New York: Knopf, 1991. N.p. Grades K-3.
   Courtesy among friends is carried too far when Bowane, the civet cat, is on his way to Tondo with the bride price for a beautiful feline. When Bowane asks Embenga the pigeon, Nguma the python, and Ulo the tortoise to accompany him to the wedding, they foolishly delay him despite the urgency of the situation. When they finally reach Tondo, the bride is already married. Although it took the four friends several years to reach Tondo, they race back to their village when chased by the irate husband. Aardema heightens the listening pleasure by maintaining the humorous undertone and imitating and repeating animal sounds.

477. Burton, William Frederick Padwick. *The Magic Drum: Tales from Central Africa.* Illustrated by Ralph Thompson. New York: Criterion, 1961. 127p. Grades 4-6.

Collected firsthand when Burton served as a missionary in the Congo, these tales capture not only the author's graceful and enticing narrative style, but also his appreciation for the role of Luban folktales in imparting knowledge and shaping values. Representative of all tale types, these stories describe local village life, explicate practical lessons and moral virtues, and embody the wisdom of the people. The stories of the trickster rabbit, Kalulu, are a case in point. Kalulu outwits larger animals by matching his intelligence with their pride and superior strength, but as soon as he oversteps the boundaries of morality and decency he is, in turn, tricked by the equally clever tortoise, Nkuvu.

478. Holladay, Virginia. *Bantu Tales.* Edited by Louise Crane. Illustrated by Rocco Negri. New York: Viking, 1970. 93p. Grades 4-6.
    Originally recorded in the 1930s by a pioneer teacher, the nineteen tales in this collection characterize the wisdom, values, and lifestyle of the Bantus of the Baluba and Lulua cultures of the Congo. Through tales of humor, trickery, friendship, and wickedness, readers will learn how people and animals face the challenges and hardships of life. As Kabundi the weasel cheats the animals of the forest during a famine, as Nkashama the leopard is justly tricked and killed by a group of monkeys, as the worthless man of poverty learns that rich or poor one cannot change others' opinions, and as Bat is disillusioned by the friendship of Sun, children learn moral lessons and a practical approach to survival.

479. Keidel, Eugene. *African Fables That Teach About God.* Book 2. Illustrated by Paul D. Zehr. Kitchener, Ont.: Herald Press, 1981. 111p. Grades 3-5.
    For someone hoping to read stories about the Zairean concept of God, the title of this collection will prove misleading. A missionary in Zaire since 1951, Keidel intends this book and her previous compilation of tales, *African Fables That Teach About God* (Herald Press, 1978), to serve as sermon illustrations and as Sunday School texts. Strictly speaking, the stories are not all fables, but an assortment of fables, realistic tales, pourquoi tales, and trickster tales. While the stories illustrate universal truths and reveal the predicaments and foibles of human beings everywhere, they are interpreted to reflect specific lessons from the Bible. Sometimes, the moral aphorism is forced on a story. For instance, "Who Put That Rope On Your Neck?" which narrates an exploit of the trickster dik-dik, is interpreted as the work of the Devil, instead of the mischievous pranks of a small animal who uses his intelligence to outwit a crocodile and a hippo. In "The Argument That Has Never Ended," the dual aspects of water and fire--which are sometimes nurturing, sometimes destructive--are ignored and these forces of nature are stated to have an absolute choice of either harm or help to others. The stories are highly didactic, and they rob the originals of their lively and philosophic qualities.

480. Knappert, Jan. *Myths and Legends of the Congo.* African Writers Series. Nairobi, London and Ibadan: Heinemann, 1971. 218p. Grades 6-12.

Organized in ten chapters, these stories reflect the mythology, religious beliefs, customs, and wisdom of the various peoples of the Congo. The selections include two epics of the Lonkundo dynasty and the foundation myth of the Alur; a dozen fables of the Ngbandi of the Northern Congo; and a variety of creation stories of the world, man and woman, and suffering and death. There are myths of the gods of the underworld and sky, stories of the relationship between humans and nature spirits, and legends of kings and priests who possess the secret of rainmaking. Prominent in the Bakongo stories is the theme of witchcraft and the punishment meted out to witches. There are also two myths that explain the presence of the white man in Africa.

481. Knutson, Barbara. *Why the Crab Has No Head.* Illustrated by reteller. Minneapolis, MN: Carolrhoda, 1987. N.p. Grades K-3.

This creation myth from the Bakongo of Zaire explains why the crab has no head. When the creator, Nzambi Mpungu, was making various animals, she got tired while working on Crab, so she asked him to return the next morning for his head. The tiny crab, thinking that he was superior to even the larger animals because Nzambi was spending so much time on him, began to boast about the magnificent head he was going to receive. All the newly created animals assembled around Nzambi's house to watch the event, but Nzambi decided to humble Crab by leaving him headless. The black-and-white illustrations are placed within a stylized decorative border that lends distance and emphasis to the moral of the story.

482. McDermott, Gerald. *The Magic Tree: A Tale from the Congo.* Illustrated by reteller. New York, Chicago and San Francisco: Holt, Rinehart and Winston, 1973. N.p. Preschool-Grade 2.

Brightly colored African designs and motifs, which seem to flow like the individual frames of a film, lend a magical charm to this Congolese fairy tale. An ugly twin brother finds strength, beauty, and love when he releases a princess and her people from a magical tree. However, he loses all when he breaks his promise and divulges the secret of his success to his uncaring family.

483. Ross, Mabel H., and Barbara K. Walker. *On Another Day. . . Tales Told Among the Nkundo of Zaire.* Hamden, CT: Archon Books, 1979. 596p. Grades 8-12.

The ninety-four tales in this volume were collected by Ross during her twenty-five years' service among the Nkundo of Zaire. Organized under the four major groupings in the Aarne-Thompson *Types of the Folktale*--Creation and Pourquoi Tales, Animal Tales, Realistic Tales, and Cumulative and Dilemma Tales--these stories are intended both for the casual reader and the serious researcher. Each section has its own introduction on the types of tales and the values they emphasize. The detailed notes that directly follow each tale provide general comments, relationship of the tale to others in the volume and citation of variants, identification of tale types and major motifs, and footnotes on literary, ethnological, and other matters of interest to the reader. For the folklorist, there is detailed information on the collection sites, methodology and scholarly tools used, details of recording situations, biographical sketches of narrators, and opportunities for further research. In addition, David J. Crowley's Foreword surveys all the collections and studies of Zairean folklore, and Ross' Introduction discusses the geography and history of Zaire, details of Nkundo lifestyle and customs, and cultural changes between 1950 and 1975.

484. Savory, Phyllis. *Congo Fireside Tales*. Illustrated by Joshua Tolford. New York: Hastings House, 1962. 88p. Grades 3-6.

Fourteen tales from the Congo were collected firsthand and translated into a pleasing style for Western readers. There are stories of Kalula the trickster hare; fables about false pride and being content with what one has; stories of heroic quests, magic, and transformations; and realistic tales of how even the poor and powerless can win great wealth through their intelligence. Prominent among the tales is "Umusha Mwaice, the Little Slave Girl," a Cinderella story which has several motifs that are present in the European version; however, once the heroine marries the chief's son, her stepmother continues to plot her death. Finally, the long-suffering Umusha Mwaice kills one of her stepsisters and serves her at a feast to her stepmother. Entertaining as these stories are, the introduction may very well dissuade readers. A note of both apology and Eurocentricism can be detected in Savory's comments on Central Africa being "the wildest and most uncivilized" region of Africa and "the uncivilized people who evolved them [the folktales] had nothing but the wilds of nature around them." No doubt referring to the Cinderella tale, he mentions the "unenlightened days [when] cannibalism was regularly indulged in certain areas," resulting in "strange" tales whose "horror element" had to be toned down. Savory is also the author of *Zulu Fireside Tales* and *Matebele Fireside Tales*.

485. Tucker, Archibald Norman. *The Disappointed Lion and Other Stories from the Bari of Central Africa*. Illustrated by John Farleigh. London: Country Life, 1937. 97p. Grades 3-6.

Ten delightful stories embody details of daily life, harmony with nature, survival against predators, and mythical beliefs of the Bari of Central Africa. A majority of the stories center around the adventures of Kidden and her family and how they outwit the wicked lion with their intelligence, with help from the trickster Bullfrog, and with magic. To capture the flavor of an actual storytelling session, Tucker has included a free English translation of the many songs that are an integral part of these tales.

While the stories are well written and highly entertaining, the Preface and Introduction reflect the racial attitudes prevalent in the 1930s. The African men from whom the author collected the stories are called "boys," and the account of Bari rural life is presented with a hint of superiority. Adjectives like primitive, queer, and quaint are used when referring to the people and the Bari language.

FICTION

486. Clifford, Mary Louise. *Bisha of Burundi.* Illustrated by Trevor Stubley. New York: Crowell, 1973. 140p. Grades 6-8.
   Set in the late 1960s, this is the story of fifteen-year-old Bisha who is torn between love for family and her personal desire to continue her education and become a teacher. Her crisis is precipitated when she completes primary school and her parents arrange to marry her to a widower with three children, because they believe his high position will ensure her father's chieftaincy of their district. With the support of a nun at her mission school, her progressive aunt, and Thomas, a childhood friend, Bisha boldly challenges their decision by applying for a scholarship to middle school. Bisha realizes the precarious social position she is caught in: dishonor to family, giving up the security of home, social ostracism, and, possibly, spinsterhood. Events move in Bisha's favor when she publicly defends her aged grandfather--the present chief of the district--against the insults of her betrothed.
   The story assumes a broad social and political dimension because Clifford elegantly juxtaposes Bisha's actions and thoughts against the history of Tutsi expansion, rigid feudal organization, cattle herding economy, and bitter ethnic rivalry between the minority Tutsi rulers and the majority Hutu laborers. The role of the Belgian mission schools is also handled sensitively. While conversion to Christianity may be the ultimate hope of the Roman Catholic Church, the nuns and priests render an invaluable service by educating young Burundians and empowering them to usher in an era of change. The conflict that Bisha experiences is a much larger phenomenon that is enacted at several levels: traditional religious beliefs versus Christianity, one-party political system versus Tutsi feudalism, formal education versus oral traditions, and nationalism versus ethnic loyalties.

487. Enright, Elizabeth. *Kintu.* Illustrated by author. New York: Farrar and Rinehart, 1935. 54p. Grades 3-5.
   The conflict centers around Kintu's fear of the jungle and its wild animals. As son of the chief, he must overcome this weakness in order to succeed as a hunter. Determined, he undertakes a heroic journey into the jungle and kills a leopard. Woven into Kintu's human predicament are details of Congolese village life, religious beliefs, and festivities. However, the author treats these details as sociological curiosities by focusing on their exotic aspects--witch

doctor, devil dances, magic, and "little black idols." The repeated references to Kintu as "black," the incongruent appearance of the witch doctor, and the chief's childish delight over a coil of telephone wire purchased from the white trader with four leopard skins and a pair of elephant tusks reflect Enright's superior racial attitude.

488. Gatti, Attilio. *Adventure in Black and White.* Illustrated by Kurt Wiese. New York: Scribner's, 1943. 172p. Grades 6-8.
This novel has all the ingredients of a stereotypical colonial adventure story: a Congolese jungle teeming with wild animals, friendly Mbuti Pygmies and the dangerous Bwa Bwa dwarfs, a World War II airbase, a European spy, and the friendship of Bob, a curious and mischievous American boy, and his Congolese friend, Loko-Moto. Gatti's superbly crafted plot unfolds the parallel stories of Bob getting lost in the jungle, Loko-Moto's search for his friend, and the sabotage at the airbase in Stanleyville. The narrative successfully balances and intertwines the three strands through descriptions and overlapping episodes, as well as maintaining the fast pace and tension of the story.
White superiority is reflected in the derogatory diction, behavior, and attitudes of the white characters. However, this blatant racism is mitigated somewhat by the friendship of Bob and Loko-Moto; by Bob's growth into an intelligent, mature, and responsible youth; and by Loko-Moto's initiative and sharp wit in rescuing his white friend and identifying the spy.

489. McGavran, Grace W. *Mpengo of the Congo.* Illustrated by Kurt Wiese. New York: Friendship, 1945. 127p. Grades 3-5.
Characters and plot are stereotyped to promote the Christian agenda of the book. As is typical of missionary stories, a Christian family goes to live in a non-Christian village to set an example of Christian fellowship and self-sacrifice. Thanks to the efforts of Mpengo's family, belief in evil spirits, superstitions, control of the witch doctor, and enmity with neighboring villages are replaced by Christianity, cleanliness, Western medicine, and schools for children.

490. Muhire, Edward. *Wake Up and Open Your Eyes.* Illustrated by James O. Okuthe. Nairobi, Kenya: Phoenix, 1976, 1989. 100p. Grades 4-6.
Set in 1945, this fast-moving story spans the life of Higiro from early childhood in Rwanda to young adulthood in Uganda. Sympathy for Higiro is created through his unhappy life with his stepmother, death of father, and encounters with drunks and cheats. However, his grandmother's love, his father's values and faith, and his love for Maria give him a positive outlook and a solid moral foundation. Regrettably, Muhire's superficial treatment does not provide descriptions of the setting or details of the psychological tensions and complex personality of Higiro. Themes of child abuse, child labor, education, adolescent sexual attraction, and political unrest are hinted at but not explored.

491. Price, Willard. *Elephant Adventure*. New York: Day, 1964. 192p. Grades 5-8.

Two experienced big game hunters--Hal Hunt, nineteen, and his brother Roger, fourteen--try to capture live elephants for foreign zoos and circuses on the dense jungle slopes of the Ruwenzori, or Mountains of the Moon, on the Zaire-Uganda border. Their efforts are thwarted time and again by the immense strength of the elephants and by an illegal group of Arabs who steal their elephants. After a series of heroic episodes, the Hunts outsmart the Arab sheik and his band and capture a white elephant.

Price, a naturalist who has led several gunless safaris in Africa's big game country and expeditions for National Geographic Society and the American Museum of Natural History, provides interesting information on the geography, giant plants and animals, and peoples of the region. Unfortunately, the book is liberally sprinkled with derogatory comments on governmental incompetence, war in the Congo, and beliefs and lifestyles of ethnic groups native to the region. The Africans assisting the Hunts are depicted as unreliable, insensitive, and generally fearful. The setting is also fully exploited for its exotica: the ability of the Watusi to jump high in the air, the "Pygmies" crawling inside the belly of a dead elephant to get meat, and an Arab hideout decorated in the grand manner of the Arabian Nights. Arabs are stereotyped as cruel, greedy, and disrespectful of the law, especially when they capture Africans for the slave market in the Persian Gulf. In contrast, Hal and Roger are saviors of the Watusi village because they stop the illegal activities of the Arabs. Not once is their own exploitation, although legal, of the natural resources of Africa mentioned. Animals are treated with more respect and courtesy than Africans.

492. _____. *Gorilla Adventure*. New York: Day, 1969. 189p. Grades 6-10.

The Hunt brothers are sent to the Virunga Volcano territory to capture a mountain gorilla and other exotic animals for the Ringling Circus. They are assisted by a thirty-man African crew and a surly Belgian who creates serious trouble. As is typical of these adventures, Price describes the habits and psychology of each animal, the best way to trap it, and the myths associated with it. However, this factual information does not make for a stilted plot. Suspense is maintained through vivid descriptions of the gorilla; activities of a gang of organized poachers; and repeated attempts on the lives of the brothers by an unknown enemy. The plot quickly reveals that the feared and ferocious animals are far from vicious, and that the real danger is posed by human greed and ego.

Undoubtedly, this is an exciting story of two heroic boys who face natural and human adversaries, but what impression will readers get of the African background? Diction, plot, and characterization relegate Africans to a passive or ineffectual role. The white protagonists--albeit only teenagers--are the leaders who catch the most dangerous animals and apprehend the poachers without much help from their crew or local officials. There is no background information on the political situation in the Congo, giving the impression that Africans are unruly and violent. There is also one instance of disregard for African life when the crazed gorilla picks up two crew members and smashes their heads together. Readers are not told whether the men died instantaneously, or whether they were in need of medical attention. Instead, the action focuses on taking the seven-hundred-pound gorilla, who has been tranquilized, to the hospital for treatment.

Other Willard Price adventures involving the Hunt family in Africa are *African Adventure* (Day, 1963), *Safari Adventure* (Day, 1966), and *Lion Adventure* (Day, 1967). In each story, the excitement of capturing live animals is contrasted with the more dangerous activities of slave traders, poachers, and slaughterers of animals.

493. Rockwood, Roy. *Bomba the Jungle Boy and the Cannibals or Winning Against Native Dangers*. New York: Cupples and Lion, 1932. ?p. Grades 6-9.

The thirteen books in this series are reminiscent of Tarzan's adventures in West Africa. The episodic plot takes Bomba from one life-threatening situation to another, and it is the alien white boy who survives better than grown African men because of his superior intelligence, strength, and courage. Even though he is only fourteen, Bomba single-handedly gains leadership of an entire tribe of Pygmies and selflessly provides for them. He is portrayed as being more mature and generous than adult Africans because of his superior racial heritage and "white blood." Africans are stereotyped as "irresponsible," "childish," and "unstable."

494. Shaw, Mabel. *Children of the Chief*. Photographs by Bernard Turner. London?: London Missionary Society, 1921. 128p. Grades 7-12.

Based on the experiences of an English missionary in Central Africa, this story recounts how the girls of Mbereshi Village are transformed once they attend the boarding school started for them. From rowdy, thoughtless, cruel, and quarrelsome girls, they become well behaved, truthful, and industrious young women. All this is accomplished only once they acknowledge the love of Chief Jesus. The narrative places the activities of the school in the context of the efforts of missionaries like David Livingstone to end slavery. Photographs of Mbereshi School, activities of its pupils, and village life illustrate the text.

495. Stinetorf, Louise A. *White Witch Doctor*. Decorations by Don McDonough. Philadelphia, PA: Westminster Press, 1950. 276p. Grades 8-12.

Based on her own and others' experiences, Stinetorf writes a moving first person account of missionary life in the Congo. The detailed, leisurely prose describes the difficulties encountered by Ellen Burton, a middle-aged nurse from rural Indiana, as she sets up a hospital in the Congo. Readers will be awed by the dangers to which she exposes herself during her twenty-five years of service. While Ellen's actions evince love and respect for her African friends and servants, and while she comes to understand their customs, her benevolent attitude and belief in the superiority of Western civilization and Christianity are equally obvious. However, the protagonist is a sympathetic character because she is selfless, dedicated, and courageous. She is made uncomfortable by the efforts of fellow missionaries to convert the Congolese, by the blatant racism and unfairness of the colonial officials, and by the crass materialism and sensationalism of the white film makers.

496. Weir, Bob, and Wendy Weir. *Panther Dream: A Story of the African Rainforest.* Illustrated by Wendy Weir. New York: Hyperion, 1991. 40p. Grades K-3.
Written and illustrated by environmentalists dedicated to saving the tropical rain forests, *Panther Dream* portrays the African rain forest, possibly in Central Africa, as a microcosm of the world. In this fantasy, Lokuli, who has been warned of evil spirits, boldly enters the forest to hunt for his starving village. He is surprised to discover a harmonious world of plants, insects, animals, and "Pygmies." When Lokuli's efforts fail, a black panther kills an antelope and gifts it to the boy, telling him to take only what is needed so that life can continue. While the message against the exploitation of nature is clear, this is an idealized picture. It is unrealistic to expect the African rain forest and its people to remain untouched by the changing economic and social conditions, population growth, and technological advancements.

BIOGRAPHY

497. Cox, L.E. *Always on the Go: Thomas Comber of Africa.* Eagle Books Series. New York: Friendship, 1944. Originally published in 1939 in England. 24p. Grades 4-6.
One of a series of biographies on Christian missionaries worldwide, *Always on the Go* recounts the pioneering journey of a young Britisher to the Congo interior. Using both jungle paths and the Congo River, Comber (1852-1887) braved the harsh environment, disease, cannibals, and unfriendly groups to establish Christian missions in the Congo. Comber is a one-dimensional character who is seen only from the perspective of his courage, steadfastness, and constant activity to achieve his goal--that is, "the white man's burden" to bring salvation to the "wild and ferocious" people of Central Africa. As in Canon Apolo's biography (see # 501), the book abounds in derogatory references to Africa and its peoples.

498. Gatti, Attilio. *Kamanda: An African Boy.* Photographs by Commander and Mrs. Attilio Gatti. New York: McBride, 1941, 1953. 200p. Grades 6-8.

This partial biography narrates the story of Kamanda's service with the Gattis on their tenth and twelfth safaris in Africa to capture and photograph wild animals. While sensitive readers will feel uncomfortable when Kamanda exchanged his royal status to perform menial tasks as a "native boy" in the expedition, Kamanda himself was unaware of the irony of his changed circumstances. It is Kamanda's curiosity, sense of discovery at visiting new geographical areas and ethnic groups of Africa, marvel at the white man's "magical" machines, loyalty to his employers, and, above all, ambition to earn the golden stripes of a chauffeur that heighten the interest of the story. While the Gattis' superior tone and benevolent attitude toward Africans are unmistakable, their affection for Kamanda and appreciation for his hard work and quick intelligence are equally obvious. Numerous black-and-white photographs of the Gatti expeditions recall the thrill and adventure of African safaris.

499. Graves, Charles P. *A World Explorer: Henry Morton Stanley.* Illustrated by Nathan Goldstein. Champaign, IL: Garrard, 1967. 96p. Grades 3-5.

The fast-moving plot, lively dialogue, and graphic descriptions will draw young readers to the life and adventures of John Rowlands, later named Henry Morton Stanley after his adoptive father in America. The biographer idealizes Stanley's character by focusing on his childhood suffering, courage and determination, and later achievements; there is no mention of Stanley's hot temperament and ruthless treatment of people. While the narrative style and illustrations are appealing, Graves' references to Africans as "natives" and the implication that they needed to be civilized by Europeans will offend contemporary sensibilities.

500. Smith, B. Webster. *Sir Henry M. Stanley.* Illustrated by John C. Gardner. Great Endeavour Series. London and Glasgow: Blackie, 1960. 67p. Grades 6-8.

This biography traces the major events of Stanley's life (1841-1904) from childhood in England, to emigration and journalism in America, to exploration in Africa, to fame and death in England. Unlike Graves (see # 499), Smith presents a balanced view of the many faults and noble qualities of this great Victorian explorer. Details of Stanley's childhood struggles with abandonment, poverty, and physical abuse provide the psychological motivation for his hardworking, self-assertive, and intolerant personality--qualities that enabled him to face the challenges of his African adventures. In addition to finding the "lost" Dr. Livingstone, Stanley traced the course of the Congo River, explored Central Africa, charted Lake Victoria and Lake Tanganyika, and assisted King Leopold in founding a Belgian colony in the Congo. While passing references are made to Stanley's autobiographical works like *How I Found Dr. Livingstone, Through the Dark Continent,* and *In Darkest Africa* and the accounts of people who had worked with him, Smith focuses on narrating the life of Stanley with a minimum of commentary.

Another biography that captures the excitement and drama of Stanley's adventures--especially his meeting with Livingstone in Ujiji--is *With Stanley in Africa* (Dutton, 1961) by Olga Hall-Quest. The tone and diction of both books reflect colonial superiority in their repeated use of words like "savages," "natives," and "children" when referring to Africans. The biographers display no knowledge or understanding of African culture and civilization, but assume a benevolent stance.

501. Yates, Pat. *Apolo in Pygmyland.* Eagle Books Series. New York: Friendship, 1944. Originally published in 1940 by Edinburg House, London. 24p. Grades 4-6.

This short biography focuses on the story of Apolo Munubi's (1864-1933) conversion to Christianity, his persecution by the Baganda and Mbonga, and his ultimate triumph in establishing Christian missions in and taking the Gospel message to various parts of Central Africa. While Apolo's strong faith and unceasing work as a missionary are noteworthy, the biography itself is one-sided and intolerant of African culture and religious beliefs. Africans are referred to as uncivilized, lazy, wild, and cruel.

INFORMATIONAL BOOKS

502. Archer, Jules. *Congo: The Birth of a New Nation.* New York: Messner, 1970. 190p. Grades 9-12.

Archer provides a detailed account of the widespread bitterness, regional politics, and unleashed violence and chaos that accompanied Congolese independence in 1960. Political rivalries and ideological differences among Patrice Lumumba, Moise Tshombe, Joseph Kasavubu, and Joseph Mobutu embroiled the Congo in a prolonged civil war, intensified the Cold War between the United States and the Soviet Union, and involved U.N. troops in a challenging diplomatic and peace-keeping effort. In trying to analyze the factors responsible for this situation, Archer traces the history of the Congo from the ancient empires of the Bakubas, Bakongos, and Balubas, to the influx of Portuguese and British explorers, businessmen, missionaries, colonials, and slavers, to Leopold II's flagrant exploitation and brutal treatment of the Congolese, to the nationalist movement and independence. Archer blames Belgium for its failure to train and prepare an educated class of Congolese for the responsibilities of independence and self-government.

For a detailed account of the history of Belgian imperialism in the Congo, especially of the excesses of King Leopold II, refer to *The Congo: A Brief History and Appraisal* (Praeger, 1961) by Maurice N. Hennessy. Also refer to Joseph Conrad's adult novel *Heart of Darkness.*

503. Batchelor, John and Julie. *The Congo*. Rivers of the World Series. Morristown, NJ: Silver Burdett, 1980. Originally published in 1980 by Wayland. 67p. Grades 3-5.

Based on their 1974 journey, the authors follow the river Congo, or river Zaire as it is now called, from its source in the hills bordering Zambia, through swamps, tropical rain forests and waterfalls, through villages and towns like Kongolo, Kisangani, and Kinshasa, to its mouth in the Atlantic Ocean. As they travel by kayak, aeroplane, train, motor boat, and car, the Batchelors combine their personal experiences with information on the major landforms, history, natural resources, wildlife, commerce and industry, religion, and people and their lifestyles. Indeed, the Congo is seen as a mighty river that is a source of power, an artery of communication and transportation, and a means of tapping the sources of wealth for modern Zaire.

The freshness and sense of discovery of the text are reflected in the photographs of the people, places, and industries along the banks of the river. Both illustrations and text link this journey to that of Henry Morton Stanley's first descent of the Congo in 1877. A glossary, bibliography, and index are included.

504. Bleeker, Sonia. *The Pygmies: Africans of the Congo Forest*. Illustrated by Edith G. Singer. New York: Morrow, 1968. 143p. Grades 6-8.

Believed to be among the oldest inhabitants of the African continent, the "Pygmies" have lived in the rain forest of the Congo for six to seven thousand years, retaining their hunter-gatherer lifestyle of a million years ago. When this book was published, there were 150,000 "Pygmies" in Zaire. In describing their natural environment, social life, and customs, Bleeker focuses on the Mbuti, a group that has resisted assimilation. Mbutis have adapted admirably to their forest home, displaying great ecological sense in the construction of huts and hunting and gathering techniques; no animal or plant species has ever been exterminated by them. Their democratic self-government emphasizes mutual respect and equal rights for all. In the absence of a leader, decisions regarding hunting, sharing food, settling disputes, and care of the young are arrived by consensus and usage. The behavior and functions of each member are clearly defined to ensure harmony in the family and group.

With the exception of trade in metal arrows and spears, plantains, millet, and manioc with villagers who live on the outskirts of the forest, Mbutis are wholly dependent on the forest for their livelihood. Hence, their religious beliefs and celebrations are associated with the forest as creator and protector. Bleeker provides a detailed account of the Molimo ceremony, a ritual honoring the dead and a thanks offering to the forest for its benevolence. Bleeker ends on a cautionary note that the Mbutis' nomadic lifestyle has been threatened by the modern realities of colonialism, deforestation, an organized central government, and postcolonial civil wars.

505. Carpenter, Allan, and Matthew Maginnis. *Burundi*. Enchantment of Africa Series. Chicago: Children's Press, 1973. 93p. Grades 6-8.

Described variously as the ''Switzerland of Africa'' and the ''land of milk and honey,'' Burundi is a country of great scenic beauty and magnificent wildlife. From its legendary past and ancient kingdoms to colonial rule and independence, Burundi has remained isolated because of its geography and the strong attachment to the family as a social unit. As the most densely populated country in Africa today, Burundi can face the challenge of feeding its people only by halting land erosion; introducing new crops; increasing production; reclaiming swamplands for farming; changing attitude toward cattle as a source of food and money, instead of as a symbol of wealth; resettlement of farmers; and wider education. The book also discusses the government, economy and resources, beliefs and customs, and ethnic groups, especially the Twa, Tutsi, and Hutu peoples. Maps, photographs, list of facts, and index are included.

506. _____. *Rwanda*. Enchantment of Africa Series. Chicago: Children's Press, 1973. 93p. Grades 5-7.
Basic information on the geography, history, government, economy, peoples, customs, and beliefs of this tiny landlocked country in eastcentral Africa is presented in an appealing manner. Anecdotes from history, a folktale, biographical sketches of three Rwandan children, description of the fast-disappearing wildlife, and conservation attempts at Kagera National Park enliven the above account. To Carpenter and Maginnis, the enchantment of Rwanda lies in its scenic beauty, pleasant climate, and varied musical styles and instruments. They view the future as hopeful because the major ethnic groups are united into one nation and the country is taking every available opportunity to develop its resources and population. The numerous black-and-white photographs are generally poor in quality.

507. _____. *Zaire*. Enchantment of Africa Series. Chicago: Children's Press, 1973. 93p. Grades 6-8.
The authors dispel the myth of ''darkest Africa'' by describing the varied and beautiful country of Zaire (formerly known as the Congo); by recounting Zairean history from the beginning of humans, to the Lunda and Kongo kingdoms, to Belgian colonial rule and independence; and by discussing the rich mix of peoples, languages, and customs. Information on the government, health and education, agriculture, mining and industry, and art testify to the efforts of modern Zaire to draw on its natural resources and culture to build a strong country. Brief biographies of three children from various socioeconomic backgrounds illustrate the opportunities available to all. Maps, photographs, list of facts, and index are included.

508. Gunther, John. *Meet the Congo and its Neighbors*. Illustrated by Grisha. Meet the World Series. New York: Harper, 1959. 260p. Grades 6-8.
In a chatty, autobiographical style, Gunther outlines the geography, history, customs, social institutions, and arts and crafts of the Congo and its neighbors during the last years of colonial rule by Belgium, France, and Britain. Generally, Gunther looks kindly on the colonists

and minimizes their excesses and racial policies. He focuses on the exotica of the region--the "Pygmies" and the Watusi "giants" of Rwanda, luxurious vegetation, and unusual birds and animals. The two most interesting chapters are on Albert Schweitzer, the medical missionary, and how uranium for the first atom bomb was acquired from the Congo.

509. Henry-Biabaud, Chantal. *Living in the Heart of Africa.* Translated from the French by Vicki Bogard. Illustrated by Jean-Marie Poissenot. Young Discovery Library Series. Ossining, NY: Young Discovery Library, 1991. 37p. Grades K-3.
Young readers are invited to a boat journey on the Zaire River from Kinshasa, capital of Zaire, to Kisangani, as this is the only navigable stretch of the 2,900-mile river. The author describes the river and the danger from water plants and shifting sandbars. The brief text and color illustrations also provide a glimpse of the passing scenes: plants and wildlife of the tropical rain forest; social life and customs of the villagers; fishing techniques; and the self-sufficient lifestyle of the "Pygmies" in the interior. The Virunga National Park, which is further inland, is mentioned for the protection it gives to the many birds and animals native to the region, especially the mountain gorillas.

510. Jones, Schuyler. *Pygmies of Central Africa.* Original Peoples Series. Vero Beach, FL: Rourke, 1989. Originally published in 1985 by Wayland. 48p. Grades 4-6.
An anthropologist who has lived in the Ituri Forest, Jones describes the environment and wildlife, complex religious beliefs, social organization, economic institutions, and the hunter-gatherer way of life of the Mbuti. He dispels the myth promoted by books and movies that the rain forest of the Congo Basin is impenetrable and steamy; Jones found it to be a cool, shady world that has sustained Mbutis so well for thousands of years that they do not need to plant crops or domesticate animals. Like Bleeker (see # 504), Jones describes their harmonious relationship with nature and their religious belief in an all-powerful creator who is the source of all good and misfortune.
In discussing the three groups of "Pygmies" (Bleeker states that there are four)--Mbuti of the Ituri Forest, Tswa of the Western Congo River and Western Africa, and Twa of the region between Lake Kivu and Lake Tanganyika--Jones regrets that very little research has been conducted on their origin and history. The earliest written accounts came from the Sixth Dynasty of ancient Egypt and from Greek and Roman historians, but then for 1,300 years there was no mention of "Pygmies" till the explorations of David Livingstone, Henry Stanley, and James Harrison in the nineteenth century. In the last thirty years, states Jones, "Pygmies" have faced many rapid changes: they are being pressured into taking up farming; their natural environment is being destroyed at the rate of 4,500 square miles each year due to deforestation and roads; and some of their traditional territory has been designated for national parks, hence prohibiting hunting.

"Pygmies" have responded to these changes by becoming increasingly dependent on village values and economy. Some work as farm laborers, live permanently on the edge of villages, and attend school, while others continue to live in the forest to hunt for the villagers. Full-color and black-and-white photographs will help readers visualize the temporary forest camps, hunting techniques, trade relations with villagers, social and cultural life, marriage and family, and music and art of the Mbuti.

For those seeking more detailed information, *The Mbuti Pygmies: Change and Adaptation* (Holt, Rinehart and Winston, 1983) by the well-known British anthropologist Colin Turnbull, who has done repeated fieldwork among the Mbuti, is recommended. Turnbull first analyzes the traditional Mbuti way of life in the Ituri Forest, and then traces their change and adaptation to wholly different customs and values from colonialism to independence.

511. Joy, Charles R. *Light in the Dark Forest: People of the African Equator.* Photographs by author. Illustrated by Walter Galli. London: Chatto and Windus, 1961. Originally published in 1958 by Coward-McCann. 96p. Grades 5-7.

Joy displays his Western bias when he describes an imaginary village in the former French Equatorial Africa. The jungle is hostile, the animals dangerous, the people superstitious and ignorant, and the lifestyle primitive. "Light" enters this "heart of darkness" with the Europeans--not with the slavers and exploiters, but with the benevolent colonials who bring the gifts of education, consumer goods, technology, medicine, Christianity, and, above all, preparation for self-government. Joy also presents an outdated theory on the origin of humans which states that groups of people migrated to all corners of the world, including Africa, from Central Asia.

512. O'Toole, Thomas. *Central African Republic in Pictures.* Visual Geography Series. Minneapolis, MN: Lerner, 1989. 64p. Grades 5-7.

Known as Ubangi-Shari while under French colonial rule, conditions in present-day Central African Republic are attributed to geography, history, and government corruption. Lack of railroads and access to oceans or seas presents a persistent barrier that hinders the country's economic growth and participation in world trade. O'Toole's detailed chapter on history and government frankly points out that the slave trade resulted in social instability, ethnic rivalry, and reduced populations in large areas of the country, hence contributing to the difficulty of developing a national identity. Colonization led to forced labor on coffee, cotton, and tobacco plantations and diamond mines, leaving the economy shattered at the time of independence in 1960. O'Toole further points out the impact of neocolonialism: French continues to be the national language even though only a small percentage of the population speaks the language; diamond export is dominated by the government, foreign companies, and smugglers whose only interest is in quick profits; and France has supported the harsh and inefficient governments of Presidents David Dacko,

Jean-Bedel Bokassa, and General Andre Kolingba in order to retain access to the country's diamond mines. It is only with a strong and dedicated leadership that the problems of official corruption and abuse of power, weak economy, poor health and educational services, and outdated agricultural technology can be overcome.

513. Pomeray, J. K. *Rwanda.* Places and Peoples of the World Series. New York: Chelsea House, 1988. 104p. Grades 6-8.

Pomeray focuses on the clash between old traditions and new ideas in Rwanda's attempt to achieve economic and social progress. Rwandan traditions stem from the Twa who settled in the region 35,000 years ago; from the farming kingdoms the Hutu established between the seventh and tenth centuries A.D.; and from the Tutsi migration between the fourteenth and fifteenth centuries. The relative isolation of the land and freedom from slave traders enabled Rwandans to develop a rigid social, economic, and political system based on a highly centralized feudal society called *ubuhake*. These institutions endured through different eras of Rwandan history from colonization by Germany and Belgium, to merger with neighboring Burundi (called Ruanda-Urundi) under mandate from the League of Nations, to independence, political unrest, and violence between the Hutu and Tutsi. The military coup of 1973 and the establishment of a strong one-party political system with Juvenal Habyarimana as president have ushered in an era of relative stability and reforms. Several programs for improving farming techniques, stimulating industrial growth, tapping the country's rich mineral deposits, and improving literacy (37 percent at present), health care, and transportation have been initiated by Habyarimana's administration. However, Rwanda's future is seen as uncertain because of firmly entrenched traditions, ethnic rivalries, lack of funds for social and economic development, increasing national debt, and dependence on foreign aid.

514. Powzyk, Joyce. *Tracking Wild Chimpanzees in Kibira National Park.* New York: Lothrop, Lee & Shepard, 1988. 32p. Grades 4-6.

Personal narrative and factual information blend happily in artist-biologist Powzyk's daily account of her brief stay in Kibira National Park, the largest area of mountain rain forest remaining in Burundi today. Interspersed with exciting incidents of bush-whacking and belly-crawling in the dense jungle in search of chimpanzees is information on the people and culture of Burundi, importance of the rain forest as a natural resource, and descriptions of the birds, insects, small animals, and plants in Kibira National Park. In addition to observing chimpanzees in their natural habitat, Powzyk discusses five other species of higher primates--L'Hoest's Monkey, Olive Baboons, Blue Monkey, Grey-cheeked Mangabey, and Angolan Black and White Colobus Monkey--that have their separate ecological niches in the reserve. Powzyk's color paintings of plant and animal life are detailed and attractive. Maps, a glossary of terms, and a chart of the vertical distribution of primate species in Kibira National Park are included as reference guides.

515. Wolbers, Marian F. *Burundi.* Places and Peoples of the World Series. New York: Chelsea House, 1989. 120p. Grades 5-8.

An examination of Burundi's land, peoples, history, government, economy, and educational and medical facilities points to the fact that Burundi is one of the twenty poorest nations in the world. Focusing on the current economic and political situation, Wolbers states that Burundi's troubles stem mainly from a burgeoning population, an annual average income of only U.S. $200 per person, an agricultural economy and depleted resources that are barely able to feed the population, internal strife between the Tutsi ruling majority and the powerless Hutu minority, and an unstable government since independence from Belgium in 1962. Belgian rule is blamed for its indifference to developing Burundi's economy and refusal to grant civil rights to Burundians during the nearly forty years of colonization. President Buyoya's military regime is attempting to improve health care and education (there is 34 percent literacy); introduce industry and more productive methods of farming; and maintain good relations with African and world nations that can help Burundi with foreign aid and trade. Wolbers believes that the future will be hopeful only if the Hutu and Tutsi can work on the problems together; otherwise, there is potential for renewed uprisings and massacres similar to those of the early 1970s. Photographs, maps, list of facts and historical events, glossary, and index illustrate and extend the text.

Southern Africa

TRADITIONAL LITERATURE

516. Aardema, Verna. *Behind the Back of the Mountain: Black Folktales from Southern Africa.* Illustrated by Leo and Diane Dillon. New York: Dial, 1973. 85p. Grades 3-5.

In her delightful prose style, Aardema narrates ten stories from the Khoisan, Zulu, Bantu, Thonga, and Tshindao languages. In these tales, both animals and human beings are engrossed in their struggle for survival, search for suitable spouses, and attainment of happiness. They use trickery, common sense, or supernatural help to fulfill their goals. Magic and supernatural aid are readily given, but when humans become proud or greedy, this help is just as easily withdrawn. The stylized black-and-white illustrations use African folk motifs.

517. Atkinson, Norman. *The Broken Promise and Other Traditional Fables from Zimbabwe.* Illustrated by Tali Geva-Bradley. Harare, Zimbabwe: Academic Books, 1989. 88p. Grades 4-8.

Sixteen fables from the Shona, Ndebele, and Venda peoples of Zimbabwe teach good behavior by encouraging people to be kind, brave, honest, generous, and hardworking. In the Shona tales, Tsuro the hare is renowned for his cleverness and skill in solving problems, but he is not the malicious Nogwaja of the Zulu tales (see # 529). Tsuro can outwit Lion and Hippopotamus, but if he becomes proud or boastful, he is tricked by Kamba the tortoise. The stories of human characters are concerned with social conduct and personal happiness. Some warn against deceit and exploitation, while others celebrate the power of love and filial duty. In "The Magic Drum," a variant of "The Pied Piper," a young girl is exploited by the village women who make her look after their children. When the young girl can no longer tolerate their ingratitude, she beats her magic drum and leads all the children into a forest pool. Atkinson's simple narration and Geva-Bradley's imaginative illustrations make the collection entertaining.

518. Berger, Terry. *Black Fairy Tales.* Illustrated by David Omar White. New York: Atheneum, 1969. 137p. Grades 4-6.

Based on stories gathered by early travelers, ten fairy tales reflect the oral traditions of various South African groups--Swazi, Shangani, and Msuto. These stories are about the quest for kingdoms and prosperity; triumph of pretty princesses who suffer untold misery; and transformation of enchanted animals. "Baboon-Skins" is the only story in which there is no magic. The heroine, Lalhiwe, uses her intelligence and kindness to overcome the infernal jealousy of her stepmother and stepsister. Realizing that her physical beauty is the cause of all the trouble, she dons baboon skins to make herself appear ugly and deformed. However, when a marriage embassy comes from a powerful king, Lalhiwe is selected because of her graceful movements and mysterious behavior.

Berger's narratives focus on the engaging storyline and heighten the suspense through description and character motivation. Details of life in the kraal, marriage customs, standards of beauty, rituals and ceremonies, and harmony with nature are respectfully presented. The only incongruous note is in the Anglicized titles and terms such as "The Moss Green Princess," "Fairy Frog," "Rabbit Prince," and "Beauty and the Beast."

519. Betjane. *Soul Brother Magqubu: A Zulu Legend.* Illustrated by L. Ncube. Dandaro Readers Series. Gweru, Zimbabwe: Mambo, 1991. 54p. Grades 2-4.

A rather lengthy preamble leads to the legend of the Zulu hunter Magquba and his European friend Jannie Pieters. The two are soul brothers whose lifelong friendship embodies mutual respect, love, and trust. The story is an eloquent tribute to the code of honor of Zulu warriors and to human understanding. The storyframe of a modern child listening to an ancestral legend symbolizes the importance of transmitting one's cultural heritage to the younger generation.

520. Chisiya (Jefrey Chisiya Cho-Mukonto III Kutchwa-Dube). *Afrikan Lullaby: Folk Tales from Zimbabwe.* Illustrated by pupils from Sheffield, England. London: Karia, 1986. 60p. Grades 2-4.

Chisiya's colloquial idiom, liberal sprinkling of dialogue, and references to the audience heighten the oral quality of these Zimbabwean tales. The tales narrate the greed and laziness of Tsuro, the hare; the patience of Chibode, the tortoise; and the stupidity of Hochi, the pig. While the animal stories embody personal qualities, the stories of human beings are about the practical concerns of wise conduct, using one's intelligence, planting crops, and selecting an appropriate husband for one's daughter. The visual interpretations by the Sheffield schoolchildren clearly point to the universal appeal of folk literature.

521. Knappert, Jan. *Myths and Legends of Botswana, Lesotho and Swaziland.* Leiden, The Netherlands: Brill, 1985. 254p. Grades 6-12.

Introductory chapters on the history, religion, languages, racial groups, and customs of the peoples of Botswana, Lesotho, and Swaziland give background information on the seventy-five myths and legends in this volume. The stories are based on the collections of French researchers and the author's visit in 1959. The selections include animal fables; creation myths that explain the origin of the first people, marriage, and fire; stories of gods and other supernatural beings; legends of the Basutho heroes, Hlakanyane and Senkatane; and realistic tales of survival, happiness and prosperity, and family harmony. "Oriakise" is an elaborate Cinderella tale that has the basic motifs of the wicked stepmother, Prince Charming, and a pair of slippers. The stories are enjoyable, but the author repeatedly interrupts the narrative to provide background information and his own interpretations of the events and characters.

522. _____. *Namibia: Land and Peoples, Myths and Fables.* Illustrated by Liesje Knappert. Religious Texts Translations Series. Leiden, The Netherlands: Brill, 1981. 201p. Grades 6-10.

Perhaps the first collection of Namibian traditional literature, this book also serves as an excellent introduction to Namibia's early history, geography, wildlife, and peoples. Separate chapters narrate the creation myths, legends, fables, songs, and proverbs of the San, Dama, Khoi-Khoi, Herero, Kwangali, Ovambo, and Ndonga cultures. Each chapter is prefaced by a discussion of the group's history, religion, language, lifestyle, and folklore.

523. Kundeya, David N. *Why Animals Live with People.* Illustrated by Hassam A. Musa. Salisbury, Rhodesia: Rhodesia Literature Bureau, n.d. 16p. Grades K-3.

This well-written tale explains how animals came to be domesticated by man. In the beginning, all the animals lived harmoniously in the forest till Imbwa (dog) killed and ate the cubs he was babysitting for Lion and Lioness. In fear, he ran through the forest looking for some animal to protect him. Dog tested the prowess of hens, ducks, goats, sheep, and cattle, but none seemed a suitable match for Lion. He, finally, went to Nzou (man) whose bow and arrow was the only thing capable of protecting him. The line drawings accurately portray the text but fail to provide any aesthetic appeal.

524. Makura, Tendai. *Why the Cock Crows.* Illustrated by Varaidzo Manzwei Makura. Village Tales Series. Harare, Zimbabwe: Zimbabwe Publishing House, 1981. 14p. Grades K-2.

This is a charming story of how the village of Kufawaedza in Zimbabwe appointed the rooster to give the wake-up call every morning. When the villagers are unable to get up before sunrise, the elders interview all the farm animals. Each animal is rejected because its voice is disagreeable, but the cock-a-doodle-do of the rooster is pleasing. Their problem solved, the villagers look forward to times of prosperity. The brisk dialogue with the animals is both entertaining and humorous.

525. Matthews, Tim. *Tales of the Secret Valley.* Illustrated by Colleen Cousins. Harare, Zimbabwe: Baobab, 1988. 40p. Grades 2-4.

Cousins' exceptional illustrations and Matthews' engaging narrations invite readers to enter the Secret Valley at Kariba, now submerged under water due to the dam on the Zambezi River. The stories narrate the origin of the Leya, Inde, and Dimba clans; Nabulo's escape from slave dealers with supernatural help; Simonje's war against the Mambo kingdom; and the fate of Namaaza, the rainmaker. The Secret Valley is a beautiful place of magical pools, enchanted animals, brave hunters, and the brain-drinking monster. Although the people and animals of the valley have been forced to move due to progress and modern technology, the tales of its mystery are immortalized in this collection.

526. Mhlophe, Gcina. *Queen of the Tortoises.* Illustrated by Hargreaves Ntukwana. Braamfontein, South Africa: Skotaville, 1990. N.p. Grades K-3.

A little tortoise is dissatisfied with her plain appearance and boring life. In her attempt to be different, she claims to be the queen of the tortoises and decides to "fly" to a meeting of the animal leaders by holding on to a stick that two ducks carry in their beaks. When her vanity causes her to speak while airborne, she falls to the ground and cracks her shell. She learns her lesson and, finally, wins the distinction of being the first tortoise to have a patterned shell. The book is beautifully illustrated and produced, but Mhlophe's text tends to be wordy.

527. _____. *The Snake with Seven Heads.* Illustrated by Hargreaves Ntukwana. Braamfontein, South Africa: Skotaville, 1989. N.p. Grades 1-5.

This folktale celebrates the love of Manjuzo, an accomplished dancer, and her husband Mthiyane, a brave hunter. The two are separated when an angry old woman transforms Mthiyane into a seven-headed snake. Manjuzo hides him in a big pot and keeps the secret from her children. In a dream, it is revealed to her that the curse will be lifted once she has danced at seven weddings. When she is at her seventh wedding, her children discover the snake and alarm the villagers who pour hot porridge on his body. Manjuzo is heartbroken to see the snake killed, but out of the burned and blistered skin emerges her husband.

Ntukwana's attractive illustrations are representative of modern art and stylized folk art; however, the lines are flexible enough to express the rhythm of the dancer, the actions of the characters, and the feelings of Manjuzo.

528. Mungoshi, Charles. *Stories from a Shona Childhood.* Illustrated by Luke Toronga. Harare, Zimbabwe: Baobab, 1989. 55p. Grades 1-4.

Two tales of Tsuro, the trickster hare, a legend, and a realistic story represent the folklore of the Shona of Zimbabwe. There is an undertone of indulgent humor as the pretensions and foibles of the characters are exposed. The legend of Kakore, a slave and rainmaker who becomes a chief, is a thought-provoking story that explores the desirable qualities of a leader. These stories have superbly crafted plots, in-depth characterization, and leisurely descriptions of setting and lifestyle. Songs and verse are frequently integrated into the narrative, especially when a hidden message, a magical formula, or a commentary on the characters or events is being communicated.

529. Pitcher, Diana. *The Mischief Maker: African Tales of Nogwaja the Hare*. Illustrated by Sally Dove. Cape Town and Johannesburg: David Philip, 1984. 64p. Grades 3-5.

Eighteen stories of Nogwaja, the trickster hare, from different parts of Southern Africa are presented as a continuous narrative. The peaceful setting of the veld is shattered by Nogwaja's antisocial behavior. He is lazy, thieving, greedy, spiteful, mischievous, shrewd, and persistent. He plays the animals against each other to his own benefit. On occasion, Nogwaja's cunning helps the community, but he gets no praise for his services.

Several pourquoi tales that offer explanations for animal traits such as the giraffe's long neck, the lion's roar, the spider's double stomach, and the leopard's spotted coat are credited to his mischief making. Even the Creator seems pleased with these modifications to His work. However, Nogwaja is ostracized because he is responsible for death, old age, and sickness among humans. Pitcher's skillful narration, descriptive prose, individualized characterization, and vigorous plots make these tales a delightful reading experience.

530. Poland, Marguerite. *The Mantis and the Moon: Stories for the Children of Africa*. Illustrated by Leigh Voight. Johannesburg: Ravan, 1979. 120p. Grades 4-8.

A common theme that unites the eight animal fantasies in this collection is the effort of the small animal to achieve heroic stature by living wisely, helping others, and being just and moral. The hopes and aspirations of the characters are so sensitively portrayed that one is absorbed in the tension and excitement of their experiences. In the title story, "The Mantis and the Moon," the small mantis expends all his energies and resources in catching the moon, so that he can ride on it across the sky and become a god. While his dreams may appear foolish, he is a sympathetic character because of his tenacious desire to excel. Poland also touchingly narrates the struggles of the underdog as he survives flood, drought, hunger, and predators. For example, Ntini, a young and inexperienced otter, grows up fast when he is separated from his grandfather during a flood. His adventures prove to be an initiation into manhood as he overcomes exploiters and his own trusting and boastful nature. The great forest is the microcosm of the world, and all the animals realize that they must live according to the destiny and nature prescribed to them by the Creator.

531. Seeger, Pete. *Abiyoyo*. Illustrated by Michael Hays. New York and London: Macmillan Publishing and Collier Macmillan, 1986. 47p. Grades K-3.

This story of a boy and his father who save their town from the giant Abiyoyo is based on a South African folktale and lullaby. Both father and son are driven out of town because one constantly clanks on his ukelele, while the other plays pranks with his magic wand. When Abiyoyo attacks the town, it is the boy's music that gets the monster dancing and the father's magic wand that makes him disappear. In gratitude, the townsfolk welcome them back. In his introduction, Seeger gives a moral and political overtone to the story by stating that through art and music the beast in all of us can be subdued and that the real monsters in our society are evils like McCarthyism. The illustrator makes a political statement of his own by peopling the town with Arabs, African Americans, Africans, Chinese, Europeans, Hawaiians, Indians, Japanese, Native Americans, and Tibetans. The boy and his father, in a sense, save the world.

532. Singano, Ellis, and Adrian Roscoe, collects. and eds. *Tales of Old Malawi.* Malawian Writers Series. Limbe and Lilongwe, Malawi: Popular Publications and Likuni Press, 1974, 1980. 106p. Grades 4-8.

This collection is the outcome of a massive effort on behalf of the University of Malawi to preserve and study the fast-disappearing folklore. The English versions retain conventions widely employed by African storytellers, especially the use of verse to convey important messages. Both realistic and animal stories are represented, but wonder or fairy tales are notably absent. Whenever magic or supernatural power is employed, it is always to emphasize a specific point or to condemn a transgression. In "The Magic Tree," for instance, all the village children are hidden and cared for in a magic tree by ancestral spirits in order to punish parents for neglecting their children. Other themes are rejecting suitors out of excessive pride, establishing an impossible bride price, and being unreasonable in one's relationships. In "The Children Left to Die," which is quite similar to "Hansel and Gretel," a man and his wife abandon their twelve children in the forest with poisoned food. Even though the parents are not punished, their behavior is presented as reprehensible. Malawian tales do not shelter readers from the harsh facts of life; instead, they are intended to regulate human conduct.

533. Vyas, Chiman L. *Folktales of Zambia.* Lusaka, Zambia: Unity, 1969. 72p. Grades 4-6.

Collected by Vyas during the turbulent period of Zambia's struggle for independence, the twenty-two stories in this book represent all the major language groups of Zambia. These stories introduce young readers to myths of creation and death, the origin of sex and bride price, gift of fire, why the creator left the earth, and explanations for animal traits. In addition, there are trickster tales, fairy tales, and realistic stories which illustrate good and bad qualities. "That Girl Had Gained" is a variation of the Cinderella story whose protagonist is prevented from attending puberty rites by her stepmother. When the young girl manages to avoid further household tasks, she is helped by an old woman who makes her chief of a wealthy village.

534. _____. *Two Tales of Zambia.* Illustrated by Gabriel Ellison. Lusaka, Zambia: National Educational Company of Zambia, 1971, 1973. 48p. Grades 4-6.

The two stories in this slim volume were recorded by Vyas between 1957 and 1960 in the rural areas of Zambia. The first story, "Sulwe the Safari," is a synthesis of short tales that explains the origin of the rabbit's tricks and how he is finally killed; however, stories of Sulwe's tricks are kept alive by the few creatures whom he had helped. The second tale, "Kapepe," is a Zambian folk epic of the Lenje hero, Mbirika, and how he won the beautiful daughter of God. Both stories are narrated in a leisurely fashion, with ample dialogue and details to make the scenes and characters come alive.

FICTION

535. Beake, Lesley. *The Strollers.* Cape Town: Maskew Miller Longman, 1987. 104p. Grades 6-8.

Winner of the Young Africa Award and the 1988 Sir Percy Fitzpatrick Award, this well-researched, sociological novel takes readers to the invisible world of "strollers," or homeless children from the townships. When Johnny cannot cope with physical abuse at home and disappointment at school, he joins Abel, aged ten, who is an experienced stroller. Abel's "family" consists of both boys and girls, brown and black, and together they provide food, shelter of sorts, and medical care for one another. For each, strolling provides the freedom and self-sufficiency that their lives at home lacked. Their main fear is getting caught by the police, getting into trouble with the wild and drunken Bergies, or being involved with the Spider Men, an adult version of strollers who engage in illicit activities. With the end of summer and a member's death due to ill-health, Johnny realizes that he cannot survive on his own. He returns home and learns the true meaning of sacrifice, friendship, and personal autonomy.

Touching though the story may be, the author oversimplifies the problem. According to the book, children leave home simply because of the warm spring weather and because strolling is daring and romantic. The situation is also blamed on the children's inability to cope with their unhappy environment--death of parents, physical abuse, abandonment by mothers, violence and student unrest, and inadequate teaching. No reference is made to apartheid, governmental policies, poverty, poor housing, unemployment, or breakup of the family. The only solution, according to Beake, is going back to school and getting an education.

536. Boyd-Harvey, Julia. *Tutti and the Black Iron.* Illustrated by Mark de Lange. Johannesburg: Ravan, 1990. 151p. Grades 7-9.

A sequel to *Tutti and the Magic Bird* (Ravan, 1980), the magic bird once again enables Tutti to participate in the daily lives of his African ancestors. The fictional time alternates between the present of an archeological expedition to Broederstroom and the past of over seventeen hundred years ago when the Bantus migrated south. Past, present, and future blend to allow the protagonist--and the reader--to marvel at the iron-making skills and technical achievements of ancient Africans; to provide a cultural context for the archeological finds; to recognize links with life in modern South Africa; and to infuse self-pride in Tutti as a black South African. The prologue makes a definite political statement when it provides background information on Tutti's life under apartheid.

537. Bregin, Elana. *The Kayaboeties.* Cape Town: Maskew Miller Longman, 1989. 90p. Grades 6-8.
This novel provides a graphic description of current racial prejudices as four white teenagers decide to enter a music contest. In their desperation to win, they invite a gifted black boy, Sam, to join their group, The Kayaboeties. As Sam cowers against the wall of their hideout, there ensues the most blatant and insensitive discussion of whether or not to admit him. Pecker, in particular, continues to treat Sam infernally through verbal abuse and gestures. The only one who shows any real concern for Sam is Charmaine, "Charlie," the narrator. When Sam is persuaded to stay secretly in the Kaya (servant's quarters) till the contest is over, Pecker's father discovers Sam and beats him mercilessly. This incident serves as a turning point in Pecker's life, who risks a severe beating by standing up for Sam. The Kayaboeties do not win a prize, but Sam receives a music scholarship for his talent. Their interracial friendship continues.
The author makes it clear that these youngsters have a very liberal and daring attitude toward race relations. Even progressive people like Charlie's parents accept "tradition" by maintaining the status quo. The plot and characters are contrived to serve the agenda that only one person at a time can be made racially sensitive. Despite Charlie's honesty and sensitivity as a narrator, one can detect her patronizing, benevolent attitude toward Sam. She uses disparaging words like "he wagged his head like a dog," and makes Sam uncomfortable by deliberately touching him. Sam, too, does not emerge as a real human being with thoughts and feelings. Except for two brief outbursts, he passively accepts his ill-treatment and agrees to be used by the group. This novel won the 1989 Young Africa Award sponsored by Maskew Miller Longman.

538. Case, Dianne. *Love, David.* Illustrated by Mario Sickle. Cape Town: Maskew Miller Longman, 1986. 124p. Grades 5-8.
Another Young Africa Award winner, *Love, David* describes the loving relationship between Anna and her older brother David, who is repeatedly in trouble for missing school, stealing, smoking cigarettes, and disobedience. Anna's love for David is sorely tested as she continues to have faith in his innate goodness. Eventually, David is caught for selling drugs and is sent to a correctional institution. He is

now on his way to becoming a well-adjusted and productive
individual.

   Love, David gives the impression that apartheid is a just and fair
system for blacks, that blacks are treated well by their white
employers, and that social agencies are humane and competent. The
author does not explore David's psychological motivations and the
impact of poverty on his behavior. While the tone is sympathetic to
David's unhappiness, he is characterized as a confused and helpless
youth. The conclusion is that David just needs to be straightened out
with firmness--maybe not with physical punishment, but certainly in
the controlled environment of the correctional institution.

539. Chimombo, Steve. *Tell Me a Story.* Illustrated by Brian Hara.
Blantyre, Malawi: Dzuka, 1992. 23p. Grades 4-6.

   Five modern stories are organized around the storyframe of a
grandfather narrating tales to his grandson. The stories, both urban
and rural, involve the exploits of a superhero who overpowers
man-eating leopards, fights the school bully, outwits a band of
marauding monkeys, and tricks the police on April Fools Day.
Chimombo's subtle humor and exaggeration provide an ironic
commentary on the art of storytelling. Had the stories been folktales,
the listener would have accepted them without question, but because
they are "realistic," he wonders about the truthfulness of the
storyteller.

540. Craft, Ruth. *The Day of the Rainbow.* Illustrated by Niki Daly. New
York: Puffin, 1989. Originally published in 1988 by Heinemann, Great
Britain. N.p. Preschool-Grade 3.

   Everything goes wrong on a hot summer day in a busy South African
city. Nerinder drops her library book, Leroy loses the earrings he
bought for his girlfriend, and Mrs. Poppodopolous loses her
husband's secret recipe for raisin cake. As a beautiful rainbow
appears after a cooling shower, each one searches for his or her
treasure in the magic spot at the end of the rainbow. By virtue of
coincidence, all three meet: Leroy finds the book, Nerinder the recipe,
and Mrs. Poppodopolous the earrings. For black, Indian, and Greek,
the rainbow is truly the harbinger of hope, the fulfiller of promises in
South Africa's multicultural society. Daly's watercolor illustrations
capture the crowds and activity of a busy city, while Craft's rhyming
text and simultaneous narration of the individual stories give the book
a mythical and universal quality.

541. Daly, Niki. *Not So Fast Songololo.* Illustrated by author. New York:
Atheneum, 1985. N.p. Grades K-3.

   Set in South Africa, Daly recreates one day in the life of a young
black boy. Malusi, who is constantly chided for doing everything
slowly, is just the right companion for his grandmother on her
shopping trip to the city. He has a memorable time with her on the
bus; he helps her cross the crowded street; and he carries her
shopping bags. However, the day becomes really special when his

grandmother buys him a new pair of tackies (sneakers) to replace his torn hand-me-downs. Daly's watercolors capture the warm and tender relationship between Malusi and Old Granny.

542. Geraghty, Paul. *PIG*. Cape Town: Maskew Miller Longman, 1988. 138p. Grades 7-9.

Michael Goodenough's secure life with Phocho, his Zulu classmate and best friend, in rural Greytown ends abruptly with his father's death. The move to the city jolts Mike into the cruel world of cramped housing and social distinctions between rural and urban, rich and poor, black and white. He suffers daily humiliation at the hands of school bullies who exclude him from their games, play rude and unkind pranks, and beat him mercilessly. His only comfort is in the friendship of Johannes, an elderly Xhosa man who tends the school grounds, and Peter, another classmate who is ill-treated. The situation changes, however, when Mike frightens four of the toughest bullies when they camp out in the forest at night. His "manliness" in the escapade finally wins him their respect and acceptance.

Geraghty draws on his childhood visits to a friend's pig farm for his convincing descriptions of rural life. Most strikingly, readers become aware of the author's superior craftsmanship as he ironically duplicates events that Mike had earlier experienced at the farm. For example, the incident when Phocho and Mike flee from a ghost is juxtaposed with the terror of the bullies when Mike scares them; and the scene when Phocho gets muddy in the river is contrasted with Mike's beating and mashing in the mud by the soccer team. Each event represents a move from the world of childhood and innocence to the unfair adult world. The simple, idyllic life ends at the farm as well when city values invade Greytown and Phocho has to face a racist society. The ending, however, is dissatisfactory: Although Mike's life has been enriched forever because of his friendship with Phocho, Johannes, and Peter, it is hinted that Mike conforms to the adult white world when he enters high school. He realizes that being a misfit only leads to powerlessness.

543. Goldie, Fay. *Zulu Boy*. Illustrated by Tessa Beaver. London: Macmillan, 1968. 104p. Grades 5-7.

The author, who has spent much of her life among the Zulus, writes simply and with feeling about Zulu lifestyle. The story focuses on Sezulu's kraal in a homeland during a severe drought. Sezulu's daughter, Mvuyana, is afraid that her upcoming wedding may be postponed and her fiance forced to go to the city to support his family. The drought also offers an opportunity to her younger brother, Umfaan, to work in the dorp as a kitchenboy. Umfaan's fear and hesitation at leaving home are overcome by this unique opportunity to advance in life and, perhaps, to move to a better job in the city. Touching as the story of Umfaan's maturation from dependency to adult responsibility may be, *Zulu Boy* fails to depict the feelings of black characters when they are discriminated against. There is mention of pass laws and segregation on beaches, but anger and resentment at such treatment is not shown. On the contrary, blacks feel extraordinarily lucky that they can serve the white *baas* in the dorp or city. While the hardships on a Zulu homeland are portrayed honestly, the author does not condemn the government for its unfair laws. The arrangement is seen as mutually beneficial to both whites and blacks.

543a. Gordimer, Nadine. *My Son's Story.* New York: Penguin, 1991. Originally published in 1990 by Farrar, Straus and Giroux. 277p. Grades 10-adult.

Like Andre Brink's *A Dry White Season* (Penguin, 1980), this political novel centers around the disruption in a schoolteacher's life caused by the freedom movement. Sonny and his wife Aila are committed to providing their children, Baby and Will, with good values, personal dignity, and cultural refinement, while still functioning within the confines of their racist society. However, when Sonny becomes involved in the freedom struggle, the chaos and danger are also reflected in his personal life: he seeks a more fulfilling sexual and intellectual relationship with a white comrade, Hannah. One by one, each family member is drawn into the antiapartheid movement; Baby and Aila join the military wing of the organization. In order to maintain the outward facade of their domestic life, each lives a double life by deceiving the other family members about his or her secret activities. The only one who is left to guard the home, both literally and figuratively, is Will, the adolescent son. However, Will also has a secret of his own. At the beginning of the novel, when he is fifteen, he accidentally sees his father in a movie hall with the "other woman." There is an unspoken pact between them to keep this affair a secret from Aila and Baby. With his mother and sister in exile, and with his family's home burned to the ground by right-wing activists, Will is finally free to participate in the struggle by recording the events he has witnessed, but which he can never publish. At the end of this intricate, postmodern novel, Gordimer reveals that Will is the author of this colored family's story, written years after the events have taken place. Their story is both intensely personal as well as an engaging recounting of the courageous actions of freedom fighters. The point-of-view alternates between the subjective first person account of Will's anger, bitterness, and jealousy toward his father and an objective third person narration of the personal and political lives of his family members.

544. Gordon, Sheila. *The Middle of Somewhere: A Story of South Africa.* New York: Bantam Skylark, 1990. 154p. Grades 5-7.

Nightmares about puff adders and bulldozers shatter the secure world of nine-year-old Rebecca when their township is declared a "black spot" and is scheduled for demolition so that a white suburb can be developed. Her parents and grandmother struggle to maintain good values at home as they fight for the basic human and social rights of their community. While they recognize the necessity of working in white homes and businesses, they are by no means passive. Through the painful departure of her friend Noni and her father's imprisonment and loss of income, Rebecca learns that suffering and loneliness are the price of freedom and human dignity. The residents' efforts to defy the government attract attention, and the decision to erase the township is postponed. Rebecca's sense of security and happiness are restored tentatively.

Rebecca's doll, Betty, serves as a powerful symbol in the story. On the one hand, the cracked and broken white doll, which was discarded by a white family, indicates the poverty and deprivation of blacks in affluent South Africa. On the other hand, Rebecca's love for this doll symbolizes her warm feelings for all races, black or white. Despite the taunts of her disillusioned older brother and the gift of a brand-new black doll, Rebecca remains loyal to Betty, her one friend through difficult times. Remarkably astute and free from bitterness, Rebecca recognizes that there are some whites who care.

545. _____. *Waiting for the Rain: A Novel of South Africa*. New York: Bantam, 1987. 214p. Grades 7-12.

This winner of the Jane Addams Peace Award is a powerful novel of interracial friendship and growing up in an apartheid society. The omniscient narrator gives the parallel stories of Frikkie, nephew of an Afrikaner farm owner, and Tengo, son of the black cook-cum-housemaid and "boss-Boy." Frikkie and Tengo have been friends since childhood; however, as they reach adolescence, Tengo becomes painfully aware of his inferior status, while Frikkie is unaware of racism, hence does not question it. To better his life, Tengo has the courage to leave the security of the farm for the pass books, overcrowding, and violence of Johannesburg. The privileged and unimaginative Frikkie matriculates with difficulty and is stationed at Johannesburg to complete his compulsory service as a policeman. A prolonged drought in the country symbolizes sterility and stasis. The literal Frikkie waits for the rain, while Tengo yearns for education to nourish and free his mind and soul.

The two opposites confront each other when a riot breaks out at a funeral service. Tengo is unwittingly caught in the fray, and he is chased by a policeman who turns out to be Frikkie. With the muzzle of a gun pointed at Frikkie, Tengo unleashes his pent-up anger and blames Frikkie for not seeing the wrong, for not questioning the system. Frikkie defends his fair treatment of blacks on the farm. After a long, tension-filled debate, Frikkie for the first time understands the just demands of blacks, and Tengo, on his part, realizes that the older generation of blacks allowed the wrongs to happen by being submissive. Their former friendship prompts Tengo to spare Frikkie's life and Frikkie not to report Tengo to the police, but the two can never be friends again. The novel is a plea for equality, friendship, and understanding between blacks and whites if the present spiritual drought in South Africa is to end.

546. Haggard, Henry Rider. *King Solomon's Mines* Harmondsworth, Middlesex, England: Penguin, 1958. Originally published in 1885. 256p. Grades 8-12.

Author of three popular adventures set in Africa--*King Solomon's Mines, She,* and *Allan Quartermain*--Haggard perpetuates the myths of savage tribes, glorious kingdoms ruled by mysterious queens, and fabulous hidden treasures. *King Solomon's Mines* is the most colonial of the three because of its stereotypical plot and characters and denunciation of African culture. Three Englishmen--Captain Good, Henry Curtis, and Allan Quartermain--travel to Africa in search of diamond mines. As soon as they arrive in Kukuanaland, they set about duping the "gullible" Africans into believing that Europeans are celestial beings from the stars by claiming to cause the eclipse of the moon. They succeed in undermining the power of Gogool, the witch doctor, who is portrayed as a hideous embodiment of evil. Social and racial superiority are maintained by treating Africans as inferior and rejecting an interracial marriage between Good and Foulata, a beautiful and intelligent maiden whom Good loves. Politically, the white characters bring peace and justice to the lawless and unruly kingdom, and a golden age is predicted when the ruler promises to introduce British ideas of government.

547. Henty, George Alfred. *The Young Colonists.* Rahway, NJ: Mershon, 1885. 281p. Grades 8-12.

A war correspondent for the London *Standard,* Henty wrote six novels set in Africa that promote the existing stereotypes; lure readers to the excitement and adventure of settling in Africa; and inculcate pride in the British empire. Set in 1877, *The Young Colonists* is an action-packed story of warfare with Boers and Zulus, hunting expeditions, prospecting for gold and diamonds, trade with "natives," and rivalry between the British and Boers for control of South Africa. These events are presented from the perspective of two young immigrants, Dick Humphreys and Tom Jackson, who volunteer their services to the British army. Henty gives a thrilling account of the British defeat at Isandhula, the second advance of British troops, and the decisive Battle of Ulundi, where King Cetawayo is finally defeated and Zululand divided into districts (see # 596). Although the British concede to Boer control of South Africa, the two protagonists are well settled in their adoptive land. The story reflects British sympathy for the "natives" and their ill-treatment by Boers. Henty also admires the highly disciplined Zulu army and the courage of its warriors.

548. Holding, James. *The Lazy Little Zulu.* Illustrated by Aliki. New York: Morrow, 1962. 32p. Grades 3-5.

Chaka is called "lazy" because he does not like to play games or work in the fields like the other boys in the village. Instead, he is an inquisitive child who likes to observe animals. One day, when his mother is very sick, his intimate knowledge of the forest enables him to earn the much-needed shilling for the greedy witch doctor. He collects a small box of tea seeds for an Englishman, because he knows where white ants store away these seeds for the winter.

Both text and illustrations present Chaka as a lively and appealing human being, but the other characters are stereotypical. The witch doctor is ineffectual as well as self-serving, while the Englishman is a do-gooder who represents Western civilization.

549. Hoppe, Charles. *Sons of the African Veld.* New York: McBride, 1947. 190p. Grades 6-10.

Niam and M'pengi, sons of two Zulu chiefs, and their white friend, Derek Blake, are involved in a thrilling adventure during World War II. The boys are asked by the police sergeant to spy on Bula, the witch doctor, and the Eurasian trader, who are suspected of spying and illegally exporting rough diamonds to the Nazis and Japanese for their ammunition factories. After a series of suspense-filled episodes, the crooks are caught and the boys are declared war heroes.

Plot, diction, and characterization reinforce the theme of the "white man's burden." Prejudicial attitudes toward Bula are obvious through derogatory words like "baboon," "old hyena," and "old buzzard." Bula is discredited as a money-grabbing fraud who takes advantage of the gullibility of the Zulus by maintaining a powerful hold on them. All the white characters use honest practices, treat Africans with respect, and administer the native territory in a tactful and sympathetic manner. The interracial friendship of Niam, M'pengi, and Derek is not a relationship of equals: Derek's superiority is reinforced throughout the adventure, while the Zulu boys regard him with affection and admiration and follow him in all his ventures, including the desecration of Bula's altar and the condemnation of their religious beliefs.

550. Howard, Moses L. *The Ostrich Chase.* Illustrated by Barbara Seuling. New York, Chicago and San Francisco: Holt, Rinehart and Winston, 1974. 118p. Grades 5-7.

This simple, yet powerful story describes the life of the San of the Kalahari Desert. The interest is focused on Khuana, a young girl who desperately wants to participate in the manly task of hunting that is forbidden to women. To realize her most earnest dream of hunting an ostrich, Khuana secretly observes the preparations for a hunt. Ironically, her lack of experience and training provide her with the opportunity to fulfill her quest. When the group is preparing to move to another camp because of water and food shortage, Khuana accidentally injures Gaushe, her grandmother, while making poisoned arrows. When Gaushe, who cannot walk with the group because of a swollen leg, is left behind to die, Khuana secretly joins her. With the younger one's strength and determination and the older woman's wisdom, the two survive and Khuana gets her chance to kill an ostrich. With plenty of rest, Gaushe's leg heals and they join their group, loaded with ostrich eggs and dried meat. They are welcomed back as loved relatives because it is a miracle to survive the desert.

The Ostrich Chase provides an endearing portrait of the loving relationship between the careless and impetuous Khuana and the patient and wise Gaushe. Khuana's character is depicted in its many facets: rebellious, loving, considerate, and feminine. Above all, Moses faithfully presents the lifestyle of the San: harmony with nature and adaptation to the desert, division of labor between the sexes, social organization and benevolent leadership, and religious beliefs and rituals. The practice of abandoning the weak is not prompted by cruelty or a lack of feelings, but by necessity and a practical attitude to survival.

551. Isadora, Rachel. *At the Crossroads*. Illustrated by author. New York: Greenwillow, 1991. N.p. Grades K-2.

Shantytown squalor, inadequate housing, poverty, and hardships do not dampen the excitement of five children who eagerly await the return of their fathers from the mines. As is typical of Isadora, she does not condemn apartheid openly, but her illustrations reveal the social inequities and strain on family life due to the prolonged absence of male relatives. Both text and pictures celebrate the black child's capacity for love, youthful exuberance, and hope.

552. _____. *Over the Green Hills*. Illustrated by author. New York: Greenwillow, 1992. N.p. Grades K-2.

This picture book describes a day in the life of Zolani, who lives in Mpane, a coastal village in the Transkei. On this special day, loaded with food and dry wood, Zolani visits Grandma Zindzi. Zolani's life, though simple, is a happy and secure one. The author presents a comfortable picture of life in the Transkei: there is plenty to eat and people barter goods in exchange for what they need. Although passing reference is made to a drought when Zindzi had to live with her family, the problems of the homelands are not depicted. The watercolor illustrations also reveal the beauty of the Indian Ocean and the plentiful farms and green hills of the Transkei.

553. Jones, Toeckey. *Skindeep*. New York: Harper & Row, 1986. 250p. Grades 9-12.

The injustice of apartheid is presented from the perspective of an eighteen-year-old white girl. At first, Rhonda is a selfish person whose main concern is to find a suitable boyfriend. However, her life changes completely when she meets a rather strange and mysterious bald man, Dave Schwartz, and the two fall madly in love. After their first sexual encounter, their feelings deepen and they go on a vacation to Cape Town. While there, both are confronted with the truth about Dave--that he is actually a colored who is passing for white. Rhonda's initial reaction is one of disgust at having been so intimate with a nonwhite, but Dave's accusation that her love is only "skindeep" leads to self-awareness and respect for the victims of racism. She defies her hypocritical family by declaring that she will marry Dave; however, Dave decides to terminate the affair in order to resolve his identity crisis. He no longer wants to be white; he acknowledges his colored family and joins the fight against apartheid.

Although the story ends on a tragic note for the two lovers, there is hope because Rhonda also joins the antiapartheid movement.

This expose of white South Africans is, unfortunately, not matched by artistic skills. The author fails to present the female protagonist as an intricate and believable character who has any serious thought beside having sex with Dave. Jones also relies heavily on dialogue and coincidence to develop the plot and place characters in revealing situations. Finally, for a novel that purports to be sensitive to the rights of nonwhites in South Africa, *Skindeep* caricatures Rhonda's black cook as a Bible-toting fanatic, instead of as a woman with feelings and individuality. This novel won the Charlotte Zolotow Award. Jones is also the author of *Go Well, Stay Well* (Harper & Row, 1980).

554. Jupo, Frank. *Atu, the Silent One.* New York: Holiday House, 1967. N.p. Grades K-3.

Both text and illustrations provide graphic descriptions of the natural environment, nomadic lifestyle, and culture of the nearly extinct Bushmen (San). A handy and tough people, Bushmen live in harmony with nature in hillside caves and use simple tools to hunt animals. Far from presenting a dry, factual account, interest is generated by the experiences of Atu, who cannot speak. Despite his handicap, Atu is treated with love by all, and he is taught to hunt like the other boys. After his first hunt, when they kill a big bull elephant, he joins in the celebrations by painting his account of the entire hunt on the cave walls. Atu's talent symbolizes the many paintings that have been preserved for centuries in the African desert.

555. Juta, Jan. *Look Out for the Ostriches: Tales of South Africa.* Illustrated by Henry C. Pitz. New York: Knopf, 1951. 177p. Grades 7-12.

Through a series of stories, Juta describes his love for his home near the Cape and the many farms and vineyards, valleys and mountains that dominate the landscape. The personal narrative is repeatedly interrupted to give the Dutch version of South African history, perpetuating the accepted myths and distortions of facts. The Hottentot (Khoi Khoi) and Zulus are seen as migrating tribes with no special claim to the land. In their wars with the Zulus and the British, the Dutch settlers believed they had "bought" the land with their blood and suffering. When the Voortrekkers went northward to escape British laws, they felt that they had discovered an ideal, mysterious world that was perfectly empty. They continued to press their claim by virtue of hard work and endurance. Similarly, when the Dutch East India Company established a "victualing station" at the Cape, the Khoi Khoi who opposed them were viewed as hostile tribes rather than as people defending their land. In describing the ruins of Great Zimbabwe, Juta fails to give credit to the Bantus for their accomplishments and engineering skill; instead, the civilization is attributed to King Solomon, the Bantu being too backward to have the skill to build the elliptical walls and oriental-looking structures. Juta displays a contradictory approach to African culture. On the one hand, Africans are seen as being one with the earth and representing the ancient harmony in their worship, and, on the other hand, they are considered inferior, lazy, undisciplined, and socially unacceptable. When viewed in the context of the racial situation in South Africa today, *Look Out for the Ostriches* encourages group pride and perpetuates animosity toward the British and black South Africans.

556. Kingston, William Henry Giles. *Hendricks the Hunter; or the Border Farm: A Tale of Zululand.* Freeport, NY: Books for Libraries Press, 1972. Reprint of the 1881 edition by Armstrong, New York. 313p. Grades 8-12.

Plentiful wildlife and big game hunting, violent attacks by Zulu warriors, witch doctors and savage Africans, and the sacrifices of white settlers characterize this stereotypical colonial novel set in South Africa. The human interest centers around the adventures of Hendricks, a trader, his white friends, and a little white boy rescued from a camp destroyed by Zulus. African characters, even the respected warrior Umgolo and Chief Mangaleesu and his wife, are treated as inferior. It is Christianity and the superior values of Western civilization that are promoted.

557. Lewin, Hugh. *Jafta's Mother.* Illustrated by Lisa Kopper. Minneapolis, MN: Carolrhoda, 1983. Originally published in 1981 by Evans, London. N.p. Grades K-3.

The author, who left his native South Africa after being imprisoned for seven years for opposing apartheid, nostalgically captures his love for his country through a series of books about a black boy whom he introduces in *Jafta* (Evans, 1981). In *Jafta's Mother*, Jafta compares his mother's attributes to nature: she is the gentle morning sun, the warm earth, the shade-giving willow tree, the cool rain, the hoopoe, and the thundering storm. *Jafta's Father* (Carolrhoda, 1983) expresses the little boy's deep love for his father and the anguish of separation. Spring, which brings new life to the village, is the season he longs for most because that is when his father returns from the factory. Rural life and festivities are further depicted in *Jafta and the Wedding* (Carolrhoda, 1983), when Jafta's sister gets married. Jafta's experiences broaden in *Jafta: The Journey* (Carolrhoda, 1984) and *Jafta: The Town* (Carolrhoda, 1984). The former book expresses Jafta's excitement in preparing for the journey and traveling by oxcart, bus, and ferry and being received by his father in town. The latter book records his first impressions of the town: the crowds are like ants near an anthill, and the noisy traffic reminds him of squealing pigs. The Jafta books maintain their romantic view of childhood by being remarkably apolitical. The evils of apartheid--pass laws, racial segregation, forcible separation of families, poor housing--are not discussed directly. Lewin describes Jafta's life faithfully and with feeling, but without commentary.

Kopper's earthtone illustrations also portray the tender emotions and solid values that are an essential part of Jafta's life. The simple lines depict the peace and serenity of rural life, while the profusion of details describe the excitement and activity of a busy town.

558. Louw, Juliet Marais. *River of the Hot Waters*. Johannesburg: Perskor, 1972. 107p. Grades 5-7.

The didactic theme of poverty and family environment adversely influencing the character of a child mars the excitement of this adventure story. When Jim Lawrie invites Danny, a poor and neglected pupil of his father, on a family camping trip to Fish River Canyon, Danny's brief exposure to a disciplined and caring family helps shape his character. He learns the importance of honesty when he confesses to hiding the lost diamonds; and he overcomes the bad influence of his criminal uncle when he exposes the activities of the diamond thieves. As a reward for his regeneration, the do-gooders promise him another trip, help for his family through the Social Welfare Department, and art lessons to nurture his hidden talents. Despite the sociological content, Louw does succeed in portraying Danny's childlike curiosity, sense of discovery, and innate goodness.

559. Mabetoa, Maria. *Our Village Bus*. Illustrated by Mzwakhe. Johannesburg: Ravan, 1985. 32p. Grades K-3.

The bus is the lifeline of a remote village in South Africa. It symbolizes the villagers' connection with the outside world: they depend on it for their schools, shopping, doctors' appointments, restaurants, and even social interaction among themselves. Yet, when the bus is stuck in the muddy road during a rainfall, it brings out the worst in the villagers; they are desperate to have it moving again in order to resume their sense of fellowship and well-being. While the text does not comment on life under apartheid, the illustrations depict empty houses, lack of activity, and stark desolation in the village environment.

560. _____. *A Visit to My Grandfather's Farm*. Illustrated by Mzwakhe. Johannesburg: Ravan, 1988. N.p. Preschool-Grade 2.

A little girl from a township enjoys the open spaces, freedom, and security of the country when she visits her grandparents. She also shares the warmth and love of her grandparents as she participates in their daily chores--cooking, milking and grazing the cows, feeding the chickens, and hoeing the fields. However, Mabetoa does not create a pastoral idyll; there is the fear of attacking hawks and jackals, weeds choking the crops, bulls fighting with each other, and a jealous hen preventing the little girl from playing with the baby chicks. Mzwakhe's illustrations, though accurate and detailed, fail to convey the liveliness and human warmth of the characters.

561. Magadza, C. H. D. *Gudo Baboon and Other Kariba Stories*. Dandaro Readers Series. Gweru, Zimbabwe: Mambo, 1991. 54p. Grades 2-4.

Eleven stories describe the changed relations between animals and humans in the Kariba region of Zimbabwe. The experiences of Gudo Baboon, James Jumbo, Janet Hippo, Bruno the Buffalo, Roger the Rogue Elephant, Ronia Rhino, and Leonard Leopard tell a sad story of human encroachment, forest fires, shooting, poaching, and food shortages. While this collection sensitizes young readers to the rights of animals, it contains some frank and distasteful comments on female and animal body parts. There is a particularly degrading reference to a European tourist's fascination for an elephant's genitals.

562. Mahanya, Morgan. *The Wound.* Dandaro Readers Series. Gweru, Zimbabwe: Mambo, 1991. 47p. Grades 8-12.
   Six short stories portray various aspects of modern Zimbabwe from the Chimurenga War, to the "amiable" relations between blacks and whites after independence, to the personal freedom and dignity of women in their affairs with men. Mahanya's restrained but rich prose reveals characters and fateful situations with subtle irony, caustic wit, and sensitivity.

563. Manzi, Alberto. *White Boy.* Illustrated by Charles Molina. Translated from the Italian *Orzowei* by Serge Hughes. New York: Macmillan, 1963. 202p. Grades 8-12.
   Through the story of Isa, a white boy, the themes of interracial friendship and enmity are explored. Amunai, a respected Swazi warrior, finds Isa abandoned in the jungle and raises him as a son, but he is unable to stop the brutality and taunting by the rest of the group. Isa is banished from the tribe when he accepts the help of Pao, leader of the Bushmen who are enemies of the Swazis. Even the Boer settlers, with whom he later lives, treat him as a savage. He is forced to give up tribal ways and has to dress, eat, and live like whites.
   This racial hatred extends to entire groups as well: Boers hate the English and Zulus; the English hate the Boers and all Africans; and the Zulus and Swazis join to fight the Boers and Bushmen. The only people who are above political ambition and racial hatred are the Bushmen, who are considered inferior and backward by the others. Isa demonstrates the same generosity toward people on the personal level: he is emotionally attached to the Swazis, Bushmen, and Boers, because he has crossed the forbidden political and social barriers. While Manzi includes numerous myths and misinterpretations of South African history, the theme of universal brotherhood is powerfully conveyed. The novel echoes with Pao's words: "when we know one another, the color of a man's skin does not matter and we can love one another."

564. Mapetere, Godsway. *The Three Men and the Bees.* Illustrated by Simon Mazenge. Dandaro Readers Series. Gweru, Zimbabwe: Mambo, 1982. 12p. Grades 2-4.
   Set in 1980, this humorous story narrates the exploits of three men who dare to enter the Cave of the Bees, called Ramashayanguvo, to gather honey. Reputed to be the best honey collectors in the region, the men make elaborate preparations for their expedition, only to be outsmarted by the bees. They dash out of the cave and into the river with thousands of bees chasing and stinging them. Their reputation is lost forever!

565. Merchant, Eve. *Ghamka, Man-of-Men*. Cape Town: Tafelberg, 1985. 107p. Grades 6-8.

Based on information recorded in historical sources and Vasco Da Gama's journal, this novel traces the movements of the Attaqua, a clan of the Khoi Khoi "tribe." While Merchant takes a refreshing approach by presenting events from the perspective of the Attaqua, she perpetuates the myth of continual tribal migrations in Southern Africa. The story begins at a crucial point in Attaqua history when their grazing lands are waterlogged and the neighboring chief refuses to honor his agreement to give them better grounds. When the inevitable war begins, Ghamka and his cousin, Xhan, have their first taste of war. Readers will identify with Ghamka's pride, fear of the first battle, sense of accomplishment, and desire to live up to the expectations of the seasoned warriors. After defeating their enemy, the Attaqua decide to leave their village and head toward the Indian Ocean. It is here that they encounter Bartholomeu Diaz in 1488 and Da Gama in 1497, and they once again move from camp to camp in search of an ideal homeland.

The friendship and rivalry of Ghamka and Xhan symbolize the complex relationships among various clans of the Khoi Khoi; while they occasionally clash, they respect each others' skills and territorial boundaries. As the rivalry between the cousins goes beyond childish competition, Attaqua begins to groom his son to be the future chief. Ghamka, on his part, acknowledges his cousin's superior hunting abilities, and together they participate in manhood ceremonies, hunting expeditions, and, eventually, search for brides. At the end of the story, Ghamka is a diplomatic and courteous prince who has proven his physical prowess, has had experiences with the "milk-faces," and is ready to assume his future responsibilities.

This historical novel is enlivened by Merchant's multitextured representation of the Khoi Khoi ethnic group and its dynamic relationship with the environment. Merchant very respectfully describes religious ceremonies, family-oriented village organization, and war methods. Also, the subtle balance of power between state and church is defined through the roles of chief, medicine man, healer, and herbalist. Merchant's prose conveys the distinctive flavor of the Khoisan language through diction and imagery. This novel won the 1985 Sanlam Prize for Youth Literature.

566. Mirsky, Reba Paeff. *Seven Grandmothers*. Illustrated by W. T. Mars. Chicago: Follett, 1955. 191p. Grades 5-7.

Both plot and characters advocate Western medicine and education for Zululand. The clash of cultures is presented through the experiences of Nomusa. When nurse Buselapi comes to their kraal, Nomusa is forced to reevaluate her traditional life. Buselapi is a Christian who has studied Western medicine, wears Western clothes, and has only one mother. Buselapi's lectures on germs, sanitation, and superstitions are juxtaposed against the witch doctor's grotesque and "meaningless" rituals to dispel the evil spirits of sickness. Conversion to Western medicine is achieved when a dirty knife is used in the ear-piercing ceremony for Nomusa's brother, and the wound festers. When Buselapi cures the boy with penicillin, the chief declares that the many useful and beautiful customs of the Zulus can coexist with Buselapi's teachings. While the efficacy of penicillin against germs cannot be disputed, Mirsky's perspective is that of a superior observer.

567. _____. *Thirty One Brothers and Sisters.* Illustrated by W. T. Mars. Chicago: Wilcox and Follett, 1952. 190p. Grades 5-7.
    As in *The Ostrich Chase* (see # 550), the protagonist, Nomusa, rebels against the narrow domestic sphere of a woman by secretly practicing the male art of hunting. She gets her father's permission to go on an elephant hunt when she finds the cow that her brother had lost and when she proves her courage by killing a wild boar. Once the hunt is over, Nomusa's feminine traits dominate and she longs for the comfort of her kraal. She is reconciled with her role in the household and community.
    Despite the feminist theme of gender roles, *Thirty One Brothers and Sisters* catalogs the exotic aspects of Zulu life: polygamous family, "strange" rituals and customs, body painting, wild python swallowing a deer, leopard pits, and poisonous cobras. The account of "Pygmies" and their lifestyle reads like an anthropological treatise which makes them appear to be more animal than human.

568. Mitchison, Naomi. *Sunrise Tomorrow: A Story of Botswana.* London: Collins, 1973. 160p. Grades 6-8.
    A typical novel of progress, the theme of Western culture versus ethnic pride takes precedence over character delineation and plot. The young protagonists, Seloi and Mokgosi, are caught between their Western education and the traditional lifestyle and beliefs of their elders. Studying to become a nurse and development officer respectively, they reject everything African as superstitious and uncivilized. However, once they witness the efficacy of traditional wisdom and medicine, they integrate their "modern" training with their African worldview. They also recognize that there are other options to formal education--on-the-job training and joining the work brigade, a self-help group working toward community uplift.

569. Mungoshi, Charles. *Coming of the Dry Season.* New Fiction from Africa Series. Nairobi, Kenya: Oxford University Press, 1972. 61p. Grades 7-12.
    Ten short stories portray the inner lives of African youth under white rule in Rhodesia. Far from idealizing or romanticizing Africans, the author relentlessly employs powerful themes and revealing episodes to expose the despair, hopelessness, hypocrisy, inner conflicts, and unfair racial treatment of his protagonists. In "Shadows on the Wall," a young boy realizes why he cannot talk to his father, while in "Coming of the Dry Season," the hero is confronted with his lack of humanity toward his mother and girlfriend. Mungoshi's psychological portrayals are enhanced by a simple yet eloquent prose that

conveys the setting in just a few brisk strokes. A more accessible collection of Mungoshi's short stories is *The Setting Sun and the Rolling World* (Beacon, 1989), which includes nine stories from *Coming of the Dry Season* and eight from *Some Kinds of Wounds* (Mambo, 1980).

570. Naidoo, Beverley. *Chain of Fire*. Illustrated by Eric Velasquez. New York: Lippincott, 1990. Originally published in 1989 by Collins. 245p. Grades 6-10.

A sequel to *Journey to Jo'burg,* Naidoo continues the story of Naledi, now fifteen, as her entire village is forcibly moved to a barren homeland designated for the Tswana. Naledi's strength and self-confidence emerge when the schoolchildren organize a peaceful protest march condemning the government's decision. Ugly scenes of police brutality, arrests, and a death occur, but the children continue the struggle and manage to unite the entire village. The authorities stop the water supply, close down the school, withhold pensions, arrest leaders, and bulldoze homes, but they cannot break the spirit of the children. Naledi is aware of a chain of resistance being forged in the fire of their anger and suffering. She feels one with the protestors in Soweto; with other ethnic groups who are also being herded into homelands to keep them divided and in check; with the black and white members of the Anti-Removal Committee; and with the newspaper reporters who are making the world aware of their plight. This is a powerful story of the freedom struggle of a people who have suffered for long, and who are prepared for torture and death. Naledi comes to understand the moral courage and efficacy of protest: it may not bring freedom in her lifetime, but it will give her dignity and a chance to exercise some control over her life and future.

571. _____. *Journey to Jo'burg: A South African Story*. Illustrated by Eric Velasquez. New York: Harper Trophy, 1988. Originally published in 1985 by Longman, England. 80p. Grades 3-5.

Thirteen-year-old Naledi and her younger brother, Tiro, undertake a heroic journey to Johannesburg, which is three hundred kilometers away, to inform their mother that their baby sister is dangerously ill. While Naledi's and Trio's courage saves their sister's life, the journey also leads to awareness for Naledi. It shatters her pride and sense of well-being when she encounters the world of pass laws, rude treatment of blacks, unfair arrests, pass raids, and separate buses. Through a young black woman they meet on the bus, Naledi and Tiro learn of the freedom movement, protest marches, and sacrifices of schoolchildren in the Soweto uprising. Upon returning to the village, Naledi is no longer confused by her mother's passive attitude: she understands the difficulties her mother and other women have to endure to provide schooling and food for their children. The system forces them to separate from their families, deny feelings for their children, and, worst of all, face the deaths of young babies. Naledi is inspired by the dream and courage of the Soweto youth to change the biased educational system, to fight for equality and human rights.

Naidoo's touching portrait of life in South Africa is based on firsthand observations. *Journey to Jo'burg* won the prestigious Child Society Children's Book Committee Award in 1986.

572. Packer, Joy. *The Glass Barrier.* Philadelphia and New York: Lippincott, 1961. 318p. Grades 9-12.

This highly complex and multilayered book is about personal, social, and political barriers. The story focuses on three cousins--Maxi, Claude, and Rema--and their endless discussions on the apartheid policies which they oppose. They sympathize with the "dark underdog" and participate in rallies and marches against pass laws, employment restrictions, and lack of freedom for the majority. Maxie is liberal, but she does not have the courage to cross barriers; while Rema seeks inspiration in the idealized, primitive Africa for her sculptures. Claude is the only true liberal who has the intellectual boldness and moral courage to label color a matter of pigmentation and taste. In contrast, their friend and neighbor, Janie, is the typical Boer farmer who is unwilling to give up his claim to the soil and to his inherited superiority over nonwhites. The other side of the racial and political barrier is represented by Fara, a colored student, who bitterly resents the racial policies of the government.

On the personal level, the characters cross barriers in marriage. Claude and Fara both go to London: Fara for the opportunities she was denied in South Africa and Claude to be himself. When they announce their marriage, they break not only social laws, but legal ones as well because interracial marriages are banned. Claude's "liberal" cousins are shocked and disturbed by his "tainting" the family bloodline. Images of barriers, fences, and cages being shattered recur as racial tensions result in the Sharpville and Langa riots, which are seen as evidence of the violent and undisciplined nature of black Africans. Even the primitive Africa that Rema exults in seems to be overshadowed by superstitions, witchcraft, and unrest. Breaking barriers, the story seems to stress, leads only to chaos and bloodshed. It could lead to a confrontation with reality and the building of bridges between races, except that the protagonists are powerless to effect change--unless they leave South Africa.

573. Paton, Alan. *Cry, the Beloved Country.* New York: Scribner's, 1948. 277p. Grades 9-12.

A powerfully evocative novel, *Cry, the Beloved Country* describes the impact of apartheid on the rural community of Ixopo. Paton's anguished cry is for the future generations of blacks and whites who will inherit the troubles of South Africa. Hailed as a prophetic novel in the 1940s, the solution it offers is still valid in the 1990s: Only love can overcome the hunger for power, fear, and revenge that control the behavior of all South Africans.

This is the story of two fathers who struggle to hold their families together despite the deaths of their sons and the separatist policies of the white oligarchy. Organized into three parts, the novel first focuses on the black community through the experiences of Stephen Kumalo, a dignified and ageing preacher. When Kumalo goes to Johannesburg in search of his sister and son, Absalom, he is shocked by the crime, squalor, deplorable working conditions, and physical and moral degradation of blacks. He also learns about militant blacks and white liberals who use varying methods to defy the system. Book II provides a glimpse into the life of a rich white landowner of Ixopo and the impact of violence on society in general. James Jarvis also comes to Johannesburg to attend the funeral of his progressive son, Arthur. Although Jarvis is governed by fear in his dealings with blacks, he is a good human being who tries to understand his son's liberal political philosophy. Ironically, the two stories intermingle when it is revealed that Absalom killed Jarvis' son, and he is hanged for the murder. With Book III, the scene shifts back to the farm. The two fathers, who have come to respect and understand each other's pain, work together to continue the legacies of their sons. Both take personal responsibility for conditions in South Africa, and together they strive to ease the burden of blacks in Ixopo. The future is seen as hopeful because their grandchildren embody the power of love.

While some modern readers may criticize the novel for its do-gooder mentality and the implication that blacks need help, no one can deny the sincerity of the author, the poetic elegance of the prose, and the strong emotional impact of the story.

574. Pohl, Victor. *Farewell, the Little People.* Illustrated by Jane Heath. London: Oxford University Press, 1968. 146p. Grades 7-12.

Based on observations of the remaining Bushmen (San) and accounts of anthropologists and archaeologists, this book provides a sociological study of the traditional life and eventual destruction of Bushmen. The story is divided into two sections, each focusing on the life and adventures of its central character. "Tsipele," set some two or three hundred years prior to the coming of Europeans to South Africa, gives an idealized portrait of Bushmen culture--harmony with nature, nature-oriented religion, wisdom of medicine men, hunting economy, family structure, manhood ceremonies, and festivals and sporting events. Their peaceful lives are destroyed by the gradual invasion of the powerful black tribes from the north. "Kasso" continues the story a hundred years later with constant warfare with the blackmen and yellowmen (Khoi Khoi) from the southwest, and the daily struggle for survival in the harsh environment of the Kalahari Desert. Ultimately, the compassionate Boer farmers protect the Bushmen from total extinction by employing them as servants. While Pohl evokes sympathy for the passing of Bushmen lifestyle, he displays an ethnocentric bias by perpetuating the myth of constant migrations of races and tribes in South Africa, and the inability of Bushmen to survive under these conditions.

575. Poland, Marguerite. *The Bush Shrike.* Johannesburg: Ravan, 1982. 115p. Grades 6-8.

Through the friendship of Anne, daughter of a prominent white family, and Josh, son of a storekeeper, Poland expresses a sense of powerlessness and hopelessness in the face of social barriers between people. Anne's and Josh's bond is sealed forever by their common joy in and love for the mysteries of the bush. Their relationship is tolerated at best because of the vast social and economic disparity between the two families. Simon, son of the rich Ogden family, expresses a more sinister reaction to Josh with his insulting behavior. Since he knows the secret of Josh's birth, he blackmails Josh's brother, Piet, into lending him money for gambling, and he drugs the horse Piet is to race. As the main story and the various subplots draw to a climactic end, everything natural and beautiful in the valley is destroyed, and the victims of racial unfairness are all displaced. Anne is deliberately sent away to boarding school when it is disclosed that Josh is the illegitimate son of the colored school teacher; Josh's dream of being a naturalist ends; the prize horse, Rostor, is killed and Piet's career as a star jockey is ruined; and the bush with all its birds and animals is burned. Poland does not openly voice her disapproval of the existing social mores in South Africa. However, through Anne's first person narrative, she delicately manoeuvres readers' sympathy for the powerless victims who, like the bush, can only rebuild over the ashes; their hearts can only let out the sad, piercing cry of the bush shrike. Poland also avoids loaded language, an ethnocentric perspective, and the common stereotypes associated with character and plot.

576. _____. *Once at KwaFubesi.*   Illustrated by Leigh Voight. Johannesburg: Ravan, 1981. 151p. Grades 6-10.
Through eight short fantasies, Poland recreates the wildlife of the bush from the perspective of the animals who live there. An overwhelming sense of nostalgia for the beauty and tranquility of nature pervades the stories. The natural harmony of the bush includes predators, battles between species over territory, and the inability of the weak to survive without help. However, the animals have to learn new skills to overcome the hazards presented by humans. Fusha, the bushpig, moves his sounder away from the mealie patch and traps of the farmer; Nzou, the old elephant, loses his pride when bulldozers denude the forest; and Lwemba, the jumping spider, moves back to the bush because he cannot survive the insecticides and roaches of the city dump. Although Poland does not make a political statement, this sociological observation of the constant movement of animal species can be read as a thinly disguised metaphor for the migration of tribes in South Africa, the power struggle among human races, and the survival of the fittest.

577. Proctor, Andre. *The School We Made.* Illustrated by Hannie Koch. Harare, Zimbabwe: Baobab, 1992. N.p. Grades 2-4.
The atmosphere of fun and cooperative learning is quickly destroyed when an insensitive and authoritarian teacher is assigned to a newly built school in a village in Zimbabwe. When the pupils and their parents organize a fair to earn money for sports uniforms--instead of buying expensive ones from the unscrupulous store owner--the

teacher learns that a village school belongs to the community that helped to build it. The story raises relevant questions pertaining to educational methodology, physical punishment, and role of business in national uplift.

578. Rayner, Richard. *Tsoko: The Story of a Vervet Monkey.* Illustrated by Lis Davis. Harare, Zimbabwe: Baobab, 1990. 124p. Grades 8-12.
    This tender story of friendship between Tsoko, a vervet monkey, and Wordsworth, a black Zimbabwean who feels kinship with animals, is based on biological facts, research at the Chipangali Wildlife Orphanage, and the experiences of people who have raised vervet monkeys as pets. Although bordering on the fantastic, Rayner's uncanny skill presents the story from the dual perspectives of Tsoko and Wordsworth. The narrative traces the adventures of Tsoko from the time he was separated from his mother because of a poacher's trap, to being shunted from one human family to another, to his inclusion in an experiment to release a band of vervet monkeys on an island in Lake Kariba. The one constant in his life is the servant Wordsworth; they communicate telepathically and call out to each other in distress. As in his earlier animal fantasy, *The Valley of Tantalika* (Books of Zimbabwe, 1980), on the fate of animals displaced by the creation of Lake Kariba, Rayner evokes compassion for the feelings of animals and reflects on the spiritual affinity between humans and animals.

579. _____. *Umboko and the Hamerkop.* Illustrated by Lis Davis. Harare, Zimbabwe: Baobab, 1988, 1991. N.p. Grades 2-4.
    This gentle story about a tuskless baby elephant raises questions of vanity and being different. While the lack of tusks does pose some practical problems for Umboko, he ignores the advice of an elderly elephant to learn to live with his disability. Instead, Umboko seeks the magical hamerkop for the gift of the longest, thickest, most curvaceous tusks. His wish is granted, but their very size makes them useless for stripping bark, digging roots, and defending himself. Ironically, although proclaimed the king of all elephants, Umboko has to be protected by man because of the great value placed on his tusks. Davis' pleasing illustrations accurately portray Umboko's feelings, immaturity, and ultimate wisdom.

580. Rochman, Hazel, selec. *Somehow Tenderness Survives: Stories of Southern Africa.* New York: Harper & Row, 1988. 147p. Grades 8-12.
    Ten fictional and autobiographical stories by both black and white writers portray life under apartheid for ordinary people. Whether black, white, Asian, or colored, coming of age under a racist regime involves suffering, violence, poverty, hunger, and imprisonment. Doris Lessing describes her sudden awareness that blacks are "persons"; Peter Abrahams narrates in excruciating detail the brutal lashing of a black boy for defying a white bully; Nadine Gordimer recounts the motherly manner in which an Indian woman risks arrest to champion the cause of the underprivileged blacks; Gcina Mhlope

reveals the plight of a young woman who has to hide in a public toilet to avoid being caught in an all-white neighborhood; and other stories describe a colored girl's sense of inferiority in a white private school and the consequences of the forbidden love between black and white. The stories are heartrending, but through them emerges the human determination to better the world, the self-pride to challenge the assaults on one's dignity, and the marvel that love and caring can survive despite the odds.

581. Rooke, Daphne. *Twins in South Africa.* Illustrated by W. Lorraine. Boston: Houghton Miflin, 1955. 164p. Grades 4-6.

The twelve-year-old twins Tiensie and Karel Van Heerden have an adventurous Christmas vacation when they visit their home in Zululand. This setting gives Rooke the opportunity to present the Afrikaner version of Boer history and the victory over the Zulu king, Dingaan. The Van Heerdens, like so many gold and diamond prospectors and cotton farmers before them, were disappointed in the soil conditions and meager rainfall in Zululand; however, they stayed to raise chickens, pigs, and cattle.

The twins' imagination is fired by stories of prospecting, especially the account of the Ernestine diamond that their father had found twelve years ago. It was stolen by his partner and hidden somewhere in the mountains, and the adventure involves its discovery by the twins. The book also describes Afrikaner family life and the close harmony between animals and humans on the farm. The established master-servant relationship between Boer and Zulu ensures that the farm is run smoothly and the servants are happy. Although the interracial friendship between Karel and Kondulu is one of mutual trust, Karel always takes the leading role. The relationship between brother and sister is also gender based, with Karel scolding Tiensie and underestimating her intelligence. In the end, Tiensie proves to be the smarter of the two when she displays tremendous presence of mind and quick thinking in rescuing the diamond from the thieves.

582. Rosenthal, Jane. *Wake Up Singing.* Cape Town: Maskew Miller Longman, 1990. 92p. Grades 7-9.

Set in 1985, this novel gives voice to the participation of white pacifists in the freedom movement. Sixteen-year-old Nicholas Mackenzie is forced to reevaluate his identity as a white South African when he is introduced to members of the black student organization. The realities of apartheid become painfully clear to Nick when he compares his privileged life to that of Zach and Mpho, two very likeable and intelligent blacks his own age. He also becomes aware of the unreasonable fear and hysteria of whites as expressed in barbed wire fences and repeated antiriot and bombing drills at school. This new insight places Nick in direct conflict with the authorities at school; with his father who is proud of his family's regimental loyalties; and with his schoolmates who accuse him of being unpatriotic.

Although the tone and theme of *Wake Up Singing* are definitely radical when compared to earlier novels published in South Africa, the open-ended plot suggests Rosenthal's unwillingness to take a definite stand. Moreover, Nick's rebellion is viewed as youthful idealism and the interracial friendship is one-sided, with the white characters protecting their black friends and volunteering their time through community service in the townships. The ending also suggests that the protagonists are really powerless against the government and police. This novel won the 1990 Young Africa Award.

583. Sackett, Elisabeth. *Danger on the African Grassland.* Illustrated by Martin Camm. San Francisco: Sierra Club; Boston: Little, Brown, 1991. N.p. Grades K-3.

The peaceful grazing of animals in Southern Africa is rudely shattered by rifle bullets fired from a jeep. A mother rhinoceros is badly wounded, but she tries to follow the stampeding animals in order to save her small calf. Although weakened by excessive loss of blood, she manages to reach safety and is renewed by rolling in a muddy waterhole. This simple story is a plea for the conservation of animals, especially the rhinoceros who is killed for its horn. The illustrations by Martin Camm, a highly acclaimed nature artist, provide details of plant and animal life of the savannas, reflect the harmony of nature, and capture the intimacy and love between the rhinoceros and her calf.

584. Sacks, Margaret. *Beyond Safe Boundaries.* New York: Puffin, 1990. 156p. Grades 7-10.

When Elizabeth Levin enters adolescence, her world extends beyond the boundaries of home and school to include upheavals in her personal life and in the country. Set in the late 1950s or early 1960s, this novel reveals the impact of South Africa's racial policies on a white family. On the personal level, Elizabeth has to adjust to a new mother, her sister Elvie's growing militancy against the government, and her own awareness of racial discrepancies. The Levins have always been "cautiously" aware of the unfair laws affecting coloreds, blacks, and Asians, and they cross the forbidden boundaries in small ways. However, their lives are completely changed when Elvie goes beyond safe boundaries to become a member of a secret antiapartheid student organization. Elizabeth's visit to her sister's apartment in Johannesburg proves to be a journey of discovery: she moves from innocence to knowledge, from naivete to maturity. Her sister, who is arrested and banned, is "smuggled" to England because it is impossible for her to live in South Africa. Unlike her sister, Elizabeth decides to protest the government's policies through her writing. This novel touchingly reveals that apartheid stifles and demeans *all* segments of South African society.

585. Schermbrucker, Reviva. *Charlie's House.* Illustrated by Niki Daly. New York: Viking, 1989. N.p. Preschool-Grade 2.

In sharp contrast with the leaking, one-roomed tin shack that Charlie shares with his mother and grandmother, the house of Charlie's dreams and creative play is spacious and comfortable. Lest the book be termed escapist, both text and pictures point out that Charlie holds on to his fantasy only with great determination because his family constantly brings him back to the realities township life. Charlie's spirit opens up the possibility of dreams and courage triumphing over adversity. However, a political message can also be detected: What is a fantasy for Charlie--basic amenities and material comforts--should be the right of every child, at least in a rich country like South Africa.

586. Scholefield, Alan. *The Young Masters*. New York: Morrow, 1972. Originally published in 1971 in Great Britain. 210p. Grades 7-10.

This long, rambling story of a white South African boy explores the theme of power from various angles. When the story begins, ten-year-old Paul is homeless after his grandmother's death and he depends on Luther, his sixty-year-old Zulu servant, to take him to his new guardian nearly eight hundred miles away. En route, Paul and Luther become victims of abuse, violence, racism, and exploitation by both rich and poor, white and colored. In the second part of the novel, Paul is well settled in a boy's school where he encounters the same power play that he had experienced in society. Paul's environment turns him into an indifferent and callous individual, but when he kicks an old "kaffir" and sees a black boy being ill-treated, he is reminded of the love and loyalty of Luther. Paul, the author makes it clear, is now part of the system, and he easily quietens his guilty conscience by gifting money to the victim of his physical abuse. The memory of Luther remains a symbol of his lost innocence.

587. Seed, Jenny. *The Broken Spear*. London: Hamish Hamilton, 1972. 175p. Grades 8-12.

The historic Boer trek to Natal is seen through the experiences of twelve-year-old Dirk, a fictitious character who accompanies Pieter Retief, governor of the trekkers, to the court of Dingaan, the Zulu king. As they cross the formidable Drakensburg mountains, Natal becomes a personal Promised Land for Dirk because he hopes it will bring him freedom from the cruelty of his foster father. Dingaan is presented as grotesque and cruel in his appearance and behavior. Despite a signed agreement giving the trekkers Port Natal and all the surrounding land as their everlasting property, Dingaan attacks their camp and kills and burns innocent families. The survivors, driven by anger and hatred, avenge the deaths by defeating the Zulus on December 16, 1838 at Blood River. Dirk is purged of hatred by the thought of his Zulu friend, by the beauty of the Zulu soldiers in their feathers, and by the loyalty and courage of his people.

This account of the Great Trek is given entirely from the viewpoint of the Afrikaners. No mention is made of the vested interests of trade, conversion to Christianity, political control, and territorial ambition. The resulting clashes with the native populations are seen as conflicts between "savages" and "civilization," with the primitive spear giving way to superior firearms. Furthermore, the trekkers justify their claim to the land by stating that it was completely uninhabited, except for a few English traders in Port Natal. Dingaan's rights to the land are seen as dubious because he had killed his half-brother, Shaka, to become king.

588. _____. *The Great Thirst.* Scarsdale, NY: Bradbury, 1971. 188p. Grades 8-12.
The story focuses on the maturation of Garib, a fictional character who belongs to the Nama nation. Under the influence of Jonker Afrikaner, the Westernized leader of the Hottentot (Khoi Khoi), Garib's young life is controlled by the desire to kill Kahitjene, leader of the Hereros. Jonker's influence is counteracted by the teachings of the Bible and by Tomarib, the wise man, who teaches moderation through mythology and folklore, but Garib is too young and immature to understand. While historians present Jonker as the Napoleon of the South and The Lion of Africa, Seed portrays him as an unsympathetic character who is vengeful, greedy, and bloodthirsty. Garib is finally disillusioned and he returns to his village and family to begin a new life. Jonker, in the meantime, is killed and his city is completely robbed and destroyed. A series of plagues--locusts, death of cattle, flood--indicate that the wrath of God is on Jonker.
Seed quite obviously presents the European view of South African history. The constant migration of various tribes, cattle raids, and wars are offset by the Christian message of love and peace. The glory and power of Western civilization are likewise presented as attractive and desirable.

589. _____. *Ntombi's Song.* Illustrated by Anno Berry. Boston: Beacon, 1987. N.p. Grades 1-4.
Set in a Zulu homeland, this picture book evocatively portrays the simple triumphs and sorrows of a six-year-old girl on her first adventure. Ntombi overcomes her fears and crosses the busy road and dark forest to buy a packet of sugar from the trading store. On her return journey, she spills the sugar when a speeding bus roars by. Undaunted, Ntombi resolves to earn money for the sugar by selling the sweet plums she had picked in the forest. When that fails, she dances to her special song to comfort herself, and some tourists pay her for the delightful performance. Ntombi finally earns the respect of her peers and elders. Seed focuses on the universal aspects of Ntombi's experience and is silent on the realities of apartheid. The rural setting is idealized with beautiful hills bathed in the autumn sunshine and the villagers content with their lives.

590. _____. *Vengeance of the Zulu King.* New York: Pantheon, 1970. 216p. Grades 6-10.
Set in 1824, this story presents a totally Eurocentric version of South African history. Southeast Africa is portrayed as being destroyed and terrorized by Shaka, king of the Zulus, whose warriors raid, kill, and burn innocent villagers without compassion. The Europeans, in

contrast, are courageous, peace loving, and kind. Under the leadership of Henry Fynn, victims are protected from the wrath of Shaka and led to the safety of the white settlement. Fynn also wins the respect of Shaka because he has the courage to challenge Shaka. Derogatory remarks are directed at the villagers for their stupidity and inability to help themselves. They gain stature only when they come under the protection of the white traders.

591. Sherfield, P. *Laika and the Elephants.* Illustrated by Gabriel Elison. N.p.: Zambia Publications Bureau, 1965. 48p. Grades 4-6.
    The popular folk motif of a human conversing with animals adds charm and special meaning to the story of Laika. Unlike Aardema's *"What's So Funny, Ketu?"* (see # 350), this is not a humorous account of the awkward predicaments caused by such a gift. Rather, sensitivity to the feelings and rights of animals is the theme of this short novel. When Laika, a young Ila herdsboy, frees a trapped elephant, he is given the ability to communicate with animals. The episodic plot recounts his many adventures in the jungle where he visits elephants, baboons, lions, and wildebeest. He learns about the nature and habits of each species and realizes that animals are more disciplined and moral than humans. Laika experiences inner conflict when the Ila organize their annual hunt. He warns the animals, but later feels guilty that the hunters had to come back empty-handed because of him. The crucial question the story poses is: Can one's love for animals be reconciled with hunting and eating meat? Sherfield's prose is engaging, but there are repeated negative references to the lack of intelligence and gossipy nature of women.

592. Stewart, Dianne. *The Dove.* Illustrated by Jude Daly. New York: Greenwillow, 1993. N.p. Grades K-3.
    The dove serves as a symbol of hope and promise to a young girl and her grandmother in rural South Africa. As in the Biblical myth, a dove appears in front of their house after a great flood and becomes Lindi's inspiration for beadwork which they sell at the Community Art Shop. This traditional art helps them to survive while they wait for the fields to dry.
    Stewart, who lives near Durban, does not make any political statements about apartheid and the reason why there are no men in Lindi's home. Daly's artwork, in contrast, silently presents the city of Durban as an economic powerbase. The beach, because of recent changes, is mixed racially; and there is a poster depicting a black child and a white child declaring that children need peace. Both text and illustrations evoke the simplicity of rural life; present the difficulties of survival; and depict hope for the future through family bonds.

593. Stock, Catherine. *Where Are You Going Manyoni?* Illustrated by author. New York: Morrow, 1993. N.p. Preschool-Grade 2.
    Manyoni's solitary morning walk to school in a faraway village offers Stock the opportunity to record the natural life of the veld in

Zimbabwe. Urban readers will fear for Manyoni's life as she passes an impala herd, zebras, a civet cat, baboons, a jackal, and a bushpig, but the author's explanatory note reassures readers that there is perfect harmony among the animals, plants, and people of this sparsely populated Venda region. The quiet and peace of the jungle scene is abruptly shattered when Manyoni greets her friend, and together they join the noise and activity on the playground.

The earthtone watercolors capture the shimmering light of the sun on the plains and the dry riverbed, the soothing dark greens of the shady kloof, the brightness of the red sandstone koppies, and the refreshing water of the Tobwani Dam. Stock has also illustrated *Armien's Fishing Trip* (Morrow, 1990), set in South Africa.

594. Thomas, Gladys. *Spotty Dog and Other Stories.* Illustrated by Albert Hess. Johannesburg: Skotaville, n.d. 47p. Grades 5-7.
Based on Thomas' personal observations and genuine concern, nine short stories capture the inner lives of children growing up in South Africa's townships. The stories reveal the simple pleasures, deep despair, disruption in family security, and daily humiliations and loss of dignity of the children. True to her mission of protesting apartheid, Thomas focuses on stark reality and does not allow for false happy endings.

595. van Wyk, Chris. *Petroleum and the Orphaned Ostrich.* Illustrated by Gamakhulu Diniso. Johannesburg: Ravan, 1988. N.p. Grades 1-4.
What starts off as a realistic story of Joseph, the dustman, turns into a fanciful and meaningless tale of a tin boy, Petroleum, created by Joseph out of odds and ends. Once Petroleum comes to life (no explanation is offered), the center of interest shifts to Petroleum's adventures with a little girl and an orphaned ostrich. The plot is poorly constructed with the characters and events thrown together haphazardly. The illustrations, however, extend the text by depicting the poor living conditions in a South African township.

596. Welch, Ronald. *Zulu Warrior.* Illustrated by David Harris. London: David and Charles, 1974. 128p. Grades 8-12.
This historical novel describes the Zulu War of 1879 when over thirteen thousand British troops were killed at Isandhlwana in trying to disband the army of Cetawayo, the Zulu king. Welch provides a graphic account of the terrain, the military tactics of the British, and the superbly trained army of the Zulus. The story focuses on the experiences of Lieutenant Robert Maryon and his servant, Thomas, who are the only survivors of the battle. They join the center column at Rorke's Drift where only one hundred British soldiers are able to withstand an attack by fifteen thousand Zulu warriors. This victory proves to be decisive because of Lord Chelmsford's reinforcements from England.

Maryon serves as an objective observer of the events. Despite the glory and heroism displayed on the battlefield, he wonders about warfare, which turns the calmest of men into bloodthirsty lunatics, and the justice of the European presence in South Africa, especially taking the best land for themselves because of superior weapons.

597. Wellman, Alice. *Time of Fearful Night*. New York: Putnam's, 1970. 158p. Grades 5-7.

This story of interracial friendship is based on Wellman's childhood in Angola where her father had a clinic and research laboratory and her mother ran a mission school. Buale, son of Chief Kombulo, and Tom, son of an American doctor, overcome numerous personal problems as they try to win the approval of their fathers. Their friendship is based on mutual respect, trust, and equality. As they enter manhood, Buale brings his training as a medical technician to his people, while Tom, enriched by his experiences in Africa, enters medical school in the United States. Wellman is careful to point out that not all whites in Angola are as cruel and exploitative as the Portuguese colonizers.

598. _____. *The Wilderness Has Ears*. New York and London: Harcourt Brace Jovanovich, 1975. 141p. Grades 6-8.

Once again, turning to her childhood in Portuguese Angola, Wellman writes a moving story of a fourteen-year-old American girl's oneness with the Angolan wilderness and her love for the Kimbutu villagers. Set on the eve of Angolan independence, the story celebrates traditional culture and opposes Portuguese rule as exploitative, selfish, and evil. When Luti is stranded in her guardian's famine-stricken village for a week, she comes to respect the Kimbutu people for their dignity and wisdom, mystical powers, ability to heal the sick and wounded, and democratic rule. Wellman's idealization of the characters and their spiritual kinship with the land emphasizes the exotic aspects of Angola.

599. Westwood, Gwen. *Narni of the Desert*. Illustrated by Peter Warner. London: Hamish Hamilton, 1967. 93p. Grades 4-6.

The lifestyle of the nomadic "tribes" of the Kalahari Desert is presented through the experiences of young Narni. It is a story of survival under the harshest circumstances: they are near starvation due to a drought; the water holes have dried; and it is exceedingly difficult to hunt for meat as the animals have fled. Narni is not satisfied with helping his mother forage for edible roots and plants, catching small animals, and searching for water. He is impatient to become a contributing male member. Narni's opportunity comes when one of his brothers injures an arm and he is asked to accompany his older brother to hunt for meat. When Narni spots an eland, he is sent to the settlement for help. Narni's journey serves as an initiation rite because he overcomes fear of snakes and wild animals, learns to control his thirst, and finds his way back after being lost. The story ends on a hopeful note with the celebration of the gift of the eland and the swarming of grasshoppers, the messengers of rain.

Through this simple story, Westwood presents a very human

portrait of Bushmen (San) as they adapt to the desert in their hunting techniques, style of building homes, food habits, and clothing. Although their environment is harsh, there is joy and laughter in their lives as they celebrate nature, sing songs, and play games of skill.

600. Wilhelm, Peter. *Summer's End.* Illustrated by Mark de Lange. Johannesburg: Ravan, 1984. 149p. Grades 7-10.
Set in a future time when all of Africa (and the earth) is in the grip of an ice age, *Summer's End* provides an indirect commentary on modern conditions. This future Southern Africa is reminiscent of precolonial times: small independent kingdoms, self-sufficient trading economy, awe of natural powers and ancestor worship, strong family unit, political organization based on the collective rule of enlightened priestlike citizens, and the quest for learning. There is no racial discrimination and the population is a happy blend of African and European physical features. The story focuses on a scientific expedition to the South Pole to investigate the presence of a mysterious fireball, which turns out to be a pyramid-shaped computer launched by a previous technologically advanced civilization. The interest, however, is focused on John Carpenter, who has just passed his initiation rite and who accompanies the team. For John, this is an epic journey of self-discovery. He is sobered by the knowledge that human civilization is only an illusion--a brief episode when the earth warms up--in the context of cosmic time and perpetual ice. He is instructed by the pyramid to use technological information wisely and not to revert to the barbarism of racial wars. This is an excellent book for critical thinking as it touches on the issues of racial harmony, problem solving, value of human language, and true progress.

601. Williams, Karen Lynn. *Galimoto.* Illustrated by Catherine Stock. New York: Mulberry Books, 1990. N.p. Preschool-Grade 3.
Seven-year-old Kondi spends the entire day collecting scraps of wire to make a pushtoy. His perseverance in designing a complicated pickup truck are evidence not only of his intelligence, but of his sense of satisfaction in accomplishing a goal. Both text and illustrations present a positive portrait of village life in contemporary Malawi.

602. _____. *When Africa Was Home.* Illustrated by Floyd Cooper. New York: Orchard Books, 1991. N.p. Preschool-Grade 3.
The author, who served in Africa with the Peace Corps, captures her love for the land, people, and culture of Malawi through the experiences of her young son. Peter is perfectly at home in his African village: he plays in the hot sun, ignoring directives to wear a hat to protect his delicate white skin; he slides down anthills and shimmies up pau-pau trees; he makes toys from the smooth white stalks of maize and wet earth from the riverbed; he chases goats and chickens, screeches at monkeys, and frightens a herd of antelope; and he enjoys eating corn paste and fish eyes from a bowl with his hands. His warmest ties, however, are with the loving people who surround him, especially his nanny, Maji (mother in Chichewa), who carried

him on her back when he was a baby. Upon completion of his parents' work, Peter is suddenly transported to the world of airplanes, skyscrapers, vacuum cleaners, hats and shoes, and forks and spoons. He longs for the bright colors and sounds of Africa. Fortunately for Peter, his parents also miss Africa, and they are able to return.

Williams eloquently portrays the feeling of powerlessness that young children experience when they are wrenched away from familiar surroundings because of their parents' jobs. Both text and illustrations strongly convey the theme that racial, cultural, and technological barriers are irrelevant to true relationships among peoples. Just as Peter's skin tans under the African sun and his soles harden by being barefooted, people can adjust to and be happy in a variety of environments.

POETRY

603. Brooks, Gwendolyn. *The Near-Johannesburg Boy and Other Poems.* Chicago: Third World Press, 1986, 1991. 31p. Grades 7-12.

Reflecting the black experience in America, this collection has two poems about Africa. In the powerful title poem, a boy from a black township expresses his sorrow at being dispossessed of his country, at his father's death and mother's plight, and at his own inferior status; yet, he is determined to carry on the struggle for freedom.

604. _____. *Winnie.* Chicago: Third World Press, 1988, 1991. 23p. Grades 6-12.

Brooks' powerful, evocative verse captures the essence of Winnie Mandela's life--as a rural girl, social worker, political activist, wife and mother, and, above all, human being who represents the collective dignity of her people. Events from history and images of death and suffering reverberate as Winnie bares her soul. Through it all emerges not a resigned or defeated woman, but a triumphant and enduring spirit who is determined to continue fighting as "truth-teller."

605. Kadhani, Mudereri, and Musaemura Zimunya, comps. and eds. *And Now the Poets Speak.* Gweru, Zimbabwe: Mambo, 1981. 178p. Grades 8-12.

This anthology of poems by a wide variety of Zimbabweans was inspired by the struggle for liberation. The poems are arranged in eight sections that trace the country's history from precolonial times through colonial domination, revolution, and, finally, to independence. Of the forty-two poets represented here, the works of Musaemura Zimunya, Charles Mungoshi, C. Hove, Samuel Chimsoro, and Godfrey Dzvairo are exceptional.

606. Mandela, Zindzi. *Black as i am.* Photographs by Peter Magubane. Foreword by Andrew Young. Los Angeles: The Guild of Tutors Press, 1978. 120p. Grades 7-12.

> Magubane's exquisite photographs of the slums on the outskirts of Cape Town and Johannesburg establish the setting and mood for Mandela's sad and poignant poetry. Written when she was only sixteen, this first book of fifty-four poems captures her anger, frustration, sorrow, love, and hope. It vents the loneliness and pain of separation from her parents; it questions the fairness of apartheid and the relationship between Christianity and the plight of blacks; and it expresses her warmth and compassion for her fellow black South Africans. The poems are not the immature ramblings of a juvenile writer; instead, they are skillfully composed to reflect maturity of thought, intensity of feelings, and hope for the future. Simple yet powerful images of death, suffering, deprivation, and joy force readers to confront the reality of being black in South Africa.
>
> The Guild of Tutors Press has also published *Black and Fourteen*, a group of Zindzi Mandela's earlier poems, and Magubane's *Riot at Soweto: This is My Body, This is My Blood.*

607. Manelisi. "If Someone Were To Ask Me . . ." In *Free As I Know*, edited by Beverley Naidoo, 102-107. London: Bell & Hyman, 1987. Grades 4-7.

> In four powerful poems, the fourteen-year-old author responds to the continuing racial inequities of apartheid. The poems are responses to questions that might be asked about his visit to South Africa. Each verse of the title poem begins with the rhetorical statement, "I would tell that person," as it matter-of-factly proceeds to describe the great physical beauty of the country and the reality of life for blacks: pass laws, difficult living conditions in shantytowns, grinding poverty, and hard labor for poor returns. "Grandad" is especially touching as it describes a visit to Robben Island where Grandfather has already served twenty-one years. The oppressive building and the physical and mental strain of the visit are contrasted with the strength that radiates from the elder. Likewise, "Shantytown" and "South Africa" also end on a positive note: the people are not broken with despair and passivity, but they have the courage and hope to think positively and to revolt.

608. Mapanje, Jack. *Of Chameleons and Gods.* African Writers Series. London, Ibadan and Nairobi: Heinemann, 1981. 80p. Grades 10-12.

> Through a variety of poems that span ten years, Mapanje attempts to give voice to his experiences and identity. Chameleon-like, he tries a number of poetic voices and tones that range from bitterness and despair to sarcasm and irony to praise for ancient traditions. The subject matter is grouped into four broad categories that center around myths of the gods and legends of national heroes, sketches from London, descriptions and legends of the Zomba plateau, and oppression of Africans by white South Africans and the Portuguese. While it is unclear if Mapanje has discovered his true self or literary

voice, he states the attempt has been a therapeutic one. The dominant impression that remains is the poet's love and reverence for Malawian traditions and his disappointment at the decay and corruption of values following independence. The Notes and Glossary explain unfamiliar terms and topical references contained in the poems.

609. Mkhize, Mlungisi. *One Calabash-One Gudu.* Braamfontein, South Africa: Skotaville, 1990. 87p. Grades 8-12.

Hitherto published individually in journals, the sixty-two protest poems in this volume were collected after the death of this young black South African poet and teacher. Mkhize's poems describe the conditions of blacks under apartheid: political inequality, unemployment, guns, prisons, lack of living space, hunger, disease, drunkenness, and death. His tone varies from frustration and discouragement to impatience and anger to inspiration and hope. These poems indicate that the only recourse left to youth is to enter the freedom struggle through riots, boycotts, protest marches, fighting, and death. In the title poem, "One Calabash-One Gudu," Mkhize implores South Africans to unify and identify with one another as Africans. He also condemns the black bourgeoisie that rejects African ways to embrace Europeanisms. His own inspiration to carry on the struggle comes from singing praises of dead heroes and invoking African ancestors and traditions to lead black South Africans to glory and liberation. In an introductory essay on protest poetry, Mkhize likens his work to the long tradition of militant literature that emerged out of the great revolutions in Russia, China, France, and America; the World War I poets who described the horrors of war; and the protest against Portuguese colonization of Africa.

610. Mtshali, Oswald Mbuyiseni. *Sounds of a Cowhide Drum.* Foreword by Nadine Gordimer. New York: Third Press, 1972. 79p. Grades 8-12.

With cutting realism, Mtshali exposes what life is like for blacks in South Africa. With frequent references to actual events, places, and people, he brings to life the world of tubercular mines; pass book offenders who suffocate to death in overheated police vans; soaring crime; and the grinding labor of blacks that has made possible the powerful edifices of the whites. The imagery is equally stark as Mtshali describes an infant baby being torn by scavenging dogs "draped in bandannas of blood"; of a crowded commuter train that "squeezes me like a lemon of all the juice of my life"; and of black identity which is like a beetle in the sand to be squashed by a white beachstroller's foot. Mtshali's world is one of shattered dreams, lost identities, inexplicable jail sentences, and longing for the good life. Images of chains and manacles, steel cages, and walls without doors, and odor of decay and excreta overpower the senses.

Mtshali's tone, however, is not accusative, whining, or bitter as he chronicles life from the perspective of blacks. He distances readers by making them gaze at reality through the curtain of irony. His artistic vision has revealed to him that fear and hate are responsible for this state of affairs. One can overcome it by soaring in spirit or by developing "marble eyes" that are immune to tears, hate, love, and anger--and color. As a philosopher, Mtshali can only hope that the meek will inherit the earth as the scripture promises, or that death will prove the great equalizer when it visits young and old, rich and poor, powerful and weak.

611. Mzamane, Lerato Nomvuyo. "Homecoming." *In Free As I Know*, edited by Beverley Naidoo, 98-101. London: Bell & Hyman, 1987. Grades 5-8.

A young black South African girl writes of how she gains firsthand knowledge of apartheid when she comes "home" for a visit on her thirteenth birthday. Having lived in Botswana, Wales, and the United Kingdom for most of her young life, Tiko's memories of South Africa are associated with the love and warmth she had received from her grandparents and aunts as a child. She can hardly contain her excitement and feeling of "belonging" as she steps off the airplane on to the soil of South Africa. However, the elation is shortlived when she, quite unaware of racial divisions, heads toward the clean public toilet marked "Whites Only," instead of to the dirty, smelly one reserved for blacks. Firmly stopped by her aunt, Tiko's sense of pride and self-worth disappear quickly.

612. Weinberg, Pessa. *Hlabelela Mntwanami: Sing, My Child!* Illustrated by Gamakhulu Diniso and Rose Cross-Striebel. Johannesburg: Ravan, 1984. 140p. Grades K-7.

The fifty Zulu children's songs in this collection, most of them written or transcribed for the first time, are part of the collector-adaptor's Master's dissertation in Musicology. The songs are arranged in ten categories based on their meanings and social functions. They are also ordered chronologically from songs for infants to those sung by and for children of about thirteen. The selection includes cradle songs, action songs, game songs, greeting songs, wedding songs, love songs, hoeing songs, history songs, and ancestral spirit songs. Each song is prefaced by the occasion for the song, the singer or singers, and relevant cultural details. In addition, each song is rendered in Western musical notation, with directions on the stylistic features of melody, text, and rhythm, and the accompanying hand clapping, arm action, and other body movements.

A detailed introductory essay provides information on Zulu history, social structure, ceremonies and customs, and European influence in order to place the songs in their historical-sociological context. The political, religious, economic, and social changes that have eroded Zulu society and the extended family unit are also reflected in the songs.

DRAMA

612a. Fugard, Athol. *"Master Harold". . . and the boys.*   New York:
Knopf, 1983. 60p. Grades 9-12.
    Fugard delicately maneuvers the tension of the play through the
revealing dialogue of the three characters: Hally/Harold, a seventeen-
year-old white boy, and Sam and Willie, two middle-aged black
servants who work in the tearoom owned by Hally's parents. Their
warm and loving relationship becomes apparent as Hally remembers
the good times he has shared with Sam and Willie from the time he
was four. If Hally teaches Sam everything he learns in school, Sam,
on his part, is a surrogate father to Hally: he helps with homework;
plays with him; comforts him when he is dejected or neglected; and
teaches him moral values. However, this happy scene in South Africa
of the 1950s is rudely shattered. Looming ominously in the
background is the fact that Hally's drunken father is to return home
from the hospital that day. Bitter because he feels trapped in an
unpleasant family atmosphere--which is not unlike the apartheid
society Sam and Willie are victims of--Hally begins to utter
disrespectful words about his father. When Sam stops him, Hally
vents his anger on Sam in a vicious and racist manner. Sam maintains
his dignity by acting the mature adult.
    This episode serves as a rite of passage as Hally moves from the
innocence and idealism of childhood to the acceptance of racial
prejudice and social power of the adolescent--a familiar motif in
South African literature. Whether or not this interracial, intergenerational friendship will transcend the change in "Master Harold's"
personality is kept deliberately vague. Sam's parting words to Hally
are that ultimately he is responsible for the choices he makes in life.
This intensely emotional play makes readers wonder if it is possible
for a lifelong relationship to snap so abruptly. At what point does a
white child begin to endorse the racist attitudes of his society?

613. Marks, Jonti. *Shaka Zulu.*   Junior Readers Series. Nairobi, Kenya:
East African Educational Publishers, 1993. 65p. Grades 6-8.
    The eventful life of Shaka from his rejection at birth by his father to
his death at the hands of his brothers is presented in two acts. Each
act is further divided into a succession of short scenes that focus on
the most dramatic and revealing moments of Shaka's career. The first
half of the play is well executed because it establishes Shaka's
emotional attachment to his mother, his psychological motivations for
revenge, and his superior intelligence, especially as a strategist.
However, readers unfamiliar with Shaka's biography will find that
Act Two gives a sketchy picture of the events and of Shaka's
complex personality.

614. Mujajati, George. *The Rain of My Blood.*   Gweru, Zimbabwe: Mambo,
1991. 100p. Grades 9-12.
    The compelling power of this play stems from the ironic juxtaposition

of the materialistic concerns of present-day Zimbabweans and the martyrdom of freedom fighters who made the good life possible. Tawanda, a crippled excombatant of the war of liberation, is rebuked by his successful brother for disturbing the peace of his fancy neighborhood by singing old war songs. Through a series of short scenes, Tawanda recalls the plight of blacks under white minority rule; the so-called humanitarian work of Christian missionaries; the leadership and exploits of a close comrade; and the execution of his friend because of betrayal by a black. Tawanda's disillusionment is understandable: the struggle to free Zimbabwe has earned him only unemployment, dependence on family, neglect, and disrespect. His dignity and glory rest in remembering the heroic deeds of the past. This play won the main prize in the 1989 National Theatre Organisation Play of the Year Competition.

615. Ndlovu, Temba Petros.   *The Return.*   Gweru, Zimbabwe: Mambo, 1990. 59p. Grades 8-12.
The play consists of a series of powerful scenes that reveal character traits through dynamic confrontations between key figures. The plot focuses on the return of a war hero six years after Zimbabwean independence, when everyone has given him up for dead. His presence causes disruption and soul-searching for both family and total strangers, especially for his wife who has remarried. In choosing the paralyzed war hero over her success-hungry husband, she symbolically rejects the evils that followed in the wake of independence--materialism, self-centeredness, governmental corruption, and moral decay. Ndlovu's ironic stance lends depth as well as controversy to the story.

616. Ng'ombe, James L., et al. *Nine Malawian Plays*. Malawian Writers Series. Limbe and Lilongwe, Malawi: Popular Publications and Likuni Press, 1976. 171p. Grades 8-12.
The plays in this collection are a testimony to the emergence of English drama in postcolonial Malawi. The fact that all nine plays were written either for the Secondary Schools Drama Festival, the university, or the Malawi Broadcasting Corporation indicates the overwhelming importance given to performances, as opposed to simply reading plays, for the stimulation of young writers. Various drama competitions encourage playwrights to write, produce, direct, and act in plays. However, competition rules restrict each play to a small cast and thirty minutes performance time. The authors have no opportunity for in-depth character development and intricate plots; instead, the theme and didactic content take precedence. Chris Kamlongera is, perhaps, the most sophisticated writer because he maintains dramatic interest by confronting his characters with powerful forces and choices. The two plays by Ng'ombe adapt mythic and folk material to denounce jealousy among co-wives; Joe Mosiwa's "Who Will Marry Our Daughter?" is an African version of the popular Asian tale of finding a powerful suitor for the Mouse Maiden; and Timpunza Mvula's "The Lizard's Tail" and Kam-

longera's "The Love Potion" examine marital relationships. "Lord Have Mercy" is a scalding condemnation of the glib assumptions of an educated, Westernized professional woman who rejects traditional African customs and values. Collectively, the plays reflect contemporary realities and the main concerns of Malawians.

Despite the strict regulations of the drama competitions, the playwrights' artistic abilities are evident in the forceful dialogue, inclusion of storytelling conventions, and a variety of technical strategies.

BIOGRAPHY AND AUTOBIOGRAPHY

617. Chidyausiku, Paul. *Broken Roots.* Gweru, Zimbabwe: Mambo, 1984. 111p. Grades 9-12.

The author describes the traditional culture of the Shona through the personal reminiscences of an elderly woman. Born before the European colonization of Zimbabwe, Munzara traces the major phases of her life from her difficult birth to advanced old age. The narrative focuses on the significance of customs in connection with childbirth, marriage, ancestor worship, training of young men and women, burial rites, and the place of a widow in her late husband's family. One is impressed by the dignity, wisdom, morality, and community consciousness of a traditional Shona village. Chidyausiku's eloquent prose and effective use of traditional songs lend immediacy to the story and engage readers emotionally in Munzara's experiences. On the social level, this biographical narrative succeeds in conveying the importance of values and heritage in daily life.

618. Cohen, Daniel. *Shaka: King of the Zulus.* Garden City, NY: Doubleday, 1973. 171p. Grades 8-10.

Shaka's career as a Zulu warrior, chief, and empire builder is evaluated against the historical, political, economic, and social background of eighteenth century Southern Africa. Shaka's success as a military genius and ruler is attributed to his ambition, courage, highly disciplined army, political astuteness, extensive intelligence gathering network, and strict regulation of sexual relationships. Cohen believes that Shaka's expansionist policy was the major cause of the *mfecane,* or upheaval caused by ceaseless warfare and migrations in Southern Africa. Shaka also changed the nature of Zulu society by giving prominence to his vast army, which he organized according to age regiments to improve fighting efficiency and to ensure loyalty to himself rather than to the clan. He further destroyed the power of the clan elders and the feared *isangomas,* or witch-finders, through regular executions and massacres. The majesty and wealth of Shaka's court is conveyed through lengthy excerpts from the writings and diaries of three Europeans whom Shaka liked and trusted--Francis

George Farewell, Henry Francis Fynn, and Nathaniel Issacs.

In assessing Shaka's complex personality, Cohen addresses the charge that he was a cruel and evil madman. Cohen is careful to point out the conditions against which Shaka's actions were performed: he used executions for discipline, but he always maintained the goodwill of his army. The psychological impact of his illegitimate birth, unhappy childhood, and rejection had a profound impact in shaping his bitter and brooding nature. Yet, he did not enjoy witnessing the killings and was a loyal friend and loving son. Military terror, states Cohen, is easy to understand as many have done it before him. If Alexander the Great, Julius Caesar, and Napoleon Bonaparte can be admired for their military genius, why cannot Shaka? Cohen believes that the continual round of brutal executions recorded by Fynn and Issacs were primarily responsible for Shaka's reputation. Casual executions were common features at the courts of many lands, and Cohen cites the examples of Timurlane, King Mindohn Min of Burma, Ivan IV of Russia, Stalin, and Hitler. Terroristic despotism was not unique to Shaka, or Africa.

619. Dachs, Anthony J.   *Khama of Botswana.*   African Historical Biographies Series. London, Nairobi and Ibadan: Heinemann, 1971. 37p. Grades 3-5.

Khama (1838-1923) ruled his people during a turbulent period when the Ngwato of Botswana were undergoing sweeping changes from traditional lifestyle to Western civilization, from African religious beliefs to Christianity, and from independent chiefdom to British Protectorate. Ironically, Khama consciously precipitated all of the above developments to avoid internal hostility and the threat of foreign control. His move was in direct opposition with the established customs of the Ngwato. Although Khama's decision produced conflict within the ruling family and curtailed his own powers when be became chief, he strongly believed that his people would benefit from Christianity and Western ideas of farming, trading, technology, and government. Above all, he tried to secure political stability and economic prosperity by avoiding warfare with neighbors like the Ndebele and Kololo and by preventing the expansion of the Boers and British companies from South Africa into his territory. Thus, Khama was able to spare his people the humiliation of forced labor, taxation, and harsh treatment that Africans suffered in South Africa, Zimbabwe, Namibia, and Zambia. Despite his typically colonial attitude, Khama is remembered for his radical reforms, his wise administration and judgment, and his generosity to the Ngwato.

620. Denenberg, Barry. *Nelson Mandela: "No Easy Walk To Freedom."* New York: Scholastic, 1991. 164p. Grades 7-12.

Nelson Mandela's life and achievements are discussed in the context of the worsening conditions of blacks under apartheid rule and their struggle to achieve freedom and political rights. From his childhood in a village in the Transkei to his involvement in the struggle,

Mandela displayed personal qualities that enabled him to lead his people in their war against apartheid. Denenberg's portrait is not an intimate one, perhaps, because Mandela was always the public figure who had sacrificed his life, his family, and his comfort for the cause. In keeping with this objective tone, the biography discusses the history of South Africa; legalized racism under apartheid; living conditions for whites in the suburbs and for blacks in homelands and townships; various antiapartheid organizations and their leaders; and the government's ruthless measures to put down opposition, especially in Sharpville and Soweto. The development of Mandela's philosophy and strategies from peaceful civil disobedience to violent protest and open revolution is seen as the only effective recourse left to blacks. Quotations from Mandela's eloquent four-hour-long trial statement reflect his passionate love for freedom and human dignity; his democratic stance in working toward a harmonious, multiracial South Africa; his intelligent analysis of the repressive measures; and his human compassion in describing the deplorable conditions in townships and homelands. For these convictions he was willing to be banned, to be imprisoned for twenty-six years, and to die. The governments of Presidents Botha and de Klerk were forced to adapt to internal chaos and international economic and diplomatic pressures by making changes--some significant, such as repealing the pass laws and legalizing opposition groups, and others cosmetic. After being freed on February 11, 1990, Nelson Mandela continued to struggle for political representation, which became a reality in April 1994.

621. Hargrove, Jim. *Nelson Mandela: South Africa's Silent Voice of Protest.* Chicago: Children's Press, 1989. 135p. Grades 6-8.
The biographer regrets that very little information is available on the ancestral village and childhood years of Mandela due to government restrictions. Nevertheless, this is not a dry, objective account. Based primarily on the speeches of the Mandelas and Winnie's writings, Hargrove presents a highly personal and sensitive portrait of the life and times of Nelson Mandela. All the major events of his life are seen from the perspective of Mandela's continual conflict with his conscience and the law. That is why he left the chieftaincy of the Thembas at the age of eighteen; joined the student protest at Fort Hare College; joined the African National Congress and later changed its resistance tactics to violent struggle; and refused to accept conditional freedom while serving a life sentence. Hargrove conveys the dynamism, courage, and strong convictions of Nelson Mandela by quoting extensively from his public speeches and trial statements.

Hargrove concludes by mentioning that Winnie Mandela built a $200,000 home in Soweto with money earned from her book, *Part of My Soul Went With Him,* and business interests. He also refers to the 1989 scandal implicating Winnie Mandela and the United Mandela Football Club, an organization of thirty black youth, with the deaths and disappearance of some Soweto youth. Winnie insisted that she was innocent. Hargrove neither draws any conclusions from nor gives the significance of the above information.

622. Hoobler, Dorothy and Thomas. *Nelson and Winnie Mandela.* Impact Biography Series. London: Franklin Watts, 1987. 128p. Grades 8-12.

Both Nelson and Winnie Mandela (now divorced) grew up in rural Transkei in families that emphasized formal education and pride in the precolonial history of South Africa. Both left their ancestral homes for the independence and opportunities that Johannesburg offered and dedicated their lives to the struggle against apartheid. Their story is also the story of the African National Congress under Oliver Tembo, Albert Luthuli, and Walter Sisulu and other organizations like the South African Communist Party and the Indian National Congress. As they fought for political and economic rights, they witnessed greater repressive measures--such as the Bantu Education Act and the creation of Bantustans--by the white minority government. Like the Hargrove biography, the Hooblers also quote extensively from the speeches, writings, and interviews of Nelson and Winnie Mandela.

This biography emphasizes the Mandelas' essentially human qualities: Nelson's strong sense of humor, majestic personality, self-confidence, devotion to friends, and buoyant outlook in the face of hardships; and Winnie's courage and pride in enduring separation from her husband, constant harassment, and imprisonment, and her difficult decision to send her daughters to Swaziland to be educated. The segments on Winnie Mandela are especially touching: her marriage had to take second place to the movement; the indignity of police raids in the middle of the night; the months of worry when Nelson went underground and could only meet her in disguise under elaborately executed plans; and the loneliness after Nelson's life imprisonment. Yet, despite her suffering, she emerged as a leader in her own right and as an international figure to whom foreign dignitaries, governments, and press have paid tribute.

623. Joseph, Joan. *South African Statesman: Jan Christian Smuts.* New York: Messner, 1969. 189p. Grades 8-12.

Based on his inclination as a philosopher and sensitivity to nature and romantic poetry, Smuts devised his theory of "the whole" which recognized definite patterns in nature and the unity of all created things. Joseph's very detailed and objective biography traces Smuts' attempts as a journalist, lawyer, politician, and prime minister to translate this holistic philosophy in the very real and pragmatic world of politics. Smuts' agenda to unify South Africa on the national front and the various nations of the world under the United Nations on the international front was prompted by this idealistic vision. Joseph is also quick to reveal the contradictions in Smuts' stance: He was a Boer who favored Dominion status under the British and fought against the British in the Boer War; and he opposed apartheid policies as well as believed in the consolidation of the white minority and the racial inferiority of Africans. As a result of this duality, Smuts was constantly attacked for his views at home and hailed as a prophet of humanity abroad because he was believed to have a deep political insight into world affairs.

624. Kaunda, Betty. *Betty Kaunda.* As told to and reproduced by Stephen A. Mpashi. Lusaka, Zambia: Longmans, 1969. 76p. Grades 5-7.

Wife of President Kenneth Kaunda of Zambia, Betty Kaunda narrates the story of her eventful life from her birth in 1928 to the security and comfort of life in the State House in 1966. Mrs. Kaunda very honestly recounts the minutest details of her early life as the first woman to become a teacher in her village of Mpika. As the wife of an important freedom fighter, she endured many hardships: the hours spent sitting outdoors with her children while political meetings were in progress in their small home; political rallies and boycotts; the constant struggle to find food and money for her family; and the painfully long absences and jail sentences of her husband. Through it all emerges the portrait of a strong, yet modest woman who grew into the role thrust upon her; she not only supported her husband's political aims, but became a champion of women's rights herself. The fame of being the First Lady of her country did not make her forget the value of family unity and the solidarity of community service. This is a touching autobiography that clearly demonstrates that great leaders are ordinary people who have made sacrifices and have faced challenges with courage and dignity.

625. Kristensen, Preben, and Fiona Cameron. *We Live in South Africa.* New York: Bookwright, 1985. 60p. Grades 5-8.

Judging by the twenty-six personal portraits in this book, South Africa would appear to be a country of immense opportunities and happiness for its citizens. The subjects represent the country's multiracial population and a cross-section of professions from archeologist and architect to housemaid and spiritualist. The portraits are convincing because they are first person interviews accompanied by superb color photographs by Kristensen. Hence, a very positive image of life for all--the Zulu maid, the Malayan architectural restorer, the Indian trader, the black township student, the white police officer, the black gold miner, and the white hotelier--is projected. While the facts of separate development in housing, businesses, and education are occasionally stated, the overall tone is one of success. In only two portraits--those of the former mayor of Durban and a minister of the Dutch Reformed Church--have serious political matters like poverty, racial integration, voting rights for the black majority, and public responsibility to create a better life for all South Africans been mentioned at all.

626. Kumalo, Alf, and Es'Kia Mphahlele. *Mandela: Echoes of an Era.* New York: Penguin, 1990. 160p. Grades 8-12.

This book, published on the occasion of Nelson Mandela's release from life imprisonment, celebrates Mandela's life and achievements. As author, professor, and freedom fighter, Mphahlele's forceful prose traces the history of the various antigovernment organizations and the leadership of Mandela, Walter Sisulu, Oliver Tembo, Steve Biko, and Winnie Mandela. He also describes the development of Mandela's political philosophy from the politics of accommodation in the fifties with his constant contact with Indian, colored, white, and communist political movements, to armed struggle under the banner of *Umkonto we Sizwe* (Spear of the Nation) in the sixties, to his role as negotiator with President de Klerk's government. Mphahlele very eloquently describes how Mandela became a symbol of freedom and hope to his fellow South Africans even from the silence of his prison cell. He became a symbol that inspired young children to resist Bantu Education and to sacrifice their lives in Soweto; he became a symbol that fired South Africans of all races to continue the fight till victory is reached; and he became a symbol around which the international community rallied to impose sanctions against South Africa. Kumalo's photographs bear witness to the behind-the-scenes and emotional aspects of the central characters. Through rare and intimate photographs of the Mandelas, Kumalo forces readers to acknowledge their humanity and the extreme pain and sacrifice that they endured. Winnie Mandela dominates these photographs with her courage and determination to carry on after her husband's life imprisonment.

627. Lantier, Patricia, and David Winner. *Desmond Tutu: Religious Leader Devoted to Freedom.* People Who Made A Difference Series. Milwaukee: Gareth Steven's Children's Books, 1991. 68p. Grades 3-5.
Archbishop Desmond Tutu's life and work are placed in the context of South African history and politics. The biography does not give a detailed account of the Archbishop's life, but focuses on his public service as a religious leader and civil rights fighter. Religion and politics are not mutually exclusive because, like Mahatma Gandhi and Martin Luther King, Desmond Tutu's philosophy was based on the teachings of his religion and nonviolent protest. To Tutu, nonviolence did not mean compromise with what he believed to be wrong. At a time when violent protest against the government was increasing, when black-on-black violence was on the rise, and when the government was taking drastic repressive measures against freedom fighters, Desmond Tutu remained steadfast in his belief that apartheid must end through love and peace. His concern was for the whites as victims as well, for living under apartheid had made them lose their humanity. The Archbishop's message is that if left to themselves individual people of different races generally get along well together. As an international figure, he advocated economic sanctions against his country as the only solution to bringing about peaceful change. For his service to the cause of peace, Desmond Tutu was awarded the Nobel Peace Prize in 1984.
  This biography has been adapted for young readers from David Winner's *Desmond Tutu: The Courageous and Eloquent Archbishop Struggling Against Apartheid in South Africa* (Exley, 1989). In this abbreviated version, the diction attempts to manipulate readers' reactions through repeated use of strong tone words like "terrible," "immoral," and "silly." The text is extended by quotations from Desmond Tutu and other antiapartheid advocates, photographs, and explanatory captions. Desmond Tutu emerges as a kind and loving man who is hopeful that equality and justice will triumph.

628. Makeba, Miriam, with James Hall. *Makeba: My Story.* Johannesburg: Skotaville, 1988. 249p. Grades 9-12.

Written with complete honesty and in a powerful, emotive style, this autobiography narrates the dramatic story of Makeba from childhood in a poor township in South Africa, to fame as an international singer in the late 1950s, to life as an exile in America, Europe, and Africa. Makeba's ability to recall scenes, expressions, and conversations with remarkable detail enables readers to identify with her struggles. Her life was full of personal tragedies: unhappy marriages, deaths of loved ones, exile from country and family, and struggle with cancer. She attributes her suffering and lonely life to the system of apartheid. Yet, her story is also one of great personal joy and triumph. She recalls the many cultural values that gave depth and meaning to her life: ritual initiation into womanhood, marriage customs and bride price, the *ukuthwasa* training of her mother, and the communication of the initiated *amadlozi* with the spirit world. Known variously as "Empress of African Song" and "Mama Africa," Makeba represented the music and politics of Africa to the Western world. The concert stage, her audience, and her message against the evils of apartheid constituted the perfect world for her. She made friends with world figures like President Kennedy, participated in the independence ceremonies of several African nations, and addressed the UN General Assembly and a UN Special Committee on apartheid. However, despite the fame and stardom, there was sorrow and loneliness for the land and people she was forced to leave behind. In the 1960s, she became a victim of white racism in America, and she settled in Guinea at the invitation of President Toure. In her search for peace, Makeba overcame one crisis after another with hope, determination, and song.

629. Mandela, Nelson. *No Easy Walk to Freedom.* Foreword by Ruth First. Introduction by Oliver Tembo. African Writers Series. London, Ibadan and Nairobi: Heinemann, 1965, 1973. 189p. Grades 8-adult.

This book commemorates ten years of Nelson Mandela's imprisonment on Robben Island. Eleven articles, one conference speech made while abroad, and evidence and addresses in court, including those at the Treason Trial and Rivonia Trial--a period spanning ten years from 1953 to 1963--have been reproduced here with a minimum of editing. Banned from speaking publicly, Mandela used his pen to spread his revolutionary message and to express his views on the Bantu Education Bill and Bantustan policy, impact of apartheid on black South Africans, labor problems, tactics to fight apartheid, civil disobedience, and the African National Congress. The introductory notes preceding each section serve to establish the historical, social, political, and personal contexts of Mandela's writings.

The Struggle is My Life (1978, 1986), another compilation of Mandela's major speeches and writings up to the year 1985 was published by the International Defense and Aid Fund for Southern Africa. This book also contains other documents relating to the South African struggle for liberation such as the ANC Youth League

Manifesto, the ANC Programme of Action, and the Freedom Charter. An introductory essay and memoirs of fellow prisoners on Robben Island further emphasize Mandela's central role in the freedom movement and his lifelong commitment to it.

630. Mandela, Winnie. *Part Of My Soul Went With Him.* Edited by Anne Benjamin and adapted by Mary Benson. New York and London: Norton, 1985. Originally published in 1984 by Rowohlt Taschenbuch Verlag, Hamburg. 164p. Grades 10-12.

This unconventional autobiography is a collection of Anne Benjamin's interviews with Winnie Mandela and her family and friends, correspondence between Winnie and Nelson Mandela, letters of family and friends, and tributes by Bishop Manas Buthelezi, Dr. Motlana, and others. This vast material has been arranged thematically to trace the life and achievements of Winnie Mandela. Where information vital to the story is not covered--such as the details of trials and lawsuits, account of the Soweto uprising, background and work of Nelson Mandela, and historical facts--the editor has provided the information in italics so that a continuous story can emerge. This extensive research, conducted under the existing political conditions and banning orders in South Africa, is a heroic achievement in itself. In her Introduction, Benjamin states that the purpose of her interviews was to find out what gave Winnie--the woman, mother, and political leader--the strength to bear what she had borne: living under a ban for the greater part of her adult life, countless arrests and imprisonment, even when she was pregnant, cross examination and torture, lack of privacy, and separation from husband, children, and family.

The emerging portrait is that of a forceful, proud, courageous, dignified, vital, selfless, and utterly human individual who was willing to sacrifice her life and happiness for the ultimate joy of seeing her country free of racism. The "autobiography" begins with Mandela's banishment to Brandfort, where she responded to the appalling conditions in the homeland by politicizing the blacks, so that instead of being forgotten, Mandela emerged as a national and international leader in her own right. Winnie provides a touching account of her married life; of Nelson's warning that she would be blamed for his life imprisonment; of her disappointment at not being able to take her daughters to school; of the indignity of having policemen enter her bedroom; of her total despair during the first few days of her solitary confinement; of her many visits to Robben Island; and of her helplessness in causing her friends and well-wishers trouble by the police. Reading this account is a powerful, emotional experience. Yet, Mandela does not feel sorry for herself. With objectivity and ironic detachment, she describes her bitter moments and humiliation. She is also conscious of becoming her own individual, instead of a carbon copy of Nelson Mandela, especially after the Soweto riots. This phenomenon is understood in the context of a black woman struggling in a male-dominated, racist society.

631. Mathabane, Mark. *Kaffir Boy*. New York: Signet, 1986. Originally published by Macmillan. 406p. Grades 10-adult.

This heartwrenching autobiography provides an insider's account of life in Alexandra, a black shantytown of Johannesburg. Beginning with his earliest memories at the age of five, Mathabane meticulously describes the life of his family: grinding poverty and hunger; back-to-back police raids when he was beaten and his mother and father dragged half naked into police vans because their pass books were not in order; unemployment and alcoholism; police brutality and street gangs; and daily reminders of their fourth-class citizenship. The resulting fear, frustration, pain, hate, bitterness, and anger distorted their lives as they strove to survive under these circumstances. It was a life that drove the young Mathabane to near suicide. *Kaffir Boy* is also the story of Mathabane's parents' heroic struggle to provide their children with a semblance of security and family life. A turning point in Mathabane's life came when his grandmother's white employer started to encourage him with books. Thus began a long association with white liberals who helped him with his education and his skill at tennis, that all-white sport. Mathabane was determined to escape from the clutches of apartheid by going to America, his Promised Land. With faith and determination, he dodged the system to train at a white club and to play in national and international tournaments. His dream was finally realized in 1979 when, with the help of tennis player Stan Smith, he won a tennis scholarship to an American university.

This autobiography is Mathabane's tool for exposing the racism and injustice in his country. He offers a double vision: he relives his experiences in Alexandria and provides an objective analysis and understanding of the effects of apartheid on blacks. *Kaffir Boy* is also a hopeful story that reminds readers that there are kind, loving people in South Africa--both black and white--who can rise above their environment to take a stand for a fellow human being and for the truth.

632. Meltzer, Milton. *Winnie Mandela: The Soul of South Africa*. Illustrated by Stephen Marchesi. New York: Puffin, 1987. Originally published in 1986 by Viking Penguin. 54p. Grades 3-6.

Based on *Part Of My Soul Went With Him* (see # 630), Meltzer traces Winnie Mandela's struggle for equal rights from her childhood in Bizana where she learned the "true" history of her people from her father, to her being drawn into the center of the freedom struggle upon meeting and marrying Nelson Mandela, to her maturation as a political leader after her husband's life imprisonment. Meltzer neither shelters young readers from the realities of apartheid, nor presents his subject as a born hero. Winnie Mandela is portrayed as a very human individual who relied on the help of others, who experienced loneliness and guilt as a mother, and who gave in to outbursts of anger and belligerency, especially when she was accosted by the policemen who watched her day and night. Quotations from Mandela's interviews allow readers to experience firsthand her gutsy nature, pride and strength, and commitment to the cause. Despite the serious subject matter, Meltzer writes an interesting story. Dramatization of key events like Winnie's banishment to Brandfort, Nelson Mandela's visit disguised as a chauffeur, and Winnie's first days in solitary confinement hold readers' interest and reveal the personality of the subject.

632a. Rogers, Barbara Radcliffe. *South Africa.* Photographs by Stillman Rogers. Children of the World Series. Milwaukee: Gareth Stevens, 1991. 64p. Grades 3-5.

Living conditions under apartheid are described through the experiences of Tumi, a twelve-year-old black girl who lives in a small room in Soweto with her mother. Text and color photographs follow Tumi through a typical school day from the time she wakes up and prepares for school, to work and play at school, to homework, shopping, and cooking after returning home. Tumi is a happy child who has a good relationship with her mother, enjoys treats on special occasions, and has dreams and aspirations for her future. The account ends on a hopeful note as Tumi is the first generation to grow up in a new South Africa that has started to relax laws that separate people according to skin color. Rogers portrays a positive picture of life under apartheid. While all the harsh facts are omitted, he admits that the lives of people in South Africa may vary according to their economic, ethnic, and environmental circumstances. A comprehensive reference section includes information on South Africa's history, geography, major cities, government, linguistic and cultural diversity, industries and natural resources, education, religion, arts and crafts, and sports and recreation. Maps, glossary of terms, suggestions for further reading, and research projects and activities are also included.

633. Stanley, Diane, and Peter Vennema. *Shaka, King of the Zulus.* Illustrated by Diane Stanley. New York: Morrow, 1988. N.p. Grades 1-4.

A simple text and full-color illustrations narrate the story of Shaka's meteoric rise to fame from his humble birth in 1787, to becoming the chief of the Zulus, to violent death in 1828. The authors focus on key events in Shaka's life to reveal his complex personality and remarkable achievements. His boyhood rejection by his father and the taunts of his age-mates led to brooding and bitterness, while the protection of Chief Dingiswayo, king of the powerful Mtetwa nation, gave him self-confidence and an opportunity to develop his skills as a warrior. Shaka's sharp intellect and single-minded devotion to a goal are apparent in the innovations he introduced in weaponry, training and organization of the army, and campaign strategies. In just ten years as chief of the Zulus, he was able to amass great wealth and extend his tiny clan into a mighty empire. Shaka is presented as a three-dimensional character with both positive and negative qualities. Although he ruled through force and fear, he could be remarkably emotional and friendly as with his mother, Nandi, and the Englishman Henry Francis Fynn. Today, six million Zulus remember Shaka with pride, and historians acknowledge his military genius by comparing him to Napoleon, Julius Caesar, and Alexander the Great.

Another notable biography for children in grades three through five is Richard Woolley's *Shaka, King of the Zulu* (Longman, 1973). In giving a detailed account of Shaka's cruelty toward his enemies and countrymen, Woolley states that Shaka was prompted by revenge, disgust for witchcraft and superstition, and, eventually, madness. The biography ends with the legend of hyenas circling Shaka's dead body and the sacrifice of Pampata, his lover.

634. Sweetman, David. *Queen Nzinga: The Woman Who Saved Her People*. Makers of African History Series. London: Longman, 1971. 40p. Grades 4-6.

The destiny of Queen Nzinga (1582-1663) is also the history of the Mbundus' resistance to the Portuguese colonization of Angola. Beginning with Nzinga's birth to Ngola Kiluanji, Sweetman presents a simple yet lively narration of significant episodes from Nzinga's life that establish her as a proud and confident ruler, brave warrior and strategist, and clever and wise diplomat. Despite the hardships and defeats, the biography emphasizes Nzinga's heroic fight to free her country. A more recent biography detailing the story of this brave African queen is Ramla Bandele's *Nzinga* (Third World Press, 1992).

635. Tutu, Desmond Mpilo. *Hope and Suffering: Sermons and Speeches*. Compiled by Mothobi Mutloatse. Edited by John Webster. Grand Rapids, MI: William B. Eerdmans, 1984. 189p. Grades 8-12.

Like Mahatma Gandhi and Martin Luther King, Desmond Tutu's compassionate ministry has the courage to speak against an immoral government and social system. His involvement in politics aims to bring about a new social order built on the foundations of equality and justice. His speeches, sermons, and letters analyze the social, political, historical, and economic conditions of blacks in South Africa. This material is grouped under four chapters. "Introducing South Africa" begins with a moving appeal in 1976 to Prime Minister Vorster to abolish pass laws, unlawful detention, and minority rule as mass scale violence may erupt if matters are not rectified constitutionally and fast. He summarizes the history of the coming of the white man to South Africa and the whites' interpretation of facts to suit their own needs. In "Liberation as a Biblical Theme," the Biblical story of Exodus is compared to conditions in South Africa. Like Moses, Tutu feels he has been called upon to pull his people out of despair and suffering and to lead them to freedom. The motif of liberation is extended to the New Testament, and Jesus is looked upon as a second liberator who came to release people from their sins and immoral tendencies. "Current Concerns" outlines the political history of South Africa under apartheid and discriminatory legislation of Race Classification, Job Reservation, Mixed Marriages, Immorality, and Bantustan Policy. Archbishop Tutu also condemns the policies of the Reagan administration for supporting apartheid and the U.S. for being appeased by the empty antiracist rhetoric of Mr. Botha. Finally, in "The Divine Intention," Tutu justifies his own involvement in politics and defines the role of the South African Council of Churches in bringing about a just society in South Africa. Once again, looking to the example of Jesus, he exhorts both blacks and whites to condemn the racial policies of apartheid and to engage in the struggle. Since this book was published, Archbishop Tutu's urgent demand for a peaceful settlement and a nonracial, democratic alternative to apartheid is becoming a reality.

636. Vail, John. *Nelson and Winnie Mandela*. World Leaders Past & Present Series. New York: Chelsea House, 1989. 111p. Grades 6-12.
The lives of Nelson and Winnie Mandela are seen from the perspective of their service to the cause of freedom in South Africa. The first six chapters focus on Nelson Mandela's life, his involvement in the African National Congress under the guidance of Walter Sisulu and Albert Luthuli, his radical change in political ideology from nonviolence to sabotage, and his life imprisonment for treason against the government. Chapters seven through ten focus on Winnie Mandela's emerging role as "Mother of the Country," as well as the movements started by Desmond Tutu and Steve Biko and the role of schoolchildren in denouncing the government's educational policy. Both Nelson and Winnie Mandela, despite the long years of separation, continued to provide sustenance and hope for each other, knowing that their sacrifice would eventually result in freedom.
This is a well-researched biography with photographs, explanatory captions, and quotations that extend the text and provide insight into the personal lives of the Mandelas. This biography, in particular, stresses the multiracial base of the struggle in South Africa by outlining the activities of organizations such as the Indian Congress-- founded in 1894 by Mohandas K. Gandhi--under leaders like Ismail Meer and Yusuf Dadoo; the Communist Party; and the United Democratic Front, a multiracial alliance of more than six hundred antiapartheid organizations. Even in 1984, when the government proposed the tricameral parliament, 80 percent of the colored and Indian population boycotted the election. Vail concludes by emphasizing the effectiveness of international pressure and economic sanctions against the South African government.

637. Van der Post, Laurens. *The Lost World of the Kalahari*. New York: Morrow, 1958. 279p. Grades 8-12.
This discussion of the physical features, history, lifestyle, and religious beliefs of the Bushmen (San) is based on the author's personal experiences. This is neither an anthropological treatise nor a reporter-like account; rather, it is an intensely private spiritual journey in fulfillment of a childhood quest. As a child, Van der Post had sensed that the very soil of his beloved South Africa was mourning the loss of the Bushmen and he had vowed to search for any remaining groups in the Kalahari Desert. As an adult, he took a team of explorers to visit the sacred rock paintings at Slippery Hills, where he communed with the spirits and "discovered" an authentic

Bushmen camp in the Kalahari interior. Van der Post's extended stay with the group provided him the opportunity to participate in and observe the daily activities of hunting, "sipping" water, family life, festivities, and affinity with nature. In his interpretation of South African history, he sympathetically portrays the extermination of the Bushmen. He sees Bushmen life and culture as being mystically connected with the soil and spirit of Africa.

638. Vyas, Chiman L. *Flight of the Eagle*. Lusaka, Zambia: National Educational Company of Zambia, 1970. 58p. Grades 8-10.
This objective analysis of the public life of Dr. Kenneth David Kaunda, first president of the Republic of Zambia, is viewed against the background of the Zambian struggle for independence. Based on interviews with Kaunda's associates and information gathered from archival sources and offices of the political parties, Vyas traces the fulfillment of Kaunda's lifelong objective--the liberation of his country and people. Vyas further illustrates that in working toward this goal Kaunda was governed by the principles of national unity, nonracialism, fair play and rule of reason, humanitarian service, preciousness of political freedom, and unity of all Africa. Photographs, excerpts from Kaunda's speeches, and a reading list are included.

639. Wepman, Dennis. *Desmond Tutu*. Impact Biographies Series. London: Franklin Watts, 1989. 157p. Grades 7-9.
This powerful biography portrays Archbishop Tutu as the conscience of his nation and as an example to the world of courage and faith. Beginning with Desmond Tutu's relatively comfortable childhood as the son of a well-respected teacher, Wepman traces his educational career, service to the community as priest, political protest, and role as international celebrity. The account especially emphasizes his involvement with politics at each stage of his life. Although sensitive to the inferior status relegated to blacks in South Africa, Desmond Tutu's contacts with whites were not all unpleasant. In fact, two shaping influences in his life were the Blaxalls who ran South Africa's first blind school for blacks and Father Trevor Huddleston, an Anglican priest who came from England in 1943 to fight against apartheid. Criticized by many for using the altar as a political platform, Desmond Tutu maintained that like the Biblical figures Isaiah, Elijah, Nathan, Jesus, and the Apostles protest against an immoral authority was in the best Christian tradition. Extensive quotations from Tutu's speeches, letters, sermons, and conversations establish his loving and caring nature, his steadfast dedication to the cause of justice, and his effervescent humor.

640. Woods, Donald. *Biko*. New York and London: Paddington, 1978. 288p. Grades 10-12.
Written as a reaction of outrage on the death of Steven Biko, this biography by Woods, a friend and admirer of Biko, was smuggled chapter by chapter out of South Africa to reveal to the world the

atrocities committed against Biko and the horrors of living in a police state. Biko, leader of the Black Consciousness Movement, died on September 12, 1977 on the floor of a prison cell after suffering torture and torment at the hands of officials and captors. Woods' boldness in investigating the circumstances of Biko's death, giving speeches to audiences throughout South Africa, and writing antigovernment editorials for his newspaper, *Daily Dispatch*, resulted in his banning order and, ultimately, voluntary exile from his country.

Using a variety of prose forms--biography, autobiography, personal anecdotes of friendship with Biko, memorials, newspaper articles, transcript of Biko's defense of nine Black Consciousness leaders in the 1976 court trial, interviews, and the lengthy inquest hearings lasting thirteen days--Woods conveys at once a passionate, analytical, and bitter account of the life of Biko and the economic, psychic, and legislative oppression of blacks. Biko is portrayed as an intelligent, charismatic, courageous, articulate, and sensitive human being who was dedicated to his principles. Initially, as a white liberal, Woods had resented the exclusion of whites from the Black Consciousness Movement and the inclusion of race as a determining factor in political thinking, but his many interviews and discussions with Biko led to a clearer understanding of Biko's political ideology. Far from being a racist or a violent man, Biko was a moderate in politics who wanted to break the psychological chains binding black South Africans, so that they could gain group power through pride, self-esteem, and identity. The account ends with a scathing indictment of the Nationalist government that first breeds an immoral system in which an innocent man is murdered and then exonerates his killers. Woods sees Biko's death as a symbolic representation of the suffering of all black South Africans under apartheid. Whether the death is physical, as in the case of Biko and thousands of others, or spiritual due to loss of pride, hope, and morale, as in the case of millions, Woods hopes this book will raise the consciousness of people worldwide. *Cry Freedom,* a motion picture, is partially based on this book and Woods' autobiography.

641. Worth, Richard. *Robert Mugabe of Zimbabwe.* In Focus Biographies. New York: Messner, 1990. 111p. Grades 7-12.

The history of Zimbabwe and the story of Robert Mugabe, Zimbabwe's complex and contradictory president, are deftly interwoven to recount the efforts of black nationalists like Nkomo, Muzorewa, and Sithole to gain freedom and build a strong and independent nation. Although trained as a teacher, the nationalist struggle drew Mugabe into the cause and he became one of its strongest and most radical supporters. As leader of the Zimbabwe African National Union (ZANU), he was successful in insisting on majority rule, which Ian Smith was ultimately pressured to accept. As the one responsible for the development of modern Zimbabwe, Mugabe improved the social lives of blacks through reforms in health care, education, and women's rights, but he abandoned his vow to control the economy by seizing white farms and redistributing them to the landless. Instead, he developed an economic policy that satisfied blacks and whites and made Zimbabwe an African success story. He championed capitalism and free enterprise by allowing white farmers and industrialists to run their businesses, with the result that today Zimbabwe produces sufficient food and has a successful and diverse industrial output. Mugabe took a forthright and result-oriented stand in all his policies, including creative measures to preserve wildlife. The most controversial aspect of his public life was in the area of internal politics and his rivalry with Joshua Nkomo, leader of the opposing Zimbabwe African People's Union (ZAPU). Mugabe and his government faced the enormous problems of bitter conflict with Nkomo; a rapidly growing population; and rising unemployment and poverty. Worth leaves readers with the questions: Will Mugabe's one-party government make him more dictatorial? How will he handle this power? Will he be able to resolve these problems in the 1990s? Black-and-white photographs, a time line, glossary of terms, and bibliography supplement the text.

INFORMATIONAL BOOKS

642. Barnes-Svarney, Patricia. *Zimbabwe*. Places and Peoples of the World Series. New York: Chelsea House, 1989. 128p. Grades 5-8.

After giving an in-depth account of Zimbabwe's geography, natural wonders, and resources, the author traces the history and development of modern Zimbabwe from Stone Age ancestors, to the Bantu civilization at Great Zimbabwe, to European imperialism and majority rule. The book provides an objective account of colonial rule. By 1888, attracted by Shona gold, the Rudd Concession succeeded in tricking King Lobengula into signing off all mining rights to the British South Africa Company. The settlers soon established themselves in Rhodesia, named in honor of Cecil Rhodes, with large farms and mining permits, while Africans were deprived of their land and pushed into reserves, generally in the least desirable locations. From the onset of colonization, the Shona and Ndebele fought for their freedom and representation. However, it was economic sanctions, international pressure, civil unrest, and emig-ration of whites that forced Ian Smith's government to agree to the principle of majority rule in 1971. Africans continued to revolt under the leadership of a variety of organizations like Zimbabwe African People's Union (ZAPU) and Zimbabwe African National Union (ZANU) till Robert Mugabe came to power in 1979, ending the fifteen-year struggle which had cost more than 27,000 lives. In 1980, Rhodesia, now called Zimbabwe, became fully independent with a parliamentary government.

Barnes-Svarney also outlines the daunting problems of education, jobs, economy, health, and adequate nutrition facing the new nation.

With its dependence on South Africa for mining and trade; difficulties in attracting foreign investments because of its socialist schemes; and ethnic rivalries between the Shona and Ndebele, Zimbabwe has survived a difficult first decade of independence. Separate chapters also provide information on the cultural aspects of Zimbabwe: major languages, family life, urban and rural life, and artistic expression through literature, sculpture, and music.

643. Bleeker, Sonia. *The Zulu of South Africa: Cattlemen, Farmers and Warriors*. Illustrated by Kisa N. Sasaki. New York: Morrow, 1970. 160p. Grades 5-7.

Bleeker surveys the history, family life, customs, religious beliefs, agricultural and hunting economy, and social and political systems of the Zulus. She states that the strength of Zulu society was based on family homesteads, or kraals, which were characterized by self-sufficiency and mutual support within the kinship groups. All aspects of their lives--upbringing of boys and girls, initiation ceremonies, marriage and *lobola* (gift), household chores, sitting arrangements, food rituals, and funerals--were strictly prescribed by social tradition to show respect for nature and the community. Bleeker frequently refers to Nguni legends to depict the living connection between oral traditions and social customs. Belief in a supreme creator and supernatural beings, including ancestors is explained respectfully.

In discussing Zulu territorial expansion, Bleeker sees the Zulus as conquerors with an efficient and well-disciplined army. Far from being war-mongering and cruel, Zulu love for peace is recorded in a legend of their ancestors who declared a truce with their enemy, the Lozi nation, in an elaborate and costly ceremony. Bleeker's sympathetic treatment is most evident in her account of King Shaka, who is portrayed as a great warrior-king, military strategist, and army commander. Like Napoleon, Shaka fulfilled his personal ambitions by uniting the Zulus and forging a great empire that extended over half of present-day South Africa. Once his ambition was achieved, Shaka sought solitude and peace. The last chapter on the coming of the Europeans and the decline of the Zulu empire is sketchy and outdated. Bleeker points out the oppressive apartheid system that has deprived Zulus of their homeland, independence, and traditional life. Illustrations portray details of living conditions and culture.

644. Brickhill, Joan. *South Africa: The End of Apartheid?* Hotspots Series. New York: Gloucester, 1991. 36p. Grades 4-8.

Four chapters give a fairly detailed account of the early history of South Africa and the foundation of apartheid; establishment of an apartheid state; resistance by numerous antiapartheid groups and violent repression by the government; and dismantling apartheid. Chapter 4 provides information on President de Klerk's efforts to remove certain obvious aspects of apartheid such as pass laws and the Separate Amenities Act; unbanning of political organizations; and release of political prisoners like Nelson Mandela. However, Brickhill points out that the basic structure of white superiority remains intact.

While it is accepted that apartheid will be dismantled, Brickhill outlines the challenges facing a postapartheid South Africa: weak economy due to high inflation and international sanctions; increasing white opposition in the form of neo-Nazis and right-wing extremists; and increasing ethnic tensions and violence in the townships, especially by the Inkatha Party led by Gatsha Buthelezi, which many believe is incited by police collusion. Maps, charts, photographs, list of facts, chronology, and glossary make the salient information accessible for quick reference.

645. Carpenter, John Allan, and Tom Balow. *Botswana.* Enchantment of Africa Series. Chicago: Children's Press, 1973. 94p. Grades 6-8.

The land and natural resources, history and government, economy and industry, and peoples and social conditions of Botswana are discussed with an emphasis on the dignity and pride of its people. As a protectorate of Great Britain, Botswana's leaders pressed for political autonomy and protection from South Africa. Independence in 1966 saw a democratic, judicial, educational, and agricultural infrastructure already in place which facilitated the young nation's future progress. As a landlocked country dependent on its four bordering neighbors for trade with and travel to the rest of the world, Botswana has pursued a neutral foreign policy for peace and economic success.

646. Chan, Stephen. *Southern Africa: The Lands and Their People.* Silver Burdett Countries Series. Englewood Cliffs, NJ: Silver Burdett, 1988. Originally published in 1988 by Macdonald. 43p. Grades 4-6.

Text and photographs outline the early history, colonial rule and independence, languages and peoples, and geography and transportation of the ten nations in Southern Africa. A special emphasis is placed on South Africa's economic and military actions to weaken and punish the eight neighboring independent nations and to keep mineral rich Namibia as its colony. South Africa is successful because it uses its military to curb the resistance groups against apartheid that are based in neighboring countries; controls the shipping routes on the Cape that are vital to Western trade; produces a very large percentage of the minerals needed by Western industry; and propagates fear of communism even though Southern African nations maintain that democracy and racial equality are most important considerations. In addition, the newly independent nations are dependent on South Africa economically. Chan also outlines the efforts of Southern African nations to unite under the auspices of Southern African Development Coordination Conference (SADCC), formed in 1976 to provide coordinated development, economic cooperation, and improved transportation in order to reduce their dependence on the racist government of South Africa. Chan insists that development of agriculture, small health clinics in rural areas, primary and secondary schools in small towns and villages, and the mining industry are imperative if Southern Africa is to become self-sufficient and strong.

647. Cheney, Patricia. *The Land and People of Zimbabwe.* Portraits of the Nations Series. New York: Lippincott, 1990. 242p. Grades 7-10.

Like Barnes-Svarney (see # 642), Cheney provides information on the geography, history, culture, and problems of Zimbabwe. However, Cheney's account of the history of Zimbabwe is more detailed and generally more sympathetic to blacks. She gives a step-by-step analysis of how Africans were divested of their land, traditional means of livelihood, and political rights under the racist white regime. As in South Africa, blacks had to register for passes to travel to their jobs in white towns. The above information is not presented in a dry or boring manner; rather, Cheney draws readers into the material by beginning each chapter from the perspective of a specific individual and extending the text with supplementary information on a leader, custom, or political fact. For example, the chapter on independent Zimbabwe includes insets on Mapfire College, a school that combines academic subjects with vocational skills; becoming a *n'anga,* or a healing spirit; witchcraft; life for workers on white farms; the judicial system; and women and the law.

Another book that presents the above information in a readable manner is Jason Laure's *Zimbabwe* (Children's Press, 1988) in the Enchantment of the World Series. Laure provides an interesting account of Zimbabwean culture as reflected in its sculpture, music, and literature; marriage and family life; and traditional religion.

648. English, Peter. *South Africa in Pictures.* Rev. ed. Visual Geography Series. New York: Sterling, 1975. 64p. Grades 4-6.

In presenting the history, government, people, and economy of South Africa, English betrays a racist attitude through misrepresentation and omission of facts, perpetuation of historical myths, and use of derogatory terms. Transkei is discussed as a model example of an independent state that has made political progress by reestablishing traditional systems of government and tribal lifestyle. English does not acknowledge that blacks have no place in the democratic process and that they are governed by the Department of Bantu Administration and Development. He states that Bantus "resist efforts" to introduce better farming and agricultural methods, but fails to mention that Bantu reserves are in arid and least productive areas of the country. Furthermore, he states that industrial development and factories are financed by the government on the edge of Bantu reserves, supposedly for the benefit of blacks, but, again, he fails to mention that in actuality this scheme is intended to draw cheap labor. The formation of these reservations or homelands is defended on the grounds that blacks have never been a homogeneous group, that the Bantus cannot be Europeanized, and that whites must rule otherwise one or two groups will dominate the government. In discussing urban life, there is no mention of the harsh realities of daily travel to work, poor living conditions, lack of choice in where blacks can live, and restricted movement because of pass laws. English states that Bantus have better educational opportunities, health services, and standard of living than anywhere else in Africa, but he does not discuss the discrepancy between the education, wages, and health and nutrition of blacks and whites. The photographs ensure the impression that blacks are a primitive and tribal people who cannot blend with the more "civilized" whites.

Another racist book that is freely available in libraries is *Let's Visit South Africa* (Burke, 1967, 1974, 1984) by Bernard Newman. It perpetuates the notion that white supremacy and the apartheid system are logical responses to the conditions in South Africa. While the objections of Africans to pass laws, the Bantustan policy, disparity between the wages and education of whites and blacks, and cheap African labor are mentioned, Newman falsifies the information through oversimplification and omission of vital facts.

649. Evans, Michael.   *South Africa.*   Illustrated by Ron Hayward Associates. Issues Series. New York: Gloucester, 1988. Originally published in 1987 by Aladdin. 32p. Grades 3-6.

The issue of racial discrimination in South Africa is faced head-on in both text and illustrations. Each two-page spread addresses a single aspect of the problem such as historical roots of racial segregation, apartheid policy, homelands and townships, education, jobs, everyday life, African National Congress, role of the church, sanctions, and reforms and reactions. While much has happened in South Africa since this book was published, it is nevertheless valuable for its direct and honest treatment of each topic and its presentation of relevant facts and statistics. It also explains why effective economic sanctions by Western powers and frontline African nations are not being imposed. The photographs, charts, and maps provide supporting information and lend a visual dimension to the book.

650. Gould, D. E. *Namibia.* Places and Peoples of the World Series. New York: Chelsea House, 1988. 96p. Grades 5-8.

Namibia is presented as a country characterized by endless struggle as a way of life: struggle against the harsh desert and semi-desert environment; struggle among the numerous indigenous groups like the Ovambo, Kackolanders, Kavangos, Herero-speaking Himbi people, San, Khoi Khoi, Bergdama, and Namas; and struggle for power between European colonists and Namibian freedom fighters. In outlining the source of these problems, Gould explains that Namibia's rich diamond, copper, uranium, and mineral deposits attracted first the Germans and then the British and South Africans. The resulting suppression of Namibians led to the disintegration of their families, tribes, and entire social structure. Small reservations were marked out for Namibians and, as in South Africa and Rhodesia, they became the source of semi-skilled and unskilled labor. From 1921, Nambia was administered by South Africa on behalf of the League of Nations; however, because of South Africa's apartheid policy, the United Nations Organization and prominent Western and African nations tried repeatedly to pressure South Africa into granting independence to Namibia. South Africa illegally continued to treat Namibia as a colony and a source of its wealth. The struggle for independence by freedom fighters and the South West African People's Organization (SWAPO), financial and military assistance by frontline states, and international negotiations proved unsuccessful.

This is an excellent introductory book on Namibia. However, while sufficient information is provided on the problems of modern farming and fishing, industrial development, and opportunities for tourism, notably absent is a discussion of human suffering due to inadequate medical care, education, health, and nutrition of the majority population. (Namibia became an independent country in 1992.)

651. Harris, Sarah. *Timeline: South Africa.* Weighing up the Evidence Series. London: Dryad, 1988. 64p. Grades 8-10.

This is a simple yet incisive analysis of historical events and processes from before the arrival of Europeans in South Africa to the 1986 declaration of the State of Emergency, which imposed severe restrictions on the press and stripped citizens of their basic legal rights. In explaining events from their religious, economic, social, and psychological contexts, Harris does not attempt to justify apartheid as moral; rather, she makes a conscious effort to present history from the perspectives of both black and white South Africans. This account is by no means exhaustive--and some might even consider it sketchy. However, the Book List and Sources section will enable young readers to explore the issues presented in greater detail.

652. Hayward, Jean. *South Africa Since 1948.* Witness History Series. New York: Bookwright, 1989. 63p. Grades 6-8.

This is a detailed and scholarly account of the politics and government of South Africa from 1948 to the 1980s. Hayward discusses the issues involved in five chapters: Struggle for Power, Advent of Apartheid, Resistance and Repression, Foreign Relations, and Clouded Future. The book provides an especially in-depth treatment of education, pass laws, migrant labor, historical connections with Mozambique and Namibia, and Botha's gestures toward reform. Hayward concludes that the problem in South Africa is not a clear-cut black versus white situation because of the varying tactics used by black resistance groups, intertribal differences and violence among blacks, tension between blacks and Asians, and the division among whites. In recent years, there has been an increase in right-wing parties on the one hand, and more whites opposing government policies by either leaving the country or struggling to change the system from within, on the other hand. In addition to numerous maps and photographs, the book includes a list of leading figures, important dates, glossary, and suggestions for further reading.

653. Holmes, Timothy. *Zambia.* Places and Peoples of the World Series. New York: Chelsea House, 1988. 96p. Grades 4-7.

Zambia's history and government, commerce and industry, and peoples and culture are examined with relation to its geographical position in southcentral Africa. Although a landlocked country,

Zambia has been linked historically to the outside world by being in the path of migrating Bantus and southern "tribes," trade routes that connected the east and west coasts of Africa, and trade in copper, ivory, and slaves with the Portuguese, Arabs, Chinese, Indians, and others. With European exploration, Zambia became the focal point of Livingstone's journeys on foot across the length and breadth of Central and East Africa; Cecil John Rhodes' search for gold and diamonds; and the British settlers' choice for a likely colony. Holmes frankly discusses how the color bar touched every aspect of the Zambians' lives under colonial rule: jobs, salaries, marriages, schooling, where to live, and where to shop. The Central African Federation, whose slogan was partnership between black and white, was actually formed to strengthen Northern and Southern Rhodesia and Nyasaland (Malawi). Under organizations such as the African National Congress, Zambia African National Congress, and United National Independence Party, Zambia led a mostly nonviolent struggle to end the federation and ultimately gain independence in 1964 with Dr. Kenneth Kaunda as president.

By following the journey of three rivers--Zambezi, Luangwa, and Chambeshi--Holmes describes major towns and cities, parks and wildlife, peoples and cultures, and mineral resources in present-day Zambia. Above all, the book emphasizes that despite its problems, Zambia has followed a humanitarian policy in assisting its neighbors (Angola, Mozambique, Namibia, Rhodesia, and South Africa) in their fight against white minority rule and a national policy of strengthening its political and economic freedom.

654. Jacobsen, Karen. *South Africa.*   A New True Book. Chicago: Children's Press, 1989. 48p. Grades K-3.
South Africa's history, geography, peoples, government, economy, education, and antiapartheid movement are presented with lower elementary children in mind. The systematic manner in which the four racial groups--Asian, black, colored, and white--are separated in the areas of housing, social life, education, and jobs is also clearly explained. Photographs and maps portray the physical beauty of the country and the stark contrast between the living conditions in white areas and in the townships and homelands designated for other racial groups. Jacobsen makes readers think about the future of South Africa and equal rights for all.

Jacobsen's *Zimbabwe* (Children's Press, 1990) presents an equally fair portrait of the land, history, government, peoples and culture, and current conditions in Zimbabwe for younger readers.

655. James, R. S. *Mozambique.*   Places and Peoples of the World Series. New York: Chelsea House, 1988. 103p. Grades 7-9.
In discussing the land, history, government, economy, and peoples, James sees Mozambique as a troubled land with many problems. Being at the crossroads of travelers and traders from the African interior, Arabia, India, Southeast Asia, and Europe, Mozambique was the seat of great empires like Mutapa and Rozwi, but its territory and

resources also became the target of exploiters and colonists. Beginning with the Arabs in the eighth century A.D. and the Portuguese takeover in the sixteenth century, Mozambique was exploited for slaves, gold, and ivory, and for five hundred years it remained a Portuguese colony. Mozambicans were forced to work on large cash crop plantations owned by the Portuguese and were forbidden to herd or plant. Hence, they were dependent on the colonial government for consumer goods as well as food. Mozambique became an independent nation in 1975 after a decade of fighting, and the Frelimo party established a socialist government based on the Soviet model.

James points out that the transition from colony to independent nation was not smooth: the infrastructure was in shambles when all but fifteen thousand Portuguese administrators, technicians, and medical personnel left Mozambique; buildings, food, medicine, and machinery were destroyed by the retreating Portuguese; continual guerrilla warfare with the armed opposition party called Renamo; and lack of industrial and economic development which led the country to declare bankruptcy in 1984. Agriculture, which still accounts for 40 percent of the total economic production, suffered due to drought and famine. Despite these problems, Mozambique followed a bold policy of Africanization at home and in its foreign policy. It supported nationalist movements in Rhodesia, Namibia, and South Africa.

The above analysis is an objective one, but it is fair to state that when discussing early Portuguese explorations in Mozambique, James repeatedly mentions hostile natives and the inhospitable environment. Numerous color and black-and-white photographs provide a multifaceted view of present-day Mozambique.

656. Kaula, Edna Mason. *The Land and People of Rhodesia*. Portraits of the Nations Series. Philadelphia and New York: Lippincott, 1967. 158p. Grades 7-12.

Although outdated, this book provides an excellent example of biased writing. Kaula's racist attitude is evident in her presenting the material from the perspective of the white minority, tacit acceptance of political institutions that guaranteed an inferior status to the majority black population, and omission of certain aspects of racism. In discussing the social structure, lifestyle, and culture of the Mashona, Kaula believes that they have lost their highly civilized arts and have become an unenlightened people who retain many "cruel and horrible customs," especially magical rites and belief in witch doctors. Europeans are seen as heroic pioneers who braved physical hardships, withstood the attacks of natives, and worked hard to bring technology and progress to the nation. The efforts of missionaries like John Moffat and David Livingstone to bring the humanizing influence of Christianity were frustrated by the hostile Bantus, whom she holds responsible for the slave trade. Cecil Rhodes is presented as a great diplomat and statesman, instead of as a cheat. Kaula fails to acknowledge the anger and nationalistic feelings of the Matabele when their land was taken from them. She says that "good government'' raised the standard of living through training programs, better farming methods, education, health services, and equal political rights for all civilized men. She does not mention that the property, income, and educational qualifications for exercising enfranchisement automatically eliminated blacks, and that blacks were deprived of their lands and put in reservations that served as labor pools for mines and farms. The nationalist organizations of the 1960s like ZAPU and ZANU are seen as an excuse for the victimization of Europeans in the name of freedom. She is afraid that franchise would result in a black government and an end to the beneficial white regime under leaders like Ian Smith.

657. Knight, Ian. *The Zulus.* Color plates by Angus McBride. Elite Series. London: Osprey, 1989. 64p. Grades 8-12.

This book is part of a series on the history, organization, appearance, and equipment of famous fighting men of the past and present. In tracing the rise and fall of the Zulu nation, *The Zulus* focuses on King Shaka's rise to power and his many conquests with the aid of an intricately structured army and a highly centralized government. Based on the diaries and accounts of British traders and army personnel in South Africa, Knight carefully recounts Zulu military tactics and training, details of the wars, regimental regalia, and weaponry. While Knight acknowledges Shaka's bravery and unsurpassed abilities as a general, he does not see Shaka's greatness as an empire builder. An equally detailed account is provided of Kings Dingane, Mpande, and Cetshwayo and their defeats at Blood River, Isandlwana, and Rorke's Drift respectively. The account ends in 1913 when Zululand became a pawn in the continuing power play between the Afrikaners and British. Knight's Eurocentric perspective is evident in his use of terms like bizarre, grotesque, and gruesome to describe certain Zulu hairstyles, clothing, and rituals, especially those pertaining to the medicine man or diviner. Also, Zulus fighting the Europeans are called ''rebels,'' instead of defenders of their land.

The text is illustrated with fifty photographs and diagrams and twelve color plates. They include rare photographs of Shaka, Dingane, Mpande, Cetshwayo, prominent Zulu chiefs, Dingane's residence, battlefield scenes at Rorke's Drift, and military weapons and clothes.

658. Lane, Martha S. B. *Malawi.* Enchantment of the World Series. Chicago: Children's Press, 1990. 126p. Grades 6-8.

Of the various informational books on Malawi published by Lerner (Visual Geography Series, 1988), Chelsea House (Places and Peoples of the World Series, 1988), and Children's Press, the last is the most comprehensive and detailed. Lane's descriptive prose provides a graphic picture of Malawi's land and resources, history and government, economy and industry, peoples and lifestyle, religion and culture, and arts and crafts. She also outlines the achievements of Malawi since independence from Britain in 1964 and the problems facing this tiny landlocked country--limited resources to speed development, growing dependence on South Africa, and uncertainty regarding President Hastings Kamuzu Banda's successor. Although the text is presented objectively, it reflects the author's personal observations and knowledge of Malawi. The numerous color photographs and black-and-white drawings are both aesthetically pleasing and representative of all facets of Malawian life.

659. Laure, Jason. *Angola*. Enchantment of the World Series. Chicago: Children's Press, 1990. 128p. Grades 7-10.

In describing the geography, history, economy, people, and culture of Angola, Laure focuses on the impact of five hundred years of Portuguese colonial rule on modern Angola. The present state of political unrest, shattered economy, lack of trained personnel, and poor state of education, health services, and transportation are blamed on the slave trade, colonization, and prolonged civil wars. The well-established ancient kingdoms of the Kongo, Dembo, and Ndgongo were disrupted by the arrival of the Portuguese in 1441 and 1483 and the almost immediate trade in slaves. A detailed account of the slave trade--and how it differed from the slavery prevalent in Africa--indicates how Angola was stripped of its best people, resources, sovereignty, and traditional lifestyle. Laure sees Angola as the perfect example of a country in the grip of neocolonialism; every aspect of its life is controlled by foreign experts: its policies, economy, health, and other services are based on the Marxist philosophy of the Soviet Union and Cuba (changes are expected to occur with the breakdown of communism in Eastern Europe); military assistance from Cuba and Russia; and technical or economic help from the United States, South Africa, Brazil, and Philippines. Laure concludes that if Angola is to achieve lasting peace and build an economy based on revenue from oil, diamonds, fishing, coffee, and other industries, the government of President Jose Eduardo dos Santos must recognize the UNITA movement and hold free elections. Superb color photographs of Angolan cities, industries, artwork, and peoples supplement the text.

660. _____. *Zambia*. Enchantment of the World Series. Chicago: Children's Press, 1989. 126p. Grades 6-10.

This book provides a more detailed account of Zambia's land, history and independence struggle, government and economy, and peoples and culture than does Holmes (see # 653). Zambian history is traced from Stone Age times (200,000 years ago), to the Bemba, Tongo, Lozi, and Lunda kingdoms, to colonization and independence. David Livingstone's role in the exploration and settlement of Zambia and Kenneth Kaunda's role in the liberation and establishment of Zambia are discussed in detail. The role of mining in the exploitation of the land and people is explained step-by-step. Zambians were systematically drawn away from farming, used as virtual forced labor because of the Hut Tax, and compelled to work in mines in other countries in Southern Africa. In contrast, the government of President Kaunda launched an aggressive policy of African Socialism, called Humanism, which attempted to strengthen the economy, improve health and educational facilities, nationalize foreign companies, and distribute wealth fairly. However, Laure points out that the collapse of the world copper market prevented these goals from being realized. He believes that Zambia needs to consider diversifying its industry and commerce, especially in agriculture and tourism. Laure lists the factors in Zambia's favor: plentiful land and water supply, hospitable climate, cheap electricity from the Kariba Dam, and a good railroad network. As a frontline state, Zambia's president took a leadership role in Africa by welcoming refugees and freedom fighters to use Zambia as a base for their operations. President Kaunda was also active in the United Nations, Organization of African Unity, and Southern African Development Coordination Conference.

661. Lawson, Don. *South Africa.* London: Franklin Watts, 1986. 88p. Grades 4-8.
Lawson's attitude toward the situation in South Africa is one of understanding--an understanding for the whites' attitude that political rights for blacks will result in the whites being driven out of South Africa, and that the present racial unrest is chiefly caused by drought, economic recession, and the drop in the price of gold. A detailed account of South Africa's geography and natural resources, history and European colonization, power struggle between Dutch and British over territory and gold and diamond mining, economy and industry, and evolution of the apartheid policy supports the above position. A separate chapter examines the changing relations between the United States and South Africa from the Carter administration to President Reagan's policy of "constructive engagement." Lawson also cites the antiapartheid activities of Senator Edward Kennedy, and the support extended to Winnie Mandela and Desmond Tutu by several American groups. While Lawson meticulously cites divergent viewpoints regarding the situation in South Africa, he distances himself from the information and does not denounce the policies of the South African government on moral grounds. Another author who objectively discusses South Africa, without condemning apartheid, is Claudia Canesso in *South Africa* (Chelsea House, 1989) in the Places and Peoples of the World Series.

662. Leigh, Nila K. *Learning to Swim in Swaziland: A Child's-Eye View of a Southern African Country.* New York: Scholastic, 1993. N.p. Grades 2-4.
When eight-year-old Nila goes to Swaziland with her parents, she writes letters to her classmates in New York City describing her life there. The letters, Nila's drawings, and photographs of her visit form the basis of this book. In a frank and straightforward manner, Nila writes of what she observes: geography, housing, culture, people and their customs, food and clothing, schooling, and work and play. Once Nila learns to swim in Swaziland, she realizes that, "You should not be afraid of what you have never done."

663. Magubane, Peter. *Black Child.* Photographs by author. New York: Knopf, 1982. 102p. Grades 6-12.

Photojournalist Magubane's black-and-white photographs are a shocking and moving record of the plight of black South African children. Whether the children are from urban townships, squatters' colonies, or homelands, their common experience is one of shattered childhood, disrupted family life, poverty and hunger, and early exposure to violence, death, and disease. The photographs also expose the social evils of apartheid for blacks: poor housing, inadequate nutrition and medical care, and exploitation of child labor on farms in Natal and East Transvaal and in urban businesses. Hopeless as these conditions are, the children are still capable of expressing simple pleasures while celebrating a birthday, playing with friends, or reciting a poem at school. They also show faith in the future by engaging in political protest, especially since the 1976 Soweto riots. Magubane's introductory essay and captions provide extensive information on the apartheid laws--such as the Bantu Education Bill, influx control laws, and migratory labor laws--that are responsible for the suffering of children.

664. Murphy, E. Jefferson. *The Bantu Civilization of Southern Africa.* Illustrated by Louise E. Jefferson. New York: Crowell, 1974. 273p. Grades 9-12.

This account of the origin and migrations of the Bantu-speaking peoples is based on the research of archaeologists, linguists, anthropologists, and scientists and information gleaned from oral histories. The history of Bantu migrations begins in 500 B.C. from their Nigeria-Cameroon homeland, to the Katanga region of the Congo in 100 B.C., to settlements in Central, Eastern, and Southern Africa. By 1500 A.D., they had covered an area of four million square miles. As they conquered the indigenous peoples and assimilated into their new environments, they developed diverse languages and cultures. However, Murphy emphasizes that the common origin of Bantu-speaking peoples accounts for the essential uniformity of their societies and worldview. Murphy gives an in-depth study of the history and government, economy and trade, farming and industry, and arts and crafts of various kingdoms like the Congo, Luba and Lunda, Zimbabwe, Buganda, Bunjoro, Karagwe, Burundi, Rwanda, and Zulu. These achievements, Murphy acknowledges, are modest compared to those of the civilizations of Egypt, India, China, Greece, Rome, and Western Europe, but he says they have to be assessed in view of the environmental difficulties of lands with comparatively meager fertility and virtual isolation from the thoughts and developments in other lands. Between 1700 and 1900, the Bantu civilizations declined in the face of competition from cheaper European manufactured goods, struggle and rivalry within African states to control trade, and European expansion for raw material and colonization. This highly researched and scholarly account is extended by maps, charts, drawings, a bibliography, and an index.

665. Ngubane, Harriet. *Zulus of Southern Africa.* Original Peoples Series. Vero Beach, FL: Rourke, 1987. 48p. Grades 4-6.

An anthropologist by profession, Ngubane's research of her Zulu background is both sensitive and honest. In tracing the formation of the Zulu empire, she states it was strengthened by sophisticated political, military, religious, economic, and family and kinship institutions. However, it could not withstand the waves of Boer settlers and their firearms despite continued resistance. In discussing the death of Piet Retief, the Voortrekker leader, at King Dingane's palace in 1838, Ngubane clearly states that each side had a different version and that mutual suspicion played a vital part in the incident. She also acknowledges the work of Christian missionaries in the areas of education and medicine. In discussing the plight of Zulus today, she points out that they are stripped of their independence and political rights in apartheid South Africa. Like other deprived black South Africans, Zulus are forced to join the migrant labor force in white cities because their land is unable to support the rural population. Their traditional kinship culture and family group has been destroyed, making them seek church organizations for support. Politically, Zulus continue to protest a system based on race, and they are actively engaged in the freedom movement under the African National Congress and Chief Buthelezi's grassroots National Cultural Liberation Movement, established in 1975 to resist making Kwazulu into a homeland. Zulus are proud of their history of continuous confrontation with the European conquerors for over a century.

Each section of the book is well illustrated with maps, photographs, and reproductions of paintings. A glossary of terms, list of Zulu words, bibliography, and index are included.

666. Nyawata, E. *The Chimurenga War.* Illustrated by author. Dandaro Readers Series. Gweru, Zimbabwe: Mambo, 1982. 16p. Grades K-2.

The causes, progress, and outcome of the Chimurenga War, the Zimbabwean war of independence against white minority rule, are presented objectively for the younger reader. While Nyawata outlines the cruelties and casualties of war for both sides, the emphasis is on glorifying the nationalistic spirit, sacrifice, and heroism of the freedom fighters and the common folk who helped them. The book is poorly illustrated and produced.

667. Pachai, Bridglal. *The International Aspects of the South African Indian Question.* Cape Town: Struik, 1971. 318p. Grades 10-adult.

As the descendant of an Indian indentured laborer and Professor of History, Pachai is amply qualified to write this well-researched history of Indians in South Africa. Although this study was published prior to the developments of the 1980s when Indians were given a small political voice and when black militants reacted violently against Indians, it nevertheless provides a detailed account of South Africa's divisive racial policies and the political status of Indians up to 1971. Beginning with Indian immigration to the sugar plantations of Natal in 1860, Pachai describes the hostility toward Indians as they

began to establish themselves as property owners and traders;
Indians' protest against injustices under the leadership of Mahatma
Gandhi; and life under apartheid from 1961 to 1971. Pachai also
gives an in-depth analysis of how the domestic "problem" of the
status of Indians in South Africa became an international issue.
Above all, this history demonstrates that the character, patriotism, and
aspirations of the Indian population in South Africa is essentially
South African. Another book that emphasizes the cultural contributions of Indians is *Traditional Hindu Temples in South Africa* (1982)
by Paul Mikula, Brian Kearney, and Rodney Harber, which is a
detailed discussion of fifty exquisite carved temples in Natal.

668. Pascoe, Elaine. *South Africa: Troubled Land.*   London: Franklin
Watts, 1987, 1992. 143p. Grades 8-12.
    In addition to tracing the geographical, historical, political, economic,
    and social causes of apartheid and racial trouble in South Africa
    today, Pascoe provides information on the recent changes enacted by
    Frederick W. de Klerk's government. She analyzes the impact of the
    various liberation movements, economic sanctions, and the growing
    dissatisfaction of white South Africans--90 percent according to the
    March 1992 referendum--on governmental policies to dismantle the
    structure of apartheid. 1989 marked the beginning of dramatic
    reforms: negotiations with black leaders; end of the state of
    emergency; freeing of Nelson Mandela and other imprisoned leaders;
    desegregation of public schools, beaches, and other facilities; lifting
    of the ban on the African National Congress; and the repeal of the
    Land Act, Group Areas Act, Black Communities Act, and Population
    Registration Act. Pascoe ends on a cautionary note because
    black-on-black and factional violence have increased, because there is
    deep-rooted mistrust on all sides, and because the legacy of apartheid
    --poverty and illiteracy for blacks--is not likely to disappear with
    political equality.

669. Paton, Jonathan. *The Land and People of South Africa.* Portraits of
the Nations Series. New York: Lippincott, 1990. 288p. Grades 8-12.
    The central focus of this book is the growing conflict between the
    bitter struggle for majority rule and the white government's
    determination to preserve white culture and identity and its fierce
    opposition to supporters of majority rule. With this theme in mind,
    eighteen individual chapters provide an in-depth examination of the
    history, geography, politics, economy, racial groups, and resistance
    and repression in South Africa. This is a study in contrasts--the scenic
    beauty of the land and the tragedy and ugliness of human suffering,
    the vast and visible differences in the wealth of the whites and black
    poverty, and the callous and cruel treatment of blacks. Paton makes a
    distinction between the situation in South Africa and the former
    European colonies in Africa because South Africa's five million
    whites are *not* colonists who plan to return to Europe in due course.
    However, the intent of the white government, and the rationalization
    presented in enacting various aspects of apartheid--such as the

creation of homelands and Group Areas Act--are clearly pointed out. Paton also strips the romance and heroism associated with the Great Trek by explaining that it was not the trek that shifted the balance to one of white dominance, but the intervention of the British and the discovery of gold and diamonds. Voortrekkers suffered several setbacks and were involved in bitter political struggles while many of their African neighbors prospered. Moreover, survival of some of the Boer communities was possible only because of the cooperation and goodwill of their African neighbors.

The text is extended by black-and-white photographs, charts, maps, an appendix on the arts and sports, and an extensive bibliography. In addition, each chapter has insets that provide valuable information on topics such as the languages and peoples of South Africa; click languages; the Zulu national anthem, "Nkosi Sikelel' iAfrika"; extracts from Jan van Riebeeck's journal; biographies of Shaka, Mosheshwe, Nelson Mandela, and Archbishop Desmond Tutu; white South Africans who oppose apartheid; and women in the freedom struggle. While Paton's approach and tone are objective and fair, he does not hesitate to denounce apartheid as "abhorrent." The text assumes an emotive and poetic quality as Paton frequently quotes moving passages by black and white poets like Don Mattera and Jeremy Cronin to express the pain, anguish, and struggle that South Africa is experiencing.

670. Stark, Al. *Zimbabwe: A Treasure of Africa.* Discovering Our Heritage Series. Minneapolis, MN: Dillon, 1986. 160p. Grades 4-6.
This book will appeal to younger readers because information on the land, peoples, history, government, lifestyles, education, and leaders of Zimbabwe is presented in an interesting manner. Numerous photographs, a list of languages of the Shona and Ndebele peoples, a glossary of terms, and a bibliography supplement the text.

671. Stein, R. Conrad. *South Africa.* Enchantment of the World Series. Chicago: Children's Press, 1986. 127p. Grades 4-6.
In introducing the land, peoples, history, government, economy, education, and arts and literature of South Africa, the controversial aspects of life in an apartheid society are discussed frankly. Both text and color photographs provide a balanced picture of the various ethnic groups, differences in lifestyles and standards of living, and the nationalistic struggle of blacks, Asians, and coloreds. The realities of apartheid are clearly spelled out: pass books, Group Areas Act, classification of races, and inferior educational and medical facilities.

Various historical myths that have been perpetuated by Afrikaner-- that the land was empty when the Boers went on their Great Trek and that King Shaka was a bloodthirsty maniac--are discredited. Afrikaners are viewed as romantics who live in the past glory of their Great Trek, in their belief that they had a sacred covenant with God, and in the achievements of Piet Retief and Cecil Rhodes. Stein also points out the irony that the Afrikaner desire for a pure white race can never be achieved because the majority of whites--especially those families who have been in South Africa for more than two centuries--have some colored blood in their heritage. The changes, or easing of apartheid, seen in cities like Johannesburg, Durban, and Soweto in the 1980s are only cosmetic and a response to international pressure and economic divestment. Stein believes that the "laager" mentality is still in operation and that Afrikaners will draw inward to resist the rest of the world. Maps, list of mini facts, important dates, and significant leaders are included.

672. Stewart, Gail B. *South Africa.* Places in the News Series. New York: Crestwood House, 1990. 47p. Grades 2-4.

Political conditions in South Africa are simply, yet thoroughly examined for the upper elementary child. First, apartheid is traced from its historical roots in the fierce independence and strict religious beliefs of the Dutch settlers, to the Boer Wars with the British, to 1948 when apartheid was officially adopted by a fully independent South Africa. Second, the apartheid system is clearly explained. Designed by Hendrik Verwoerd to keep South Africa's white race pure, three hundred separate laws were established to ensure that whites would have the best jobs, finest living areas, and, because they were the only group that could vote, control of the government. Next, Stewart discusses the fight for freedom from the formation of the African National Congress and the Pan-African Congress, to the leadership of Nelson Mandela, Steven Biko, and Desmond Tutu, to the launching of strategies like strikes and sit-ins, nonviolence, and the black consciousness movement. The white government's violent reactions are evidence of government and police brutality and the determination of blacks to face death and suffering for their cause. Finally, Stewart discusses the effectiveness of economic sanctions against South Africa.

Since 1986 there has been some progress: blacks are no longer required to carry passes; it is not illegal for blacks and whites to marry; and blacks can use "white" park benches, beaches, water fountains, and hospitals. However, Stewart emphasizes that no real change can come until every South African can participate in the government by voting. Frederik de Klerk, the new president, has promised peace and justice.

673. Steyn, Hendrik Pieter. *The Bushmen of the Kalahari.* Original Peoples Series. Vero Beach, FL: Rourke, 1989. 48p. Grades 4-6.

Anthropologist Steyn discusses the history, hunter-gatherer economy, culture, social groupings, marriage and child-raising customs, and religion of the Bushmen (San), who lived in large areas of Southern Africa for at least twenty thousand years. They developed a unique lifestyle that responded to their various environments: the wet coastal regions, the dry Karoo shrubland, the grassy plains of the Highveld, and the bare Namib and Kalahari deserts. Using stone tools and objects made of bone and ostrich shells, they lived in small family groups by hunting animals, gathering edible plants and honey, and coping with water and food shortages. They have left behind thousands of prehistoric rock art sites that depict their lifestyle, animals they hunted, religious rituals, and aesthetic sensibilities. With the arrival of white settlers in 1655, Bushmen were--over a period of three hundred years--pushed away from their territories in the Drakensberg mountain range, southeastern Transvaal Province, and northwestern Cape Province. Numbering only an estimated fifty thousand today, Bushmen live mainly in the Kalahari Desert region which includes portions of Botswana, Namibia, and Angola. Their survival as a distinct cultural group is once again in danger because the protective isolation of the desert has been broken with the opening up of large portions of the Kalahari to cattle farmers, prolonged war in Angola and enlistment in the army, and rapid absorption as labor by black and white farmers who own Bushmen land. With only the Central Kalahari Reserve in Botswana and the Bushmanland in Namibia positively protecting their land rights, the traditional lifestyle of Bushmen is threatened with extinction.

A glossary of terms, description of the various click sounds in the "Bushmen's" language, suggestions for further reading, and an index are included.

674. Tessendorf, K.C. *Along the Road to Soweto: A Racial History of South Africa.* New York: Atheneum, 1989. 194p. Grades 8-12.

This examination of South African history takes an understanding approach to how and why the country became an "unmelting pot" of black, brown, yellow, and white races, with the thin white layer on top enjoying all the economic, political, and social privileges. The account begins with the Bantu migrations nearly two thousand years ago and the subjugation of the San and Khoi Khoi. Tessendorf continues the discussion with the founding of the Dutch East India Company and slavery, settlement and colonization, bitter rivalry between the British and Dutch for power, rise and fall of the Zulu nation, the roles of Cecil Rhodes and Paul Kruger in establishing the basis of apartheid, immigration of Indian labor and Mahatma Gandhi's fight for civil rights, and the demands of the African National Congress for equal rights. These phases in South African history clearly show how a firm belief in superior and inferior races led to the stagnation of society into racially segregated layers with each supposedly fulfilling its destiny separately. In 1976, Tessendorf contends, the Soweto schoolchildren's protest against the Bantu Education Act destroyed the myth that the "lesser breeds" are relatively happy under white law. Soweto is viewed as a symbolic turning point in South African history because it began the dynamic process of rearranging the varied racial strata. However, Tessendorf's detailed analysis fails to emphasize the role and significance of the numerous antiapartheid organizations prior to the Soweto uprising.

Tessendorf's readable prose includes quotations from the diaries, speeches, and writings of historians and leaders. The text is illustrated with maps, charts, drawings, and photographs. The index and bibliography will assist the serious researcher.

675. Tonsing-Carter, Betty. *Lesotho*. Places and Peoples of the World Series. New York: Chelsea House, 1988. 95p. Grades 5-7.

> The discussion centers on the impact of geography on Lesotho's history, industry, agriculture, rural lifestyle, and dependence on South Africa for jobs, electric power, and consumer goods. It is the mountain peaks of this beautiful country, also known as the "Switzerland of Africa," that prevented King Shaka and the Boers from completely destroying it in the nineteenth century. The Basotho nation under the leadership of King Moshoeshoe I retreated to the mountains to ensure their sovereignty. Modern Lesotho is a combination of old and new: a Western-style judicial system combined with the traditional *pitso*, or open-air assembly, in villages, towns, and cities to discuss major issues; mission schools and the National University of Lesotho; traditional medicine and modern health clinics and hospitals; and Basotho customs and rituals in Christian services. The book makes it clear that the only way Lesotho can maintain good relations with South Africa *and* continue to be a refuge for people fleeing oppression is by strengthening its economy, health and education, commerce and industry, and transportation and communication. The United Nations and large international donor organizations have spent millions of dollars in foreign aid to help Lesotho become self-sufficient.

> With the intention of attracting future tourists, both text and photographs portray the breathtaking scenery, modern amenities in the capital city of Maseru, nature trails, handicrafts, music and dance, and the centuries-old "Bushman" paintings.

676. *Two Dogs and Freedom: Children of the Townships Speak Out*. Johannesburg: Ravan Press/The Open School, 1986. 55p. Grades 5-7.

> This book is a poignant collection of writings and drawings by children of the townships. These youngsters--ranging between eight and fifteen years of age--provide a graphic picture of their nightmarish lives: police searches, school raids, bullets fired at children, rape, neighborhood violence, death, and poverty. Yet, being children, they are not discouraged; they look forward to a bright future when they will have freedom, quality education, and equal rights in Azania. In the simple words of an eight-year-old, "I would like to have a wife and to [sic] children, a boy and a girl, and a big house and to [sic] dogs and freedom."

Appendix: List of Distributors

Africa World Press, Inc.
P.O. Box 1892
Trenton, NJ 08607

African Art Museum Shop
Smithsonian Institution
950 Independence Avenue, SW
Washington, D.C. 20560

African Book Collective
The Jam Factory
27 Park End Street
Oxford OXI IHU
England

Baobab Books
P.O. Box 567
Harare, Zimbabwe

East African Educational Publishers
Brick Court House
Mpaka Road/ Woodvale Grove
P.O. Box 45314
Nairobi, Kenya

Everyone's Place
African Cultural Center
1356 W. North Avenue
Baltimore, MD 21217

Ghana Publishing House
Ghana State Publishing Corp.
P.O. Box 4348
Accra, Ghana

Griot Booksellers, Inc.
3102 Milford Avenue
Baltimore, MD 21207

The Institute of Karmic Guidance
P.O. Box 73025
Washington, D.C. 20056

Jacaranda Designs Limited
P.O. Box 76691
Nairobi, Kenya

Lake Publishers & Enterprises
P.O. Box 1743
Jomo Kenyatta Highway
Kisumu, Kenya

Longman Zimbabwe
Tourle Road Ardbennie
P.O. Box ST 125
Southerton
Harare, Zimbabwe

Mambo Press
P.O. Box 779
Gweru, Zimbabwe

New Beacon Book
76 Stroud Green Road
London, N4 3EN
England

Oyo International, Inc.
1390 Bedford Avenue
Brooklyn, NY 11216

Phoenix Publishers, Ltd.
3rd Floor, Coffee Plaza
P.O. Box 18650
Nairobi
Kenya

Ravan Press
P.O. Box 31134
Braamfontein 2017
South Africa

The Red Sea Press
15 Industry Court
Trenton, NJ 08638

Sea Island Information Group
P.O. Box 10628
Silver Spring, MD 20914

Shrine of the Black Madonna
13535 Livernois
Detroit, MI 48238

Southern Africa Media Center
630 Natoma Street
San Francisco, CA 94103

The Text Book Centre
P.O. Box 47540
Nairobi, Kenya

Zimbabwe Publishing House
P.O. Box 350
Harare, Zimbabwe

Author Index

Includes authors, translators and editors.
Numbers in index refer to individual entries, not pages.

Illustrator Index

Includes photographers as well as artists.
Numbers in index refer to individual entries, not pages.

Title Index

Numbers in index refer to individual entries, not pages.

Subject Index

Numbers in index refer to individual entries, not pages.

About the Author

MEENA KHORANA is Professor of English at Morgan State University. She is the author of *The Indian Subcontinent in Literature for Children and Young Adults: An Annotated Bibliography of English-Language Books* (Greenwood Press, 1991). Her publications have appeared in *Children's Literature, Writer and Illustrator, Library Trends,* and the Children's Literature Association's *Quarterly* and *Proceedings.* Dr. Khorana has also contributed articles to *Beacham's Guide to Literature for Young Adults, Lion and the Unicorn, Magill's Literary Annual, Twentieth-Century British Children's Writers,* and the Modern Language Association's *Teaching Children's Literature.* She is currently working on *British Children's Writers, 1800–1880.*

ISBN 0-313-25488-5

HARDCOVER BAR CODE